Table of Contents

Dear Tracy,

Thank you so much for your assistance with this project. I am so grateful that you took the time + effort to help me raise awareness for women's rights, agency and autonomy in creating a rich her-story.

I do support your endeavours with The Maiden Factor. And please know that you can call on me to assist in any way that I can.

Warm regards,
Ray

Sports Highlights

*A History of Plays Replayed
from Edison to ESPN and Beyond*

RAY GAMACHE

SECOND EDITION

McFarland & Company, Inc., Publishers
Jefferson, North Carolina

LIBRARY OF CONGRESS CATALOGUING-IN-PUBLICATION DATA

Names: Gamache, Ray, 1952– author.
Title: Sports highlights : a history of plays replayed from Edison
to ESPN and beyond / Ray Gamache.
Other titles: History of sports highlights
Description: Second edition. | Jefferson, North Carolina :
McFarland & Company, Inc., Publishers, 2023. | Revised edition of:
A history of sports highlights. ©2010 | Includes bibliographical references and index.
Identifiers: LCCN 2023034450 | ISBN 9781476692289 (paperback : acid free paper) ∞
ISBN 9781476650791 (ebook)
Subjects: LCSH: Television broadcasting of sports—United States—History. |
Sports journalism—United States—History.
Classification: LCC GV742.3 .G36 2023 | DDC 070.4497960973—dc23/eng/20230807
LC record available at https://lccn.loc.gov/2023034450

BRITISH LIBRARY CATALOGUING DATA ARE AVAILABLE

ISBN (print) 978-1-4766-9228-9
ISBN (ebook) 978-1-4766-5079-1

Front cover: (top highlight) Washington player-manager Bucky Harris
attempting to steal home in a game on August 13, 1925 (Library of Congress);
(bottom highlight) Tampa Bay quarterback Tom Brady preparing
to pass in an NFL game on November 14, 2021 (All-Pro Reels)

Printed in the United States of America

*McFarland & Company, Inc., Publishers
Box 611, Jefferson, North Carolina 28640
www.mcfarlandpub.com*

Acknowledgments

To the staff of the Philip Merrill College of Journalism for their patient and kind service.

To the administration of the Philip Merrill College of Journalism for providing me with the means to pursue my dreams.

To A.R. Hogan, who provided me with a wealth of materials gleaned from the television archives at the Library of Congress.

To the staff at the National Archives II.

To Maurine Beasley, whose tireless encouragement, consideration and attentiveness made the experience so rewarding.

To my mother Rachel and sister Aline for encouraging me to set sail on this adventure and whose love guided me to new shores.

To Jane, my guiding light and love, without whom none of this would matter.

To Captain Jim Vander Schaaf for helping me navigate my discussion of sailing matters and to Commodore Paul Visich of the WBFYC for back-up of archival materials.

Preface

This book traces the emergence of sportscast highlights as the dominant news frame in electronic sports journalism. Sports highlights emerged as an important vehicle to convey sports events as a result of the technological, economic and social changes that impacted media systems. Changes in technologies do not provide the entire story of the highlight's development and deployment as a news frame, so this book also explains the importance of those protocols that express the intricate relationships between media producers, sports leagues and organizations, and audiences. It argues that sportscast highlights are not a recent development, given their prominent use within a news context in every medium from early news film actualities and newsreels to network and cable television to today's new media platforms.

As an example of sports journalism history, this book investigates each medium's contributions, not so much as discrete phenomena, but as a relational totality. As a macro-level history, the book necessarily takes a long-term view of the processes of historical change. Additionally, this methodology utilizes intertextuality and discourse analysis as analytical strategies to question whose interests were served from the evolution and deployment of sportscast highlights, who benefited from the narratives represented through the news frame, and whose interests were consolidated with its commoditization. This study analyzes primary and secondary sources related to sportscasts, including early sport films and actualities, newsreels, network and cable programming, and new media content.

The importance of this book stems from the prominent position sports media in general, and sports journalism in particular, occupy within the political and cultural economy of late capitalism. The book's significance is also evidenced in the considerable impact the broadcast networks (e.g., ABC, CBS, FOX, and NBC), cable sports networks (e.g., ESPN, Fox Sports Network, Versus), specific sport channels (e.g., Golf Channel, Tennis Channel), and professional sports league networks (e.g., MLB Network, NFL Network, NHL Network) have had on the proliferation of sportscasts, moving us from a trustee model of spectrum scarcity to one of conglomeration and convergence based on digital plenitude. That plenitude is comprised of traditional genres based on appointment consumption like live broadcasts, news programming and talk radio and continuing on to a digital virtuosity based on platform agnosticism in which handheld mobile devices provide instant gratification. In

1

short, we've moved from the *Gillette Cavalcade of Sport* and *Camel News Caravan* to *ABC's Wide World of Sports* to the World Wide Web, YouTube, Facebook and Twitter; from Grantland Rice, Ring Lardner, Red Smith, and Bill Stern to Curt Gowdy, Chris Berman, Stuart Scott and Dave Zirin; from the Four Horsemen of the Apocalypse and Tinker to Evers to Chance to "Rumblin' ... stumblin' ... bumblin'" and "Cool as the Other Side of the Pillow"; from the "Thrill of Victory and the Agony of Defeat" to the Ecstasy of Communication; from modernism to postmodernism.

What has remained constant despite the many changes to the media delivery systems, the sports, the athletes, and the journalists has been our reliance on and fascination with sports highlights. In that sense, sports highlights have become a genre unto themselves, and one could spend a lifetime, if one were so inclined, watching them on YouTube, which now stands as a seemingly limitless cosmos of highlights. Because of the ubiquity of sports highlights, it is important to understand the impact sports media and electronic sports journalists have had in influencing and reflecting cultural trends related to national identity, race, gender, and ethnic relations, as well as political, economic and international affairs.

I'd like to say I became interested in writing about sports highlights on December 7, 1963, the day Lindsey Nelson described the first instant replay during the Army-Navy game, but that would be a stretch since I was 11 years old at the time. More specifically, my interest in sports was cultivated by my father, an avid sports fan with whom I spent countless hours watching and arguing about sports. That interest deepened after seeing my byline in the sports pages of the *Nashua Telegraph* as a high school student, but it was only after deciding to enter the doctoral program at the University of Maryland's Philip Merrill College of Journalism that a smoldering interest finally had life breathed into it. While many people helped refine my interest, two accomplished scholars and mentors and one book deserve mention. Dr. Maurine Beasley, noted journalism historian, directed my dissertation research, and Dr. David L. Andrews, noted scholar in the sociology of sports, challenged me to stake out my own ontological and epistemological ground. The book that made me realize something more needed to be written about sports highlights was Charles Hirshberg's *ESPN25: 25 Mind-Bending, Eye-Popping, Culture-Morphing Years of Highlights.* It wasn't the hyperbolic title that galvanized my attention, but the premise that ESPN, the self-proclaimed "Worldwide Leader in Sports," perfected highlights that lit my fuse and pointed the way.

This resulting book employs a historical framework whose concern is not specific individuals and events, but larger forces that shaped those people and events. The book is based upon primary and secondary sources related to sportscasts. Analysis revolves around a number of early films, located and available at the Library of Congress, Washington, D.C. Newsreels have been analyzed, covering the years 1929–1952. A collection of Universal Newsreels are available at the National Archives in College Park. The Library of Congress also has an extensive collection of NBC radio and television programming log books and public relations news releases that were utilized. While there are almost no extant copies of early sportscasts, the log book and news releases provide valuable information about their creation, production and dissemination. Another important source of information resides in national newspapers and trade journals related to television.

Cable programs such as ESPN's *SportsCenter* are still being broadcast, so a purposive sample of one week during each season (i.e., spring, summer, fall and winter) was analyzed to establish the audio and video conventions of the sportscast. In addition, this study has accessed a number of Web sites utilizing the sportscast highlight form in order to analyze the deployment, packaging and functionality of the content. It has considered utilization of the highlight form by the professional sports leagues, media organizations and providers of wireless mobile services. Issues related to commoditization and marketing have been explicated.

Lastly, an extensive number of newspaper articles have been utilized to delineate the social, economic, legal and technological changes that impacted the development of the sportscast highlight news frame. Given the dearth of archival television programs available for research, newspaper articles were an invaluable source in establishing what sports programs were televised.

While there is relatively little scholarship that explicitly traces the history of sports highlights, a number of scholarly books and articles informed the author. Most notable among those are Charles Musser's *Edison Motion Pictures, 1890–1900: An Annotated Filmography*, which provides a comprehensive guide to early Edison films. In the first volume of his *History of the American Cinema*, titled *The Emergence of Cinema*, Musser offers a compelling account of the social, technological and economic factors that contributed to the formation of early American cinema. Gordon Hendricks' *Origins of the American Film*, a compilation of three works—*The Edison Motion Picture Myth* (1961), *Beginnings of the Biograph* (1964), and *The Kinetoscope* (1966)—is instrumental in detailing the contributions of W.K.L. Dickson and the Latham family to the development of early film. The most detailed study of boxing's relationship with film is Daniel J. Streible's dissertation, titled *A History of the Prizefight Film, 1894–1915*, recently published by the University of California Press as *Fight Pictures: A History of Boxing and Early Cinema*.

Raymond Fielding's *The American Newsreel: A Complete History, 1911–1967* offers a comprehensive overview of the history of the American newsreel, although his analysis of sport focuses more on event coverage than on the routinization and standardization that characterized the newsreel sports segment. In *King Football: Sport and Spectacle in the Golden Age of Radio and Newsreels, Movies and Magazines, the Weekly & the Daily Press*, Michael Oriard argues that newsreels were instrumental in popularizing football and that newsreels were a forerunner of ESPN's *SportsCenter*.

Several works explain the importance of television in the development of sports. Benjamin Rader's *In Its Own Image* presents a rich critical analysis of the early years of sports telecasts, although it provides little about cable television's impact or the importance of the highlight form to sportscasts. Similar in style and scope to Rader's book is Ron Powers' *Supertube: The Rise of Television Sports*. Published in 1984, the same year as Rader's work, Powers' book explores the changes television forced upon sports, especially in terms of economics. Roone Arledge's *Memoir* provides anecdotal information about the development of ABC Sports by the person most responsible for its development. Bill Rasmussen's *Sports Junkies Rejoice! The Birth of ESPN* offers a detailed account of his role in creating the cable network. A more comprehensive and detailed study of ESPN is available from Michael Freeman, whose *ESPN: The Uncensored History* is based on interviews, company documents, handwritten notes, diary entries and media accounts.

Several book chapters deal directly with sports highlights. In "'Highlights and Action Replays'—Ideology, Sport and the Media," Alan Clarke and John Clarke examine key processes through which the media interpret sporting events and provide viewers with the frameworks of meaning with which to make sense of the event. In "Cool as the Other Side of the Pillow," Grant Farred argues that the commentary produced by ESPN's *SportsCenter* anchors is a distinctive type of sports discourse permeated with a penchant for hipness. In the article "Sport on Television: Replay and Display," Margaret Morse analyzes the impact of technical innovations like slow motion and instant replay in television broadcasts of American football, arguing that such innovations distort time and space to the detriment of the game's overall geometry.

The emergence of the sociology of sport as an academic discipline in the 1980s fostered a wealth of research on the relationship between sport, media and society. Garry Whannel's *Fields of Vision* argues that television affects the ways in which we perceive and make meaning of sports. David Rowe's *Sport, Culture and the Media: The Unruly Trinity* focuses on the organizational structures and professional ideologies that shape the production of media sports texts and the way audiences deconstruct sports images and information. His critique is particularly relevant to a discussion of how the sportscast highlight form is deployed. *Sport and Postmodern Times* brings together a number of North American and European scholars whose work examines sport and its significance in the construction and diffusion of dominant cultural meanings and values. Several chapters confront the issues related to sport, representation and the postmodern mediascape.

Several works that do not deal with sport directly informed this study's discussion of the changing protocols related to media. Timothy W. Luke's *Screens of Power* investigates the politics behind how cultural, economic and social meanings are created. His discussion informs the political and cultural economy of sport media forms. Although E. Ann Kaplan's *Rocking Round the Clock* focuses on the rock video genre, her arguments about postmodernism, spectatorship and advertising are certainly applicable to the aesthetic issues confronted in this study. In *Promotional Culture*, Andrew Wernick delineates the unfolding relationship between the intensive and extensive development of the market as an organizing principle of life, emphasizing the impact of promotion on the objective side of culture. Henry Jenkins' *Convergence Culture* offers a cogent discussion on the collision of old and new media. Of particular interest to this study is his explication of convergence, participatory culture, and affective economics.

There is a dearth of scholarship specifically devoted to the issues and contexts in which sports journalism, media and popular culture intersect. Raymond Boyle's *Sports Journalism: Context and Issues* argues that sports journalism has been implicated in the construction of various sports discourses connected to wider issues of gender, race, ethnicity and national identity. David A. Klatell and Norman Marcus' *Sports for Sale* is not wholly devoted to sports journalism; they explore several issues that stem from the entertainment ethos of sportscasting—biased reporting, conflict of interest, time-shifting, and the lack of enterprise reporting.

Understanding how sports highlights evolved out of the technologies and became the means through which producers couch the visual and verbal languages of sport affect is what distinguishes this book and its historical-cultural lens. By tracing the evolution of sports highlights as a news frame, this book adds to our understanding of sports journalism and serves as a praxis for educators to prepare the next generation of sports journalists.

Preface
to the Second Edition

By the time I proposed a new edition of this book in the spring of 2022, I had recognized that the profound changes impacting sport media from cultural, economic, and technological perspectives warranted analysis.

The most significant development reflecting media's obsession with highlights has been the utilization of video replay to adjudicate sporting events. While timing and touch technologies have been in use for much longer, the deployment of video review or replay undoubtedly marks a new level of reliance on technology to ensure that a final outcome was not the result of an obvious human error. The need to guarantee that the result is not tainted has implications for sport leagues and governing organizations as well as media and gambling operators. In order to maintain the veneer of integrity, all aspects of the event or game are monitored and recorded, and obvious errors in officiating are corrected. Preserving the neutrality of written rules by using visual evidence and technological precision has become another of sport media's functions, shaping the discourse.

This quest for certitude and integrity comes at the very same time media regularly embeds promotions for sports betting into televised sportscasts, the direct result of increased sponsorship of professional teams by gambling operators. Techniques including logos on uniforms, gambling-sponsored segments, and on-screen displays of betting odds among others are routinely threaded into the presentation. Sponsors enhance brand recognition and avoid ad-skipping. This marketing trend is manifested in the arena or stadium experience with the addition of free Wi-Fi allowing fans to bet while watching the game in person. New arenas accommodate fans who want to bet on multiple events by providing devoted gambling areas. High stakes bettors are no longer characterized as social misfits but as celebrities within today's culture of risk, players willing to go all in based on an analytical approach that sees sporting teams and players as investment strategies.

This risk-averse sensibility also characterizes the athlete-adventurers featured in sport documentaries that serve as long-form narratives establishing and documenting sporting achievement beyond the immediacy of live events. Fascination in firsts—the very idea of conquests over nature—has remained a source of sports mythmaking, despite having to carry the albatross of imperialism. The road from *The Ascent of Mont Blanc* (1902) to the IMAX presentation of *Shackleton's Antarctic Adventure* (2002) reflects that fascination, and over the course of a century, while technology has only enhanced the spectacular nature of the experience, the focus on human endeavor in an existential struggle remains a compelling draw. It's why 15 million people watched the BBC's broadcast of *The Old Man of Hoy* in 1967 and why millions more watched Alex Hannold free solo climb Yosemite's Half Dome in 2011 on *National Geographic Live.*

These long-form narratives are rooted in an economy of death that serves as the ends and means to cinematic gratification, transferring the thrill of athletic achievement into a concentrated moment of exhilaration meant to maintain that which is of commercial value. That gratification, in effect, is what a highlight satisfies, perfectly suited to a TikTok world in which hyperscale networks push what's important based on algorithms coded with racial, class, and cultural biases.

A history of sports highlights is arguably more relevant now than it was over a decade ago, as the technologies and demands of Big Data surreptitiously suppress individual choices and manufacture consent within a simulacrum that effaces attempts at subversion.

Introduction:
The Highlight Mythmaking Machine

Today it is almost impossible to access sports media without being inundated with highlights. Regardless of the platform (e.g., television, the World Wide Web, hand-held mobile devices), or the venue (e.g., home, sports bar, stadium or arena), all deliver sports highlights as news, teasers, and programs at an ever-increasing rate. It's hard to imagine being at a live sporting event or watching the live broadcast of a sporting event without highlights being shown on jumbotrons and television sets. Highlights have not only become one of the primary means through which sports teams, leagues and media inform and entertain their audiences, but they have also become an intrinsic part of the sports themselves in the form of "Instant Replay," allowing coaches and players to contest on-field decisions by officials. In this sense, the technology that enabled highlights has changed the way sports are officiated, the way live sports are broadcast, and the way journalists construct news.

No longer are sports limited to a three- or five-minute segment that dominated network and local newscasts. With the launching of ESPN in 1979, sports news became a never-ending cycle of scores, updates, previews and promos—all thanks to video recorders that made highlights easily accessible. Highlights have supplanted the sports pages, sports magazines and radio as the easiest way to follow sports and its stars. Whereas 1920s' sports writers like Grantland Rice, Ring Lardner and Paul Gallico were the mythmakers of Babe Ruth, Bill Tilden, Jack Dempsey and Bobby Jones, and television brought Mickey Mantle, Johnny Unitas, Bill Russell, Muhammad Ali, and Arnold Palmer into the living rooms of most Americans, highlights are what made Michael Jordan, Wayne Gretsky, Andre Agassi and Tiger Woods into the megastars who transcended their sports and became icons of sports marketing. Sports have become ubiquitous in our culture and sports stars have replaced political and business leaders as the most important and recognizable persons on earth. It certainly wasn't always this way. So the question must be asked: How did we arrive at this juncture in which sports have become the first and foremost cultural capital? How do highlights help create today's legends and myths?

This book traces the many developments that contributed to the evolution of the sportscast highlight as the primary means of communicating about sports and athletes. In this regard the term *highlights* refers to those texts created with established visual and audio techniques and conventions that generate meaning and create affect. Whether one chooses to describe highlights as a news frame, genre or aesthetic form, the sportscast highlight has been, and continues to be, used to communicate narratives about sporting events and the athletes who compete within them. In this sense, highlights are both form and content, serving as both frame and image within which narratives are presented and preserved. Highlights are those segments that capture historic achievement (e.g., world's record), as well as those sterling examples of individual or team athleticism (e.g., slam dunk) that produce the "wow factor," and even those oddball follies that defy categorization.

Types of Highlights

Basically, highlights fit into two distinct categories that come together to meld into a third. First, there are those highlights whose images largely derive their meaning from their context. For example, the highlight selected as the greatest in a 2008 Entertainment and Sports Programming Network (ESPN) contest, "Greatest Highlight with Chris Berman," was Mike Eruzione's game-winning goal in the 1980 Lake Placid Olympic Games. Although the goal-scoring sequence offered neither outstanding athleticism, nor compelling visuals, it captured a significant sporting moment for an American audience, namely, victory over the highly favored hockey team from the Soviet Union. Even if one did not know that Eruzione's goal was not scored in the gold-medal winning game or that it wasn't scored against the USSR's top goal-tender or that the USA's other goals by Mark Johnson were more dramatic, what's important about Eruzione's goal was that it conveys the ultimate blow of David defeating Goliath. Not knowing the Cold War context of a group of erstwhile amateurs going up against a mighty, state-funded juggernaut robs Eruzione's goal of much of its meaning and significance. Arguably, understanding the context of the "Miracle on Ice" gives that highlight its meaning. Second, there are all of those awe-inspiring images whose meaning is not at all dependent on the context or backstory. For example, Lynn Swann's acrobatic catch in Super Bowl X was a great individual play regardless of the game's outcome. No context is necessary to appreciate the catch, and the images can be appreciated for the power, grace and beauty of the athleticism. The catalogue of these highlights is as wide as the firmament of athletic genius. You can picture them in your imagination: MJ or Doctor J launching from the free-throw line and soaring in for a slam dunk, Bobby Orr or Wayne Gretsky rushing end to end, Gale Sayers taking a punt back all the way. Knockout punches, towering home runs, game-winning goals, touchdown runs and pass receptions are the staples that are delivered as Play of the Game, the Week, the Year. The third category offers great plays at crucial moments. These are iconic sports highlights—game-winners, buzzer-beaters, golden goals: Bill Mazeroski's ninth-inning home run; Franco Harris' "Immaculate Reception"; Dwight Clark's "The Catch"; Bobby Thompson's "Shot Heard Round the World"; Diego Maradona's "Hands of God" goal; Secretariat's Belmont Stakes run. It is not by accident that many of these plays have their own specific or generic identity (e.g., the Hail Mary pass).

Sportscasts

To trace the evolution of highlights as they were developed and deployed within various aspects of a sportscast, it is useful to differentiate between the two main types of sportscasts: (1) the live coverage (i.e., accounts and descriptions) of a sporting event and (2) news- and entertainment-oriented programming based on sporting events. The first category includes all the national and international, professional, collegiate, interscholastic and club sporting events (e.g., Olympics, World Cup Football, Wimbledon, Kentucky Derby, NFL, etc.) that are disseminated live via an electronic delivery system.[1] The second includes all emanations of sports news—film actualities, newsreel sports segments, televised sports news programming, Web site content, sport documentaries, and content delivered via mobile devices. These two main sportscast genres have been communicated by a variety of delivery systems. While the changes in delivery systems, or technologies, are important to consider in the evolution of highlights, they function as only one aspect of how media systems operate. Media systems serve within the broader nexus of information and entertainment conglomerates. In short, media use the various delivery systems to not only disseminate content, to gather data, and to establish social and cultural practices. As a result, it is equally important to consider the social, economic, legal and material relationships that accompany the dissemination of sportscast highlights.

Sportscast highlights, as both form and content for various media, have changed as media's protocols have changed. While the delivery systems of sportscast highlights have changed, what has not undergone significant change is the highlight form itself. In short, sportscast highlights evolved from refinements in audio and video techniques, resulting in enhanced production values. Not surprisingly, sportscast highlights have been adapted and appropriated by news organizations, as well as sports teams and leagues, to capture, preserve and embellish not only decisive moments of sporting events and athletic achievement, but also in establishing and maintaining their identity. In so doing, these entities have utilized highlights to carry ideological messages about whose stories and what values are worth communicating while dismissing or obscuring others. *Who* is in the highlight is as important, if not more important, as *what* is in the highlight.

Explaining the changes in technologies and protocols that have shaped sporting discourse, transmitted cultural values, and promoted affective economics involves an analysis of the visual and audio techniques that constitute the highlight. Arguably, the most important technique is the creation of a visual shorthand through the use of condensation and remediation.[2] Creating the news frame involves editing down hours of footage to find a part that serves to represent the whole. The sportscast highlight frame condenses a two- or three-hour sportscast and reframes those images with auditory conventions (e.g., narrative commentary and canned music) to generate a new meaning context. Highlights can be presented in such a way as to guide the viewer to the "correct" interpretation and feeling state about the performance or play, despite the fact that viewers are almost always disparately positioned and rarely interpret the highlight's meaning in the same way. A towering home run can be seen as a great swing or a fat pitch.

Changes in the technologies were accompanied by changes in protocols for both sportscast producers and audiences. Highlights changed the way sportscasters and electronic sports journalists performed their jobs. For example, with the introduction of in-game replays in the early 1960s, sportscasters' accounts and descriptions of live sporting events became increasingly more technical and analytic, lending a greater scientificity to the commentary. The role of the sportscaster changed from one who informed to one who entertained. When videotape recorders allowed for instant replays, montages were used to amplify the spectacle and generate more in-game promotions. In turn, the commercial imperative reshaped institutional values and professional practices of electronic sports journalists. The relationship between sports journalists and the leagues, teams and players was characterized by marketing co-promotion and a vested interest in protecting each other's financial investments.

Technological changes also impacted the protocols of sportscast viewers. In the early 1890s viewers experienced the sportscast highlight form alone, looking through a viewer mounted on the top of Kinetoscope machines, what were known as peep shows. Only a few years later, projectors allowed for viewing in cinemas (i.e., nickelodeons), opera houses, fairgrounds and anywhere a screen and projector could be set up and powered with electricity. Similarly, early television viewing was largely a communal affair as bars and taverns capitalized on the new medium by offering sportscasts to patrons. The home became the primary place to watch when television sets became affordable for individuals and families. The viewing experience for home audiences changed again with the proliferation of new delivery systems. No longer did viewers depend exclusively on the television schedule since sportscast pay packages allowed for access almost anywhere and anytime, thanks to personal computers and mobile phones. Media and sports leagues discovered they could generate another revenue stream by delivering sportscast content to an audience of one, bringing the viewing experience full circle.

Highlights have a long history. While it is important to acknowledge that illustrations were used in early sporting magazines like *Bell's Sporting Life*, *Spirit of the Times*, and the *Police Gazette*, highlights as we know them today can best be traced in the context of visual electronic media. Specifically, sportscast highlights start with some of the earliest Edison films, which included staged boxing matches, as well as actualities of live sporting events. Later, newsreels helped to standardize the routines utilized by cameramen and the sports segments created in the production offices by editors. Next, early television developed the conventions and production practices used in the presentation of live sporting events and sports news programming. In the early 1960s, televised sportscasts were enhanced with special effects techniques like instant replay.[3] The emergence of cable networks like ESPN and the Cable News Network (CNN), which began airing nightly half-hour sportscasts in 1979 and 1980 respectively, saturated the electronic sports media market and introduced the concept of the "sports junkie."[4] Lastly, new media offered yet another set of delivery systems and protocols that changed the ways audiences accessed sportscasts. Each medium made important contributions, not so much as discrete phenomena, but as the relational totality which the term implies.[5] Put another way, film, newsreels, network and cable television, and new media are very closely aligned in terms of the technologies and protocols that contributed to the development and deployment of sportscast highlights.

Why Highlights?

Highlights are important in large part due to the prominent position sports media in general and sports journalism in particular occupy within the political and cultural economy of late capitalism. Significantly, it is within the sphere of culture where the key economic processes of production, dissemination and exchange occur, connecting cultural production to the late-capitalist world of making products, supplying services and generating profits. Since cultural factors are central to economic processes, then sport and sports media clearly occupy a central position in the larger process that is reshaping society and culture. Highlights, as media texts, are positioned at the very center of our culture: they may not be material, yet billions of people consume them in quantity, and media corporations expend billions of dollars to supply them.[6]

Understanding how sportscast highlights became the means through which producers couch the visual and verbal languages of sport affect sheds light on our cultural and media history.

The significance of highlights can also be seen in the considerable impact the national and regional sports networks (e.g., CBS, NBC, ESPN, Fox Sports Net) have had on the proliferation of sportscasts. The sportscast landscape changed drastically with ESPN's presence on cable systems, as its daily newscasts grew from 15 minutes (originally titled *SportsNight*) to 60 minutes (*SportsCenter*). Additionally, when ESPN began broadcasting 24 hours a day in 1980, sports programming became an all-the-time feature of American culture. Little wonder, then, ESPN research in 2003 showed an average of 94 million Americans spent 50 minutes a day or almost six hours per week with ESPN media.[7] Not surprisingly, ESPN has staked its claim to revolutionizing sports broadcasting and the American experience with sports. In a 2004 book published by ESPN, titled *ESPN25: 25 Mind-Bending, Eye-Popping, Culture-Morphing Years of Highlights*, author Charles Hirshberg argues:

> And it did so by adopting, and perfecting, an underutilized, unappreciated method of communication: the sports highlight…. ESPN has made highlights the primary means by which the patterns and stories of sports are revealed. It's a perfect medium for modern America.[8]

Hirshberg's contention that sportscast highlights have been "underutilized and unappreciated" is patently overstated, given the very prominent use of highlights in both journalistic and non-journalistic sports programming since the very beginning of film. Additionally, the contention that the highlight form is "a perfect medium for modern America" raises questions about whose stories are told and what values are being promoted through that particular media form.

Although ESPN has doubtlessly changed the landscape of sports broadcasting, it's important to consider the changed context within which American electronic sports journalism has been organized and produced, as well as the changed model of consumer behavior shaping programming and marketing strategies.

Electronic sports reporting has arguably changed from one that predominantly informs to one that primarily entertains by employing highlights to present increasingly dramatic and spectacular sports images. The greater the affect, the easier it is to maintain audience satisfaction. If Hirshberg's description—"A good highlight is at once a poetic distillation of athleticism and a carnival barker's holler for your attention, a shameless effort to keep you from pressing that damned remote"—is even remotely accurate, then this "shameless effort" to maintain the audience not only dictates which highlights are presented, but also skews the aesthetic techniques toward more spectacular and viscerally generating highlights.[9] Operating within a postmodern market culture, sportscasts create rather than satisfy needs. This can be referred to as the sport of desire—the non-stop parade of new products, increased sensations and market branding. The media constantly feeds this desire but never quite allows the consumer to feel fulfilled by the images.[10] With highlights, the communication system captures, in this case, sport reality in its entirety so that the viewer becomes fully immersed in a virtual image setting of slam dunks, towering home runs, vicious sacks and fist-pumping athletes. Not having seen the live broadcast doesn't matter because experiencing the highlights becomes more real than the actual event. Ultimately, however many highlights are shown, the viewer is never satisfied, instead being fixated on a perpetual present of a constantly revolving array of myth-making narratives—game recaps subsumed within pastiches of spectacular plays removed from game context, hyped promotional images untethered to any meaning other than what to watch next. By pandering to what Hirshberg calls "Incredible Shrinking Attention Span and its cut-to-the-chase-and-show-me-what-you-got values," networks like ESPN may have found an easy way to rationalize their form of broadcast journalism, but calling it the "perfect medium for modern America" trivializes the product it purports to celebrate.[11]

Lastly, issues of representation remain central to electronic sports journalism, as well as political, economic and international affairs. This stems from the idea that sport and mediated presentations of it operate within a discourse permeated with symbolism and metaphor. In order to analyze the extent to which mediated presentations of sport impact the formations of race, ethnicity, gender and national identity, it is necessary to consider particular social, cultural and historical contexts. Rather than applying universal theories of sport, ethnicity and racism, particularly when examining the production and consumption of electronic news reportage of sport, it should be noted that a clear linkage of relationships connects the roles played by media, sports leagues and audiences. The positioning of the sports world in the social construction of news within both the layout of newspapers and the segmentation of local television news programs offers an important clue about our culture and a direct bearing on the coverage of sport, race and ethnicity. In major newspapers, sports are strategically set apart from other types of news, a world unto itself with its own set of priorities, its own set of news values and a self-sufficiency that other types of news only wished they could duplicate. The newspaper sports section and the televised sports segment have their own internal ranking of big and small stories, their own climaxes, fillers, features, brights and commentary.

This positioning within electronic news media reflects the general place of sport in our culture as a well-defined enclave, one of whose major attractions is that it has little or no relation to the rest of the news. With the arrival of cable sports news programs, televised sports journalism truly set itself apart from the rest of the news. These programs have had an immediate impact on local stations and the way they cover sports, since programs like *SportsCenter* serve as the linchpin for local sportscasters in much the same way that network news programs serve as models for local newscasters. Many local network affiliates, especially those in metropolitan areas that have professional sport franchises, have created their own sport-specific programs modeled after those on ESPN. Not surprisingly, highlights provide the means to attract and maintain an audience. Thus, tracing the evolution of the sportscast highlight provides historical perspective on what might appear to be a distinctly postmodern aesthetic. The better we understand this important sport news frame, the better we can understand the way sportscasts have been, and continue to be, deployed to shape cultural and social values.

Preview of Chapters

What was the history of sports highlights? What were the conditions of their production and reception? This book details the significant technological, legal, social and economic factors in the evolution of this news frame from the earliest days of film until the first decade of the twenty-first century. Throughout this long period of time, highlights remained an important journalistic tool that served important functions.

Chapter 1, "Knockout Rounds and Rounding Marks," explores how early sport film actualities contributed several key components to the evolution of the highlight form—an operational aesthetic that established production practices for the presentation of sport, the popularization of a performance culture that relied on spectacle and sports celebrities, and the marketing, packaging and diffusion of sport content in the form of highlights for cultural consumption. With its ability to capture movement, whether in the form of a horse race, yacht racing on the water, or boxers in a ring, film proved highly popular with the public before the turn of the twentieth century. Significantly, producers quickly learned how to package and promote the most important action and use it to attract an audience.

Another key aspect related to film's operational aesthetic was its use of an on-stage narrator or commentator. Although this development stemmed from the tradition of illustrated lectures, it was used to legitimize sports. For example, having a commentator diffused boxing's unsavory aspect by suggesting that the exhibition could be appreciated for its "genteel style of presentation."[12] Ultimately, however, film actualities featuring boxing became a victim of their own success and of a racial ideology that would not allow the wide presentation of film showing a black champion. Racial ideology was fully realized with the filming and exhibition of the 1910 world heavyweight championship bout between Jack Johnson and James Jeffries.

Chapter 2, "The Habit of Highlights," explains the importance of routinization and standardization in the ways newsreels were produced and viewed. Newsreels built on the advances of film actualities by nationalizing sports within an ideology of hegemonic masculinity, by refining audio commentary, and by increasing the sense of spectacle in capturing the activities of cheerleaders and fans. Sports became one of the three basic kinds of news for newsreels. Sporting events fell into the category of scheduled events, and could be readily counted upon for content, an important consideration when newsreels went to a twice-a-week schedule. With commentary provided by the era's leading sports radio announcers, newsreels contributed to building a national identity in which sport had a central place. That central place was occupied almost exclusively by the dominant male white culture.

Chapter 3, "Bad Habits," delineates the way highlights were employed to create a national culture that focused on the accomplishments of white athletes. Blacks and women were marginalized in most newsreel coverage of sports. Black athletes were to a large extent rendered invisible. Portrayals of women athletes upheld an ideology of hegemonic masculinity in which contact sports were exclusively a male preserve. While this was not a direct product of the aesthetic form of highlights, it points to the impact producers had in shaping the ideology that form manifests. Ultimately, with the advent of television, newsreels lost their hold on viewers, who increasingly watched sporting events as they unfolded on their home sets.

Chapter 4, "A Dream of Carnage and the Electronic Monster," analyzes early sportscasting as an exclusively live medium, transmitting images and sound from one space to another in real time. Viewers watched telecasts that originated from a studio or remote locations, and broadcasters developed the conventions of live coverage of sporting events. Considerations related to the production of sporting events had implications in the development of sports journalism's institutional structures and professional values that shaped the representation of national identity, gender and race. Because coverage of live events was the preserve of the networks' news divisions, conflicts and institutional jealousies within broadcasting arose almost from the very beginning of television production of live sporting events. Thanks to the use of kinescopes, television networks contributed to the development of highlights for newscasts by constructing programs that offered the viewers highlight packages, profiles of sport stars and in-studio interviews. Many of the program formats that remain in vogue today were developed between 1947 and 1960.

In Chapter 5, "The Agony and the Ecstasy of Communication," videotape's deployment as a means to create instant replays is considered, illustrating its immediate and profound impact on sportscasts. The videotape recorder, developed by the Ampex Corporation in 1956, allowed network and local television stations to incorporate highlights more easily into sportscasts. However, it wasn't until 1963 that Tony Verna of CBS developed the means to incorporate instant replay into a live sportscast. Verna's contribution revolutionized the industry and provided the technology that would make the highlight form a means of paramount importance for all live and news-oriented sportscasts.

So pervasive did the use of videotape technology become that it changed not only what fans could see of a game, but it also altered the role of announcers from color commentators to analysts. Even more significantly, the technology changed television's role in relation to the sports it covered. That participation occurred in the way that the technology literally became a part of many sports (e.g., football, hockey, soccer and tennis) in terms of on-field officiating decisions. Equally important from a journalistic perspective, videotape changed the way sports news was packaged and delivered. Until the arrival of videotape, scores and statistics were the primary discursive ingredients of the sport newscast; with videotape, highlights became the focal point.

Chapter 6, "Sports Junkies, Junk Journalism and Cathode Ray Sterilization," explicates cable television's role in saturating the television schedule with sports, fragmenting the audience, driving ratings down, and creating Friday afternoon fire sales for advertisers. The result was predictable: by the mid–1980s no station, cable or broadcast, was making money telecasting sports. Competitive bidding invariably drove up the broadcasting rights for major sporting events. With the advent of cable, television's use of the highlights changed not only the way events were telecast, but it also impacted the stadium and arena experience, long regarded as the last bastion against television's encroachment on the sporting spectacle. Additionally, cable television changed the way sports journalists performed their jobs—both in terms of coverage of live events and in the reporting of sports news. Most notably, the presence of women journalists in the press boxes, announcing booths and locker rooms altered the dynamic of the sports-media relationship. By the time ESPN celebrated its fifteenth year of broadcasting in 1994, the boundaries demarcating sports journalism as information and as entertainment had been blurred beyond recognition. The sports junkie's loyalty was largely predicated upon an operational aesthetic in which the highlight form had become the networks' *sui generis*.

Chapter 7, "The Little Shop of Highlights," explicates ESPN's appropriation and commodification of the highlight form as *SportsCenter* became the network's flagship program. While *SportsCenter* doubtlessly made highlights its primary means of communication, *SportsCenter*'s ubiquitous place in American sports journalism is considered in terms of its formation and development, its constitutive elements, and its offshoots, namely, the "This is *SportsCenter*" advertising campaign and a reality show, *Dream Job*.

Chapter 8, "The Real Virtuality for an Audience of One," explores the developments in new media that reshaped the sports mediascape by providing new technological means of delivering and accessing sportscast highlights. Over the past two decades, sports broadcasters, fans, athletes and the leagues have all been impacted by the changes, especially those precipitated by the development of new delivery systems (e.g., World Wide Web and mobile devices). However, because the integration of new media with coverage of major sporting events involved not only changes in technology, but also social and cultural practices, it is important not to attribute too much to technological changes.

To comprehend the dynamics of the new sports media landscape, it is necessary to consider the changed context of sportscasting and the changed model of consumer behavior or affective economics, a model "which seeks to understand the emotional underpinnings of consumer decision-making as a driving force behind viewing and purchasing decisions."[13] In this model, cultural protocols and practices related to media can be seen as dynamic for both producers and consumers. Today, new alliances between broadcast and cable networks, technology companies, and wireless mobile phone providers have forestalled television audience fragmentation and helped to build a new fan base for sports by offering Internet pay packages, enhancing production values for live coverage of major events, and providing more infotainment, especially highlights.

Chapter 9, "Replay and the Façade of Certitude," investigates the use of technology to adjudicate sporting events, based on a case study of the 2018 FIFA World Cup final match between Croatia and France. Replay serves as an exemplar of remediation within the communicative logics of sport media. That theoretical framework provides the basis for unpacking how replay functions not only within sport media discourse but also within a broader cultural context. Given sport media's key locus within the entertainment industry, the use of replay is a key technological innovation that has brought even more consolidation and coordination between sport media and the sport leagues and organizations. In this sense, replay is media's contribution to maintaining the veneer of integrity, promulgating "presumptive justice," the notion that the outcomes are fair and that justice has been served. The area in which replay has had the greatest impact is officiating. Replay resides at the intersection of the jurisprudence of sport and sport media production, challenging the ontological authority of field officials who now have to cede part of their epistemological privileges—superior view and specialist skills—to off-field or booth officials, armchair arbiters armed with high-definition, digitized video and the promise of revelation. The use of replay has become the last best option for sport media to protect its vested interest, namely, the rights to broadcast, by providing the façade of certitude. By imagining that media can guarantee the integrity of the game, replay has become a false idol of error-free measurement and its counterpart, false transparency. Because both media and sport organizations have embraced gaming and gambling, the importance of integrity has only increased. Achieving the flawlessly officiated game by ever-increasing presence of technology only sends us further into the reaches of corporatized, globalized media conglomerates whose main interest is profit, not integrity of the game.

Chapter 10, "Dead Reckoning and the Discourse of Deviation," analyzes the growth of the sport documentary as an important vehicle for media to promulgate mythmaking. This chapter argues that the genealogy of endurance ocean sailing (EOS) documentaries that chronicle women's sailing achievements offers an opportunity for critical inquiry into sport media's representations of contemporary issues related to gender, communion with the natural world, historiography, and sport culture. By unpacking the changing attitudes about women's participation in a male-dominated sporting culture, it is possible to analyze how sport media through cinematic practices and discursive tropes have provided viewers with a transcendent experience that emphasizes the performative aspects of the sailor who faces death and danger to resist the existential angst of postmodern life. Particularly relevant to these documentaries is their engagement with the past, an intertextual referencing that binds them together, blending meanings that can be re-produced and re-mobilized to further larger ideological aims and to reinforce the shared sense of achievement concentrated in values that maintain the status quo and enhance commercial gain.

Chapter 11, "Big Data and the Gamblification of Sport (Media)," explores changes to the sport-media ecology, spurred by the processes of digitalization, globalization, and commodification and by the convergence of these processes with datafication and hyperscale networks. No better instance of how big data works can be illustrated than the collusion between media organizations, betting operators, and sport entities as embodied in the wearing of betting organizations' logos on FIFA team jerseys, which are shown during coverage by television cameras that, in effect, provide maximum exposure for those brands and blur the lines between entertainment, advertising, and data harvesting. The need to harness the power of big data has only intensified the interdependencies between the Internet and media communication networks, facilitating the digital realization of data as an emerging global format and creating new centers of power, based more on control of data than on control of content.

Chapter 12, "Highlights and History," delineates the major factors that contributed to the emergence of sports highlights, and it considers the importance of highlights in terms of the formation of a cultural hegemony, the standardization of sportscasts, the commodification of highlights, the codification of a canon, and the impact of changing viewer protocols.

CHAPTER 1

Knockout Rounds and Rounding Marks

The first medium featuring sports that contributed to the evolution of sports-cast highlights was film. Those contributions emerged in the two decades (1870s and 1880s) before the arrival of film technology thanks to sports like horse racing and boxing, which borrowed promotional techniques and organizational structures from show business entities like vaudeville and the circus. These techniques included the use of road managers, booking agents, and advertising men. Known as the sporting and theatrical syndicate, this association of entrepreneurs was closely linked to the press, another institution that would have an important cross-promotional relationship with sports and films.[1]

Additionally, early Edison films captured sporting activity—some staged and some actualities—by utilizing production techniques, as well as marketing and exhibition strategies, in ways that were distinct from other film subjects. Early sporting films not only provided the content required to display the technology's capacity to capture motion and save it for audiences, but they also demonstrated film technology's operational aesthetic, which means the ability to capture a live event and represent it in a way that leads the spectator to question how the technology works.[2] This fascination with film technology encouraged spectators to become consumers of the technology, and in turn the films became cultural capital, which acts as a social relation within an exchange system that ultimately confers power and status.[3]

Another consideration stems from the ways that film enhanced the status and earning capabilities of sport celebrities, whether represented as hero (e.g., Gentleman Jim Corbett) or as villain (e.g., Jack Johnson). Film not only facilitated the dissemination of information about sport stars, but it also provided an important source of income to those stars. For example, boxers received royalties from their fight films and earned considerably more than they did from the fights themselves. Previously, fighters earned income by giving exhibitions and appearing in vaudeville shows. Even when states made boxing illegal, they did not prohibit the presentation of fight films in peep show parlors and nickelodeons.

Film technology lent an air of veracity to the representation of sporting events. Before film, sporting events were reported in newspapers and magazines or recreated on stage, but the representation involved the subjective interpretation of the reporter or performer. Because of film's capacity to document actual events, the filmmaker's role was to record an event without interpreting, allowing audience members to form their own opinions about the event. This observational cinema or *cinéma vérité* was further enhanced by the use of an expert commentator, who often was positioned to the side of the screen and offered running commentary, a precursor to today's sports broadcaster.

Lastly, producers and exhibitors played important roles in the marketing of film content, and editorial control became a contested area between them. Owners of Kinetoscope parlors did not buy just anything, but viewed new subjects frequently and carefully decided what to purchase and present. Some Kinetoscope parlors employed multiple machines to exhibit the different rounds of a staged fight, usually six. Although exhibitors could purchase entire films for a set price or single rounds, the knockout round was often the only one sold.[4] A viewer's having to pay ten cents at each machine to see each round of a fight ultimately inhibited the success of the Kinetoscope. Nonetheless, the packaging and exhibiting of knockout rounds became an important marker on the road to sportscast highlights. Film's ability to capture movement, whether in the form of a horse race, yachts racing on the water, or boxers in a ring, proved to be highly popular with the public, creating opportunities for a shared culture.

Sport in the Pre-Film Era

The relationship between sport and its dissemination through visual media emerged as a continuation and transformation of magic lantern traditions that had originated in the seventeenth century and gradually took shape along with the invention, development and deployment of nineteenth-century communication technologies such as the telegraph, telephone and phonograph. Models for early moving pictures can be traced back to wall paintings and illustrated books, both of which employed series of images to tell a story. Arguably, the dissemination of sports via media was also an extension of a visual entertainment tradition (e.g., circus, burlesque, variety theater, etc.) that emphasized an entertainment ethos related to display and spectacle rather than story-telling.[5] Another part of the changing cultural system that fostered a fascination for sports and their visual representations was played by post–Civil War sporting magazines, which anticipated newspapers, radio and television in capitalizing on the public's growing interest in sport. As early as 1872, Frederic Hudson, in his book *Journalism in the United States*, admitted that magazines "unquestionably give more information on the subjects they treat than the general newspaper can."[6] Even before Richard Kyle Fox assumed editorial control of the *National Police Gazette* in 1877, lurid illustrations and photographs were being utilized to exploit the sensationalized themes of crime and sex.

To those themes, Fox integrated the world of sport, especially boxing, so that the *Gazette*'s coverage of the Ryan-Goss fight of 1880 resulted in a run of 400,000 copies and justified the journal's subtitle as *The Leading Illustrated Sporting Journal in America*.[7] These and many other achievements within a long, dynamic process were necessary to help shift the cultural milieu from pragmatic, business-oriented technologies to a consumer-oriented one.[8] It was the conjunction of these lines of development that would ultimately produce the first filmed sports highlights.

While sporting magazines and newspapers were cultivating a fascination for sporting events and athletes, attempts to capture and project motion were being conducted in the laboratories of Muybridge, Edison and Marey. In February 1888, Eadweard Muybridge met Thomas A. Edison in the latter's West Orange, New Jersey, laboratory to discuss combining Edison's phonograph with his zoopraxiscope to project a series of painted images onto a screen, a process that Edison ultimately deemed impractical and inconvenient. Eight months later Edison wrote the first of his caveats about projecting motion pictures. However, it was not until Edison met Étienne-Jules Marey at the 1889 Paris Exposition that he formulated the ideas for a machine that "passed a tape-like band of film past a camera lens, halting and then exposing a single frame of film for a brief fraction of a second, after which the strip was again moved forward, until the next frame of film was halted in front of the lens and likewise halted."[9] After several experiments with cylinders, Edison and his camera specialist William Kennedy Laurie Dickson enlisted William Heise for the project, largely because Heise had expertise in moving tape-like strips of paper through a machine. In the spring of 1891, their experimentation produced a horizontal-feed kinetograph camera and Kinetoscope viewer, which used three-quarter-inch wide film. Of the seven films known to have been made with this camera, the last captured two men boxing.

Edison, who had recently returned from Chicago where he had been asked to provide some electric novelty for the World's Fair exposition, was quoted in a *New York Sun* story of May 28, 1891, that he had a machine being perfected that would allow viewers to sit in their own parlor and see and hear opera singers. Not content to satisfy the more refined tastes and knowing what had already been produced in his Photographic Building, Edison added:

> That is only one part of what the machine will do. To the sporting fraternity I can say that before long it will be possible to apply this system to prize fights and boxing exhibitions. The whole scene with the comments of the spectators, the talk of the seconds, the noise of the blows, and so on will be faithfully transferred.[10]

Edison's comments anticipated a level of sophistication that became characteristic of the "Up Close and Personal" production values of Roone Arledge at the American Broadcasting Company (ABC). Edison clearly understood that boxing, wrestling and strong men were the sporting content that could most effectively be captured by a motion picture camera. Part of this was grounded in Edison's fascination with boxing and the fact that newspaper and magazine coverage had already lent a degree of legitimacy to prize fighting, despite its illegal status in many parts of the country.

In fact, after the last bare-knuckle championship fight in which John L. Sullivan defeated Jake Kilrain (ring name of Joseph Killion) on July 8, 1889, in Richburg, Mississippi, Governor Lowry vowed to prosecute Sullivan and even offered a thousand-dollar bounty. The state of Mississippi indicted Sullivan for the offenses of prize fighting and assault and battery. Tried and convicted of the first charge, Sullivan and his lawyers appealed that decision on the grounds that the nature of the crimes had not been adequately specified in the indictment, that the fight had not been public and that the law required two defendants be charged.[11] Although the court reversed the first decision and quashed the indictment, the entire ordeal cost Sullivan more money than he had won by defeating his opponent, and he vowed never again to fight under the old ring rules. The press played up both sides in the unseemly affair, exploiting the bout to sell newspapers and decrying the fighters' flaunting of the law. Typical was the coverage found in *Frank Leslie's Illustrated Newspaper*:

> The spectacle of two bruised and battered ruffians dodging about the country, to escape the officers of the law, was in itself sufficiently demoralizing, without the addition, in print, of the story of their debaucheries and their low brutalities: and the two together, as illustrative of prevailing popular tendencies, certainly afford little ground for confidence as to the future dominance of the better forces in our life as a people.[12]

Once cleared Sullivan toured North America with a theatrical troupe performing the melodrama *Honest Hearts and Willing Hands*, written especially for him. After a lackluster tour of Australia in early 1892, Sullivan was goaded into issuing a challenge to face "any and all bluffers who have been trying to make capital at my expense,"[13] according to Marquis of Queensberry rules. Among the opponents to whom Sullivan was willing to give preference—all white fighters—was a young Californian named James J. Corbett, with whom he had previously sparred.

That the first heavyweight championship fight to be settled with gloves would be a legitimate media spectacle was testified by the fact that the articles for the $25,000 purse and $10,000 side bet were signed at the offices of the *New York World* and not the *Police Gazette*. The battle between Sullivan and Corbett was scheduled for September 7, 1892, at the Olympic Club in New Orleans, which was equipped with electric lights and a canvas mat. The New Orleans city council had authorized Queensberry rules fights in March 1890, with stipulations that no liquor be served, that no bouts be staged on Sundays, and that promoters contribute fifty dollars to charity.[14] Additional evidence of boxing's transformation from a sport dominated by gamblers to one in which entrepreneurs seized control was seen in the person of Corbett's manager, William A. Brady. Having a background in show business instead of the ring, Brady soon became a theatrical and motion-picture promoter, one who clearly recognized boxing and bicycle racing as extensions of the entertainment field.

In addition to the heavyweight championship fight, the Olympic Club organized and publicized a triple-main-event card over three nights, billed as "The Carnival of Champions." The card included a lightweight title fight between champion Jack McAuliffe and Billy Myer on September 5, and the next night a featherweight championship bout between Jack Skelly and George "Little Chocolate" Dixon.[15] The latter fight, in which the black champion defeated his white opponent in eight rounds, drew calls from both the *Daily Picayune* and the *Times Democrat* that the Olympic Club cease staging interracial matches. Although no hostile reaction was reported to have occurred at the Olympic Club, segregation became the law of the land within four years.

Press coverage of the heavyweight championship fight was extensive. Weeks before the fight, the *New York Herald* declared that "the events on hand are of national and international importance."[16] The *Chicago Daily Tribune* reported that "now men travel to great boxing contests in vestibule limited trains; they sleep at the best hotels ... and when the time for the contest arrives, they find themselves in a grand, brilliantly lighted arena."[17] The *Times Democrat* noted that New Orleans was packed "with visitors of all classes, from the millionaire to the baker to the fakir. Politicians, lawyers, merchants and gamblers elbowed each other in all public places on comparatively equal terms."[18] The 10,000 fans who filled the Olympic Club were not the only ones anxious to see the fight, hyperbolically called the "clash of the Titans." In almost every major city in the country, thousands of interested fans jammed into theaters, hotels and newspaper offices to receive telegraphic reports of round-by-round descriptions "read aloud and shared for a moment in an instantaneous national culture."[19] On top of the Pulitzer Building in New York, a red beacon was poised to signal when the fight went Sullivan's way or a white one for Corbett. The national information network of telegraph, telephone and newspaper communication provided instantaneous results of the fight. Not only did Corbett's victory signal a change in the titleholder, but it also ushered boxing out of a saloon-centered, gambler-controlled subculture and into the larger modern landscape of big business, mass media, and capitalist ideologies.

The Kinetograph, the Kinetoscope and the Black Maria

Less than a month passed after the Corbett-Sullivan fight before Dickson and Heise were testing the design of their motion picture camera. In October 1892 they shot four new films which used film whose width had been adjusted to one and nine-sixteenths of an inch (approximately 35 mm). The subject matter for three of the four films was sports—boxing, fencing and wrestling—and selected frames were subsequently published in the October issue of *The Phonogram*, which clearly articulated the Kinetograph's importance, noting that viewers need not resort to seats in the open air to see events:

Those who are interested in swift-running horses can see a race going on in Sheepshead Bay or Monmouth, without leaving New York and just here let it be remembered that this instrument may play a most useful part, for in a close race where a few inches of space turns the scales, it will take down just what happened faithfully; and the kinetograph will also record with fidelity all that takes place at prize fights, baseball contests and the noise, stir and progress of games.[20]

Significantly, this passage not only heralded the kinetograph's technological achievement in settling sporting disputes, anticipating the use of photo finishes and instant replay, but it also suggested the camera's ability to capture the ambience of sporting events, similar to Edison's comments for the *Sun* article published in May 1891.

Having achieved a working camera, the Edison Company set about in late December 1892 to construct a studio specifically designed for motion picture production. The Black Maria, so named because it resembled the black paddy wagons that brought prisoners to jail, was constructed between December 1892 and January 1893. In his *History of the Kinetograph, Kinetoscope & Kinetophonograph*, Dickson related that the "exigencies of natural lighting" and "the lack of a suitable theatrical stage"[21] necessitated the construction of this revolving building that could follow the rays of the sun. The Black Maria measured 48' × 10' to 14' × 18' overall, and swung suspended on a central vertical axis over a graphite pivot to accommodate the need for sunshine, although nearly all Black Maria subjects were shot close to noon.[22]

Although Edison had entered into an agreement to supply A.O. Tate with 25 Kinetoscope machines for use at the World's Columbian Exposition of 1893 in Chicago, production progressed slowly. By early May George Hopkins of the *Scientific American* examined the Kinetoscope in anticipation of demonstrating it at the annual meeting of the Department of Physics of the Brooklyn Institute of Arts and Sciences. This became its first official public demonstration, and although it did not include sound as promised, *The Brooklyn Standard Union* story offered an interesting account:

The Instrument which was exhibited, however, only presented the moving picture without the noises accompanying. But even in this form it was startling in its realism and beautiful in the perfection of its working.... The pictures taken by the camera can scarcely be distinguished from one another, so slight is the difference between successive views. This explains the continuity and unbroken character of the scene as presented in the kinetograph.[23]

Only one Kinetoscope was sent to Chicago and displayed in the Edison exhibit there, and the first parlor was not ready for the public until April 14, 1894.

In anticipation of the grand opening, the pace of film production in the early months of 1894 picked up considerably. One film, *Fred Ott's Sneeze*, was made specifically for publicity purposes to illustrate an article that appeared in the March 24 issue of *Harper's Weekly*. The other films capturing athletic movement included *Athlete with Wand*; *Amateur Gymnast, no. 1*; *Amateur Gymnast, no. 2*; *Men on Parallel Bars*; and *Boxing Match*. The most significant films of this period, however, included three films of Eugen Sandow, body builder and strong man, shot on

March 6, 1894. Sandow, one of the most popular theatrical stars, was at the time appearing at Koster & Bial's Music Hall, and his appearance at the Black Maria initiated the commercial phase of Edison's motion picture work. Dickson relates in his *History* that Sandow's chest expansion was 14 inches. "The greatest expansion ever known at the Olympic games was six. This is demonstrated in the kinetograph series, together with the more remarkable feats relating to the action and uses of the various muscles, such as the lifting of three-hundred pound dumb-bells at arm's length over his head."[24] Despite Dickson's seemingly overblown contention about expansion, the making of the *Sandow* film marked an important break from past efforts and introduced a relationship between the motion picture world and a performance culture, of which athletic performance would become increasingly popular.

The next major development occurred later that summer with the production of two fight films for the Kinetoscope Exhibiting Company,[25] controlled by Samuel Tilden, Jr., Enoch Rector and the Latham family—Woodville and his sons Otway and Grey. The Lathams proposed the exhibition of prize fight films in enlarged Kinetoscopes that could accommodate approximately 150 feet of film, almost three times as much film as the standard Kinetoscope. The enlargement involved the addition of spools to the spool bank, a stronger motor and changes to the Black Maria's interior, including the addition of padding on the walls and ropes on three sides of the 12-foot square ring. The rounds lasted a minute with seven or eight minutes in between rounds to load more film into the kinetograph. Newspaper accounts noted that several attempts to enlist fighters had been made before June 14, but those attempts proved unsuccessful.

Although titled *Leonard-Cushing Fight*, it is important to consider this production in the Black Maria as distinctively different from a legitimate fight documented by a motion picture camera. Rather, this match was a staged boxing exhibition, limited by the constraints of the camera and the Black Maria space. Nonetheless, the *Leonard-Cushing Fight* was indeed marketed and advertised as a legitimate fight, evidenced by the descriptions in various catalogues. For example, the Maguire *Catalogue* (1898) noted, "This fight consists of six rounds between Mike Leonard, the very popular and well-known pugilist … and Jack Cushing. It was an actual contest, and is full of hard fighting. It has proved a popular and interesting subject."[26] The Edison catalogue of July 1901 called it "an actual six-round contest between Mike Leonard … and Jack Cushing."[27] The Maguire and Baucus catalogue of 1897 read: "Each of the above spirited boxing contests consists of SIX live rounds with 'knock-out' in the last."[28] By emphasizing that this was an "actual" fight with "spirited boxing" and "full of hard fighting," the producers were obviously attempting to dispel the notion that this was a pseudo-fight, and to present it as a novelty worth the 60 cents a viewer paid to watch all six rounds. Although the fight garnered considerable newspaper coverage, it seems doubtful that viewers expected a legitimate boxing contest. Nonetheless, this graying of boundaries between films of legitimate fights and those staged fights set up for the camera undermined the legitimacy of both the motion picture industry and the sport of boxing until the 1920s.[29]

While problems did surface when exhibitors attempted to pass off recreations as the real thing, no evidence suggests that customers entering a peep show parlor were duped into paying for anything other than a staged fight. More significantly, the Latham scheme of serializing the presentation in machines that offered viewers three times as much film for twice the cost of the standard nickel-slot Kinetoscope created a viewing experience that emphasized the knockout as climax. The marketing ploy was readily picked up and disseminated by the press, evidenced in the *New York World*'s report:

> The theory is that when in the first round he [viewer] sees Mr. Leonard, to use his own language "pushing Mr. Cushing in the face," he will want to see the next round and the next four. Thus he will pay sixty cents for the complete kinetograph [sic] of this strange and unheard of fight.[30]

Believing that viewers would pay to see "a fight to the finish," the Kinetoscope Exhibition Company opened a parlor at 83 Nassau Street in Manhattan that was devoted exclusively to showing the *Leonard-Cushing Fight* on the new model (150-foot capacity) Kinetoscope. However, the relative obscurity of the fighters, both of whom were from Brooklyn, and the fact that viewers could opt to pay for only the knockout round contributed to the lack of success of the Lathams' parlor. Not surprisingly, the knock-out round of a fight was often the only one sold. Nonetheless, the marketing of fight films by selling rounds remained in vogue into the first decade of the twentieth century and marked a necessary step in the formation of highlights as a way to attract viewers.

Regardless of how viewers interpreted the film, the *Leonard-Cushing Fight* also drew the notice of authorities. An article in the June 16 edition of *The Sun* noted that the Grand Jury in Essex County was being convened to "investigate a reported prize fight, something which was certainly meant to appear to be a fight to a finish took place in the grounds of the Edison laboratory at Orange on Thursday morning."[31] Although no formal charges were brought against Edison, concerns about the presentation of fight films continued as the technology improved and ultimately was used to capture actual boxing contests.

With the help of Enoch Rector and Samuel Tilden, Jr., the Lathams attempted to arrange a bout that featured heavyweight champion Jim Corbett. After winning the heavyweight championship from John L. Sullivan in 1892, Corbett had not defended his title and fought only one exhibition against British champion Charlie Mitchell in January 1894. Speculation swirled that Corbett would fight Peter Jackson of the British West Indies, but nothing came of that, in part because Corbett, like Sullivan, had promised not to break the color line and fight a black fighter for the championship. Newspaper accounts reported that Edison's company had offered $15,000 for the Corbett-Jackson fight, but the fight never materialized.

Nonetheless, Corbett was enlisted, for a fee of $4,750 to fight "a clever Trenton heavyweight" Peter Courtney, who had supposedly "stood up against" Robert Fitzsimmons.[32] That Corbett's appearance at the Edison complex was a carefully choreographed promotion was evidenced by the fact that the fight was staged on the seventh of September[33] (the second anniversary of Corbett's knockout of Sullivan), by Edison's presence at the Black Maria to greet the champion, and by the numerous newspaper accounts documenting the entire affair from Corbett's arrival at the ferry dock at 8:15 a.m. to the celebrations at Johnny Eckhardt's. Clearly, journalists from the *Police Gazette* and the *World* were complicit in assisting the Edison Company's marketing of this supposed genuine fight, the latter providing a series of drawings that were recorded by the newspaper's "artist at the scene."[34] Although the *Sun*'s lead graph notes that "the fight was in the interests of science," the outcome never was in doubt. In the *Sun*'s summary of the fourth round, the reporter notes, "It was now a certainty that Courtney would not last the six rounds...." Even as Courtney toed the mark to begin the next round, "he knew very well that Corbett would sooner or later knock him out, but he didn't flinch a particle, and faced the music like a man." In the climactic sixth round, "Jim had to finish him, however, as a matter of business...."[35] For the purposes of the film, the knockout occurred on cue.

Dickson served as the producer for the filming of *Corbett and Courtney before the Kinetograph*, and Heise worked the camera. The Black Maria's improvised ring was enlarged to "14 feet square, roped on two sides, the other two being heavily padded walls of the building. The floor was planed smooth and covered with rosin."[36] Five-ounce gloves were used, although the gloves were changed to smaller ones because they blocked the fighters' faces from the camera. Footage of the fight shows Corbett laughing while deflecting Courtney's wild swings, possibly in the fourth round, when the *Sun* reported that "Corbett clinched him and then laughingly threw him off."[37] Each of the six rounds lasted a little longer than one minute, appropriate lengths for the Latham-enlarged Kinetoscope.

As soon as newspaper accounts of the Corbett-Courtney fight were published, Judge Depue instructed the Grand Jury "to look into the Corbett fight in West Orange, before Edison's Kinetoscope, and find an indictment if the law has been violated."[38] The following day, Edison spoke to a reporter for the *Newark Daily Advertiser*, dismissing the incident:

> I don't see how there could be any trouble about that fight. Those kinetograph people take pictures of anything that comes along. They have to do it, and we don't interfere with them....
>
> Certainly I did not understand that a prize-fight was to take place, and it was not a prize-fight in any sense of the word, as I understand it.... I have been told that the men wore five-ounce gloves....
>
> I was not there. I have my business to attend to up here, but I have seen some of my men who were there and they say that the contest was similar to others, except that Corbett being one of the principals there was more interest in it.
>
> There was no knocking out done. It was simply a boxing match for a show for which these men were paid, and nothing more.... I should certainly not permit any fight to a finish in my place under any consideration.[39]

This constituted almost the entire printed article and illustrates Edison's careful manipulation of the situation, distancing himself from the immediate proceedings, claiming not to have been there and not to have interfered with the kinetograph people, who produced an exhibition similar to others. Edison also clearly differentiated this "boxing match for a show" from a "fight to a finish," although that distinction was meaningless when it came to marketing the fight for public consumption, at which point it again became an actual fight with knockout. Edison doubtlessly knew that the controversy surrounding the making of this staged film enhanced the public's desire to see what all the fuss was about. Not surprisingly, then, *Corbett and Courtney Before the Kinetograph* became the most widely seen Kinetoscope attraction, even after projected film replaced peep shows in popularity. The exhibitions earned Corbett considerable royalties; the agreement stipulated that he receive $150 per week (later reduced to $50) for each set of films on exhibition in the Kinetoscopes, the sum of which reached $13,307 by August 1896 and eventually exceeded $20,000.[40]

Projection of Actualities

The progression from peep show to projection owed as much to the conditions related to audience comfort as to technological innovation. Woodville Latham testified that almost as soon as the Edison Kinetoscope Company began showing fight films in the enlarged Kinetoscopes at their parlor on Nassau Street in Manhattan, Otway and Grey heard viewers express a desire to see the films projected upon a screen.[41] Such a projection enabled several possibilities. For one, the audience would see a larger, if not life-size, representation of the subject matter more clearly and more conveniently. Second, rather than experiencing the film individually, viewers seeing a film projected upon a screen shared the experience with others. Third, projection offered the possibility of exhibiting an entire sporting event instead of an abridged version necessitated by the Kinetoscope's limited capacity. Projection also benefited the exhibitor in that parlors needed only one projector, reducing the wear and tear on both film and projector. Showing a film to many viewers at one time reduced costs and increased revenues, expanding the exhibitor's range for distribution since more parlors across a wider territory could be opened with far fewer projectors.

By autumn of 1894, the Lathams were conducting experiments on a new projection system under the auspices of the Lambda Company, headed up by the Lathams, Eugène Lauste, and William K.L. Dickson, who would resign from the Edison laboratory in April of the following year. These experiments resulted in a new camera and the Eidoloscope projector, a demonstration of which was given at the Lambda Company offices (and workshop) on April 21, 1895. An illustration of the demonstration appeared in the *New York Sun* the very next day with a caption that read:

"Enlarged Kinetoscope Pictures Thrown on a Screen." According to the *Sun* article, the projected image was about the size of a window sash, although "the size is a matter of expense and adjustment."[42]

It is ironic that the Lambda Company's first production with the projection system that was so instrumental in capturing actualities involved the re-creation of a fight between Young Griffo (Albert Griffiths) and Charles Barnett on the rooftop of Madison Square Garden in early May. The film included no more than eight minutes of action—four rounds of a minute and a half with thirty seconds of rest between rounds—which was not significantly different than Kinetoscope fights. What was different was that the action was shot without interruption. With an added loop to the camera—known as the Latham Loop—the capacity for continuous shooting was limited only by the amount of film housed in the film magazine.

The Latham Eidoloscope made its debut on May 20, 1895, in a small storefront theater at 156 Broadway. The first commercial audience for projected motion pictures saw a reproduction of the Griffo-Barnett fight. A broadside for the fight related several key components about the exhibition, as well as a summary of the fight. The broadside noted that the reproduction was "Life Size" and that "During the Exhibition the Audience Will Be Comfortably Seated" and "This is the first practical exhibition of subjects showing Actual Life Movements on a screen ever made in the world."[43]

A *World* article from late May lauded the advantages of the Eidoloscope, noting that viewers will no longer "have to squint into a little hole" to see the life size presentations. "It is all realistic, so realistic indeed that excitable spectators have forgot themselves and cried, 'Mix up there!' 'Look out, Charlie, you'll get a punch,' 'Oh! What do you think of that Mr. Barnett?' and other expressions of like character."[44] The article's point about viewers responding to the realistic images, despite being a representation of a re-created fight, was significant because it showed that in the absence of a commentator, viewers supplied commentary themselves. In the next important fight film, the *Corbett-Fitzsimmons Fight*, commentary would be provided for them. The article also noted that the audience sat comfortably and saw "fighters hammering each other, circuses, suicides, hangings, electrocutions, shipwrecks, scenes on the exchanges, street scenes, horse-races, football games, almost anything, in fact, in which there is action, just as if you were on the spot during the actual events."[45] In fact, those actual events included a horse race at the Sheepshead Bay track and several wrestling bouts on the roof of the *Police Gazette* building.

Latham's Eidoloscope Company exploited territorial rights for the projector and exhibited projected films in Chicago's Olympic Theater in late August before moving on to the Cotton States Exposition in Atlanta where they encountered competition from C. Francis Jenkins and Thomas Armat, whose Phantoscope was technically superior in the use of an intermittent mechanism. By the end of 1895, Jenkins and Armat had a falling out, but not before the latter had enlisted the interest of Raff & Gammon, who worked to secure rights to the Phantoscope for Edison. The machine was given a new trade name, the Vitascope, formed from the Latin *vita*, "life," and the Greek, *scope*, "to see," somewhat ironic since this machine eventually sounded the death knell for the Kinetoscope, the first commercially successful motion picture machine. Kinetoscopes would disappear from the American scene by the turn of the century.

When the Vitascope debuted on April 23, 1896, showing six films at Koster & Bial's Music Hall on Thirty-Fourth Street and Broadway, it initiated a new phase in entertainment culture. In addition to the continuous band of 50-foot or 150-foot films spliced together and shown repeatedly, the Music Hall band provided accompaniment to the projected images. The representation of real scenes produced a heightened sense of realism. An article from the *New York Mail and Express* from April 24 captured this in detail:

> One could look far out to sea and pick out a particular wave swelling and undulating and growing bigger and bigger until it struck the end of the pier. Its edge then would be fringed with foam, and finally, in a cloud of spray, the wave would dash upon the beach. One could imagine the people running away.[46]

This produced congruence between the projected image and the everyday world as viewers knew and experienced it directly. The Vitascope remained a novelty in that most of the filmed actualities were devoid of a narrative. The exceptions were those sporting events like the 1896 Suburban Handicap that the Vitascope, more mobile and sensitive to light, captured on site rather than in the confines of the Black Maria studio.

The Edison Manufacturing Company's footage of the 1896 Suburban Handicap was the first American film of a horse race.[47] That also made the Suburban Handicap the first remotely shot sporting actuality to be projected for commercial distribution in the United States. The film debuted at Keith's New Theatre in Boston in late June, less than a week after the running of the race. A *Boston Herald* article of June 30 explained that the "portion of the picture showing the field was somewhat obscured by the dust raised by the racers, but the *finish of the stretch*, showing the judges' box and grand stand crowded with spectators was extremely realistic"[48] (emphasis added). Arguably, the race's finish constituted the most important part of the race and the most natural part to capture on the 150 feet of film shot (approximately one minute), although it was not the only portion of the race captured. This testified to a deliberate, conscious decision on the part of the producers—James White and Raff & Gammon—to guarantee that cameraman Heise captured highlights of the race. An editorial in the *New York Herald* from June 24 added more details, including the fact that the "day was perfect overhead" and that "the race itself was anybody's until the horses were nearly home."[49]

The team of White and Heise also shot the 1897 Suburban Handicap at the Sheepshead Bay track of the Coney Island Jockey Club. This race was also filmed on a 150-foot strip and included several views of the event—the parade past the stand to the starting post, the horses running past the stand, the finish, and the weighing out. The four-shot structure marked this Suburban as particularly noteworthy, although not so significantly different from the previous year's film apart from the parade. Since the 1896 film is no longer available, a direct comparison is not possible, although only the pre-race parade seems to have been added, according to the *Boston Herald* account. Both films were framed by editorial decisions about composition, and since a 50-foot strip "showing the start and finish and weighing-out as above"[50] was also available, the process of selecting and editing to create highlights of the event was certainly accomplished. The process is a synecdoche in that through the use of condensation and re-contextualization, a part was used to represent the whole.[51]

The Corbett-Fitzsimmons Fight Film

When Bob Fitzsimmons knocked out Jim Corbett in Carson City, Nevada, on March 17, 1897, to win the heavyweight championship of the world, three hand-cranked cameras loaded with thousands of feet of film were situated at ringside in a specially designed wooden house to capture the entire spectacle. The fight was financed and promoted by a Dallas entrepreneur and sporting man, Dan Stuart, and filming of the event was produced by the Rector-Tilden partnership, which had successfully brought off the Corbett-Courtney exhibition for the Kinetoscope Exhibition Company but was now operating under the aegis of the newly formed Veriscope Company.

Organizers of the Corbett-Fitzsimmons fight had to overcome considerable difficulties before being able to stage the fight. Finding a venue for the fight proved to be one of the most difficult hurdles. In October 1895, Stuart unsuccessfully attempted to stage the championship fight in Texas only to be thwarted when the governor and legislature quickly enacted a law making prizefighting a felony. A similar scenario unfolded in Arkansas, and soon thereafter Corbett announced his retirement. The title then passed to Peter Maher, who knocked out Corbett's sparring partner Steve O'Donnell on November 11, 1895, despite the fact that Fitzsimmons had easily outclassed Maher three years earlier. In turn, Fitzsimmons knocked out Maher on February 21, 1896, in 95 seconds in a ring constructed on a sandbar in the Rio Grande, although no film of the fight was taken due to a light rain and insufficient light. With Fitzsimmons touring the vaudeville circuit as champion, the debacle on the Rio Grande prompted Corbett to come out of retirement and proclaim himself champion despite a lackluster four-round draw against Tom Sharkey. Only after intense lobbying was Stuart able to convince Nevada lawmakers to once again legalize prizefighting.

By the time an agreement for the fight, including film rights, was signed, the commercial potential for fight films had increased dramatically as a result of the development in projection by the Eidoloscope, Phantoscope and Vitascope. Boxing became the first sport to realize considerable profits from motion-picture reproductions, complementing the profits reaped from paid admissions, betting, and theatrical exploitation of prizefighters' celebrity status. Importance of the event's filming was evident in a *Boston Herald* headline that read, "The Kinetoscope Will Dominate Wholly the Arrangements for the Holding of the Battle."[52] Stuart even tried to alter the size of the ring to 22 feet square when he realized the Veriscope camera might not capture the action in one of the corners, where, as fate would have it, Corbett fell in the 14th round during the controversial knockout sequence.

While the 11,000 feet of two and three-sixteenth-inch-gauge film stock with a wide-screen format shot by Enoch Rector's specially built cameras on March 17, 1897, was being developed for exhibition, a variety of religious and reform groups lobbied Congress to enact legislation that would ban not only prizefighting but also images and reports of fights. Fearing that such a broadly written bill would result in censorship of newspapers and magazines, Congress took no action on the proposed legislation. Even though a number of state legislatures also considered banning fight films, few enacted laws prohibiting the exhibition of fight films. Several factors contributed to the defeat of such legislation, including boxing's popularity, the absence of any clear conception of what constituted cinema, and the Veriscope Company's effective publicity and promotional campaign.[53]

Exhibition of the *Corbett-Fitzsimmons Fight* was noteworthy on several counts. Even before the film was made available for the public, Stuart screened the film for the New York press, generating considerable publicity about the film's content rather than the technology. As such, each of the fighters made claims about what camera showed. In this regard, the company's name, Veriscope or truth-viewer, proved beneficial in playing on the controversies stemming from the fight's outcome. A *New York World* article noted that the camera proved to be "a triumph of science over the poor, imperfect instrument, the human eye, and proves the veriscope camera is far superior."[54] The possibility that the camera could prove whether or not Fitzsimmons had been down for a ten-count in the sixth round and whether or not Corbett had been fouled in the decisive fourteenth round added to the film's attraction.

The exhibition of the *Corbett-Fitzsimmons Fight* debuted on May 22, 1897, at the Academy of Music in New York City. The film, with a running time of almost two hours, was soon offered as a stand-alone feature in many large theaters of major urban centers. As a representation of an actual event, the film was both legally and socially acceptable viewing material for an audience that cut across cultural and economic lines. In Chicago, where the film enjoyed an initial run of nine weeks, admission ranged from 25 cents for a gallery seat to one dollar for the orchestra. As such, the theater seat served as a replacement for the ringside seat, creating an alternate way of spectating this sport. Over time, the film was exhibited in various other amusement places—fairgrounds, resorts, amusement parks, storefronts, and midways—almost anywhere a screen could be hung and electricity provided. Despite newspaper reports that detailed the flickering and vibrations that proved trying to the eyes, prompting efforts to improve both prints of the film and the projecting machines, the *Corbett-Fitzsimmons Fight* remained a premiere attraction thanks to effective publicity and distribution, topicality and mode of exhibition.

One of the noteworthy aspects of the film's exhibition was its use of an expert who stood on-stage and provided running commentary. These experts varied from location to location, and undoubtedly the nature of their commentary also varied in terms of content and quality. Nonetheless, their descriptions of the fight's key moments, especially its controversies, fueled the audience's experience and drew considerable reactions, as evidenced in various newspaper reports. For example, the *New York Tribune*'s article of May 23, 1897, noted:

> In the sixth round, when Fitzsimmons was brought low for a few seconds, the crowd became so much excited that the lecturer who was explaining incidents had to give it up and let the spectators understand the rather complicated situation the best they could. He managed to get in just a word of explanation when it was nearly over.[55]

The same article related that when Corbett was knocked out in the final round, spectators cried out, "Where's the foul? Where's the foul?" The fight's ending, in which Corbett crawled out of the camera's view, no doubt left many viewers wondering exactly what had happened.

The live narrator's presence was important for at least two reasons. The narrator connected the fight film exhibition to the tradition of the illustrated lecture and thereby helped to assuage the concerns of those for whom boxing was an anathema by suggesting a more refined mode of presentation used in illustrated lectures on the lyceum circuit.[56] Also, the spoken commentary rendered musical accompaniment unnecessary and doubtlessly inspired spectator yelling, cheering and generally playing the counterpart to the actual ringside spectators. Perhaps even more telling is the idea that in the use of an expert to provide commentary, sports announcing was born. Given the fact that within two years, several broadcasters, including Marconi and De Forest, would attempt to provide newspapers with live reporting of an international yacht race off Sandy Hook[57] via wireless technology, the assertion is not without merit. Details and significant moments that today's technology brings out in close-ups were emphasized by the narration and accurately illustrates the importance of this exhibition innovation in the development of an sportscast convention.

The *Corbett-Fitzsimmons Fight* grossed approximately $750,000 with profits exceeding $120,000 after the fighters received their percentages, marking it the first motion picture blockbuster. More important, the fight's film proved that a mass audience would pay to see a presentation of an actual event and that a privileged commentator could be used to guide viewers to the correct interpretation and feeling state, a function performed by today's expert analyst who communicates insider information through intonation, interpretation and assertion, with the help of technological innovations like the Telestrator.

Issues

Although motion picture companies continued to film sporting events, as well as their recreations and reenactments, these undertakings were not without problems along various technical, social and legal fronts. Seeking to follow up on the success of the *Corbett-Fitzsimmons Fight*, the American Vitagraph Company attempted to photograph the Jeffries-Fitzsimmons fight, scheduled at the Coney Island Sporting Club on the night of June 9. That the film industry was having a direct economic impact on the boxing world was evident in a July 29, 1899, article by Sam C. Austin for the *Police Gazette*, titled "Lively Bidding for the Jeffries-Sharkey Fight." Noting that any club wanting to stage this championship fight needed both money and motion-picture facilities, Austin argued that the exhibition of fights "has moved beyond the experimental stages ... [of the] indistinct and unsatisfactory"[58] Corbett-Fitzsimmons fight film and that the potential for the upcoming fight was enormous:

> To such an extent has the photographing of movable objects been perfected since then that a wholly satisfactory result may be obtained, and considering the amount of interest that is now being taken in pugilistic affairs an exhibition of a genuine championship fight, such as the one forthcoming [Jeffries-Sharkey], ought to profit its promoters to the extent of several hundred thousand dollars.[59]

Although Austin's claim that the photographing of movable objects, both staged and outdoor events, had been perfected was overstated, the same could certainly not be said of photographing live indoor events.

To capture this indoor event, 24 lamps were erected over the ring, but the engine that was supposed to provide the necessary watt output failed to generate enough horse-power.[60] *The Phonoscope* reported that only half of the lights powered up. "The light was perhaps equal to about four of the lamps burning as they should have burned, and the Kinetoscope films developed out innocent of any marks that would suggest a negative." The magazine blamed the fiasco on inadequate planning and "demonstrates the advisability of preliminary trial before risking an installation on an important venture."[61] The piece concluded by underscoring the fact that with more time to properly install and connect the equipment, the venture could be successfully accomplished. The Edison Manufacturing Company offered "the six important rounds, including the knockout ... faithfully reproduced"[62] with the actual fighters for $150, but not before Siegmund Lubin's reproduction beat them to market, which even the Vitagraph Company used for a time.

When Jeffries and Sharkey met in a heavyweight championship fight of 25 rounds on November 3, 1899, at the Coney Island Sporting Club, the lighting issue had been resolved from a technical standpoint. Despite shooting more than seven miles of footage on the largest film stock, two inches by two-and-three-quarter inches, Biograph's production team encountered different problems. Some were self-inflicted and others "surreptitiously" imposed. The 350 miniature arc lights needed to illuminate the ring for Biograph's cameras almost roasted the fighters. After the fight, Jeffries decried the lights, telling the *New York Herald*, "No more picture machines for me. The intense heat from the electric lights bothered me considerably and made me very weak at times."[63] Additionally, the cameras failed before the final round was completed, so that a reenacted ending had to be filmed some time in the 17 days before the film was ready for exhibition. This diluted Biograph's contention that they alone were offering the "only complete and accurate pictures" of the fight.[64]

Biograph waged an intense publicity battle in order to fend off Lubin's faked fight reenactment and American Vitagraph's fragments shot with cameras that had been smuggled into the arena by Edison and Vitagraph's men, despite the presence of Pinkerton security hired to forestall such an infringement. Although Vitagraph's pirated version was copyrighted the next day by James H. White as *The Battle of Jeffries and Sharkey for Championship of the World*, the American Mutoscope and Biograph Company launched vigorous legal and publicity campaigns to prevent exhibition of the pirated film. Biograph took out an advertisement in the *New York Clipper*, offering the Edison Manufacturing Company $5,000 if it could dispute the fact that their pictures of the fight "are anything more than fragmentary snap shots of a few rounds, taken by cameras surreptitiously smuggled into the Coney Island Sporting Club and worked secretly."[65] A similar amount was offered to Lubin, although he countered by offering $10,000 to anybody who could prove his reproduction was not copyrighted. Lubin offered both a 15- to 20-minute version of the entire fight, and a six-round highlight film. Interested exhibitors were even provided with free samples via mail. Unfortunately, fake fight films contributed to the dissolution of public interest in the real sport, which continued to struggle under the shadow of corruption and deception.

Although Biograph's exhibition of the *Jeffries-Sharkey Fight* met with financial success, the tour was short-lived in comparison to the *Corbett-Fitzsimmons Fight*. One contributing factor was the changed reception that existed in 1899–1900. Unlike its predecessor, this release did not engender calls for legislation and censorship. Rather, by the dawn of the twentieth century, editorial control became an area of contention between manufacturers and exhibitors. The Edison Company had assumed greater editorial control in the production and marketing of its films. For example, the film of *President McKinley's Funeral Cortege at Buffalo, New York,* was a 400-foot "series" consisting of four separate films brought together through dissolves, introduced in the printing process.[66] The same process was employed for America's Cup races, filmed in early October 1901, as they had been in 1899.

The America's Cup yacht races between "Columbia" and "Shamrock I" in 1899 and between "Columbia" and "Shamrock II" in 1901, the latter owned by Sir Thomas Lipton, drew considerable newspaper coverage. The *New York Times* reported on October 21, 1899, that "large and demonstrative" crowds gathered in front of the newspaper offices along Park Row to read the bulletins of the race's progress, "impeding the progress of street cars and invaded City Hall Park for a considerable distance." The crowds who gathered were both business men and "idlers who stood through the nearly four hours the race was in progress."[67] The races also provided an opportunity for Marconi to demonstrate his wireless technology. According to the *Proceedings of the United States Naval Institute* by the United States Naval Institute, the tests found that the "coherer, principle of which was discovered some twenty years ago, [was] the only electrical instrument or device contained in the apparatus that is at all new."[68] A new technology was again tested through coverage of a live sporting event.

The films of the 1899 America's Cup, produced for Edison by J. Start Blackton and Albert E. Smith, captured select moments from each of the races. At least two were taken of the first race, contested on October 16, 1899. The first 100-foot film showed the "two yachts rounding the stakeboats and jockeying for a start."[69] The second film was given no description, although it had an alternate title, *"Columbia" and "Shamrock" Tacking*, which might be the name of another film that was not copyrighted.[70] For the third and final race, three films, each 100 feet, were taken; the first two show the two yachts rounding one of the outer marks. The third, titled *"Columbia" Winning the Cup*, captured the decisive moment of the race. The Edison Film catalogue of July 1901 described the action: "As the 'Columbia' crosses the line, followed closely by the 'Shamrock,' we see the steam from the whistle of the Light Ship announcing the well earned victory of the American yacht."[71]

These America's Cup films are important examples of how film was used to capture sport actualities. First, that the Edison Manufacturing Company created a series with the 1899 and 1901 America's Cup races illustrated a desire to create and market a composite story of a sporting event comprised of multiple parts. This strategy continues to be employed to market DVDs that tell the story of a team's victory (e.g., Super Bowl, World Series) or the story of a specific event (e.g., 2002 Salt Lake City Olympics, 1981 Wimbledon). Additionally, the decision to capture the decisive moments of a race that featured 90-foot yachts rather than attempting to capture the event in its entirety necessarily involved strategic planning, coordination, and timing. It also pointed to a completely different aesthetic than had been employed for filming fights. In capturing actual performances that unfolded in time, films of sporting events like boxing worked against conventions of the presentational approach that dominated early cinema.[72] However, because of their length, their movement across a fixed course over open water, and their slow progress, these America's Cup races lent themselves to highlight framing that could better represent the whole by capturing specific aspects of the race, namely the start, rounding marks, and the finish, signified by a cannon shot once the winning boat crossed the committee boat's bow. This deliberate presentation of key moments was arguably the most important marker in the evolution of sportscast highlights. Lastly, these films served as standards against which to measure newsreel coverage of the

America's Cup races featuring J-boats in 1930, 1934, and 1937, as well as television coverage of the 12-meter boats starting in 1958, particularly the 1983 and 1987 America's Cup competitions. This process of putting together excerpts of actualities that had already taken place and editing in more recent film was also used to promote and publicize the Jeffries-Johnson heavyweight championship fight in 1910. More and more, film was being used not merely to capture an actual event, but also to generate publicity for an event that had yet to occur.

Bifurcation

By the time the Chicago Fight Picture Company put together excerpts and knockout rounds from the recent fights of both Jim Jeffries and newly crowned champion Jack Johnson and sold it as *The Making of Two Champions (1909–1910)*, both the film industry and the sport of boxing were in the midst of considerable change. During what was known as the Nickelodeon Era (1905–1915), the motion-picture industry changed from a loosely structured entertainment syndicate to a big business model based on mass production by a limited number of production companies. These studios ultimately changed both their product, concentrating on feature-length fictional films rather than short subjects, and viewing spaces, replacing storefront nickelodeons and peep show parlors with ornate theaters that showed only films. Rapid growth in the film industry is also evidenced in the proliferation of the first trade magazines—*Views and Film Index* (April 1906), *Moving Picture World* (March 1907), *Moving Picture News* (May 1908), and the *Nickelodeon* (January 1909). As Streible notes, "Amid this expansion, American Progressivism also simultaneously implemented its age of reform, critiquing and regulating the practice of cinema as it did most other social institutions."[73] This concentration on social betterment forced the film industry to reassess its relationship with sporting entities, especially prizefighting.

In the first decade of the twentieth century, sports also experienced considerable growth as a source of popular entertainment. This growth was, in part, fueled by the continued proliferation of sporting magazines, the development and expansion of sports sections in newspapers, and the continued filming of sporting events for distribution within the growing motion-picture industry. The symbiotic relationship between these two industries generated tremendous enthusiasm by producing a constant flow of publicity through co-promotional activities. An article, titled "Pictures and Pugilism," which appeared in the December 18, 1909, issue of *Moving Picture World*, captured the essence of this relationship:

> The fortunes of the prize ring are apparently interwoven with those of the moving picture. Without the moving picture your modern prize fight would be shorn of most of its financial glamour and possibilities; without the prize fight the moving picture would not appeal to so many people as it apparently does.[74]

This joint venture to film and exhibit sporting actualities had to contend with reformists who continued to rail against the barbarity of prizefighting, still struggling to shed its reputation as a brutal, savage blood sport with no socially redeeming value. Ultimately, the only spark needed to incite the move toward censorship and the banning of fight films was provided when Jack Johnson became the heavyweight champion by defeating Tommy Burns in 1908. As long as there had been a white heavyweight champion and the social hierarchy was maintained, the exhibition of fights was tolerated, even, at times, celebrated, especially when the feature showcased a popular champion like Gentleman Jim Corbett or Jim Jeffries.

For black boxers, especially those who won championships, defeating white fighters in the process, acceptance was given as long as the black fighter maintained a semblance of assimilation. As already noted, when Jack McAuliffe won the lightweight championship in New Orleans in 1882, newspapers demanded that boxing clubs no longer stage inter-racial bouts. Because John L. Sullivan and his successors maintained the color line, no black heavyweight had been afforded the opportunity to upset that hierarchy. Although the social hierarchy did not allow a black heavyweight champion, film played an important role in creating a space where black athletes demonstrated their talents. The camera captured these performers without cultural preconceptions. Johnson, however, not only upended the social hierarchy, but in his dominating ring presence and his flouting of social conventions by carrying on relationships with white prostitutes (e.g., Hattie McClay 1907; Belle Schreiber 1908) and marrying a white woman on two different occasions (e.g., Etta Duryea 1909; Lucille Cameron 1912), Johnson was cast as a threatening menace to the ideology of race.

Even before Johnson won the heavyweight championship, the news of a black boxer defeating a white sparked considerable violence. As the telegraphed returns of the 1906 fight between Gans and Nelson were read at various sites, the furor of a black boxer beating a white fighter erupted in street violence. A *New York Times* article for September 5, 1906, with the headline "Almost a Lynching Over Gans's Victory," reported on several incidents:

> There were half a dozen fights in different parts of town, which were brought about by the success of the negro pugilist. In at least one instance the trouble almost grew into a lynching. In another case a stonecutter who had applauded the decision in the negro's favor in a saloon in Williamsburg was followed from the place and assaulted by three men. He may die from his injuries.[75]

The films of Gans' victory did not generate the same type of mob behavior, in part because venues for the exhibitions were segregated and alcohol was not served. Two years later, when Nelson knocked out Gans, the films grossed over $100,000, a dramatic increase attributable to both an increase in the film market and to the idea that white audiences desired a white fighter to regain the championship belt.

Consideration of Johnson's fight films—Johnson-Burns 1908, Johnson-Ketchel (Stanislaw Kiecal) 1909, and Johnson-Jeffries 1910—involved issues related to those racial policies that governed public life. One immediate result of *Plessy v. Ferguson* (1896) was the racial bifurcation of public infrastructure and accommodations. As such, black and white public spaces for seeing the Johnson films were separate and unequal. Although Johnson defeated Burns for the heavyweight title on December 26, 1908, the film did not premiere until March 21, 1909, at the Chicago Auditorium where it played for two weeks for overwhelmingly white audiences. Promoter Hugh D. (Huge Deal) McIntosh provided the commentary, which often included calls, first uttered by Jack London, that the smile be removed from Johnson's face and that Jeffries, who had retired undefeated and therefore still the rightful champion, come out of retirement to restore the championship to the white race. White public outcry was accommodated by including footage of the *Jeffries-Sharkey Fight* of 1899, the moment of Jeffries' greatest glory, to the Johnson-Burns film. This appendage served another purpose in addition to appeasing white panic; namely, it provided marketing impetus for a Johnson-Jeffries "Battle of the Century."

Johnson's ascendancy to the heavyweight championship came at a time of increased political activism within segments of the black community, especially related to the film industry. During Johnson's reign atop the boxing world, 1908–1915, efforts included attempts by blacks to redefine stereotypical portrayals of black characters in theater and cinema, and debates about racial grounds for film censorship. Activists called for both access and autonomy, challenging segregation of exhibition venues and establishing independent, black-run movie houses. Coincidental to Johnson's capturing the heavyweight championship was the founding of the National Association for the Advancement of Colored People (NAACP) by W.E.B. DuBois and others in 1909. Along with the *Chicago Defender*, NAACP leaders spearheaded efforts to integrate Chicago's movie theaters, a campaign which was also taken up in Harlem.

While there certainly was an expansion in the number of black-only movie venues during this time, the exhibition of Johnson's films often lagged behind exhibitions in white-run movie houses. Because McIntosh alone controlled the rights to the *Johnson-Burns Fight*, there were fewer advertisements for black theaters showing the film, indicating a lack of timely prints of the film. A similar situation did not occur when the films of the Johnson-Ketchel fight were made in October 1909, in part because the prints were controlled by the Motion Picture Patents Company (MPPC) and in part because Johnson himself demanded possession of the fight's prints.

The Johnson-Ketchel Fight generated both sensation and abhorrence. The extant prints of the film provided ample evidence that for most of the fight Johnson and Ketchel were engaging in a 20-round exhibition more than a fight to the finish, cashing in on a money-making opportunity. As the fifth in a series of "Great White Hopes" that Johnson had fought and easily defeated since March 1909, Ketchel had earned a reputation as a fearless fighter. However, for most of his career Ketchel fought as a middleweight, and he was physically no match for Johnson. In fact,

Ketchel was provided with lifts and padding to add girth to his stature for publicity photos. The film showed that for the first 11 rounds, Johnson toyed with the smaller man. Then in the 12th round, Ketchel caught Johnson with a punch to the head, sending him to the canvas. As quickly as Johnson went down, he got up and quickly lunged at Ketchel, catching him with a vicious punch to the mouth that knocked him unconscious and left several of Ketchel's teeth embedded in Johnson's glove. The film showed Johnson pawing at the glove, as if to remove the teeth.

Reception of the *Johnson-Ketchel Fight* ranged along the racial divide, accelerating white fears with images of black power and offering black audiences "a laudable antidote to the pervasive negative stereotypes of popular culture."[76] Neither black nor white audiences reacted monolithically, however. Black critics questioned the fight's highly suspicious ending, which appeared to one columnist as choreographed for the cameras:

> If this Johnson-Ketchel fight wasn't a pre-arranged affair, there was some awful clever catering to the moving picture machine…. After the supposed blow Johnson went down on his hands and toes, rolled over backward on one hand, and facing the moving picture machine all the time; then, seeing that Ketchel was waiting for his cue, he jumped up and rushed at Ketchel like a wild man…. The referee stood squarely over Ketchel, counting him out, and all three were in full view of the moving picture machine.[77]

In addition to concerns about playing to the camera, black critics were also beginning to question Johnson's exorbitant lifestyle. Conversely, not all whites viewed the film within a racial discourse. Regardless of their attitudes about race, white fans of the sport doubtlessly appreciated Johnson's boxing skills. When the fight film was shown at Hammerstein's Victoria theater, *Variety* reported that Joe Humphreys provided commentary that focused on the fistic and economic details rather than race.[78]

Those reports included details about the Jeffries-Johnson fight, the contract of which was signed on November 30, 1909, a little more than six weeks after the Ketchel fight. Promoter George Lewis "Tex" Rickard lured Jeffries out of retirement, thanks in part to the largest purse for a championship fight, $101,000, with the fighters splitting two-thirds of the movie rights and each receiving a signing bonus of $10,000. The fight, originally scheduled for July 4, 1910, in San Francisco, was moved to Reno, Nevada, when in mid–June California Governor James N. Gillett withdrew his support, bowing to pressure from civic and church leaders. According to a *New York Times* article from December 5, 1909, details of the "moving picture clause" occupied a considerable portion of the negotiations and was finally "stricken out of the articles and incorporated into a separate agreement."[79] That separate agreement included the formation of a stock company, the J. & J. Co., to handle the fight's pictures. The MPPC ultimately bought up both boxers' shares of the net film profits, paying Johnson $50,000 for his third and Jeffries $66,000, as well as buying Rickard's share for $33,000. The *Times* article reported that profits would exceed $300,000.

In addition to the MPPC coverage of the event, numerous independent film companies shot footage of the boxers preparing for the bout. Significantly, these films contributed to the pre-fight publicity so important in generating interest and building an audience not only for the event itself, but also for the films that followed. Comprised of excerpted segments, or highlights, from previous fight films and edited footage of training and sparring sessions, these publicity films constituted an important step in the sportscast highlight form's evolutionary process, serving as precursors for not only newsreel segments, but also for the pre-game and post-game programs, as well as for Video News Releases (VNR) that became staples of the sports broadcasting industry half a century later.

Backlash and Bans

Production values of the *Johnson-Jeffries Fight* were not particularly noteworthy, for despite a veritable cadre of cameras outfitted with special lenses being used by member companies Vitagraph, Essanay, and Selig, the film utilized most of the conventions of earlier fight films. Cameras were stationed on a platform thirty feet west of the wing and shot the action from that distance. One difference from earlier fight productions was the allocation of a panning camera to follow Jeffries, "framing the white boxer as protagonist and privileging white spectatorship."[80] Jeffries, however, was unable to match the ring skills of the younger, more agile Johnson, who not only controlled the action, as he had in other fights, but was also seen talking to his opponent, as well as to Corbett and Sullivan, both of whom served as handlers in the Jeffries corner. Another significant aspect that the camera captured was that during the climactic sequence in the 15th round after Jeffries had been knocked down three times, Jeffries' handlers entered the ring (Corbett included), preempting the final knockout ten-count. This caused referee Tex Rickard to declare Johnson the winner and new champion rather than allowing Jeffries to be knocked out as he surely would have been. A similar, more intrusive ending had occurred in Australia when Johnson defeated Tommy Burns to win the championship in 1908. In that bout, Australian constables forced cameramen to stop filming so that the knockout of Burns was not recorded. These incidents marked only the beginning of what became a vigorous campaign to censor the films of Johnson vanquishing the Great White Hope(s).

In the immediate aftermath of Johnson's victory, jubilant blacks celebrated and whites lashed back, and the ensuing race riots left a number of people dead. In a July 6 *New York Times* article, titled "Bar Fight Pictures to Avoid Race Riots," the *Times* listed seven cities where at least ten fatalities resulted from fights occasioned by the Johnson's victory. The article also noted that Washington, D.C., Atlanta, Baltimore, St. Louis, and Cincinnati were among the cities that decided "not to permit the exhibition of the pictures."[81] Despite the numerous calls for bans on the film of the fight, few decried the overt racial furor being played out in cities and towns across the country. The actual number of blacks killed as a direct result of white vengeance over Johnson's victory has never been accurately documented. More telling perhaps, neither newspapers and magazines, nor church and civic leaders decried the behavior of white citizens for their actions. Rather, blame was placed on the sport of boxing or on black demonstrations of empowerment. The easiest target to censor was invariably the fight's film.

On July 6, the *New York Times* also reported that William Show, general secretary of the United Society of Christian Endeavor, had issued a formal statement in which he declared "that Independence Day had been dishonored and disgraced by a brutal prizefight: that the moral sense of the Nation had been outraged, but that this evil was as nothing compared to the harm which will be done by allowing children and women to view the production of the Jeffries-Johnson fight by moving pictures."[82] Significantly, this declaration against the fight film invoked a paternalistic tone of protecting women and children from viewing the film, despite the fact that women and children were certainly not the primary audience for fight films. In fact, the literature suggests that other than the *Corbett-Fitzsimmons Fight*, few women sought admittance to fight films.[83] Church leaders like James Cardinal Gibbons, Archbishop of Baltimore, echoed a similar concern, namely, that the pictures would have a desultory effect on women and children. "If the pictures of this contest were permitted, I am sure hundreds of children would see them, and what would be the result? Their morals would not only be contaminated, but they would have the wrong ideal of a true hero."[84] Although not explicitly stated, the message was clear: Johnson could never be considered a hero. Implicit was the idea that it was up to the white race to lead the way "to confer these gifts of civilization, through law, commerce, and education on the uncivilized."[85] A legal challenge was issued by Mayor Patrick Henry McCarthy of San Francisco, who claimed: "Inasmuch as the contest resolved itself into a prizefight pure and simple and was not a boxing match, the exhibition of the moving pictures would be as unlawful as the fight itself."[86] The entire episode marked a nadir in American sporting history.

Attacks on the *Johnson-Jeffries Fight* film did not go unchallenged. The *New York Times* reported on July 7 that the "moving-picture syndicate owning the rights to the Johnson-Jeffries fight films will resort to the courts of the several States to determine their right to show the pictures."[87] Black newspapers and clergy also added their voices to those advocating for the films to be shown, often pointing out the hypocrisy of the situation. The *St. Paul Appeal* asked, "Who believes for one minute, that had Jeffries been the victor at Reno, there would have been any objection to showing the pictures of him bringing back 'the white man's hope?'"[88] Similar stances were taken in black press editorials and cartoons, noting that the film of Johnson's victory would have beneficial effects for the political and psychological well-being of black citizens.

When New York City's mayor had made it clear that the film would not be banned, offers from theaters and houses of amusement poured into the MPPC offices on Fifth Avenue. With promises from the film's producers and the MPPC that the films would be carefully handled, meaning "the shows will be stag,"[89] the *Johnson-Jeffries Fight* escaped total censorship for some time. Exhibitors, in practicing class, gender and race controls, were able to show the film and charge steeper prices for admission. This meant that not all of Johnson's supporters, especially those in black communities, got a chance to see the *Johnson-Jeffries Fight*. For the next several years, Johnson held the heavyweight championship. Unable to find anyone who could defeat Johnson in the ring, those who sought to dethrone Johnson used the Mann Act, which forbade, under heavy penalties, the transportation of women from one state to another for immoral purposes, to prosecute and jail him, forcing him to leave the country.

The first attempt to ban fight films, as well as telegraphed descriptions of fights, was introduced in the U.S. Congress in May 1910 by Representative Walter I. Smith (R–Iowa). Although that effort failed, two years later, another bill was introduced by Representative Thetus Sims (D–Tenn.) early in 1912. Southern Democrats pushed through the legislation, which was modeled after existing federal control on obscene publications (e.g., birth control, abortion literature). With the Sims Act of 1912, passed on July 31, 1912, Congress used its constitutional power to regulate commerce by forbidding interstate transport of fight films. Because motion pictures were considered commerce, they came under the purview of the federal government. Federal intervention served a dual purpose of raising concerns about the moral effect of boxing and the impact of Johnson's ascendancy to heavyweight champion. That the Sims Act was motivated by racial ideology was evidenced by the demagoguery deployed in the debate. On July 19, two weeks after the fight, Representative Seaborn A. Roddenbery (D–Ga.) delivered a speech in which he called Johnson "an African biped beast" and that failure to take action against "black-skinned, thick-lipped, bull-necked, brutal-hearted African"[90] would lead to another civil war. Ironically, those who had been longing for Johnson's defeat were denied the opportunity to see the bout with Jess Willard in 1915 that ended Johnson's tenure as heavyweight champion.

Conclusion

The ban on boxing films did not mean filmmakers no longer sought to capture and disseminate sporting events. In the years that followed, leading film companies continued to capture actualities with their newsreel divisions, which began in 1911, one year before the Sims Act became law. By that time, other sporting events had captivated the public's imagination on both national and international stages. Major league baseball began playing its World Series in 1903 and baseball was captured on film as early as 1906. Another sport that grew in popularity at the turn of the century was college football, which the Edison Company captured on film during 1903. Still another sporting spectacle that grew in popularity was the modern Olympic Games, which began in 1896. In short, sporting events served as important content for the newsreel divisions of the major film studios.

What is especially important about the formation and development of what today is called the sport-media-commercial complex was not merely the technological improvements that allowed cameras to stage or capture live sporting events. Rather, all of the various constituencies played key roles in the evolution and development of the sportscast highlight form. Arguably, far more is known about the ways that inventors, promoters, exhibitors, journalists, athletes, civic and church leaders attended to the consumption of sport culture than about the audience. It is difficult to ascertain who watched sport films and what they thought of them. Economics limited the access to films by the poorer members of the working class and the poor. Drawing its audience from across the upper, middle and working classes, films sought to accommodate people of diverse financial status.

It should not be assumed that the audience was comprised of males only. While the films showing the physique of Sandow, as well as the fight films featuring Corbett and Jeffries, were primarily intended for male patrons, these films almost certainly "held considerable erotic interest for women spectators."[91] At least a few women asserted their independence by visiting theaters showing fight films and other sporting events, especially those that offered matinees.

While many factors determined the composition of the audience, it is also important to understand that control of the places of exhibition was as contentious as the controlling of the content. As the motion-picture industry became financially lucrative, not all entities shared equally in the profits. The system of selling the rights by states spawned highly competitive practices among exhibitors seeking to capitalize on topical films. States rights owners also faced considerable difficulties in recouping their investments in specific film properties. The sheer number of motion picture enterprises, especially in the early years of projection, exacerbated the difficulties of making profits from exhibitions. As the MPPC gradually gained more and more control over the distribution of feature-length fictional films, fewer independent companies were left to compete.

This concentration of control in the hands of the studios ultimately pushed sport films from the feature to the news actuality. With feature-length fight films no longer legal, sports became an important source and a regular part of the newsreel. As such, capturing highlights of a sporting event was established as the new operational aesthetic, one that remained an integral part of the newsreel genre, even as radio broadcasting became the vehicle for capturing and disseminating a live sporting event.

Chapter 2

The Habit of Highlights

By the time the Sims Act was enacted in 1912, barring the interstate transportation of fight films for commercial exhibition, the cinema industry had already entered into the second phase of newsreel development with the release on August 8, 1911, of the first American-produced newsreel by the French-owned Pathé Weekly. An announcement in the July 29, 1911, issue of *Moving Picture World* signaled the beginning of a weekly newsreel in America, "issued every Tuesday, made up of short scenes of great international events of universal interest from all over the world."[1] That regularity became a hallmark of the newsreels, allowing them to become a vehicle for news that the audience came to expect. As already established by newspapers and magazines, news sustains itself through form and habit.[2] Sporting events became a mainstay of the newsreels precisely because they were scheduled throughout the calendar year. Because of the way newsreels presented sports, highlights became the dominant news frame.

Several factors related to production and distribution facilitated the establishment of the weekly exhibition of filmed news. The ready availability of serviceable cameras, projectors and film stock allowed a sufficient number of producers that had become competent in the field of cinematography to chase down and capture dramatic events that whetted the public interest for spectacle. Additionally, the public's interest in film entertainment had been firmly established, evidenced by the fact that in the United States the number of cinemas grew from nine thousand in 1908 to almost fourteen thousand in 1914.[3] This growth would not have been possible without a very large number of people having acquired the habit of attending the cinema. The ability to exhibit reproductions of actual events anywhere a darkened space and a projector could be brought together transformed the economic basis of entertainment from a local commodity of theatrical performance to a national and international industry. Clearly, it was the large production companies with world-wide connections that had the resources to produce news films to satisfy the public's insatiable appetite for this new medium of communication in which the wonder of the moving image supplanted the magic of acting.[4]

Film's ability to affect an audience *en masse* had both positive and negative implications for the development of the newsreels as journalism. On the one hand, newsreels were capable of exerting tremendous influence; on the other hand, newsreels were confined by the limitations of the motion picture camera being employed within the context of a news organization trying to capture its news on the fly, often rendering that coverage superficial and entertaining. Despite those limitations, watching newsreel coverage of sports joined attending sporting events, as well as reading about athletic contests in the print press and listening to games on the radio, in creating a common popular culture centered around sports.[5] One component of that popular culture was being in the public eye, which now meant being seen.

That sports was to play an instrumental role in the development of the newsreels became apparent when Birt Acres and Robert Paul filmed the Epsom Derby on June 3, 1896, and projected it the following evening at the Alhambra, a popular theater and music hall located on the east side of Leicester Square in the West End of London. Getting the filmed version of topical events that interested the public had been missing from other cinematic presentations of actualities. Equally importantly, the coverage of sporting events proved that film communicated aspects of an event that could not be captured by print media at the time or by radio when it emerged over the next two decades. News films of boxing, horse and yacht races, and athletic (i.e., track and field) competitions evoked a greater degree of emotional involvement from the audience than printed words or illustrations by supplying moving images of the event, despite the fact the results were already known. As such, evocations of crowd responses demonstrated the power of newsreels to reduce the importance of individual critical assessment and substitute a collective response by the audience.[6]

Sports lent themselves to the formulaic approach employed by newsreel cameramen. The major producers obtained the greatest access to events throughout the world thanks to their network of cameramen and their operational bases throughout the globe, as well as to the private exchange agreements among them, which guaranteed both financial and technical advantages and curtailed challenges from local producers. This system of gentlemanly competition resulted in a general increase of productivity through routine and standardization.[7] Before the newsreel era, the earliest news films were shot in 50-foot and 150-foot segments. These were followed in the first decade of the twentieth century by 300-foot topicals, also known as actualities. When newsreels supplanted topicals in the market, they retained their standard length and stayed that way until their ultimate end in 1967. Because a cameraman had a limited amount of film to shoot, every shot had to be a highlight. The formula can be seen in almost any newsreel sports segment. Getting footage of a college football game begins with a general view of the stadium to establish the venue, followed by a shot closer to the field, then by a shot of the crowd cheering, a shot of a crucial play, a close-up of the star player, and end with the reaction shot of jubilation and celebration. Cameramen were not expected to capture footage in sequence, and close-ups were often edited into the final edited reel.

When the first all-sound newsreel was premiered by Fox Movietone News on October 28, 1927, at the Roxy Theater in New York City, it contained highlights of the

Army-Yale football game at the Yale Bowl and the rodeo in New York City. Sound newsreels necessitated a more complex approach to editing to insure synchronization and sound levels. In early sound newsreels, microphones were strategically positioned to capture the sounds of the bands and cheerleaders, and canned footage of cheering crowds and football pageantry were edited into the game action.[8] As newsreel editors became more comfortable and ambitious with the sound-on-film process, commentary was used to enhance the excitement of sport segments. Commentary was often provided by the some of the period's leading sports radio announcers, who became among the most widely known personalities in the nation. More importantly, those commentators and their emphatic delivery helped make the sports stars even more identifiable, putting a face on the mythic while establishing the period's cultural values and attitudes.[9]

One of the most significant developments regarding the relationship between newsreels and sports revolved around securing the exclusive rights to film a sporting event. Piracy and re-enactments had plagued early film actualities, and these illegitimate practices continued unabated for many years. Perhaps the most glaring illustration of this continuing problem occurred in October 1923 with the filming of "The International," a match race between Kentucky Derby winner Zev and Epsom Derby winner Papyrus at Belmont Park. Pathé paid $50,000 for the exclusive rights to the race, but the event was pirated by cameramen from Fox Movietone and Hearst's Metrotone. They exhibited their film of the entire race—5,000 feet of it—a full week before Pathé's legitimate newsreel reached the screen. The issue of securing the rights to important sporting events did not end with the Zev-Papyrus race; in fact, the practice of charging film companies for access to footage of the Olympics took root in that same year, 1923, and greatly contributed to casting the Olympic Games as a commercial commodity.

Just as the newsreel sports segment became the prototype for today's sportscast highlights, the newsreel companies also served as the prototype for today's multinational corporations. It was this economic aspect of the cinema industry which, more than any other factor, characterized the history of newsreels, inextricably linking the development of film as journalism to the development of film as entertainment.[10]

Routines and Standards

Sports coverage by newsreels was predicated on routines—by both producers and viewers, who flocked to the cinema on a weekly and then semiweekly basis expecting to be entertained. At the height of newsreel popularity in the 1930s, sports accounted for 20 to 25 percent of the footage, and weekly attendance of over 100 million meant an estimated audience of 20 million for each of the five major newsreel distributors.[11] Producers crafted sports segments filled with highlights by combining newspaper headlines with footage of actual events, staged shots, archival material and eventually commentary. Another aspect of the routine revolved around the standardization of the visuals, which used a sequence of shots taken before and after the action, juxtaposing shots of the event's location with close-ups of participants as well as intermixing real shots of the crowd and the event with re-enactments. Lastly, sports segments followed the progression of the sports seasons, heeding the calendar in a very predictable fashion—ski jumping in the winter, horse racing in the spring, baseball in the summer, and football in the fall.

The newsreel sports segment relied on a combination of scheduled events, breaking news, and human interest stories that often featured child golfing prodigies, female wrestlers and all kinds of crashes. Comparing a sample of Universal International Newsreels from the beginning of the sound period—1929, 1931, 1932 and 1933—with those from the years following World War II—1947, 1948, 1949 and 1951—not only provides an overview of what the newsreel sports calendar encompassed but also reveals a narrowing of the range of sports covered as certain sports like college football and Major League Baseball and events like horse racing's Triple Crown, the Olympics, and Wimbledon came to dominate coverage. Being able to count on scheduled events afforded newsreel editors opportunities to dispatch cameramen to cover breaking news as it arose as well as to find those human interest stories that highlighted the bizarre, the unusual and the spectacular. Significantly, coverage was characterized by picture content, not interpretation, meaning the newsreels celebrated athletes and events but largely avoided controversy.

The newsreel sports calendar in the early 1930s was far different than it would be in the early 1950s, especially during the winter months. In the earlier period, viewers were more likely to see newsreels about speed skating, ice boat racing, ski jumping and dog sled racing during January, February and March than viewers in the later period. Although 1950s viewers were treated to some traditional winter sports like ski jumping and speed skating, their coverage began with highlights of college football's bowl games and featured sports that were growing in popularity, including figure skating, college basketball, indoor track and field, speed boat racing and professional golf tournaments. Horse racing was one sport that retained a favored position in both time periods, as thoroughbred racing from Florida (Hialeah) and California (Santa Anita) was covered, as well as the Grand National steeplechase from England. It is worth noting that steeplechase racing, which often featured spectacular falls as horses and riders attempted to jump barriers, offered the visual material that newsreels sought. Although not in season, baseball, usually in the persons of stars like Babe Ruth and later Joe DiMaggio, received ample coverage in March as teams began spring training. Several factors contributed to the wide assortment of winter sports covered in the early newsreels, including the absence of two key professional leagues—the National Hockey League and the National Basketball Association—as well as limited coverage of college basketball's NIT and NCAA tournaments.

Adding spice to the mix of winter sports highlights was 1930s coverage of oddities like water-ski polo, aquatic ballet, inner tube races down mountains as well as 1950s coverage of roller-skate hockey, barrel-jumping, cliff diving, and motorcycle racing on ice. Neither time period refrained from odd and exotic events, including women wrestling men, child golfers performing trick shots, kick boxing, and mass gymnastics. Any event that featured a world record performance, spectacular crashes in the snow or daredevil stunts on the water or ice was certain to be included. While the winter season offered sporting events that depended on the elements, the spring months featured events involving speed, daring and teamwork. The schedule revolved around horse racing's Triple Crown—including the Kentucky Derby, the Preakness Stakes and the Belmont Stakes—as well as English races like the Epsom Derby, the Grand National steeplechase and the Ascot Gold Cup. Other sports' top races such as the Boston Marathon, the Indianapolis 500, America's Cup racing, and speed boat racing's Gold Cup were also covered. In fact, races of all kinds—from crew and air racing to bike and race walking—were captured. Part of racing's lure for the newsreels stemmed from the fact that starts and finishes were relatively easy to catch as highlights.

What constituted a sports highlight in either period was dictated by the need to distill an entire event into the newsreel's scale. In other words, until 1945 cameras were capable of filming continuously for no more than ten minutes, so capturing a race's finish was easier to time than attempting to capture the scoring of a goal, touchdown or home run. Even after the introduction of 16 mm safety film, newsreel companies could not afford to film most events in their entirety or for long stretches to secure the decisive moment-of-truth plays. For that reason, racing of almost any kind was captured, especially because it offered at least one decisive moment, the finish, which was combined with the start and almost any other part of the race to suggest a complete story. Add to that establishing shots of the crowd and a reaction shot of the winner celebrating, and the reel was complete, economically and efficiently captured. Except for the shortest races, usually track and field's sprints and hurdling events, editors preferred transforming what had been captured into a highlight by allowing the headlining and commentary to maximize the affect and importance of what the viewer was seeing. Capturing significant plays was often more about luck. With racing, cameramen relied on the knowledge that if they captured the finish, they had a highlight.

Just as the coverage of most any race was standardized, so too was the coverage of those summer sports in which individual athletes were the focus. Newsreels presented highlights of the major tennis and golf championship events, focusing on the stars of those sports. Arguably, neither of those sports lent themselves to the spectacular footage that characterized coverage of auto, bobsled, or speed boat racing. Lacking visually exciting crashes, these sports rarely offered dynamic, spectacular action. Given the technical and economic limitations, capturing the moment-of-truth shot in golf or decisive point in tennis proved exceedingly difficult for any cameraman shooting a Wimbledon final or the final round of the U.S. Open Golf Championship.

Not surprisingly then, coverage focused on the stars of those sports, including Bobby Jones, Walter Hagen and Babe Didrikson Zaharias in golf and Bill Tilden, Suzanne Lenglen and Helen Wills Moody in tennis.

The formula for those sports used at least one familiar technique of juxtaposing action shots with close-ups, although the key was capturing the final point or putt, the handshake between competitors, and the trophy presentation, culminating with a close-up of the victor. For example, Universal's highlights of the 1930 women's final at Wimbledon featuring two Americans, Helen Wills Moody and Helen Hull Jacobs, set the stage by showing the two women before the final, then presented a rally of several shots, culminating with the final handshake at the net. Moody was then shown holding the trophy, and lastly, viewers were provided a close-up of her on board ship as she was returning home.

Moody was certainly a favorite of the newsreels, evidenced by the coverage of her marriage in December 1929 titled *Life's Doubles*, her 1924 Olympic gold medal in tennis, her many Grand Slam victories, and her exhibition match against the eighth-ranked American male player, Phil Neer, whom she defeated on January 28, 1933, in San Francisco. In 1933, the newsreels also covered the last match she played at the U.S. Open, in which she retired during the final against Jacobs due to a back injury. At the time, Jacobs was leading in the third set. Because Moody felt the press and fans treated her harshly at the U.S. Championship, she never played the tournament again.

That the focus of the coverage was squarely on the star athlete is further evidenced by another piece taken during the 1930 Davis Cup Challenge Round contested at Stade Roland Garros in Paris, France, between the United States and France, the three-time defending champion. Using the formula described above, the piece focused on Tilden's victory in the first singles match, a four-set victory over Jean Borotra, one of the legendary Four Musketeers who helped France hold the Davis Cup from 1927 to 1930. Significantly, Tilden's victory was headlined, no doubt because it was the first and the only match won by the United States that year, but also because it was Tilden's final match as a member of the U.S. Davis Cup team. Even after Tilden turned professional, he remained a favorite of the newsreels.

Golf posed a comparable set of problems for cameramen attempting to capture highlights. Like tennis, golf features a large number of shots over the 18 holes, and it is difficult to know exactly when a competitor will make a winning or spectacular shot. For this reason, golf coverage most often showed the eventual winner teeing off on the first hole of the final round, followed by shots of the crowd swarming toward a green, and the competitors taking turns putting on the final hole. The final sequence typically included the final putt, the handshake and the trophy presentation with a close-up of the winner.

This formula is much in evidence in the newsreels that captured Bobby Jones' historic Grand Slam in 1930, with victories in The (British) Open Championship, the U.S. Open Championship, the U.S. Amateur Championship and the British

Amateur Championship. The coverage of Jones winning the British Amateur followed this formula, providing shots of Jones teeing off for the final round, as well as the final putts and the hoisting of the trophy. Universal's headline provided the drama: "Bobby Jones Victor in British Amateur After Close Finish." A month later, the Universal cameraman was able to capture the ultimate shot in the 72-hole event held at the Interlachen Country Club. Positioned as the first segment of the newsreel for July 14, 1930, the segment showed Jones teeing off for the final round with a comfortable five-shot lead. By the final hole that lead had almost completely disappeared, thanks in part to a double-bogey on the penultimate hole when Jones uncharacteristically hit a wayward drive into a water hazard.[12] After his second shot to the final green, Jones, clinging to a one-shot lead over MacDonald Smith, was left with a long, 40-foot putt that had to travel over a mound up to the hole. The camera was rolling as Jones lined up the shot, got into position and struck the ball with his putter. The film showed the ball rolling over the mound toward the hole and then disappearing.

Although no audio is available with Universal's footage, the *New York Times* story provided a comparable dramatization.

> Now was this the time for Calamity Jane, his renowned putter, to deliver a telling blow and deliver it he did. His ball went up the hill, over the top and into the hole for a birdie 3 which left Mac Smith with the impossible to do. As Bobby's ball made its way toward the hole there was utter silence, but when it disappeared into the tin a shout that could be heard to the utmost limits of the course went up.
>
> Jones had won again—the only man in the history of the game to gain the two British championships and one of the two American championships in the same year. All that now remains for him to do in order to accomplish a feat that probably will never be equaled in golf is to win the American amateur at Merion next September.[13]

Given the fact that Jones went on to complete the Grand Slam, a feat which has never been duplicated as the *New York Times* reporter aptly predicted, the Interlachen putt is arguably one of the most significant sports highlights ever captured on film. When Jones completed the Grand Slam by defeating Eugene V. Homans in the final of the U.S. Amateur Championship at the Merion Golf Club, Universal featured it as the lead story on September 29, 1930.

Jones, Tilden and Moody were not the only stars to shine in the newsreel sports galaxy, for despite the ban on boxing films, the newsreels continued to provide coverage of champion boxers. For example, in February 1930 the cameras were rolling as soon as Jack Sharkey knocked out Phil Scott, actually capturing Sharkey raising his arms in victory. Not being allowed to film the fight did not discourage the newsreels from capturing pre- and post-fight footage. Being limited to previewing fights and showing the aftermath served as important precursors for the wrap-around programs that were later adopted by television producers for coverage of many sports, especially college football. That boxers remained sport celebrities is not surprising given the stature they had achieved prior to the Sims Act; in fact, boxing was arguably the most important sport in terms of generating what famed sportswriter W.O. McGeehan called "ballyhoo" in referring to the excessive attention given to sport by a network of publicists and press that rivaled the attention generated for Hollywood's stars.[14]

The most significant change in coverage from the 1930s to the 1950s can be seen in the increased coverage of team sports during the autumn months. Although baseball's fall classic, the World Series, had been and would remain a showcase event in the 1930s during early October, in terms of the number of segments, college football dominated newsreel sports coverage. In October 1931, for example, Universal devoted two segments to the World Series and two segments to college football. Two years later, those numbers had not changed significantly, three World Series segments to two college football segments. Although a World Series might last a minimum of four games, coverage usually spanned at least two newsreel dates—a Wednesday and Saturday—and if the series lasted through the seven-game maximum, it spanned three dates, as it did in October 1951.

However many segments were devoted to the national pastime, baseball posed at least one problem that cameramen had difficulty overcoming; namely, following the ball. For example, Universal's segment on the 1930 World Series, titled "Record Crowds See Cards and Mackmen Battle for Title," illustrated the camera's limitation. The segment attempted to capture action, but the shots of hits and base runners at times resembled a Buster Keaton comedy. Not being able to follow the ball also characterized early television coverage of baseball, and it was not until cameras were improved and better positioned that baseball coverage caught up to the other sports in terms of aesthetic quality. In 1934, the newsreels began covering baseball's other glamour event, its mid-summer All-Star game, which lent itself to cut-ins of star players and shots of celebrities in the crowd.

Several factors contributed to the significant rise in the number of newsreel segments devoted to college football. For one thing, the schedule of college games, beginning in September and ending on New Year's Day with the bowl games, was made far in advance, publicized in every section of the country, and intended to provide stimulating rivalries. Additionally, the fact that the games were played on Saturday afternoons meant that the newsreels could process and edit footage of several top games from across the country for Wednesday newsreel release and even provide same-day coverage of one Saturday game for newsreel cinemas in New York City. Lastly, the pageantry and spectacle of college football provided newsreels with the kinds of action shots, cheering crowds, and band and card section choreography upon which they relied. Little wonder, then, that the newsreel coverage of the Army-Navy game became a favorite, thanks in large part to in large part to the mascots, the military and political dignitaries in attendance, and the formations of uniformed cadets and midshipmen cheering boisterously. The sheer number of segments provides ample evidence of the newsreels' increased coverage of college football. For example, Universal increased the number of college football segments during November from six and four in 1931 and 1933 respectively to thirteen and sixteen in 1947 and 1949. So entrenched were the newsreels' routines in terms of both calendar and technique that in 1952 a UNESCO study reported that no major changes in methods of selecting and presenting sport segments occurred during a quarter-century (1927 to 1952), which included almost the entire period of sound newsreels.[15]

Access and Rights

While the routines and standards of newsreel sport segments were largely a product of the lack of competitiveness that characterized the later years, the same cannot be said for the formative years of the silent newsreel era. Competition between news film producers was intense even before the introduction of Pathé Weekly in 1911, evidenced by the attempts to pirate such events as the Jeffries-Sharkey championship fight in 1899. In those early years securing exclusive news material in advance of competitors sprang from motives that ranged from prestige to economic survival. The acquisition of exclusive rights by one company invariably precipitated surreptitious attempts to capture the event by competitors, and piracy of sporting events was commonplace.[16] At the heart of the issue was the idea of whether or not sporting events were news, the rights to which Pathé, in particular, argued, "could no more be properly sold to a newsreel company than they could be sold to a newspaper association."[17] Perhaps no single sporting event illustrates the lengths to which competing companies went to pirate an event, as well as the attempts to counter pirating, as the match race that took place at Belmont Park on October 20, 1923, between Kentucky Derby winner Zev and Epsom Derby winner Papyrus.

To state that this match race, christened "The International," received as much ballyhoo as the Sir Barton—Man o' War match race in 1920, would not be an overstatement. The Belmont Park Jockey Club was offering one of the two gold cups to be awarded to the winner, the main trophy being worth $5,000. As the *New York Times* reported, "This will be a permanent trophy and it is hoped will continue for all time as a challenge cup to serve for the turf as the America's Cup does for yacht racing and the Davis Cup for lawn tennis."[18] The Jockey Club also assumed responsibility for selecting the thoroughbred to represent the United States in this race by sponsoring what it called the American Trial Sweepstakes, scheduled for late September at Belmont Park. When Zev injured himself in winning the Lawrence Realization Stakes at Belmont Park on September 10, 1923, and could not participate in the American Trial Sweepstakes, the matter was thrown into considerable dispute.

The dispute over which American horse the Jockey Club would select drew the attention of many people, including Brigadier General William Mitchell, assistant chief of the U.S. Air Service, who wrote a letter to August Belmont, Chairman of the Jockey Club. Published in the *New York Times* on October 1, 1923, Mitchell's letter explained that the entire country was thrilled by the announcement that the race had been arranged and even those who cared nothing for racing "looked upon the announcement as an excellent method of cementing relations between the two great English speaking peoples … worth more than years of activities in diplomacy, propaganda and other things which are now taking so much money and efforts…."[19] Conceding that Papyrus had been the unquestioned choice to represent Great Britain, Mitchell expressed the view that he and many people who cheered the original announcement "are dumbfounded by the manner in which your club has chosen or rather has neglected to choose the American standard bearer."[20] Mitchell outlined the merits of the leading contenders, especially Zev—winner of that year's Kentucky Derby, the Withers, the Belmont Stakes, the Paumonok, and the Rainbow Handicap, as well as the aforementioned Realization Stakes—and My Own—winner of "every race in which he was entered, including the Fort Edward Handicap, and galloping away from Harry Payne Whitney's Bunting in the Saratoga Cup."[21] My Own's owner, Admiral Cary Grayson, had offered to race Zev "at any place, any time, with or without a purse, the whole matter to be left to the decision of the Jockey Club." Mitchell argued that if Zev were not fit to race in the American Trial Sweepstakes on October 6, then "the committee cannot justify the selection of him for the big race on Oct. 20…. The condition of a horse last Spring or Summer cannot be controlling for a race in October. It seems to me that the question should be settled without delay … or the public should be given very good reasons in support of your decision."[22]

Mitchell was doubtlessly disappointed when the Jockey Club issued a statement on October 5 in which it named its top three horses: Zev, My Own and Untidy. As the *New York Times* reported, "This means that Zev, if he remains fit and well, will be the horse…. The definite choice of Zev sets at rest any speculation as to the chances of My Own outranking him for the honor and puts an end to the controversy which has been raging for the past two weeks."[23] The Selection Committee's decision may have put an end to the controversy for the present, but only two days before the race, Admiral Grayson was contacted by the committee and "directed by Major Belmont to ship My Own immediately to Belmont Park and [told] that the shipment of his colt is being provided by the Jockey Club."[24] Perhaps the Committee had been unimpressed by Zev's workout the previous Sunday, even though it was reported that the horse had come through that work in good shape. More likely, the Committee became alarmed and "was put in an embarrassing position by a malady of uncertain diagnosis that affected Zev."[25] That malady proved to be a skin irritation that did not impact Zev's overall conditioning.

Given the race's importance, it certainly made good business sense that Pathé News, despite having fought so hard against paying for exclusive rights to sporting events, paid $50,000 for the rights to film the race. They doubtlessly knew their competitors would attempt to pirate the event. In fact, as the *New York Times* made clear in an article published the day following the race, Pathé went to considerable lengths to keep its rivals from acquiring footage of the race:

> A smoke screen thrown up on the far side of the course, opposite the grand stand, and the dancing motion of two enormous reflectors over there were observed with much curiosity, it

is true, by the spectators on the lawn and in the crowded grand stand.... The spectators also had evinced interest in five airplanes which, from some time before the first race at 2 p.m., had been twisting and cavorting over them.[26]

The reporter explained that these were not part of the overall scenery, but "were barriers arranged by the racing officials and employes [sic] of a motion picture company which had bought the privilege of taking pictures of the race to prevent other film companies from doing likewise." Despite these efforts, described hyperbolically as "world war tactics," the other companies got pictures of the great event "right under the noses of the men who had been delegated to prevent their doing so."[27]

Fox Movietone and Hearst Metrotone accomplished their goal of surreptitiously shooting film of the race by stationing cameras both inside and outside of the track. For one company, "every available house in the vicinity of the race course from which motion pictures could be taken with long distance lenses was hired ... and then arrangements were made to get camera men inside the track to take pictures as the two horses were battling for victory."[28] The article added that one of the companies paid $600 to a house owner with a clear line of sight with the second turn and the start and finish line. Not to be outdone, the other company "paid for the privilege of erecting a 'crow's nest' in a clump of trees directly overlooking the grand stand." Not satisfied with this, the company also "arranged to have an automobile and a delivery truck drive right into the race course at points between the third and fourth turns on the left of the grand stand and near the first turn on the right." Lastly, they enlisted "two motion picture actresses who were seated at vantage points in the grandstand with small cameras concealed in ornamental handbags, resting on the rail in front of them."[29] The article explained that these "actresses" merely had to press a button in each camera until the horses had passed beyond them.

To combat these efforts, Pathé utilized various means to keep its rivals from acquiring film of the race. These included setting off "'smoke pots' to spoil the plates of those interloping camera men and [using] reflecting mirrors to prevent any rival camera man in the interior of the race course from snapping phases of the race." The smoke pots, set off as soon as the horses entered the track from the paddock area and paraded past the grand stand, were followed by cars pulling "two large mirror reflectors, glaring in the sunlight, bouncing up and down as they made their way along the outer rail on the opposite side of the track ... in an effort to blind the lenses of the rival cameras." Detectives were stationed at the entrances in an attempt to keep rival cameramen out. While one rival "effected a perfect disguise and took one of the large motion picture cameras into the inner field merely through the medium of wearing a black derby hat," another, disguised merely with a false moustache, was nabbed when "this added adornment came loose just as he was undergoing the scrutiny of a scout for the concessionaire."[30]

The episode, as reported by the *New York Times*, raises several interesting points. For one, the article was based almost entirely on unnamed sources, no doubt to protect the identity of these "interlopers," as they were referred to in the article, raising questions as to the validity of what these sources told the reporter. It seems likely that while some of these tactics were employed, the subterfuge was invariably exaggerated, especially considering the fact that by 1923 newsreel cameramen had acquired a reputation for daring and bravado in their quest to capture footage of important events. The article reported that it was "considered unprofessional" for a cameraman to wear anything but a cap on his head, yet no mention was made of the dubious ethics of pirating what another company has paid the rights to film exclusively. Lastly, Emanuel Cohen, editor of the Pathé News, was identified by name in the article's final paragraph, only because he issued a statement explaining that Pathé had secured the exclusive right to take film of the race from Benjamin Irish, owner of Papyrus, who was granted the motion picture privilege in his agreement with Belmont Jockey Club. Doubtlessly, the Jockey Club granted Irish the exclusive film privilege to this event as an inducement to get him to ship his horse across the Atlantic Ocean. Perhaps, too, because Pathé's international home was based in London, that company invariably had the inside track to secure exclusive film rights to the event. In England, companies routinely paid for the rights to film important sporting events; however, securing the rights to an event of public importance was not common practice in America. That Pathé, which had so vigorously fought against paying for rights in America, changed course for this particular event becomes understandable given the Jockey Club's decision to cede rights to Irish.

On October 21, 1923, the *New York Times* ran a listing of "This Week's Photoplays," including the Zev-Papyrus race at the Rialto, and a day later, the Strand's presentation of the race was reported in an article under the heading "The Screen." This film showed Zev "gradually plowing his way ahead of the British winner, and at the end slow-motion pictures of the race, which give a wonderful idea of the speed of the two horses."[31] Also noted were the shots of the crowd, hurling their hats high in the air. This certainly followed the standard newsreel formula of editing in crowd shots reacting to an event's outcome. That either Movietone or Metrotone had such a well-edited version available only two days after the race seems plausible, despite the fact these companies were showing the race a week before Pathé.[32]

Fascination with the incident continued for more than a week, evidenced by several articles the *New York Times* ran that reported reaction in England, thanks to wireless and special cable. The day following the race, the *New York Times* reported that when the race result was announced on the screen in the cinemas "there were groans of disappointment, and then the program went on."[33] The next day another article noted that a (London) *Times* correspondent wrote that Papyrus' defeat surprised no regular followers of racing there, noting no other result "was ever possible, and the whole episode, with its alarums and excursions in the American press and the cinema rights, savored more of a prize fight between two heavyweights than a horse race of any sort."[34] Finally, on October 28, 1923, the *New York Times* ran a lengthy article, titled "Resourceful Camera Men," which noted that in England, events similar to what had happened during the Zev-Papyrus race occurred regularly. Ultimately, as a result of this episode, the practice of purchasing exclusive newsreel rights to sports events in the United States came to an abrupt end.

Although it is difficult to estimate what, if any, impact the piracy that marred the filming of the Zev-Papyrus match race had on securing the rights to filming other sporting events, later that year the *New York Times* reported that "the French Olympic Committee has just signed a contract with a private French firm granting it the exclusive moving picture and still picture rights for both the Winter sports at Chamonix and the Summer games at Colombes."[35] The article reported that the decision was reached after "a long investigation and study into the situation" led to the conclusion that the "great number of cinema men and photographers likely to be attracted to the games would interfere with the effective carrying out of the program."[36] An article that appeared in early January 1924 noted that it would be impossible for judges, timekeepers and umpires to perform their duties if newsreel cameramen were allowed to do as they wished. This decision, issued shortly before the initial Winter Olympic Games in Chamonix, France, set off a vigorous protest by American and international newsreel companies. A similar scenario had unfolded before the 1920 Antwerp Games, but because of the clamor, organizers allowed the newsreel cameramen and photographers access. The Organizing Committees for the 1924 Olympic Games in Chamonix (winter) and Paris (summer) held fast, however, and their November decision may, in part, have been influenced by what had happened at Belmont Park in late October.

As preparations for the 1924 Paris Olympic Games began, difficulties arose, especially relating to the rugby tournament, scheduled for May, prior to the other athletic contests. On May 8, the *New York Times* reported that Franco-American relations had been strained "over the determination of the American players to take their own photographs of the match with Romania Sunday for documentary and training purposes, despite the insistence of the French Olympic Committee that exclusive contracts already had been let to French firms for all photographic work in connection with the Olympic Games."[37] The issue quickly reached an impasse, prompting team manager Samuel Goodman to threaten to leave the Games if permission were not granted. After a meeting between Goodman and Alan Muhr, the assistant general commissioner of sports, Muhr issued a note explaining that the private company who owned the right to make pictures of all Olympic contests would allow "your official photographers to make pictures of both Rugby matches in which the Americans are engaged, under the condition that these pictures are purely for record and educational purposes."[38] Goodman's threat to "prevent the French company's men from filming the rugby matches participated in by the Americans unless American photographers were allowed the same privilege" apparently convinced the French Olympic Committee, "which promised to break its contract with the moving picture concern having the concession, or to pay it 100,000 f[rancs] forfeit money in order to allow American photographers to work."[39]

When a similar ban was announced before the 1928 Olympic Games to be held in St. Moritz (winter) and Amsterdam (summer), American newsreel companies appealed to the U.S. Department of Commerce "to make an unofficial protest against the action of the Amsterdam Olympic Games committee."[40] What especially vexed the American newsreel companies was the fact that the film rights had been sold to the UFA Company, a German company, and this marked the first time since World War I that the Germans were participating in the Olympic Games. In their appeal, the newsreel companies complained of having to pay exorbitant rights fees to film the Winter Games. By May, the newsreel companies were "formally protesting … against the attempt to sell the exclusive American news-reel rights for $60,000."[41] The companies contended that charging for film footage ran counter to journalistic precedent and practice and that they should be entitled to the same privileges and consideration as the press. In addition to this contention was the threat that the American public would not have an opportunity of seeing its Olympic athletes in competition, a scenario similar to what had happened in England when British companies refused to make any pictures of the 1924 Olympic Games. Such threats were repeatedly met with a statement that the rights for America could be purchased for the set price. When the newsreel companies took their protests directly to Amsterdam, they were "served notice that no photographer from any foreign newspaper or newsreel would be permitted to enter the Stadium."[42]

Except for those Olympic Games hosted in the United States—1932 Summer Games in Los Angeles, 1932 Winter Games in Lake Placid, and the 1960 Winter Games in Squaw Valley—American newsreel companies were required to pay for access to film showing the Olympic Games. The argument asserting their right to cover the Olympic Games free of charge was based on the premise that they were covering a news event. Conversely, Olympic organizers recognized that the distinction between news coverage and entertainment was a difficult one to distinguish. Furthermore, there was no way to prevent news organizations from editing their coverage into commercially viable packages that would detract from sales of the official Olympic film, long a staple of each Olympiad. This impasse culminated in a major showdown before the Melbourne Games of 1956, which ultimately led to a major revision in the *Olympic Charter*, known as Rule 49, regarding the selling of publicity rights and distinguishing between news coverage and live television rights, which by that time had become the primary source of income for the International Olympic Committee. Rule 49 stipulated that television networks seeking exclusive rights to more than the nine minutes of royalty-free daily coverage granted to all television and cinema news agencies would have to pay for the enhanced level of programming.

Conclusion

The newsreels were crucial to the development of sports highlights. Their importance is rooted in the routines and standards that produced sports news packaged as entertainment. Newsreel sports segments not only established what constituted a highlight, they also codified a hierarchy of teams and individual sports that were preferred. The more important the event, the more coverage the newsreel companies provided. Not only was there a clear preference for name events (e.g., Wimbledon, the Olympics, the World Series), but also for star athletes (e.g., Bobby Jones, Helen Wills Moody, Babe Ruth, Babe Didrikson).

Watching newsreels from the early 1930s and 1950s also reveals the reluctance of the newsreel companies to depart from their clearly established formula. Newsreel sports segments from the 1950s were not significantly different than those from the 1930s in terms of how the major sporting events were covered. Shot composition, editing and commentary of sporting events and sports stars established the highlight's aesthetic of distilling an event into a series of shots that brought the people and places into the neighborhood cinema. With this technique, newsreel cameramen created a condensed sporting discourse that reached a wider audience than any other sport media.

Newsreel companies sought the same rights and access to sporting events that print journalists and photographers enjoyed, yet these companies handicapped themselves with a superficial formula that relied on the entertainment rather than the journalistic value. Despite the limitations imposed by the workings of a motion picture camera and of news organizations that rarely challenged the status quo, newsreels provided viewers with a range of sporting events and athletes that became highly predictable. Even though viewers might have known the results of the events they were watching, the highlights presented in the newsreels evoked a greater degree of emotional involvement than print media offered. Unfortunately, that emotional involvement only reinforced the unequal distribution of power based on class, race and gender.

CHAPTER 3

Bad Habits

In the decades between the two world wars, newsreels helped to establish athletes as the heroes and heroines of a burgeoning consumer culture, comparable in stature to the Hollywood movie actors that followed the athletes onto the screen. Athletes became recognizable commodities within a national sporting identity, an identity largely based on a strict separation between whites and nonwhites, and reinforced the unequal distribution of power based on class, race and gender. While the newsreels reinforced existing attitudes about culture, class, gender and race, they rarely attempted to change those attitudes.

Sports highlights became a staple of the newsreels because sporting events were regularly scheduled events that offered easy-to-digest entertainment featuring sports stars who had become increasingly important after World War I. While sports reporters like Grantland Rice, Damon Runyon, Ring Lardner, Westbrook Pegler and Paul Gallico were instrumental in elevating the status of sports stars in the 1920s, the newsreels intensified the public's desire for those stars by bringing them from the agate type of the printed page to a larger-than-life stature that only the movie screen could display. Within this framework, both newsreel and newspaper economics were determining factors in turning the nation's attention from the carnage and horrors of war, President Woodrow Wilson's campaign for a League of Nations, and a Communist Revolution that promised a workers' paradise to the more parochial and mundane pursuits of recreation and sport. Newsreel sports segments provided a seemingly endless stream of national heroes, supplanting pre-war heroes from politics, business and science. Confronted with the uncertainty that accompanied changes brought on by women's suffrage, the Palmer Raids, prohibition, and the great Black Migration, people turned to sports to find heroes, and newsreels capitalized on that burgeoning interest. Not only had military preparedness introduced soldiers to a number of sports, but sports also replaced a physical closeness to the outdoors with different forms of recreation and organized sports.

As post-war economic prosperity surged in urban settings, sports promoters and sports media began creating competitions and events such as the Golden Gloves, the college all-star football game and baseball's All-Star game. Having a vested interest in promoting and presenting sports in a positive light, newsreel sports segments were increasingly infused with ballyhoo, hero worship and an idealized notion of the importance of sports. Media critics like Silas Bent and John R. Tunis decried the cozy relationship between the sports organizations and media, believing that the media overemphasized the glorious and magnificent while turning a blind eye to sport's unseemly underbelly. Myth-making in the service of movie attendance meant that newsreels manufactured empathy between fans and their heroes. In this way, the newsreels created a world inhabited by heroes who reassured everyday Americans that the extraordinary accomplishments of magnetic personalities provided meaning for a nation of faceless masses. Newsreels used sports stars to enhance profits by providing a vicarious escape from everyday concerns. In this way, the sports segments of newsreels were instrumental in not only extending the popularity of cinema as a burgeoning cultural form, but also in creating and diffusing overarching narratives that established sports as an important national cultural tradition.

Newsreels also maintained the positioning of sports as a specialized field within journalism while attempting to legitimate their own status as practitioners. Like their counterparts in the press boxes, newsreel cameramen and editors developed their own particular codes and practices that distinguished them from other journalists. As such, they can be seen as members of an interpretive community who not only shaped their professional identity, but also defined appropriate practices. Meaning derived from knowledge about these shared practices helped members of the newsreel community to validate themselves, especially in comparison to the status that sportswriters had achieved by the 1920s. Arguably, that decade served as an important time in establishing newsreel sports segments as a specialized unit within the larger community of sports journalists. The means that they used to create that distinctiveness was sports highlights, which offered a completely new way of appreciating sports and sports stars. Not surprisingly, even the venerated Grantland Rice, the decade's leading sportswriter, adopted the medium, supervising the production of Sportlight Films, which offered monthly, ten-minute newsreels featuring athletes.[1] Newsreel sports highlights were effectively employed to capture the exploits of star athletes, fixing them as recognizable markers of excellence and lending them an aura of universality that became imprinted upon a collective memory and national culture.

By 1949, surveys showed sports was the most popular newsreel segment, not only because it captured the spectacle and pageantry of events, but also because it helped nationalize sports by providing moving images of major sports heroes who had rarely before been seen by sports fans outside of the areas where they played.[2] Newsreels were not wholly responsible for creating a distinctly American sporting identity, nor were they responsible for perpetuating a dominant masculine sporting identity extolled in the era's sports discourse.[3] To a large extent this discourse evolved over a period of time when the modern Olympic movement was initiated by Baron Pierre de Coubertin in 1896 and continued throughout the twentieth century. The Olympics were appropriated by those advocates of nationalistic athletic prowess as a means of celebrating the melting pot character of the United States, and the newsreels provided the perfect medium for celebrating that character. As their popularity grew, newsreel sports highlights became so formulaic that they never changed in more than 50 years, playing up themes related to celebrity, nation (melting pot), gender and race to maintain the dominant cultural hegemony.

Nationalism and a National Culture

Part of the reason why securing film rights to the Olympic Games was such an important issue for American newsreel companies in the 1920s revolved around the ways that both the newsreels and print media used the Olympic Games to foster a national culture. For example, after only the second day of the 1896 Olympic Games, the *New York Times* reported, "One thing is believed to have been established, and that is that the future of the Olympian Games has been decided, and that they will henceforth take their place among the noted events of the athletic world."[4] The American press quickly seized upon these noted events and crafted stories that proved to themselves and the rest of the world that American athletes possessed the character and make-up of an exceptional people, capable of showing others the path towards social, economic and political enlightenment. The symbolic relationship between athletic success and national vitality became a cornerstone in the drive for a national culture. According to press accounts, American victories at the Olympic Games stemmed from the country's egalitarian ideals, its Protestant work ethic and social justice in all aspects of life.[5] By the turn of the twentieth century, sport discourse had become one of the key sources in shaping national identity. The American press even devised a means of keeping score of the Olympic Games—only the track and field events were counted—so that in 1908, for example, even though Great Britain won far more medals during the entire competition, the American press proclaimed the United States team victorious based on their achievements in track and field.

Formulating a national identity did not happen at once; rather, the process evolved over the course of several Olympiads. The earliest teams were principally composed of eastern collegiate athletes and members of clubs like the New York Athletic Club. During the very first modern Olympic Games held in Athens in 1896, notions of American athletic success cast in national terms were attributable in part to foreign commentators. For example, one Greek newspaper described American athletic prowess as attributable to their mixed blood "join[ing] to the inherited athletic training of the Anglo-Saxon the wild impetuosity of the red-skin."[6] These representatives of America were also lauded for their enterprise and their skill. G.S. Robertson, a British participant in the 1896 Athens Games, commented on the effort of the American team, attributing the team's participation to "the natural enterprise of the American people and to the peculiarly perfect method in which athletics are organized in the United States."[7]

In 1900, the *New York Times* simply referred in headlines to the participants as "Our Athletes in Paris" and "American Athletes Win." Held in conjunction with the Paris Exposition, the 1900 Olympic Games ran into several problems. One stemmed from the scheduling of several sporting events on a Sunday, which the *New York Times* reported "is the day of all big sporting events in France," but which aroused "a strong feeling of the American colleges from [against] participating in Sunday games."[8] The other was the scheduling of several track and field events on the same day as the annual review of the troops of Paris by the President at Longchamps, resulting in a sparse crowd of not more than a thousand spectators, most of whom, the *New York Times* reported, were American:

> Two small stands only were provided for the spectators, and only one of these was fairly filled, chiefly with bright, young American girls, who wore the colors of the various American colleges competing and gave unstinted applause as their countrymen secured victories. A portion of the leading stand was reserved for Americans, and it was gaily bedecked with the Stars and Stripes.[9]

As evidenced here, sport served as an institution to socialize both American men and women in gender-specific roles—men to compete and women to support them by cheering them to victories. The *New York Times* concluded that the primary "feature of the meeting was not only the number of events the Americans won, but the ease with which they outstripped their competitors, often finishing first and second, laughing side by side, and in a canter."[10] That the participants would be laughing and not running at full speed draws attention to the lack of competitiveness in certain events.

Americans exhibiting an air of superiority became a staple of Olympic myth-making, culminating in the most mythologized story of American Olympic bravado, which purportedly occurred at the opening ceremony of the 1908 London Games. During the parade of nations, American flag-bearer Ralph Rose refused to lower the American flag before English royalty, reputedly growling that "this flag dips for no earthly king."[11] Perhaps this was done in retaliation when the American flag was not displayed in the stadium for the opening ceremony. Other commentators have suggested that Rose, of Irish descent, was irked that the English had refused to allow the Irish to participate as a separate team. From this event the mythology of never dipping the American flag before a foreign leader at an opening ceremony took root, despite evidence that the flag was dipped at both the 1912 Stockholm Games and again at the 1924 Paris Games.[12]

The theme that dominated media portrayals of American athletes competing in Olympic competitions to forge a national sporting identity was the image of the melting pot, a term that served as the title of Israel Zangwill's popular 1908 play. The idea that America effectively assimilated the various ethnic groups into a unified athletic team was used by Progressives as an explanation of American athletic prowess, as well as in a more general sense to explain away the debilitating effects of industrialization, urbanization and immigration.

The melting-pot image was certainly fostered by the American media and officials of the American Olympic Committee. For example, in 1912, Edward Bayard Moss, a leading sports journalist, anointed the U.S. Olympians as "America's Athletic Missionaries," who represented a "heterogeneous gathering [of] lawyers, physicians, policemen, Indians, negroes, [sic] Hawaiians, college men, school boys, clerks, mechanics, and, in fact, entrants from every walk of life."[13] A *New York Times* photograph from July 26, 1908, titled "Tewanima the Indian competitor in the Marathon Leads the Fourth of July War Dance," illustrated the conflicting ideology that characterized the melting-pot imagery. On the one hand, Tewanima, a Hopi who was enrolled at the Carlisle Indian Industrial School, is shown performing a war dance for his laughing teammates. Upon returning to the United States, Tewanima and another Carlisle Olympian, Frank Mt. Pleasant, were greeted by President Theodore Roosevelt, who told the two athletes that he was "glad to have this country represented abroad by a genuine native American."[14] On the other hand, the use of the stereotypical "War Dance" by a stoic, noble savage possessing natural athletic ability to illustrate those democratic ideals that recognized no class or racial distinctions was typical of mainstream press representations of American Indian athletes, especially the Carlisle school football team.[15]

That the democratic ideals personified in America's melting-pot Olympic team were not completely realized became painfully evident after the 1912 Stockholm Olympics when double gold medal winner Jim Thorpe, a teammate and classmate of Tewanima at Carlisle, was stripped of his medals by the American Olympic Committee (AOC) and the Amateur Athletic Union (AAU) when it was discovered he had played professional baseball several years earlier. The AAU explained Thorpe's mistake in terms of his Indian identity, seemingly separate from his being an American winner of two gold medals. In an editorial, the *New York Times* lamented not Thorpe's disgrace but the disgrace "which he has brought upon his country—with the derision and denunciation which all Americans will long have to hear from the foreign critics."[16] Neither the AAU nor the AOC expressed much sympathy for Thorpe when they informed him that ignorance was no excuse. The final irony of the situation played itself out in 1982 when Florence Ridlon, the wife of Thorpe biographer Raymond Wheeler, discovered that Olympic rules stipulated that any contestation of a medal won must be filed no later than thirty days after an event has been completed. Petitioning the IOC for the return of Thorpe's medals, Wheeler and Ridlon told the IOC: "Gentlemen, with all due respect, ignorance of the general regulations for the 1912 Olympics was no excuse for illegally divesting Jim Thorpe of his awards."[17]

American newsreels made nationalism an integral part of their Olympic presentations, especially in the 1932 Olympic Games, hosted by two American cities: Lake Placid (winter) and Los Angeles (summer). These constituted the first Olympic Games the United States had hosted since 1904 when the Games were included as part of the St. Louis World's Fair. The Olympics first attracted British newsreel companies in 1908, but it was not until the 1920 Antwerp Games that American newsreel companies decided to film the competitions. Faced with the prospect of paying for rights to show the Olympics in 1924 and again in 1928, newsreel companies limited coverage, especially when the American team fared poorly in Amsterdam. Nonetheless, Fox Movietone News publicized its coverage as "one of the highlights of its fall offerings."[18] For the 1932 Games, four American newsreel companies were granted rights to shoot footage, including Pathé, Paramount, Fox-Hearst and Universal. In addition to sponsoring special showings of feature films and social gatherings that included motion picture stars, the studios released segments that included highlights of the day's events, including slow-motion footage.[19] The 1932 Games were touted by the media as "Depression-busters," infusing money and creating jobs during a time of considerable economic distress, leading AOC President Avery Brundage to proclaim, "It is a remarkable fact that in this unprecedented period of financial and industrial distress there has been practically no disturbance, disorder or social unrest."[20] Although glossing over the depression's impact, Brundage enlisted the support of many companies that used the Olympics to market their products, including Standard Oil, Union 76 Petroleum Company, Nisley Shoes, Kelloggs, Weiss Binoculars, Safeway and Piggly Wiggly.

Universal's coverage of the 1932 Winter Games in Lake Placid presented the Olympics as a competition between nations. This idea of winning the Olympics, originally based on a method of scoring devised by the media, continued to be employed. In its first Olympic Games segment on February 4, 1932, Universal used a formulaic headline: "Shea's Sensational Skate Victory Gives Olympic Lead to US."[21] A week later, the newsreel presented two key victories by American athletes—one in speed skating and the other in the two-man bobsled event. As the headline makes clear, these "Thrilling Victories Clinch U.S. Triumph in Winter Olympics."[22] In its last segment about the 1932 Winter Games, Universal showed ski jumping, not because Americans won medals—the Norwegians swept the top three places—but because the event featured several spectacular crashes. The final contest shown was the four-man bobsled event in which the American quartet raced to victory, purportedly sealing overall victory for the U.S. team. Sixteen years later during its coverage of the 1948 Winter Games in St. Moritz, commentator Ed Herlihy contradicted the claim of victory in the 1932 Olympics. In describing Dick Button's victory in men's figure skating, Herlihy announced that Button's victory provided precious points for the American team, helping it secure third place, "the strongest showing of any American team" at the Winter Games.[23]

The idea of winning the Olympic Games as a nation also dominated coverage of every summer Olympiad. For example, at the 1932 Los Angeles Games, Universal focused on that aspect in almost every one of its headlines: "U.S. Maintains Lead in 10th Olympiad as World Marks Fall,"[24] "U.S. Increases Lead in Olympics as More World Records Fall,"[25] and "U.S. Athletes Add to Overwhelming Lead in Xth Olympic Games of 1932."[26] This aspect of winning the Olympics has remained an important theme in the American media's coverage, although the idea of winning has changed slightly from a scoring system in which points were tabulated to a system of counting medals. Rather than celebrating traditional Olympic ideals of participation and universality, the media often focused on creating heroic myths and nationalistic pride.[27]

While the media certainly created heroic myths in their coverage, the newsreels did not completely ignore Olympism and Olympic ideals. Newsreel coverage highlighted the pageantry of the Games, giving considerable attention to the opening and closing ceremonies. The opening ceremonies of the 1932 Los Angeles Games, for example, merited "Special" coverage in which every aspect was presented— the parade of nations, greeting from American dignitaries, release of the pigeons as a symbol of peace, the athletes' reciting the Olympic oath, and lighting of the Olympic flame. In fact, Universal repeated several of the same segments, a technique that had been employed in early film actualities of fights to lengthen the reel. Another aspect of Olympism that received treatment was sportsmanship. In its coverage of the St. Moritz Winter Games of 1948, Universal's commentator noted the "tempestuous start" to the Games, in which "fist fights and sabotage imperil the Cold War developments over eligibility."[28] As a result of this dispute over the use of professionals, ice hockey was not officially recognized that year, although Universal ended that week's segment with a shot reminding viewers that the Olympic "torch burns brightly with hope that nations will foster friendship through continued sportsmanship."[29] Another display of sportsmanship was prominently used in one segment from the 1948 London Games featuring the men's 4 × 100-meter relay race in which the winning American team was disqualified for an illegal baton pass, giving the host nation its only gold medal. After the Americans protested the decision, race officials, using slow-motion filmed footage, reviewed the disputed exchange and reversed their decision. Herlihy noted, "The gallant British team relinquished the crown to the Yanks with true Olympic sportsmanship."[30]

While the Olympic ideal of sportsmanship received attention, it often was overshadowed by international ideological posturing and intense national pride. For example, at the 1952 Helsinki Games, with the arrival of a team from the Union of Soviet Socialist Republics, Cold War politics were added to the formula. In describing the parade of 67 nations, Herlihy explained that this was "the first Russian team since the days of the czar, forty years ago, and the political implications of their presence overshadow the sporting side."[31] In the same reel, the commentator noted that Finland, "the little nation that pays its debts," is "still struggling under the yoke of Russian reparations.... Finland is proud host of the athletic pride of the world."[32] Significantly, the Soviet team was identified as the "Russian" team, and the hammer and sickle icon was not prominently displayed in any footage of the Soviet team, although several Soviet athletes were shown on the medal stand with the CCCP emblazoned on their uniforms. In its final segment featuring the Helsinki Games,

Universal noted the contributions of American swimmers to the team's point total. This allowed the American team, the commentator explained,

> to win the unofficial team title, overtaking the Russian team in the closing days of the Games. The Soviet news agency, TASS, is telling its readers the Russians won the Olympics. Those at Helsinki, and especially the American swimmers, whose victories contributed greatly to our Olympic triumph, know better.[33]

For the next four decades, the ideological battle between communism and capitalism characterized an Olympic rivalry that resulted in boycotts, allegations of professionalism, and charges of cheating, all of which undermined Olympic ideals. In fostering a national sporting identity through the Olympics, the newsreels commodified its coverage in ways that reinforced a cultural hegemony. They accomplished this by structuring their coverage to highlight national sporting traditions and defining the boundaries of accepted behaviors within sporting practices, meaning American amateurism was acceptable while state-sponsored, Soviet professionalism was not. The newsreels enabled Olympic advocates to diffuse values-laden messages about ideology and culture to the wider sporting audience.

Cultural Hegemony

Newsreel sports highlights were dominated by a cultural hegemony that marginalized women and minority athletes. The newsreels, to a large extent, followed the print media in reflecting and reinforcing traditional roles for women in American culture. Women's sports newsreel features were created within a context of gendered power relationships in that they were almost entirely filmed by men, edited by men and had commentary written and provided by men.[34] That images of women were almost entirely produced through the male gaze to accommodate male interests and desires is testified by the fact that Pathé's in-house *Hints to News Film Cameramen* noted that "only the most strikingly beautiful specimens should appear."[35] For example, in Universal's coverage of the 1948 St. Moritz Games, Barbara Ann Scott is identified as "Canada's Pretty Ambassadress" and "Queen of the Flashing Blades."[36] That she was not an American was less important than the fact she was an attractive blonde. Jean Shiley, a participant in the 1932 Los Angeles Games, received praise for being "the prettiest girl of the American track team."[37] Having a strict company policy meant that newsreel coverage of women's sports was framed by a patriarchal male discourse which defined the ways that audiences thought about women's sports. While approximately half of the general newsreel stories featuring women were related to sport, the percentage of women's sports newsreel segments ranged from five to seven per cent of all sporting newsreels.[38] Additionally, women's achievements in sports were projected as part of a marginalized, separate sphere. For example, women's sports were often introduced with headlines and phrases such as "Gals Get into the Act"[39] and "And Now Something for the Ladies."[40] In a similar way, the commentary almost always referred to women athletes as girls, and members of the U.S. Olympic team were called "Uncle Sam's Nieces."[41]

Newsreel sports highlights featuring women athletes focused on the socially elite, white, heterosexually feminine women. Not surprisingly, the more genteel sports such as tennis, golf and figure skating figured most prominently with commentary extolling the grace, style and elegance of athletes such as Suzanne Lenglen, Helen Wills Moody, Althea Gibson, Carole Heiss and Peggy Fleming. When Helen Wills married in 1929, Universal used that event to illustrate the idea that beyond winning Grand Slam tennis titles, Wills Moody, like the women watching her, was first and foremost a woman and wife. A woman's role as wife or mother often overshadowed her athletic accomplishment. When Universal showed Andrea Meade Lawrence winning two alpine skiing gold medals in the 1952 Oslo Games, commentator Ed Herlihy emphasized her marital status along with her technical expertise, telling viewers, "The pretty Vermont housewife swept down the steep slope with flawless perfection."[42] By focusing on a Lawrence's role within a heterosexual relationship, the newsreel reinforces patriarchal values, emphasizing the idea that she would not undermine the dominance of masculinity in sports.[43] Even for a publication like the *Woman Citizen*, which had long been the voice of the women's suffrage movement, sports provided an opportunity for a woman to enhance her sexual appeal as much as her political right. Public discourse about women athletes fostered this duality—emancipated and sexually appealing—as a way of reassuring men that these new women were still alluring.[44]

The first sports that the newsreels and print media used to focus attention on the physical attractiveness of women athletes were swimming and diving. These two sports were introduced into the Olympic Games of 1912, although the American Olympic Committee (AOC) resisted the inclusion of women until 1920. In 1914, in a meeting at the New York Athletic Club, the AOC went on record as being opposed "to women taking part in any event in which they could not wear long skirts."[45] Ironically, when the AOC finally allowed women on the 1920 Olympic team, the committee failed to field a U.S. tennis team to compete in the much anticipated tennis tournament that featured France's Suzanne Lenglen. Instead, the U.S. team included one female figure skater and fifteen women swimmers and divers. American women dominated the 1920 Antwerp Games, winning all three medals in four of the five women's events. Ethelda Bleibtrey won three swimming gold medals and Aileen Riggin and Helen Wainwright each won two gold medals.

In both the 1920 Antwerp Games and the 1924 Paris Games, photographs and newsreels of American women swimmers and divers dominated coverage. Not only did these two sports showcase the athletes' grace and rhythm exhibited in their performances, but they also allowed photographers to show them in their bathing suits and commentators to use the terms "mermaids," "naiads," and "water sprites" as discursive motifs to accentuate their other-worldliness. Bleibtrey, Riggin and other women swimmers were featured in a special Sunday picture section of the *Pittsburgh*

Press that was removed from textual articles about American Olympians, appearing in their swim-suits under a headline that accentuated their physical attractiveness, "A Bevy of Fair American Mermaids."[46] In the 1924 Olympics, Caroline Smith, winner of the gold medal in diving, was described in terms suggesting it was her beauty rather than her athletic accomplishments that won over the highly partisan French crowd: "With her beautiful figure standing out impressively against a blue sky and a smile of unassuming confidence on her face, she sailed so gracefully in the high dive that she inspired the first real tribute that a French crowd gave to an American during the entire games."[47]

Newsreels also expressed reservation and anxiety when women athletes ventured into iconic masculine sports. Women were not allowed to compete in Olympic track and field events until 1928 when a five-event program was begrudgingly introduced. This inclusion was doubtlessly the belated reaction to the first Women's Olympics held in Paris in 1922 and sponsored by the *Fédération Sportive Féminine Internationale* (FISI), which proved so successful that the International Olympic Committee was forced to drop its resistance to women's participation. Of the events that were introduced in 1928, the women's 800-meter run drew the most criticism. Despite the fact that Germany's Lina Radtke broke the world record by seven seconds, sports journalists drew attention not to that achievement but to the exhaustion of the runners as they crossed the finish line, decrying the race as a "spectacle [that] proved ... such events are not right for the Olympics."[48] Paul Gallico also lamented seeing women exerting themselves: "If there is anything more dreadful aesthetically or more depressing than the fatigue-distorted face of a girl runner at the finish line, I have never seen it."[49] Not surprisingly, the 800-meter run for women was dropped from the next Olympics, and women did not compete in all the distance running events until 1988 when the women's 10,000-meter run was introduced.

As women's sports became more prominent, the newsreels struggled to reconcile the incursion by women athletes into male preserves, reflected in newsreel titles such as "What's next girls? Cross-country running, the latest sport to be taken up by women" and "Should women box?"[50] While newsreels did document certain women's achievements, like Gertrude Ederle's swim across the English Channel, other presentations made light of gender-bending activity. Universal segments like "Girl Mat Gladiator Wins Smashing Bout with Man Rival" and "Woman Champ Defeat Man Rival in Bowling Clash" showed women were capable of defeating men at their own games; however, such a characterization assumed that a woman's athletic capabilities peaked at a certain level. When an athlete exceeded that level and intruded the male preserve, the media portrayed that as a gender anomaly or a female impossibility.[51]

The case of Mildred "Babe" Didrikson offered insight into the masculine ideology that governed sport. Didrikson's performance at the 1932 Los Angeles Games, in which she won two gold medals and a silver medal in the three events in which she competed, challenged the idea that women should not participate in rigorous athletic competition. The media responded in typical fashion, referring to her as a "slender, brown-haired Texas girl."[52] The media diminished Didrikson's accomplishments by noting that while her victories were impressive, they did not help secure victory in the all-important scoring competition for the men's track and field competition. Didrikson was also characterized as a "Viking girl" and "Amazon," capable of a primitive rage.[53] An athlete like Didrikson had the capacity to upend traditional patriarchal perspectives, and the easiest way to marginalize her was to create a separate category, one that implicitly questioned her femininity. Significantly, when Didrikson expressed her desire to join the women's golf tour, the media immediately printed pictures of her in a dress. By taking up golf, considered a more appropriate game for women, Didrikson was cast in a role that highlighted her femininity, reducing the threat.[54]

Just as the newsreel presentations of women athletes was characterized by a conflicting discourse of sexual appeal and nationalistic fervor, the presentation of America's black athletes was characterized by a discourse that sought to avoid controversy by presenting their contributions in a factual manner. With their formulaic approach, newsreel highlights encapsulated events by capturing their superficiality, using sequences with high cutting rates to bring more action and potency to reduce the audience's critical participation. Scholars have identified five historical stages of news about minorities: exclusion, threat, confrontation, stereotypical selection, and integrated multiracial coverage.[55] Except for rare occasions when an individual athlete was identified as "Buckeye Bullet" (Jesse Owens in 1936), "the flashy Negro Back" (Bernie Jefferson in 1938) or "sensational Negro back" (UCLA's Kenny Washington in 1939), race was largely ignored, rendering black athletes invisible in terms of their racial identity, especially within professional sports that openly barred them.[56] However, in amateur sports like track and field, particularly in the Olympics, black athletes who won medals could not be totally excluded from coverage in newsreels or the mainstream press, although that coverage largely reinforced traditional patterns of racism.

As early as 1904 when George Poage won two bronze medals, one for the 200-meter hurdle and the other for the 400-meter hurdle, becoming the first black to win an Olympic medal, black athletes contributed to America's national sporting identity. Unfortunately, Poage's victory at the St. Louis Olympics, held in conjunction with the World's Fair, was couched within the prevailing racial attitudes, as organizers had built segregated facilities for the spectators. The contributions of blacks and American Indians in early Olympiads were explained under the "melting pot" paradigm that celebrated these victories as evidence of the democratic ideal of inclusiveness. When black athletes like Eddie Tolan, winner of two gold medals in the 1932 Los Angeles Games, and Jesse Owens, winner of four gold medals in the 1936 Berlin Games, emerged as star performers, a new paradigm emerged, one that began to proclaim the physical superiority of the black athlete.[57] This dialectic, in which white athletic prowess was aligned from superior intellect, will power, and scientific training while black athletic prowess was aligned with natural ability, closeness to nature, and superior physicality, was incorporated into a double-edged discourse that promoted national identity while marking racial differences.

Universal's coverage of the 1932 Los Angeles Games, for example, showed Tolan's victories in both the 100- and 200-meter sprints, Ralph Metcalfe's silver and bronze medals in the same races, as well as Edward Gordon's gold in the long jump. Unlike the print media, which gave these athletes nicknames like "Negro flash," "dusky little thunderbolts," and "two streaks of black lightning," the newsreels tended toward understatement, focusing more on the point totals contributed toward the U.S. team score. By using commentary to frame these victories within the overall team victory, the newsreels avoided having to explain the total absence of blacks from the American Olympic Association or the American Olympic Committee, and the absence of any black coaches or managers.

Other coverage was blatantly racist in nature. For example, in November 1931, Hearst Metrotone News featured a game between two Norfolk, Virginia, high schools. In this piece titled "Colored Gals Get Football Fever," the newsreel's commentator refers to the "dark shadows" playing on the field and to the "red hot mama that keeps the crowd a-sizzling, and every time her man makes a couple of downs, she starts a ragtime chorus."[58] A football is carried "in a watermelon clinch," one team's shift is "better than pork chops," and one of the captains calls "the magic signal, 'Come seven, eleven.'"[59] Shown in movie theaters across the country, this newsreel, like others produced by Hearst's company in the early 1930s, played on demeaning stereotypes that pandered to ignorance, bigotry and intolerance.

Not all portrayals of African Americans were equally distasteful, thanks to the work of black journalists. The most positive newsreel portrayals of them can be found in All-American News, a newsreel founded by Claude Barnett in 1919. Barnett also founded the Associated Negro Press in 1919, and sports played an important part of the black press' appeal to its readers, providing a narrative that captured the explicit drama of triumph over inequality, of resilience over despair, and of power over prejudice enacted by its athletes.[60]

Conclusion

Occupying a central position in popular culture, newsreel presentations of sports and their athletes operate within a frame permeated with symbolism and metaphor. Newsreel highlights continued the trend established in the print media of mythologizing sports heroes for the general public. Through their highly edited, action-oriented format, newsreel highlights shaped audience responses in a way that was more interesting, more active, stronger and quicker than the stories that appeared in newspapers and magazines. With their ability to generate more interest and more pleasure in the athletes, newsreel highlights depicted sports celebrities as larger than life figures performing in the service of their nation.

Newsreels used highlights to transform narratives about sporting events into palatable segments with easily identifiable heroes and villains, framing their presentations within a discourse that furthered a national culture. By focusing on the transcendent nature of competition and elevating sports stars to the status of national heroes, newsreels helped to maintain the status quo while sidestepping any journalistic responsibilities in covering issues related to gender, race and ethnicity. In doing so, the newsreels perpetuated sport's place in reproducing social inequality. Depictions of women and minorities were largely patriarchal. Only the most attractive female athletes were considered for inclusion; black athletes had to be nonthreatening. These athletes were expected to manifest and uphold the dominant culture's values and morals at all times. If they attempted to challenge those roles, they were marginalized or rendered invisible. Not surprisingly, newsreels maintained the idea that politics should be kept out of sports.

Newsreel highlights celebrated and entertained, never digging very deeply beneath the surface, generating interest with an emphasis on affect. By anchoring the audience's response in recognizable stars, experiences and pleasures, newsreel sports highlights maintained an entertainment ethos in which stars are presented as the culture's leaders, guiding the audience to the correct feeling. By adding meaning, an appealing sport celebrity encouraged fans to generalize their appreciation from the athlete to an endorsed product or brand. Sports stars appeared in the newsreels because they evoked an emotional response from their audiences and because the newsreels and sports organizations benefited from these peoples' visibility. In eliciting crowd responses, the newsreels had a power "which it did not bequeath to its successor, television."[61]

Chapter 4

A Dream of Carnage
and the Electronic Monster

Any indication that television would become the medium within which the sportscast highlight developed into the most important form for disseminating sports news was certainly not evident when the first steps in bringing sport to the public through the camera eye or "magic window" were taken.[1] That some of the initial steps were taken by Vladimir Zworykin, a Russian scientist who had fled post–Bolshevik Russia and who eventually came to work for the Radio Corporation of America (RCA) and its president, David Sarnoff, another Russian immigrant, helps to explain the lore of television's mythological genesis. Beginning in 1933, Zworykin and his assistants took photographs of daily activities and special events conducted in and around his Camden, New Jersey, lab. Among the earliest photographs of images captured on the television screen are a pair related to sports—one taken of a football game that shows one team about to score a touchdown and the other a long shot of a baseball game.

These images do not represent an actual broadcast of sport; rather, they illustrate the effect that different scanning rates had on picture clarity.[2] Additional steps were taken in August 1934 by another important figure in television's development, Philo T. Farnsworth, a part of whose demonstration of the world's first electronic television system showed a scrimmage between members of the Philadelphia Eagles outside the Franklin Institute.[3] Coming more than five years before RCA unveiled its television system at the 1939 World's Fair in New York City, these tenuous steps provided little evidence that television was about to become the primary vehicle for sports broadcasts across the world, let alone that it would displace existing media—newspaper, film and radio—as the medium people chose to enjoy consuming sport.

The first stage of television's development and deployment of sportscast highlights spans the period from 1934 through 1959, covering experiments and early telecasts of sporting events before World War II through the introduction of videotape into television broadcasts and re-broadcasts of sports programming. In its early years, television was almost exclusively a live medium, transmitting images and sound from one space to another in real time. Viewers watched as events unfolded in the studio or from remote locations. In terms of presenting sporting events, this marked a considerable difference from the technology of film, which was unable to transmit a live event to viewers in real time. Until 1939, sports fans in America either watched an event at the site or listened to a radio broadcast, which might originate from the event's location or might be the skillful recreation of an announcer working from Western Union reports rather than live coverage.[4] Listening to those radio broadcasts was not the same experience as attending or being able to watch a game, despite the skill of radio announcers in capturing the drama and stimulating excitement. Nor could newsreel highlights provide the immediacy and wholeness of being at a stadium, despite offering visual stimulation. Only being at a live event or watching on television was capable of providing the complete visual experience. If seeing truly is believing, then only television could bring viewers to remote sporting events in real time.

Sporting events became a favorite subject of early television producers for many of the same reasons they had become a staple of the newsreel and radio industries. Sporting events, scheduled well in advance throughout the year, offered dramatic spectacle that appealed to ready-made fans. Having learned the operational aesthetic of both film and radio, these fans quickly adapted to a new technology that was accessed in the public sphere of the neighborhood tavern or in the private sphere of the home. Producing a sporting event for telecast was accomplished as efficiently and economically as a studio program, especially in the case of sports like boxing, which became the medium's most popular televised sport. That popularity stemmed, in part, from the controlled environment in which the bouts took place, as well as the fact that boxers occupied a prominent position among sport celebrities. Thanks to the prizefight's inherent drama, neither scripts nor rehearsals were needed.[5] Similar production considerations contributed to the popularity of televising pseudo-sports like professional wrestling and roller derby.

Additionally, the production of televised sporting events had implications in the development of sport journalism's institutional structures and professional values that shaped the representation of national identity, gender and race. Because television's coverage of live events was the preserve of the networks' news divisions, conflicts and institutional jealousies arose almost from the very beginning of television production of those live sporting events. Not only were there questions about the allocation of resources and personnel, but other questions surfaced about television's role in reporting the events and promoting them to guarantee that sponsors and advertisers realized a return on their investments. Analyzing how sports broadcasting came to utilize a blend of entertainment, promotion, reportage and controversy to build an audience that attracted sponsors and advertisers constitutes one of the overarching themes of television's early ventures into sportscasting.[6] As sports promoters and the professional sports leagues partnered with television broadcasters, conflicts of interest were but one of a formidable set of obstacles that encumbered sports journalists. Early on-air announcers not only had to sell the game, but also the sponsor's products. If a station bought the rights to a team's games, the announcers often avoided criticizing their contractual partners. Control over the descriptions and accounts of a sporting event may have belonged to the broadcaster in theory, but in practice that control was shared between the broadcaster, the team and league, and the sponsors and advertisers. As rights became more expensive, cooperation was as important as the amount of money that blind bidders put forth.

Not only were sportscasters faced with questions about the need to satisfy the responsibilities of the journalism profession while producing coverage that was mutually beneficial for their contractual partners, but they also had to produce television that attracted and maintained an audience via a medium whose technology paled in comparison to film in terms of picture size and quality. While the public had certainly acquired a taste for watching newsreel coverage of sports, no one knew for certain whether or not the public would be satisfied watching any sporting event on a screen that ranged in size from 2 × 3 inches to 6.75 × 9 inches.[7] Not only was it difficult to follow a baseball or hockey puck, but the signal, especially in outlying areas, was not always clear.

The primary advantage that television capitalized on was its ability to show a live event; for while newsreel viewers often knew the outcome of the sporting event's highlights they were watching, television offered the opportunity to see the event as it unfolded. In the early days of sportscasting when the question of television's impact on attendance at sporting events was still being debated, *New York Times* columnist Arthur Daley explained that television catered to sheer creature comforts:

> It eliminates long trips to stadia or arenas; you just walk across the room and twist a dial. It eliminates crowding, pushing and those hard wooden seats; you sprawl out in an easy chair with all the elbow room you need. It eliminates the uncertainties of the weather; as far as is known, blizzards, rainstorms and the broiling rays of summer sun don't invade the living rooms.[8]

Daley noted that while some believed that television was not a threat because it could not convincingly capture the atmosphere and excitement of being at the stadium, others understood television's potential to satisfy spectators and give prominence to major sports at the expense of lesser ones. Perhaps the most prophetic pronouncement Daley included came from one promoter who said, "Radio has made sports fans, but television will only make television fans."[9] The implication was that viewers would be satisfied as long as they were entertained, regardless of whether the entertainment program happened to be a sporting event. In 1939, only one broadcast was needed for producers to realize that a single camera was not enough to cover a baseball game. That broadcast began a never-ending process of presentational refinements that led to multiple camera positions, new camera technologies (e.g., mobile, tracking, miniature and blimp), on-screen graphics, and faster editing. Several decades were required but television became the medium to popularize sport as mass entertainment.

Lastly, television furthered the importance of highlights by developing news programs that offered viewers filmed highlight packages, profiles of sport stars and in-studio interviews. On the one hand, the networks converted successful radio programs into content for television. For example, NBC recast a radio show, *The Colgate Sports Newsreel*, as *The Gillette Summer Sports Newsreel*, a replacement for *The Gillette Cavalcade of Sports* program. Offering "round-the-world coverage of the biggest sports stories,"[10] the program included headline sports events, sound-on-film interviews with leading sports personalities, and topical features. The networks also attempted to complement their live broadcasts with studio programs. For example, all four television networks—NBC, CBS, ABC and DuMont—televised sports news round-up shows as well as pre- and post-game shows to accompany their live sports broadcasts between 1947 and 1952, many during prime time. Although none of the shows lasted for more than a season, dismissing these programs as totally inconsequential because none lasted very long would be short-sighted. These programs served as important forerunners for not only the shows like the *CBS Sports Spectacular* (1960) and *ABC's Wide World of Sports* (1961) that replaced them, but also for the sport news programs that are so ubiquitous in today's sports programming schedule.

Prime Time Coverage

Television's broadcasting of sports followed a similar trajectory to the media that preceded it, especially radio. This trajectory included the broadcasting of live sporting events, and both NBC and CBS radio networks assigned the description and accounts of sporting events to their news departments.[11] That the distinction between news and sports became blurred beyond recognition was attributable, in part, to the use of the most prominent on-air commentators like Graham McNamee for both types of events. In this way, Walter Cronkite served as host for CBS's coverage of the 1960 Squaw Valley Olympic Games, and Roone Arledge, who headed up ABC Sports through numerous successes including *Wide World of Sports* and *Monday Night Football*, was selected president of ABC News. Not surprisingly, the public's perception of broadcast sport as entertainment contributed to the blurring of journalism with entertainment.

In 1939, the first American sporting event to be telecast was a collegiate baseball game in which Princeton University defeated Columbia University at Baker Field by a score of 2 to 1 in ten innings, which, the *New York Times* reported, "consumed 2 hours and 15 minutes of television's time."[12] A mobile television van from station W2XBS, which later became WNBC-TV, transmitted the accounts and descriptions via ultra-short waves to a transmitter atop the Empire State Building, which were picked up at the World's Fair and other receivers throughout the area. This telecast had followed efforts by Universum Film AG (UFA) at the 1936 Berlin Olympics and by the British Broadcasting Corporation (BBC) the following year when its first broadcast was transmitted from Wimbledon. Although the baseball game's picture quality by the one camera positioned on the third base side of the diamond ranged from blurry—players described as appearing like "little white fliers"—to clear—the skyline of apartment buildings "sharply defined" in the background—telecasting quickly improved with the addition of a second and third camera.[13] As the *New York Times* noted in September 1939, "Four or five cameras will be used before long and then baseball as a motion picture will be in the air to stay, providing, of course, that some scheme is evolved to protect the gate."[14] In addition to the dearth of television sets in the public, the main impediment to the acceptance of televising live sporting events was the need to protect the gate, a team's main source of revenue.

That boxing was destined to become television's favorite sport to broadcast was evident from the very first televised fight at Yankee Stadium on June 1, 1939. Because this bout was covered during television's experimental period, "no fee was charged by the promoter for the rights to telecast,"[15] Orrin E. Dunlap, Jr., reported in the *New York Times* several days later in his review of the televised fight. Dunlap watched the telecast "in a darkened room at Great Neck on Long Island, about twelve miles beeline from Yankee Stadium," which was "like sitting in a front row seat."[16] Within the first few paragraphs of his review, Dunlap favorably compared the experience to listening on the radio or seeing highlights of the fight in newsreels. "To see a prize fight telecast is 10,000 times more interesting than listening sightless to a broadcast announcer. The telecast batters broadcasting into the category of the silent film." Interestingly, Dunlap relegated radio to the status of silent film, another visual medium, rather than to another auditory medium like the phonograph, which could not capture live what radio was capable of capturing. In fact, in the next paragraph, he noted that "this seeing by radio is far more exciting than watching a belated and cut newsreel of such warfare, because here the result is in suspense, it may be revealed at any moment."[17]

Dunlap pointed to the size of the boxing ring, the two contestants being within an arm's length of each other, and the well-lighted ring as reasons for the telecast's success. Later, he admitted that the television image was not sharp enough yet to reveal graphic details like swollen eyes and cuts. Dunlap recommended against sending two fighters into the televised ring in the same colored shorts, which suggested that the black and white picture alone was not enough to distinguish between the fighters, who were of similar builds. That Dunlap did not describe the bruises each fighter suffered—Baer's badly cut lower lip required four stitches and Nova's right eye was swollen shut and had a cut that required three stitches[18]—also strongly intimated that the picture quality was not particularly clear. Not surprisingly, then, Dunlap admitted that while the sights and sounds of the event came alive, "it is still considered necessary that a sports commentator sit alongside the camera to thread the illustrated story together."[19] Noting that the commentator had to be attentive to every blow because the public was seeing exactly what he saw, Dunlap praised announcer Sam Taub for his "colorful reporting job. His words fitted every whack."[20]

Dunlap aptly summarized the televised bout's importance, identifying that "television uncannily projects intimacy into the performance" so that the fighters seemed "to be slamming in the family circle, not for the 16,738 huddled around the ring under June's starlit canopy."[21] Dunlap also correctly surmised that televised boxing would do for sales of television sets what radio broadcasting had done for radio sales, noting that once television sets were mass produced, the price would inevitably come down. He also predicted that "eighteen years from now, in 1957, fistic classics will be projected on wall screens, and no doubt a coast-to-coast audience will surround the arena."[22] Pronouncing boldly that the first American televised bout had provided evidence galore that boxing was a natural for television, Dunlap did not mince his words. "Carnage has been a dream of television.... There is no dodging of reality, for television is already recognized as an instrument of truth. Seeing is believing."[23] Coincidentally, the same thing had been proclaimed about film, and like the older technology, television, as an instrument of truth, would also be manipulated and compromised.

Only after World War II did television attempt to build a stable programming schedule. In 1946, for example, NBC and DuMont broadcast for only an hour or two per night and not at all on Saturdays. Two years later, sports, most notably boxing, figured prominently in the early prime-time schedules. This was attributable to the fact that the networks had very little idea what programs the public wanted to watch. Additionally, with few stations operating and the cost of building studios in which to create original programming costly, television turned to boxing, which afforded an economical alternative to the studio program, with production costs running approximately $2,500 per program.[24]

The first regularly scheduled television sports program, known as the *Cavalcade of Sports* and owned by the Gillette Safety Razor Blade Company, featured boxing from St. Nicholas Arena in New York City on Mondays from 9 to 11 p.m. and from Madison Square Garden on Thursdays from 9:15 to 11 p.m. The show had made its debut on Mutual Radio in 1941 with the broadcast of the Joe Louis–Billy Conn heavyweight championship fight, thanks to the enterprising work of A. Craig Smith, who paid only $14,820 for the rights to the fight.[25] Smith also secured the rights to the World Series and baseball's All Star Game for Gillette, which it retained into the mid–1960s. Bob Stanton served as the announcer for the *Cavalcade of Sports* program until 1948 when he was replaced by Ray Forrest, who remained with the program for only a year. Jimmy Powers took over the role in 1949, and remained while NBC aired the program until 1960 when it was dropped. ABC then picked it up, moved it to Saturday nights, and continued airing it until 1964. In total, the program broadcast over six hundred nights of boxing. The *Cavalcade* enjoyed one of the longest runs in television history, and in March 1955, the *Gillette Cavalcade of Sports* was awarded an Emmy for Best Sports Program at the seventh annual awards ceremony of the Television Academy.[26] That marked the last time the academy included Best Sports Program as a category until 1979 when a number of sports categories were awarded in a separate ceremony.

Despite its success on television, the *Cavalcade of Sports* was also broadcast on radio. Ads, which read like press releases and included photographs, regularly appeared in New York newspapers the day of the broadcast. The writing for these ads emphasized the local draw, "Jawbone" Jake LaMotta or "Rock-a-bye" Rock Graziano. The ads also promised plenty of action, "a slam-bang affair" or "a blistering battle."[27] The ads always ended with the same two paragraphs, the first identifying the radio station (WJZ, WHN) and the second providing the Gillette logo and jingle. It read: "And remember, men…. LOOK sharp! FEEL sharp! BE sharp! Use Gillette Blue Blades with the sharpest edges ever honed."[28]

By the time Gillette attached its company name to the television program's title in 1948, the *Gillette Cavalcade of Sports* had become one of the most popular programs with the neighborhood tavern audiences throughout New York City.[29] Interestingly, the fees to broadcast the program rose dramatically when Madison Square Garden demanded $200,000 for the rights during that television season.[30] A year before, the DuMont network experienced "a considerable increase in fee" to broadcast fights from the Jamaica Arena in New York City, a point that showed, as *New York Times* reporter Jack Gould reported, that "apparently not all boxing promoters are worried over the possible inroads of television on the box-office receipts of pugilistic events."[31]

In addition to its weekly coverage of boxing, Gillette also secured the rights to the world heavyweight championship bout between Joe Louis and Jersey Joe Walcott for $100,000. The *New York Times* reported that the deal between Gillette and the 20th Century Sporting Club "occasioned some surprise along Radio Row, since previously a television contract for a major bout had been made directly with a broadcaster rather than with a sponsor."[32] No doubt this surprise stemmed, in part, from the fact that NBC had enjoyed considerable success with the broadcasts of other championship fights, particularly the Louis-Conn fight in 1946, which Gillette had also sponsored. The broadcast's success caught the attention of advertising agencies, which noted the achievement by the industry "to bring forcibly to the attention of the public the practical value of television."[33] As the trade magazine *Broadcasting* noted, this practical value largely revolved around the introduction of new consumer products.

NBC did, in fact, broadcast the Louis-Walcott rematch, scheduled for June 23, 1948, in Yankee Stadium. A display ad that appeared in the *New York Times* on the scheduled day of the fight conveyed the importance of not only the fight, but also of the telecast as a means of promoting the NBC television network, its news and entertainment programs and its sponsor. In the advertisement's copy, NBC noted that "tonight's fight—like the last three World's Heavyweight Championship Bouts—will be seen on the NBC Television Network…. WNBT in New York."[34] Coverage of the fight was yet "another in the parade of exciting events which make NBC television's No. 1 Network."[35] Since the fight was scheduled to coincide with the Republican National Convention, NBC made sure to note that, in addition to the fight, viewers could "see *complete* television coverage of the convention."[36] The year 1948 marked the first year television provided coverage of the national political conventions, which eventually led to the development of nightly network news. The ad did not mention that the fight was being televised over NBC (coaxial) lines through its outlets in Washington, D.C., Philadelphia, Baltimore, Schenectady, Boston, and Richmond. However, it did mention that coverage of the fight and convention was to be broadcast to home receivers in the Midwest, thanks to "the first public demonstration of stratovision."[37]

Stratovision was a technology, developed by Westinghouse with the backing of the Glenn L. Martin Company, which utilized a B-29 Superfortress, orbiting 25,000 feet above Pittsburgh, to receive the television signal directly from WMAR-TV in Baltimore and send the signal to an area over 500 miles in diameter.[38] The bomber was outfitted with an eight-foot mast on its vertical stabilizer to receive programs; the signal was then sent from the antenna to the cabin and on to the broadcast antenna, which projected 28 feet down when in operating mode. Stratovision was successfully used to broadcast coverage of the Republican convention on June 23, the night of the scheduled Louis-Walcott fight, although the fight was twice postponed due to rain. While the rain played havoc on the fight's schedule, television did not deter people from attending. The *New York Times* reported that 42,667 people paid $841,739 at the gate to see the bout on June 25, noting that receipts would have surpassed the $1 million mark had the inclement weather not forced the postponements and refunding totaling more than $100,000. The newspaper also reported that 18 members of the Walcott family, including the fighter's six children, gathered in the Walcott home to watch the fight via television.[39] That the broadcast garnered considerable coverage in the press suggests the gathering importance of the medium in American culture.

Boxing was not the only sport to appear in prime-time in the late 1940s. In terms of quantity, 1948 marked a high point in the number of programming hours devoted to sports, accounting for 27 of the 83 hours broadcast. The second most popular sport was basketball, which was offered on Saturday nights during prime time by three of the four networks. In addition to its Saturday night broadcast, CBS offered a game on Monday nights. One can only wonder what prompted the networks to commit over nine hours of their schedule to a professional sport that had certainly not taken root with the sporting public, evidenced by the fact that, by all accounts, college basketball was more popular, with double-headers often offered at Madison Square Garden. That three networks scheduled games at the same time on the same night proved to be not only overly ambitious but not well suited for prime-time programming, lacking boxing's popularity.

By 1949, the television audience had grown considerably. In that year, the *New York Times* published another article by Jack Gould that included a television map of the United States, which showed that television was available in areas populated by 60,000,000 people.[40] The report also noted that there were 1.5 million sets, with a regular audience of 6 million. Although coast-to-coast broadcasts were still more than two years away, Gould predicted that by 1953, "television looks forward to serving 19,000,000 families and a total audience of 50,000,000."[41] Gould noted the continued improvement in television set manufacturing and the increased variety of programs, of which sports, "as a ready-made attraction, retain their hold on a large part of the audience."[42] The most pressing problems were economic, Gould explained, commenting that the television networks were yet profitable, production costs were running high and on-screen talent had not yet organized and instituted a union contract. Despite those imponderables, Gould explained that the main concern of the industry was directed toward satisfying public demand.

In 1950 television viewing choices greatly expanded, as network prime-time offerings increased from 90 to 109 hours. Sports accounted for only 11 per cent of that total, or 12 hours and 30 minutes, down from nearly 27 hours in 1948 and 15 hours the previous year.[43] While many decried the impact television was having on attendance at sports events, others realized that sports were becoming a far less important source of network programming but more important for local television stations. In this regard, television was merely following the precedent of radio. In a *New York Times* article, Sidney Lohman presented two reasons for the decline in the number of hours devoted to the network televising of sports events: "(1) a growing reluctance on the part of promoters to permit the televising of their shows, and (2) the elimination of choice nighttime viewing periods as more time segments are sold for sponsored shows with long term contracts as opposed to the seasonal fluctuations in sports events."[44] Lohman and others aptly recognized that while sports had played an important role in helping television gain a foothold into American popular culture, that role changed significantly after 1950. Two decades would pass before sports re-appeared in prime time with ABC's *Monday Night Football*.

The impact of television on sports journalism was immediate and long lasting. With their descriptions and accounts of sports events, the networks were largely responsible for reinvigorating sports journalism, including newspaper sports pages. While broadcasting indirectly spurred sales of newspapers and magazines, it also had the effect of allowing sportscasters to shirk journalistic responsibilities. As more local television and radio stations broadcast the games of local teams, the audience expected a certain familiarity with the announcers, many of whom remained with the same team for years. That familiarity bred anything but contempt. In fact, television audiences came to see the announcers and reporters as a part of the home team, not expecting them to be unbiased and uncomfortable with overt criticism of the team or management.

A Byers Market

By the time Walter Byers assumed the position of executive director of the National Collegiate Athletic Association (NCAA) in 1951, college football attendance had experienced television's impact in much the same way as the major professional sports leagues. Attendance had surged briefly after World War II, but then declined in each season from 1950 through the 1953 season. Another seven seasons passed before attendance reached the same level as in the 1949 season. Television was blamed for falling attendance, especially after the University of Pennsylvania and Notre Dame University signed contracts with ABC and DuMont respectively to allow telecasts of all their home games for the 1950 season. In September of that year, the *New York Times* reported that New York City viewers would have "a choice of five different games each Saturday during most of the season and three night-time Friday games in addition."[45] CBS was telecasting the home games of Army, Navy and Harvard; WABD carried Notre Dame's home games; ABC televised the home schedule of Pennsylvania; WOR-TV was televising a slate of games but had not decided on which teams at the time the article was published; and WPIX was to televise Yale's five home games at Yale Bowl and Fordham's two home games at the Polo Grounds. The night games were also carried by WPIX and featured Boston College's home games, to be played at Braves Field in Boston.

Only the Big Ten Conference banned televised games entirely, and attendance at those games dropped less than the national average. Other colleges across the country were at liberty to negotiate deals with local television stations, and with no restrictions and not much money offered, it was definitely a buyers' market. Those conditions precipitated considerable angst within the NCAA, especially after two studies—one conducted for the NCAA by the Crossley Corporation in 1948 and another, requested by the NCAA's newly formed television committee, by the National Opinion Research Center (NORC) of the University of Chicago in 1950. The former concluded that viewers rated watching games on television to be equal or superior to watching them from the stands, and the latter concluded that attendance would have been at least 40 percent higher had no games been televised.[46] Swift action was taken.

At the national convention in January 1951, the NCAA decided to try a program of total and partial blackouts, enabling the NORC to make a comparative study of television's impact on attendance.[47] With television coverage limited to seven regular season games in each region and three nationally televised games, NBC announced in August 1951 that 50 affiliates would carry its slate of games, including "the majority of Big Ten universities, most of the Ivy League and some colleges in the Southern and Southeast conferences, as well as numerous large independent institutions."[48] If NBC was not terribly specific in terms of which schools would be participating in the broadcasts, it was attributable to the furor that the NCAA plan had engendered, including bills introduced in a number of state legislatures that required the "games of their respective state universities be televised"[49] and a charge from one governor that the NCAA was engaging in an "illegal conspiracy."[50] Having paid $700,000 for the rights, Westinghouse Electric Corporation used its national advertising agency to arrange the slate of games. To complement its telecasts, NBC also introduced pre- and post-game shows for the 1951 season as a means to keep viewers informed about traditional rivalry games the network chose not to broadcast.

To its credit, NBC dealt with the issue of television's impact on attendance head on. In October and December of 1951, NBC offered two simulcast programs about college football on Theodore Granik's *American Forum of the Air*, a public affairs program that aired on Sundays at 2:30 p.m. The first program was billed as a debate, titled "What's Wrong with College Football?" and offered the opinions of four experts: K.L. Wilson, Commissioner of Athletics in the Big Ten Conference; Avery Brundage, president of the American Olympic Committee; Arch Ward, sports editor of the *Chicago Tribune*; and Marshall Smith, sports editor of *Life* magazine.[51] In December, another group, also composed of collegiate athletics administrators and sportscasters, discussed the question of whether there was too much football on television.

Things hardly improved the next year when the NCAA Television Committee sold the rights to NBC for $1 million with the stipulation that no college would appear on the air more than once. A week before announcing the deal, NBC named Lindsey Nelson as assistant director of sports and David M. Camerer as coordinator for the NCAA football television coverage.[52] When it announced the deal on July 29, NBC noted that "under controls as outlined by the National Collegiate Athletic Association,"[53] it would telecast a single game coast-to-coast on 11 of the 12 Saturdays from September 20 through November 29. Tom Gallery, NBC's sports director, explained that the schedule of games would be announced after extensive field tests were conducted to guarantee remote pickups. Gallery noted, "We hope to bring games of national and intersectional significance from stadiums that, heretofore, have been 'out-of-bounds' for full network transmission."[54] The other Saturday would be devoted to televising regional and local games. In August, however, NBC announced that General Motors would sponsor the television broadcasts of the college football "television game of the week"[55] on 11 consecutive Saturdays, noting as it had in the previous release that "there will be no 'blackouts' this year."[56] This marked the first venture of General Motors into television broadcasts of sporting events. NBC designed special letterhead for the "College Football News" press releases that went out for each of the 11 telecasts. It dropped its pre-game film show in 1952, but retained its post-game show.

Having achieved a measure of control over the telecasts, the NCAA's Television Committee added to the price for the television rights. To the list of conditions, it included the right to approve all network play-by-play announcers. Byers wanted to make sure that announcers refrained from any mention of the NFL, and NBC allowed this dubious editorial intrusion, which went on into the 1960s.[57] Through the remainder of the 1950s, the NCAA's Television Committee exerted more control on telecasts and undermined the popularity of its signature sport on television in an attempt to save attendance figures.

The NCAA's policy of restricted telecasts was not well received. In November

1952, *New York Times* reporter Jack Gould called the telecasts "dull viewing.... It is almost a sure bet that if there is a dull game around it will turn up on TV."[58] Gould explained that the decline in quality of college football on television stemmed from the NCAA's attempt to curb the impact television was having on attendance at the games. What was troubling was the manner with which the NCAA had elected to cope with the problem. Part of the problem related to picking the games in June, which Gould thought was nonsense. "The individual team's quality can only be judged after the season's start. What may be the interesting games on a succeeding Saturday may be known only a week ahead."[59] Getting the maximum number of colleges on the air was "as silly as its schedule-making" because "the teams commanding national interest always have been relatively low."[60]

Rather than adhering to a rigidly fixed schedule put together in the spring, the NCAA should focus on telecasting the best game available, Gould argued. He maintained that presenting one important game a week would not destroy college football nationally. Not announcing which teams would be shown until the Wednesday or Thursday before the game was important, he argued. "With uncertainty until almost the last moment over what game would be on the air, the sale of tickets could be protected."[61] Admitting that a nationally televised game might adversely impact attendance of a local game, Gould reasoned that a solution was available by moving the telecast of the "game of the week" to a Saturday night. "This would satisfy the TV fan, protect all the country's other games from the financial standpoint, and remove a constant source of argument."[62] Gould concluded that whatever solution the NCAA decided upon, "for a change it might abandon its essentially negative approach to the medium and see if a little sensible imagination cannot accommodate it."[63] Gould's warning proved prophetic. Not only did Byers' iron grip on controlling the schedule and other aspects of the telecasts not solve attendance issues for almost another decade, but college football also lost the popularity contest as professional football gradually became more popular with football's television viewers.

The Electronic Monster

Regular season broadcasts of National Football League games on CBS did not begin on a league-wide basis until 1956. Before this time, individual teams negotiated contracts for the rights to their games but realized next to nothing in profits. In fact, in 1948 the Chicago Bears televised six home games and because the team had to pay two of the stations to transmit the broadcasts, the Bears lost $1,750 in the venture.[64] Having reached the championship game in 1949, the Los Angeles Rams sold the rights to their 1950 home games to the Admiral Television Company with one important stipulation: Admiral would compensate the Rams if attendance did not increase by ten percent. Despite having one of the most potent offenses in league history, attendance fell from an average of 49,854 to 26,804, costing Admiral $307,000.[65]

With the Western Conference title game against the Chicago Bears blacked out in Los Angeles, the Rams drew 83,501 fans to the Coliseum, ending the television experiment on the local level.

In 1951, NFL Commissioner Bert Bell decreed that league teams could not sell broadcast rights to home games, which the U.S. Department of Justice challenged as an unlawful restraint of trade. Assistant Attorney General H. Graham Morison articulated the Justice Department's position, noting that the NFL's policy was "a denial to the people of their right to see football games."[66] As expressed by Morison, the Justice Department's premise that the public should not be denied "their right to see football games" ran counter to the entire commercially-based American broadcasting system and was positioned closer to the British and European systems.

On November 12, 1953, U.S. District Court Judge Allan K. Grim issued a ruling that limited the constraint in certain peripheral areas—within a 75 mile radius—but it specified no interference with telecasts outside that area.[67] The ruling also prohibited the blacking out of radio, and it disallowed Bell's powers "to approve or disapprove all contracts made by the league teams for the telecasts or broadcasts of their games."[68] The NFL had unsuccessfully argued that because it did not engage in interstate commerce, it was not subject to the anti-trust laws. Grim rejected that argument, holding that radio and television is an interstate industry, and "the league's policies interfered with the conduct of its business."[69] Significantly, Grim's ruling did not address the status of the league. Only a few days earlier, the U.S. Supreme Court had ruled that MLB could continue to enforce its reserve clause in players' contracts because it was not an interstate business.[70] The NFL, Bell noted, had "won the most important part of its case because the league's most vital need is the protection of the home gate if we are to continue our existence."[71]

In reviewing the decision, *New York Times* columnist Arthur Daley offered commentary that was clearly laced with sarcasm, especially in regard to the government's position that the public had a "right" to the games. "The Government had claimed that the play-for-pay boys violated the anti-trust laws by not giving away their products on video for free-to-all comers."[72] Although noting that the decision sounded ridiculous to a non-legal mind, Daley took another shot at the government by pointing out the hypocrisy of that position. "The Government didn't demand that Westinghouse and other pro football sponsors give away their products for free. The gridiron folks were the only patsies."[73] Daley aptly surmised that the decision was tremendously important and that it opened up possibilities for other sports, particularly baseball. "The diamond game slowly is being strangled to death by the electronic monster and yet the baseball folks were too scared to make a move until the suit against the gridiron game was settled."[74] Daley concluded by bringing the Grim decision into perspective with the Supreme Court's decision to uphold MLB's anti-trust status. "The world of sports has got so many green lights in the last few days that it's beginning to resemble a St. Patrick's Day parade."[75]

Daley's assessment of the baseball situation was confirmed over the next decade.

Even though MLB attendance was not adversely impacted by televised games, attendance at minor league games was, in fact, devastated. According to statistics compiled by William O. Johnson, over 40 million Americans attended minor league contests in 1949. A decade later, that number plunged to 13 million and then to 10 million by the end of the 1960s. The number of minor league teams dropped from almost 500 in 1949 to approximately 150 in 1969.[76]

The Grim decision was the first of several important legal cases that shaped the broadcast landscape of televised sports over the next several years. Emboldened by the decision, Bell then imposed stipulations within the contract the NFL had signed with CBS that "CBS News shall instruct its cameramen and camera crews to make every reasonable effort to avoid training any television camera on any fights among or injuries to the players."[77] Significantly, Bell did not restrict print journalists from reporting on any such events. However, Bell insisted that radio and television had to be held to a higher standard because broadcasting was a matter of public interest. "We don't want kids sitting in the living room to see their heroes trading punches. That doesn't teach good sportsmanship."[78] Significantly, Bell's invocation of protecting children echoed the very same concerns that had been used to bar fight films.

News and Information Programs

Even before the development of videotape, television did not rely on the broadcasting of live events alone. Beginning in the late 1940s, the networks developed a number of programs that featured sports news, information, interviews and highlights from game action. The process of gleaning highlights from film was time-consuming and required several steps before copies could be dispatched to subscribing stations that carried the programs. These programs, referred to as kinescopes, were syndicated to a network's affiliate stations. Byers, who began his career by working for the Big Ten Conference in the late 1940s, prepared highlight kinescopes of Big Ten Conference football games for distribution in the Midwest. He described the process required to produce a highlight reel.

> During Sunday evening, I ran through countless yards of 16-mm black-and-white film from Saturday's games to select the best plays. Then the lab editor made a work copy of the edited version, which I viewed for purposes of writing the script. The announcer would then put a voice on the master print, the lab would hurriedly print the 26 1/2-minute Big Ten highlight film, and copies would be dispatched to subscribing stations in the seven-state Big Ten territory.[79]

The process had certainly been established by years of newsreel production, and viewers had come to expect news in this manner. Significantly, the newsreel highlight formula had considerable impact on the production of sports news for television.

In 1948, ABC, CBS and NBC introduced sports news programs. CBS offered the *Sportsman's Quiz*, hosted by Don Baker and Bernard Dudley. Sponsored by the magazine *Sports Afield*, this five-minute filler, first seen on Mondays from 8 to 8:05 p.m., posed and answered questions about hunting, fishing, conservation and wildlife. Dudley served as the program's host and posed the questions. Baker provided the answers, using drawings, pictures, diagrams and other visual aides to illustrate his responses. Viewers were encouraged to send in questions of their own.[80] The program moved to Friday nights in August 1948 where it remained until January 1949 before moving to Mondays at 7:10 p.m. The DuMont network introduced a similar, but more ambitious, half-hour program, the *Fishing and Hunting Club*, in September 1949, which aired on Friday evenings from 9 to 9:30 p.m. Hosted by Bill Slater, this program offered demonstrations and interviews with various outdoor experts and enthusiasts. In January 1950, the program was re-titled *Sports for All*, but it was discontinued in March of that year. This type of hunting and fishing program was fully realized in 1965 when ABC introduced *The American Sportsman* with Curt Gowdy as host and enjoyed an 18-year run.

ABC was next to introduce a sports news program in August 1948. *Sports News with Joe Hasel* was a 15-minute summary of the sports news of the world. Hasel provided scores and commentary for the edited film highlights, and he conducted interviews with notables from various sports. ABC tried the program on Saturday evenings at 7:30 p.m. from August through January before moving it to Friday evenings at 9:30 for two months and then to Tuesday evenings at 7:15 for another two months. ABC also introduced a half-hour collection of filmed short subjects on various sports and sports personalities, titled *Sports Camera*, in September 1950. The following year it was reduced to a 15-minute program, and in December was renamed *Sports on Parade*. Similar in format to these programs, CBS's *Your Sports Special*, with reporter Carswell Adams and former major league umpire Dolly Stark, first aired in October 1948 on Friday evenings and then varied from two to five nights per week in January 1949. The program's ambitious schedule, offering viewers daily news and interviews, provides evidence that the networks were searching for a format that would complement their live telecasts of sports. The use of a studio host also characterized NBC's five-minute program, *Sportswoman of the Week*, which aired in 1948 from September 9 until December 2. Conceived as a documentary about a different notable woman each week, the program changed to a straight interview show, hosted by tennis champion Sarah Cooke. The program was first called *Girl of the Week*, echoing the newsreels in referring to women athletes as girls.

Later, in September 1949, CBS tried a 15-minute weekly sports news program on Tuesday evenings, *This Week in Sports*, which offered "newsreel highlights from various events, films of outstanding individual plays and short profiles of well-known sports personalities."[81] This program, which aired from September through mid–December, covered the end of the baseball season, the World Series, most of the football season, and the beginning of the basketball season. Arguably, based on this description, highlights of individual plays constituted the main focus rather than a recitation of scores and statistics. That the visual element served as the primary focus provides an indication of how television developed its news-oriented programs around highlights.

In October 1950, ABC began offering a half-hour highlight show of a major college football game, titled *Game of the Week*, and hosted by Bill Fisher. After a two-year hiatus, ABC brought the program back in 1953, and although it retained the title, the program featured highlights of Notre Dame's football games. This had been precipitated in part by the NCAA's decision to restrict universities from negotiating their own deals. Because no college could appear on NBC's telecasts more than once and given Notre Dame's national popularity, it is not surprising that ABC created a vehicle to show all of that university's games. The program replayed almost the entire game, excluding inconsequential plays, with Harry Wismer and Ford Bond serving as announcers. The program lasted only one season. Several years later in 1957, ABC offered the *All-American Football Game of the Week*, a highlight program of one major college game played the previous Saturday. It seems likely that given the exorbitant cost of videotape, which had been introduced for commercial use earlier in 1957, the program was produced using kinescopes.

On Friday nights, Joe Hasel hosted *New York Giants Quarterback Huddle*, a program that was syndicated as *Pro Football Highlights*, which offered extensive highlights of the previous week's New York Giants game, as well as interviews with players and discussions of news and issues about the NFL. Although it aired neither program in 1951, DuMont brought back the Giants highlight program in 1952 and used Coach Steve Owen as host. Although the program only lasted for two seasons, the format served as the prototype for the type of program that many local television stations offered in most every NFL city and surrounding markets. In 1957, ABC offered a half-hour highlights program of the New York Giants games, and two years later began to offer "a full-length videotape replay of the game that had been played earlier that day."[82] This marked an important development in the use of videotape technology as a means of time-shifting, which had first been used with radio broadcasts a decade earlier. In the mid–1950s the Ampex Corporation of Redwoods City, California, developed a visual version of its system, and its new four-head Quadruplex system was first used in American television on November 30, 1956, in Los Angeles.[83] The Ampex videotape recorder (VTR) being used at this time did not allow for cutting and editing, so the program would have to be aired in its entirety. Chuck Thompson and Howard Cosell provided the commentary for this 1959 videotaped program.

Cosell hosted another sports news program in the late 1950s, titled *Sports Focus*. This 15-minute program aired on weekdays from 7 to 7:15 p.m. on ABC. Cosell summarized the day's news in the sports world, also providing personal commentary on controversial issues, which became his signature contribution to sports journalism. At a time when the relationship between sports journalists and athletes was nothing if not cozy, Cosell was different stylistically from other sports broadcasters, more confrontational with those he featured on camera and many off camera. Although not as well known as his later work on ABC Sports, especially his *Monday Night Football* announcing, *Sports Focus* allowed Cosell to hone the journalistic techniques with which he widened the public agenda on sports.

Another important consideration related to the highlight show format was how the professional leagues attended to their game highlights. The NFL once again showed that it intended to pursue its own course. In 1965 the NFL took an important step to securing control over the highlights of all its games when it entered negotiations with Blair Motion Pictures, owned by Ed Sabol, who suggested to Commissioner Pete Rozelle that the league bring his company in-house as a promotional vehicle. At the NFL meetings in the spring of 1965, the owners agreed to buy Blair Motion Pictures, which had shot the previous two championship games, and renamed it NFL Films. That fall, NFL Films dispatched two cameramen to every NFL game. One camera captured the game from a press-box-wide perspective and the other from the field was used for close-ups.[84] The move proved highly profitable to both the league and to CBS, whose many affiliates bought into a syndicated program, the *NFL Game of the Week*, which not only built up the league's rich archive of action but propelled the game's popularity into the public imagination thanks to its enhanced production values that captured the sport's raw power and graceful beauty. John Facenda lent his distinctive baritone voice to do the voice-overs, and a media spectacle was born around professional football. In addition to syndicated features like *NFL Yearbook*, *Inside the NFL*, *NFL Week in Review*, *NFL Action* and *Great Teams/Great Men*, NFL Films created a half-hour highlight movie for each team each year. In comparison, MLB did not introduce its first syndicated series, *This Week in Baseball*, until 1977.[85]

These programs were ambitious attempts to deliver sports news at a time when sports fans got most of their news from the newspapers or listened to news programs like the *Colgate Sports Newsreel* on the radio. In terms of delivering visual highlights of sports, the programs also directly competed with newsreel sports segments, ultimately hastening their demise. Once the local and network stations began offering nightly news programs, which invariably included a sports segment, most of these television programs became obsolescent, although some of the formats were brought back by local stations and later by cable stations. To their credit, television producers refined the formula and techniques that newsreels had established with highlights, and despite the limitations associated with kinescopes, they fully recognized and featured highlights as an integral part of news programming, intimating how important highlights would become once a newer technology allowed full integration of highlights into live broadcasts and news programs.

One key development that contributed to the way sportscasts are presented today was the decision by NBC to add pre-game and post-game shows to its broadcasts during the 1951 college football season. Additionally, on September 22, a week before it began coverage of its slate of regional football games, NBC aired a half-hour special, *Football Kickoff, 1951*, which featured several Ivy League coaches "to tell what can be expected during the coming season."[86] NBC's 15 minute pre-game show, sponsored by General Tire & Rubber Co., was hosted by well-known broadcaster Ted Husing, who commented "on the players and strategy of the competing teams."[87] In addition to previewing each Saturday's top match-ups, Husing interviewed a leading coach or football expert. This use of expert opinion became a lasting characteristic of sportscasts, especially after baseball pitcher Dizzy Dean began announcing games in his own highly personal and vernacular style. More importantly, NBC's pre-game show made use of "film clips of notable contests of last season."[88] The week between games afforded enough time to select and edit film to use for these kinescope highlights. However, because television had not yet developed the technology to create instant replays and slow motion, the post-game show was restricted to "an up-to-the-minute roundup of the latest scores of the day of games played across the country."[89] Nonetheless, in developing these programs in which edited highlights played such a prominent role, the networks established key institutional practices of the modern sportscast.

Conclusion

Television networks and local affiliates utilized coverage of sports to fill broadcast schedules. Both live sportscasts and sports news and information programs figured prominently in the early weeknight prime time schedule (1946 to 1952) and the daytime weekend schedule from 1947 to the present. In its formative years, television had a deleterious effect on attendance at sporting events, and both the professional leagues and the NCAA struggled to find a way to use live telecasts and highlight shows to build and maintain its audience for events. It has been clearly established that the more important the sporting event, the less impact television has on attendance. However, for sports like boxing, the sheer number of telecasts impacted gate attendance.

In presenting the accounts and descriptions of sporting events, the television networks continued using many formats and announcers from film, radio and newsreels. More significantly, television maintained the widely held belief that broadcast sports were entertainment programs, staged to attract an audience to whom sponsors and advertisers offered their products and services. This belief had lasting implications in terms of broadcast sports journalism's institutional values and practices. As the costs to broadcast rights for sporting events escalated, the teams and leagues were rarely confronted with controversial topics other than what happened on the field. Despite this commercial imperative, television attempted to develop news and information programs that moved discussions beyond what was merely good for the game. Relatively little success was achieved with these programs. Part of the reason for the programs' relatively quick cancellations can be attributed to an audience that had come to expect all sports news to look like newsreel sports segments. Perhaps, too, television executives and sponsors feared how the audience might react to hard-hitting sports news.

In the post-war period, sports provided television with programming that was relatively inexpensive to produce. As the television industry relied more and more on variety programs to fill its prime-time schedule, live sports telecasts were relegated to the weekends. This shift from prime time to the weekends for sports programming marked the beginning of the networks' strategy to secure the largest audience for its telecasts of sporting events. The strategy of attracting an audience primarily comprised of males for weekend telecasts of both live and news-related sports programming was greatly aided by the development of videotape. Videotape was first used to re-broadcast professional football in 1959. Two years later, ABC introduced the first slow-motion highlight during halftime of a college football game. In December 1963, CBS used instant replay during game action, and in the following year slow motion and instant replay became regular features of most major sporting broadcasts, thanks to the Ampex Corporation's videotape-recording machine. Its impact on sportscasts was immediate and profound. Network and local television stations more easily incorporated highlights into their sportscasts. The highlight revolution was born.

CHAPTER 5

The Agony and the Ecstasy of Communication

Sports highlights came of age in television's second stage of development from 1956 through 1979, covering those years when videotape was first used in broadcasting up through the beginning of cable television. The videotaping of television shows for rebroadcast triggered a revolution that allowed for time shifting, which meant the recording of programs so that they could be broadcast live in the Eastern Time Zone and again three hours later in the Pacific Time Zone.[1] Equipment (e.g., optical film recorder, embossing on uncoated aluminum) to record radio broadcasts had been available from the very beginning of broadcasting; however, it was not until the Ampex company started work on an American version of the Magnetophone tape recorder, developed in Germany in the mid–1930s, that recording technology moved toward magnetic tape. Examples of the German technology had been sent back to the United States during World War II, and because the Germans had not secured U.S. patents, the technology became available in the U.S. and other countries.[2] Bing Crosby's *Philco Radio Time*, which aired on ABC, is often credited as the first radio show to be played back from an edited recording in 1947, although scholars point out Mutual had prerecorded shows in the mid–1930s. Many other shows followed Crosby's example as the networks dropped their restrictions on transcribed shows, so that by the early 1950s, canned shows were the norm.[3]

Arguably, videotape had an even greater impact on television. Until its initial demonstration at the 1956 convention of the National Association of Radio and Television Broadcasters in Chicago, a film recording, or television transcription, was made of every "live" commercial television program on a network.[4] All of those films, known as kinescopes, were filmed by a movie camera positioned directly in front of a picture tube while a live program was in progress. The program was then shipped to stations not linked by the network's coaxial cable. The prevalence of kinescopes was due, in part, to the number of non-interconnected television stations in many cities. For example, a program like *One Man's Family* was presented live on 28 stations, and then presented as a kinescope on 34 additional stations.[5]

According to an RCA Victor engineer, in May 1949 the networks were using 250,000 feet of film for kinescopes every week in New York City alone, and a 1951

New York Times article estimated that the television industry needed 550 million feet of film to meet weekly demands. By 1954, the television networks were using more film on a weekly basis than all the Hollywood studios put together.[6] NBC and CBS were the largest distributors of film transcriptions—the former shipping 44 hours of programs weekly and the latter 42 hours. Each of the networks distributed approximately 1,000 film prints to stations every week, and after the films completed their rounds, the Eastman Kodak Company bought back the film at a salvage rate of seven cents per pound.[7] Val Adams of the *New York Times* also noted some of the "gremlins" that plagued the distribution system of kinescope film prints. "Once a station affiliated with the A.B.C. network ran off an entire kinescope film before it discovered the show belonged to N.B.C. One network sent a station Part 1 of a certain program and Part 2 of a separate program, the station telecasting both parts as the same show."[8] Given the costs and gremlins, it was not surprising that after seeing the Ampex demonstration, CBS immediately ordered three videotape recorders and announced it would "eliminate its kinescope film recording process in Hollywood when the tape recorders are delivered."[9]

The use of videotape also had a lasting impact on sports coverage. In 1959 a New York City television station began broadcasting full-length videotape replays of college football games that had been played earlier in the day. More importantly, with videotape technology, broadcasts of live sporting events could be recorded and played back during the event, or for later news segments, sports round-up programs, and on-air program promotions.[10] Although slow-motion was a technique that had been introduced in sports films like the 1897 Corbett-Fitzsimmons heavyweight championship fight, it was not until halftime of an ABC broadcast of college football on Thanksgiving Day 1961 that a slow motion replay was used, predating the BBC's use during coverage of the Grand National steeplechase.[11] Finally, arguably the most important innovation was the introduction of instant replay during CBS's broadcast of the Army-Navy game on December 7, 1963.

So pervasive did the use of videotape become that it changed not only what fans were shown during a broadcast, but it also altered the role of color commentators, as well as the way sports news was packaged and delivered on television. Before the arrival of videotape, scores and statistics were the primary discursive elements of the sportscast; with videotape, highlights became the focal point. Even more significantly, the technology changed television's role in relation to the sports it covered, ultimately becoming a participant in the game.[12] Television's participation occurs in the way that instant replay is used to confirm or overturn on-field officiating decisions.

Videotape also resulted in enhanced production values that characterized television's broadcasting of sports. Those production values were necessitated by the increased rights fees the networks paid for sporting events. Because sports helped draw an audience to television and spur the sale of television sets, securing the rights to premiere sporting events became more expensive, spurred, in part, by a pair of legal rulings. The first was a 1936 FCC ruling that stipulated that the baseball teams and not the broadcasters owned the rights to disseminate the product.[13] The second came to be known as the *Sports Broadcasting Act of 1961* (15 USC 1291), which allowed professional sports leagues to negotiate broadcasting rights collectively, without fear of anti-trust legislation.[14] Before these rulings, stations secured the broadcast rights for sporting events directly from individual teams at a relatively inexpensive rate. Once television helped popularize sport, however, the professional leagues, as well as organizations like the International Olympic Committee, came to depend on the revenues from selling network television broadcast rights to offset escalating staging costs and players' salaries. To justify their investment, the networks translated the higher rights fees into more sophisticated production values to attract larger audiences, which, in turn, allowed them to charge sponsors more expensive advertising rates. The networks enjoyed considerable control through the 1970s until the arrival of cable and the fragmentation of the television audience.

In addition to technological, legal and economic factors that impacted sports broadcasting, a philosophical change about production was articulated by ABC's Roone Arledge in a memo prepared during the summer of 1960. Shortly before ABC began telecasting college football on Saturday afternoons, Arledge composed a memo in which he delineated his vision for how he wanted to cover sports. Arledge provided a summary of the memo's major themes in bold letters mid-way through the document: "WE ARE GOING TO ADD SHOW BUSINESS TO SPORTS!"[15] Invoking the entertainment ethos of show business was Arledge's way of reconfiguring the relationship between televised sports and the audience. Arledge felt that the best way to "take the viewer to the game" was to "utilize every production technique that has been learned in producing variety shows, in covering political conventions, in shooting travel and adventure series to heighten the viewer's feeling of actually sitting in the stands and participating personally"[16] in the experience. The memo outlined the concepts that came to characterize ABC's "up close and personal" coverage of sports. What Arledge articulated in this memo not only served as the template for ABC's live coverage of college football, the Olympics and *Monday Night Football*, but also for the omnibus program that would be "Spanning the globe to bring you the constant variety of sport: The thrill of victory and the agony of defeat, the human drama of athletic competition."[17] That program was *ABC's Wide World of Sports*.

Lastly, as television matured, the relationship between televised sport and viewers changed in several ways. In the early days of television before many individual homes were equipped with sets, programs were shown in restaurants, bars and neighborhood taverns. The installation of television sets in taverns changed the dynamic of that social space. Intruding into a space of amusement that already had regimented practices and behaviors, television changed how taverns were aligned with other working-class diversions, provoking protests from motion picture exhibitors and sport team owners.[18] Taverns also created a distinct market for large screen television, spurring the development of "direct view" systems for public viewing.[19] As a means of viewing live sporting events within a public space, the television in taverns engaged the viewer with both the spectacle and the context of that viewing.

When the number of home television sets increased rapidly in the 1950s and 1960s, the production values of sports broadcasting became more sophisticated and for the home viewer more entertaining. The entertainment ethos impacted sports journalists' roles in the presentation of live events and its coverage of those events during sports newscasts. The television networks' view of sports did not change with the growing commercialization of sports, and the complex ties between sport, media and business were largely unreported by broadcasters who had a vested interest in portraying sport in a positive light and fostering a set of social and sporting values for a range of ideological and economical reasons.[20]

A Bombshell Starts It All

The project to develop the first videotape recorder began in 1951 at the Ampex Corporation laboratories in Redwoods City, California. In its early days, the project was a rather low priority and was suspended twice—the first time in May of 1952 and again in June of 1953—in favor of other high priority company programs. In fact, as Charles Ginsburg, one of the engineers, noted, the project enjoyed no continuous status until August 1954, although "a certain amount of progress had been made on specific problems by means of some very minuscule man hour and money allotments, some authorized and some bootlegged."[21] Eventually, a report was drafted that included a request for time to make modifications on the machine that became the Mark I. By the end of August, Ginsburg and Charles Anderson demonstrated the Mark I for an Ampex management committee, which approved authorization for the allotment of more time on the project. The project team was expanded to include Fred Pfost, Shelby Henderson, Ray Dolby and Alex Maxey, in addition to Ginsburg and Anderson.

Although Ginsburg related that the work did not "flow from divine inspiration or a miraculous break through,"[22] several major innovations—including varying tape tension and redesigning the individual magnetic heads—keyed the recorder's development. By the end of 1955, the team demonstrated their improved model, which Ginsburg described as "a rather crude looking wooden cabinet containing a metal top plate and a few electronic units, which operated in conjunction with two partially filled 19-inch standard equipment racks."[23] Having achieved considerable improvements in resolution and in signal-to-noise ratio thanks to the shift from fast-moving tape to fast-moving heads, the team was instructed to package its machine more attractively and to prepare a "surprise demonstration" at the National Association of Radio and Television Broadcasters (NARTB) Convention in Chicago, scheduled for April 1956. That improved packaging resulted in the Mark IV, which was successfully demonstrated to a group of thirty Ampex people in February 1956, whose response "shook the rafters of the building with shouting and hand clapping."[24]

Before demonstrating the Mark IV at the NARTB Convention, Ampex invited representatives from CBS, ABC, CBC and BBC to see the new invention. NBC's parent company, RCA, was in the process of developing its own videotape recorder. Bill Lodge of CBS was impressed enough to invite Ampex to give a showing at the annual CBS Affiliate's Meeting, scheduled for the day before the opening of the NARTB Convention. In addition to the demonstrations in Chicago, Ampex decided to stage a simultaneous demonstration of the videotape recorder for the press at its Redwood City headquarters using the Mark III model. Despite almost constant refining, on the night before the affiliates meeting when Lodge saw the pictures the engineers were getting, he declared they were not good enough—the signal-to-noise ratio was too low and the noise banding was unacceptable.[25] This time the team decided better tape was needed, and an emergency call was made to the chief physicist at Minnesota Mining and Manufacturing, better known as 3M. A total of ten minutes of new tape was produced overnight, rushed to the Minneapolis airport and surreptitiously passed to an Ampex employee on board a Chicago-bound airliner.[26]

With two hundred CBS network affiliate representatives gathered, Lodge delivered a speech that was taped using the Mark IV. One attendee described what happened:

> After a brief introduction from Bill, we were looking at pictures of ourselves on the monitors not only taken just seconds before, but of a quality that was hard to realize was actually electronically duplicated and not "live." It took a few seconds before we realized the significance of what we had seen, and then, for all the world like a football crowd cheering Doak Walker or Bobby Lane trotting off the field after the winning touchdown, the entire audience rose to its feet and applauded spontaneously.[27]

That the audience's reaction was compared to a cheering football crowd points to the importance sports had assumed among television broadcasters and industry representatives.

In his front-page story for the next day's *New York Times*, Val Adams reported that the introduction of the device, the only one ready for commercial use, was "bound to set off long and arduous jurisdictional battles between various motion picture and television unions."[28] Adams detailed the differences between the Ampex recorder and RCA's model, which had been first demonstrated in 1953, although that device used far more half-inch wide tape. Whereas the RCA recorder's 19-inch reel could only record a quarter-hour program, the Ampex device could record 65 minutes of program on its 14-inch reel. Despite the recorded picture's clarity, one minor distraction was noted. "Tiny white streaks shot across the screen here and there, indicating flaws in the recording."[29] In spite of this flaw, in a follow-up story the next day Adams reported that broadcasters and reporters who saw the demonstration were amazed at the clarity of the tape-recorded picture. CBS, which placed an order for three of the recorders, said that the first application would be for delayed broadcasts. By the end of the convention, Adams reported that 73 recorders had been ordered, which represented gross sales of $3,800,000.[30]

Although RCA presented "the first public demonstration of moving color pictures recorded on magnetic tape"[31] in October of that year, the entire tape-recorded portion lasted only two minutes. By the end of November, CBS used the Ampex VR-1000 monochrome Video Tape Recorder to present a delayed broadcast of *Douglas Edwards and the News* on the West Coast, marking the first time that any video tape had been broadcast.[32] In December, the *New York Times* reported that CBS had conducted a closed-circuit test in which *Art Linkletter's House Party* program, recorded the day before as the live show went on the air, was fed from Hollywood to CBS headquarters in New York City. CBS also disclosed that it was planning to record the *Arthur Godfrey's Talent Scouts* program on tape and release the taped version to West Coast viewers at its usual hour. In the same story, Val Adams reported, "By coincidence, engineers and executive of the National Broadcasting Company also witnessed a private demonstration here yesterday of Ampex tape."[33] In January, NBC began daily telecasting of a live show, *Truth or Consequences*, from a pre-recorded magnetic tape, and in April, ABC began using the Ampex VR-1000 monochrome Video Tape Recorder for delayed broadcasting at the beginning of daylight savings time.[34]

Within a month, NBC and CBS combined to present almost 20 hours of tape-recorded programming weekly, and on April 1, it was reported CBS "quietly transmitted a magnetically recorded version of 'Cinderella' to the West Coast last night, marking the first time ninety consecutive minutes of tape-recorded images have been telecast."[35] The *New York Times* article does not explain what was meant by "quietly transmitted," although the playing of tape-recorded feature length films more than likely brought to the fore jurisdictional issues between the motion picture and television unions. The *Times* story also noted that the technical flaw of the white flash across the screen, or drop-out, was at a minimum. Engineers had determined that the flaw causing the drop-outs was in the tape and not the recorder.

The impact of the Ampex VR-1000 VTR was felt by television network producers, who no longer had to create and distribute thousands of kinescopes, and by millions of viewers, who no longer had to watch an inferior picture of programs shown live elsewhere. As a book published by 3M explained in capital letters: "TAPED TV LOOKS LIVE, WHEREAS FILMED TV LOOKS FILMED," and "TAPE CAN BE PLAYED BACK IMMEDIATELY, ERASED, RE-USED, EDITED."[36] The technical benefits to broadcasters were almost immediately incorporated into programming, including creating time lapses, dissolves, and special effects, as well as allowing for immediate review of performances and for flexibility in covering events and scheduling production. It was 3M's third point, however, which proved to have long-term implications, especially for archivists. Because video tape cost $306 for a reel, almost three times as much as film, the only way to make it cost effective was by reusing it time and again. What broadcasters in the 1950s considered important was not longevity and stability but durability. The question was not about archiving a tape for posterity, but whether the tape was durable enough to offer recordings without a loss of quality visible to home viewers.[37] Additionally, tape stock was often defective, so once a good tape was identified, having successfully recorded a program already, that tape would necessarily be reused, regardless of what had been previously recorded on it. Lastly, since most of the early videotape recorders were actually prototypes, they were hand built, meaning their record and playback heads were not compatible with other machines. A tape recorded on one machine could only be played back on that same machine.[38] Unfortunately, these factors contributed to the loss of a tremendous amount of early television programming.

The Coup d'NBC

Even before the arrival of videotape, CBS used kinescopes to get around the NCAA-imposed restrictions of televised games during the 1951 football season. On August 19, 1951, Val Adams reported that CBS "will film a selected college football game in its entirety on Saturday afternoons this fall and televise a one-hour condensation of the contest twenty-four hours later" and that some Sundays would offer "highlights of two games rather than one."[39] Since NBC owned the rights to televise one NCAA football game per week that season, CBS was using a highlights program to get around the newly-imposed restrictions and NBC's contractual exclusivity to televise college football live. Adams noted that CBS planned to use Red Barber and Dr. Mal Stevens to "offer 'live' commentary with the specially edited films."[40] This technique of offering "live" commentary over an edited film had its antecedent in "live" radio broadcasts of baseball games done from Western Union transcripts. It also became commonly used for sporting events that were videotaped and then edited for television omnibus programs.

In 1959 ABC used videotape to present a full-length replay of a college football game played earlier that day. The more important use of videotape for sports broadcasting, however, was its utilization for telecasting omnibus-format programs like the *CBS Sports Spectacular* and *ABC's Wide World of Sports*. This latter program had, in part, been made possible as a result of ABC's securing the rights to NCAA football on March 14, 1960, at New York City's Royal Manhattan Hotel. On that day, NBC's Tom Gallery, not recognizing any competitors, submitted his bid to the NCAA believing that no one was bidding against him. However, ABC had someone waiting in the wings to offer its bid in the person of Stanton Frankle, who waited until Gallery had submitted NBC's bid before stepping forward and presented the NCAA's television director ABC's bid.[41] That coup, master-minded by Tom Moore and Ed Scherick, whose Sports Programs, Inc., company served as the foundation upon which ABC Sports was built, was not the last time ABC pilfered from the older network. The ascendancy of ABC Sports was largely attributable to Scherick's bringing together a team that included Chet Simmons, Roone Arledge, Chuck Howard and Jim Spence.

Having secured the rights to NCAA football, Scherick and Moore attempted to develop a low-budget, regularly scheduled weekly program for the second quarter of the broadcast schedule, from April through July, featuring videotaped sports events that people would not mind watching on a delayed basis. They believed such an omnibus program would not only satisfy the needs of their affiliates, who were exasperated by the lack of ABC sports programming, but would also attract sponsors. Faced with the daunting prospect of having almost no money to secure the rights to established events and no idea how to sell the idea for a sports program without a name, Scherick approached Arledge and instructed him to find events they could tape between April and September. In turn, Arledge told Chuck Howard, his production assistant, to develop a list of events during that time period. When Howard questioned how he was going to do that, Arledge instructed him to venture over to the NBC library and look through microfilm of *New York Times* sports sections by posing as Pat Hernon, who, while working at an NBC affiliate, had introduced Arledge to Scherick. Arledge knew Hernon never used the library, and Howard found everything he needed to compile his list in the NBC library.[42]

Scherick then sent Arledge to the annual board meeting of the Amateur Athletic Union (AAU) in January 1961 where he secured the rights to all AAU events for $50,000, including track and field, gymnastics, swimming and diving, and the Soviet Union-American track meet. Getting advertisers to commit to a program still without a name proved difficult even when Scherick and Arledge promised agencies opportunities to advertise on NCAA football in the fall. Unable to secure sufficient sponsorship and facing an absolute deadline of March 31, Scherick was rescued by a not-so-unlikely hero, A. Craig Smith and the Gillette Safety Razor Company. When $30,000 of Gillette's advertising budget that had been earmarked for the *CBS Sports Spectacular* suddenly became available after a rival shaving cream company bought an extra minute of advertising time, Gillette's agency went to Scherick with the money. On the same day, R.J. Reynolds also decided to buy advertising on a yet unnamed and largely undeveloped program. Scherick and Arledge suddenly had enough sponsorship. Finally, Chet Simmons suggested the name *Wide World of Sports*, adapted from NBC's popular program, *Wide, Wide World of Entertainment*. Once again NBC provided an integral ingredient for ABC's fledgling sports programming.

Parades and Charades

While *CBS Sports Spectacular* may have served as a model that ABC adapted to suit its new program, the omnibus or magazine-style format had been conceived by the BBC. For example, the mid-week program *Sportsview*, introduced by Peter Dimmock in 1954, was created with the intention of combining filmed material with a studio host to offer commentary and conduct interviews. Later, in 1956, the BBC brought out another program, *Match of the Day*, which made extensive use of videotape, and was "built on the back of the BBC's exclusive deal with the Football League for edited filmed highlights."[43] Finally, *Grandstand*, introduced by David Coleman in 1958, brought together "previously disparate live outside broadcasts from sport under one umbrella programme, and was invariably structured around horseracing."[44] All of these programs predate the American programs, so it is reasonable to assume American producers were at least aware of them. Even if American producers were not aware of them, the omnibus format resembled the newsreels in terms of the variety of sports presented.

In March 1961, Scherick sold Sports Programs, Inc., and all its properties to ABC, including *Wide World of Sports*, for $500,000 in stock. After becoming the second largest individual stockholder at ABC and its vice-president in charge of sales, Scherick never again produced a sports program for the network he rescued from the television doldrums. In drawing up the guidelines for *Wide World of Sports*, Scherick wanted no staged events or exhibitions, demanding that the events be legitimately contested and resolved in the show. Although those guiding principles were followed, production values that emphasized place and personality characterized the presentation of *Wide World of Sports*.

Shot live on videotape for airing on a later Saturday, *Wide World of Sports* made its debut on April 29, 1961, with Jim McKay (McManus) serving as host and reporter. Over its 20-week run that spring and summer, *Wide World of Sports* truly did span the globe by going from Acapulco, Mexico; to Le Mans, France; to Nagoya, Japan; to Moscow, Russia; to cover 25 different events in 15 different sports.[45] Also important were the technical innovations—capturing divers from the bottom of the pool as they entered the water, using the creepy-peepy hand-held camera to show Soviet and American track and field athletes joining hands as they paraded across the infield and in 1965 transmitting the Grand Prix from Le Mans via the Early Bird communications satellite.[46] Arguably, the element that made *Wide World of Sports* successful can be traced to its emphasis on human interest. That included not only a veritable parade of athletes who became well known—Olga Korbut, Evel Knievel, Dorothy Hamill, and A.J. Foyt—but also those cliff divers, barrel jumpers, demolition car drivers and others in marginal sports whose competitors were unknown. One such athlete, Yugoslavian ski jumper Vinko Bogataj, became an iconic figure who personified "the agony of defeat" in the show's opening sequence, aired each and every week. At the show's 20th anniversary celebration, Bogataj was the only individual performer to receive a standing ovation, although in his own country, he was neither a hero nor well known.

Although the program was almost canceled after its first run in 1961 because of low ratings, *Wide World of Sports* broadcast over 800 shows and over 1,200 hours of sports in its first 25 years.[47] The program also spawned several spin-offs, the most notable being *The American Sportsman with Curt Gowdy.* The pilot aired in May 1963 on *Wide World of Sports* with a segment that featured Gowdy and angler Joe Brooks fishing for trout on the shores of Lago General Paz near the Argentine-Chile border. Gowdy and Brooks were paired against two Argentine fishing guides in a pseudo-competition in which a scoring system was used to quantify who caught the most fish, the largest fish and other firsts. Not only can the legitimacy of the competition be questioned, but before long all three networks were producing other spin-offs that focused more on celebrity than competition. Shows such as *Superstars, The Women Superstars, The World Superstars, The Superteams, Challenge of the Sexes, Celebrity Challenge of the Sexes, Dynamic Duos, US Against the World, The Battle of the Network Stars,* and *The First Annual Rock 'n' Roll Sports Classic* became the vogue of the self-absorbed 1970s. These pseudo-competitions harkened back to the earliest staged fights in Edison's Black Maria, an attempt to generate audience interest in sports stars and entertainment celebrities for a strictly commercial end. The phony packaging so inherent in these staged and heavily edited programs soon extended beyond televised sports as reality programming firmly took root in prime time television in the 1990s.

Videotape and communications satellites certainly changed the way the American networks approached telecasting sporting events that originated in Europe and the Far East. The most common solution was to offer the event on tape-delay, as *Wide World of Sports* often did, or to offer same-day tape-delayed coverage, especially for World Championship and Olympic events. Time-shifting effectively solved the problem of not having to telecast an event (e.g., Australian Open tennis championships) at 3 a.m. when most Americans would not be watching. When time-shifting was used, one journalistic issue surfaced, namely, the restriction of news of the event's outcome before the videotape was scheduled to air. While the producers of *Wide World of Sports* often counted on their audience not knowing the results of many events, the problem of other news organizations reporting the results has become more pronounced in today's nonstop news cycle.

Moreover, the practice of recording events on videotape was also used when time was not the issue, but the event's length did not fit into the program's time frame. Videotape allowed producers and editors a way to edit down long events to fit into a specified time frame. The event was videotaped in its entirety with announcers providing commentary as the event unfolded. That tape then was edited to eliminate long, boring or inconsequential stretches. To create a seamless, tightly edited product, the announcers re-narrated the edited version on videotape, which greatly enhanced announcers' ability to predict what had to happen for an athlete to win or provide commentary that sounded spontaneous but could have been well rehearsed. In this way, television created the appearance of providing live and objective descriptions and accounts, when in fact the product was stripped of its liveness in favor of an artificial, scripted package in which suspense, sequence and narrative

were manufactured. The practice raised questions about whether or not this constituted the best use of the technology or a flagrant disregard of journalistic standards.

A-synchronicity

The question was in part answered in the early 1960s after communication satellites—Telstar in 1962, Syncom III in 1964 and Early Bird in 1965—were used to
broadcast television across the oceans. In the *New York Times*, Jack Gould reported
that the successful transmission of French and British television signals on July 11,
1962, would spur governmental agencies and the networks "to prepare for the new
era in global communications" in which television would become "the dominant
medium for speaking directly to the peoples of the world."[48] Gould explained that
the Kennedy Administration attempted to separate the problems of international
television from those of domestic television. Those domestic problems had lingered
ever since FCC Chairman Newton N. Minow characterized a great deal of television
programming as "a wasteland."[49] Broadcast executives were also concerned about
the costs of trans–Atlantic transmissions and "that as a practical matter Telstar programs will be limited to major news events with Television stations on both sides of
the Atlantic deciding what they would carry."[50]

In a separate story published on the same day, the *New York Times* reported that
Japanese officials and scientists were impressed by Telstar's success. Ichiro Matsui,
an Olympic official in charge of television planning, said that the Telstar project "is
a very hopeful sign for live televising of Olympic events, but there are still a number of problems to be solved."[51] In August, the *Times* reported that the United States
and Japan had agreed to hold technical talks to determine whether live broadcasts of
the Olympics might be possible. Conspicuously absent from these preliminary discussions was any mention of network executives and to what extent they would be
involved in the endeavor of international cooperation.[52]

In January 1964, the *Times* reported that "urgent studies" were being conducted by the newly formed Communications Satellite Corporation (COMSAT)
to see whether the next Syncom satellite, Syncom III, scheduled for a July launch,
"might be able to transmit pictures sufficiently improved so that commercial broadcasts would be possible."[53] Manufactured by the Hughes Aircraft Company, Syncom
III would orbit at the geo-synchronous altitude of 22,300 miles above the Equator,
which would allow for continuous live broadcasts because the satellite would keep
pace with the Earth's west-to-east rotation. Previously, satellites could only transmit signals while in line of sight with both coasts, usually for less than an hour.
Because of the synchronous orbit, Syncom III would remain at a fixed point in
range of both the Japanese and California coasts. Despite these promising developments, Richard Witkin reported NBC was planning "to fly films by jet across the
Pacific. Events would go on the air here anywhere from 10 to 14 hours after they took

place."⁵⁴ Although plans for at least some live coverage had been discussed for several months, there was still only "an outside chance that television audiences here will have extended live coverage of the Olympic Games in Tokyo this fall."⁵⁵

Prospects for live coverage of the 1964 Tokyo Games remained dim after a test was conducted in late April by representatives from NASA and NBC. The test used Syncom II, hovering near the West Coast, to relay pictures from an antenna at Fort Dix, New Jersey, to the satellite and from the satellite to a powerful receiver at Andover, Maine, before being relayed to NBC studios by coaxial cable. The *New York Times* reported, "Officials of both organizations adjudged the pictures not of standard commercial quality but adequate for brief broadcasts of important events."⁵⁶ Not surprisingly, the Japanese representative, Dr. H. Uyeda, was more enthusiastic about the quality of the reception than the U.S. representatives. Underscoring the sensitivity of the negotiations, the State Department was reported to have written to COMSAT, which served as the carrier responsible for setting up a receiving station on the West Coast, "asking it, in the national interest, to look into the possibility of live TV coverage of the Olympics."⁵⁷ Providing live coverage of the Olympic Games may have been deemed "in the national interest" by the State Department, but it was not of considerable interest to NBC's executives.

When the 1964 Tokyo Games opened on October 10, 1964, NBC provided live coverage of the opening ceremony on the East Coast of the United States from 1 to 3 a.m. The broadcast was relayed by the Syncom III satellite, which had been launched into a synchronous orbit in July and provided pictures that Jack Gould described as extraordinary. "They were so rich in detail that they often seemed superior to pickups made under ideal lighting conditions in studios."⁵⁸ Although President Johnson and Secretary of State Dean Rusk hailed the plan for live Olympic telecasts as "a stimulus to friendship between peoples," NBC balked at the plan, explaining that long before anyone knew Syncom III would be aloft and working, the network had to schedule its Olympic broadcasts. That schedule included an arrangement providing exclusive coverage for four major sponsors. NBC also blacked out live coverage on the West Coast "to avoid interfering with commercial programming, including the *Tonight* show with Johnny Carson."⁵⁹ NBC offered no further live telecasts of the Tokyo Games.

The incident provides ample evidence that the commercial interests of NBC were asynchronous with the desires of the State Department, the Japanese Embassy in Washington, D.C., and the COMSAT. In a scathing review titled "When TV Lost the Olympics," *New York Times* reporter Jack Gould lamented the recurring problem between "the exciting wonders of science and the harsh practicalities of commerce."⁶⁰ Gould noted the significance of the experience—the remarkable progress of electronic transmission of signals, as well as overcoming the element of time—in terms that he admitted were idealistic. "The potential of Syncom 3 and its successors as instruments for advancing world unity and understanding was so vividly apparent that one's imagination inevitably ran off in all directions."⁶¹ While all the organizations that had worked so tirelessly to collaborate on a scientific endeavor between countries expressed disappointment, David Sarnoff, chairman of NBC who was in Japan for the Olympics, "could not understand the adverse reaction from Washington."[62] Gould scoffed at the notion that the incident could be rationalized by contractual provisions, however valid they might be. "Such is the importance of TV and the international interest in the medium that it becomes a commentary on American values when the rest of the world hears that this country makes a moment of history subordinate to the fate of a cluster of advertising spot announcements in California."[63] Gould berated NBC for neglecting its trusteeship of the public airwaves and its failure to recognize that at times national interest will inconvenience commercial schedules. Calling for new and broader perspectives, Gould concluded succinctly, "Isolationist TV is a contradiction in terms."[64] Despite Gould's condemnation, NBC's coverage of the 1964 Tokyo Games, comprised of tape-delayed, highly edited filmed highlights, was a harbinger of the way NBC would present later Olympics, even after all technological barriers had been surmounted.

Scoring Again and Again

In addition to allowing tape-delayed telecasts, videotape was a technology that afforded more noteworthy uses in telecasting sports. Arguably, the most significant use of videotape in sports telecasting was the development of instant replay. As early as 1955 George Retzlaff, head of sports for the Canadian Broadcasting Corporation (CBC) and producer of *Hockey Night in Canada*, experimentally used a "hot processor" to develop a kinescope (film) recording of a goal within 30 seconds for "almost instant" replay.[65] Although he used the process in a live telecast, he had not forewarned MacLaren Advertising, which expressed displeasure at not being able to promote the new feature. Additionally, the Montreal studio, one of two Canadian studios that produced *Hockey Night in Canada* each Saturday, was not equipped to produce such a replay, and the CBC had a rule that hockey productions from both centers had to look alike. Retzlaff did not use the technology again.

A year later, ABC announced that it had installed a speeded-up process for recording a live television program on film and playing it back within an hour.[66] Several years later, Roone Arledge related that while in Japan to secure the rights for the Japanese All-Star baseball game, he watched a samurai epic and became intrigued by a scene filmed in slow motion. After returning to the United States, he explained what he had seen to one of his engineers, Bob Trachinger, who sketched out how to produce slow-motion effect with television. Arledge explained: "We'd tape the action, and as it replayed on an orthicon camera tube, tape it again with another camera running at half speed. Voila, we'd have slow motion."[67] After considerable experimentation and refinement to eliminate the picture flickering and drop-outs (i.e., lines running through it), Arledge debuted the special effect during halftime of a college football broadcast on Thanksgiving Day 1961. The replay of a made field goal originated from a videotape machine in New York City rather than the ABC remote truck. The following weekend, Arledge's production team again utilized the effect, showing a 70-yard scoring run in which the player appeared to move "with dreamlike grace.... Watching, I saw the future open up before me."[68] However, Arledge's memory of instant success was only partially reliable in that ABC refused at that time to allocate a budget to develop the technique any further.

Instant replay was first used during CBS's telecast of the Army-Navy football game on December 7, 1963, after Tony Verna, a director, solved the problem of how to rewind and replay videotape immediately after a play. Verna explained:

> In those days there were no such things as footage counters or electronic readouts. It wasn't like film. When we rewound the tape we didn't know where we were. I finally ordered one of my technicians to coordinate a "beep" tone to the point at which the quarterback took the snap.[69]

Attempts to employ the technique during the early parts of the game failed until Verna and his technicians finally cued up usable footage of Army quarterback Rollie Stichweh scoring a touchdown. Verna reminded announcer Lindsey Nelson that he would have to explain the replay. Taking his cue literally, Nelson said to the audience: "This is not live! Ladies and Gentlemen, Army did not score again! They did not score again!"[70] During the following season, instant replay became a regular part of sports telecasts.

Instant replay's impact on sports telecasts was significant, compressing space and distorting time through slow motion and repetition.[71] When instant replays are shown, time is manipulated in order to dramatize and analyze action that has just occurred. Instead of bringing perspective to the game's overall geometry, instant replay tends to frame the action around the ball and only those in its immediate vicinity. Not only is the overall geometry of the game lost in the camera's myopic gaze, but the television screen itself becomes a canvas on which multiple, fragmented images are displayed. Highlights have the effect of removing events from one time frame and deploying them in another. This transformation of televised sports means in one sense that the highlights are no longer subject to the laws of linear space and uni-directional time. With slow-motion instant replay, the world of speed and violent collisions are transformed into a dance-like beauty.[72] Television's production of live sporting events was the best and easiest way to showcase broadcast technology. Producers used the capital investment that went into those enhanced production values to attract a large enough audience that would satisfy advertisers. Those production values included a complex combination of title montages, music, amplification of field noises, collages, superimposed graphics, rapid cuts, computer simulations, color arrangements, and shocking images.[73]

Highlights that featured slow-motion instant replays can also be seen as part of a move toward more sophisticated analysis by sports announcers. These highlights allowed for the analysis and appreciation of complicated choreography, the nuances of which were normally inaccessible to the television viewer. Instant replays also presented the commentator(s) with the opportunity to judge individual performance, evaluating it as well as setting it in statistical and biographical perspective. While the play-by-play announcer's role remained largely unchanged, the color man became responsible for the more spectacular aspects of the game and for conveying the enthusiasms of the crowd vocally.[74] This dual capacity has justifiably lent special effects innovations and the accompanying discourse an aura of insider information unavailable to anyone who either has not played the sport or who lacks training in highly technical aspects of that sport.

The camera's ability to capture mistakes was not always welcomed at sporting events. Thanks to visual evidence that captured conclusively errors in the judgments of officials, umpires and referees, by the end of the 1920s sports promoters had moved to bar slow-motion cameras from sporting events.[75] In 1961, at almost the same time that Arledge introduced slow-motion replays during halftime, the *New York Times* reported that a local television station would show "TV highlights of the disputed Notre-Dame–Syracuse football game last Saturday.... The sponsored half-hour will include shots of the field goal by Notre Dame that became the point of contention for Syracuse."[76] Invariably, with more and more slow-motion instant replays came more disputes related to officiating. The technology allowed announcers and home viewers to second-guess decisions made by on-field officials. As camera and replay technology improved, the use of instant replay not only served to entertain the viewer, but it also became an active participant in the conduct of sporting events. In the case of professional and collegiate football, hockey, tennis and basketball, instant replay is now part of how many sports are officiated with the replay system used to determine whether or not an official's call should stand.

Segmentation and Copromotion

Videotape and special effects techniques allowed for other uses besides in-game replays. Other notable uses of videotape occurred in the preparation of highlights for inclusion in the sports segment of newscasts and on-air promotions for both network sports events and entertainment programming. Any sporting event can be shown as it unfolds and then be repackaged and used in various ways, separated from the audio commentary and incorporated into other programs. With the advent of videotape, the use of the sportscast highlights was greatly facilitated. One of the most prevalent ways that highlights were used was in newscasts. The positioning of sports in the social construction of news within local television news programs offers important clues about culture and has a direct bearing on the coverage of sport, identity, race, gender and ethnicity. Like the newspaper sports section, sports segments in broadcast news have been set off from others news.[77] Television news' positioning of sports followed the pattern that was established in the newsreels.

Within that positioning, sports stories were, and continue to be, reported based on traditional values related to timeliness, proximity, impact and human interest. To those traditional news values must be added the availability of videotaped material in highlight form, shot either by the television station itself, provided by the local sports teams, or acquired directly from the networks.

This positioning of sports within the televised newscast also reflected the general place of sports in our culture. Despite having little relation to the rest of the news, sports news has been able to maintain its special status. Even before the advent of cable stations devoted strictly to live sports broadcasting and news programming, local television stations included scores and highlights, breaking news, and previews of upcoming events. Despite having a distinct advantage over newspapers in being able to provide same day scores and highlights, the sports segment within television newscasts was often cut to accommodate breaking news. Sports news ended up on local newscasts because network sports news programs in the late 1940s and early 1950s failed to attract enough of an audience to hold a prime-time slot. The sports segment only remained a viable part of the newscast primarily because it provided coverage of local sports teams. Perhaps because of the narrow range of news historically covered by television stations, sports ranked at or near the bottom in most late twentieth-century research polls as to why people watch local television news.[78] For example, in a 1998 poll conducted by the Radio and Television News Directors Foundation, the percentage of people (two percent) who watched local news because of sports matched those that said they watched because there were no other choices on television.[79]

The business of televised sports is to deliver a large audience to the advertisers. As such, the leagues and teams, advertisers and broadcasters share an interdependence in developing and maintaining an audience interested in watching sports. Accomplishing this requires a blend of news, entertainment, and promotion to generate interest in the product. Controlling this blend has largely become the preserve of sports management and sports public relations specialists, who interpose themselves between journalists and team players and coaches in order to maximize return on sponsors' investments. These tightly controlled conditions impact sports journalists in several ways, including selection of on-air announcers, the tendency to avoid criticism of contractual partners, and the practice of giving prominence to those events being broadcast by particular stations.

Until Roone Arledge stood up to NCAA executive director Walter Byers, the NCAA attempted to exert pressure on the networks in terms of which announcers did the telecasts. The NCAA was not alone in this regard. Not only have teams and television stations cooperated to make sure announcers refrain from undue criticism of the league, team, owner and players, but announcers have been enlisted to serve as the spokesperson in advertising campaigns featuring local companies. Some even have their own endorsement contracts with advertisers. Because advertising and sponsorship commitments are negotiated long before a sporting event is telecast, advertisers are alert to a team's changing fortunes. Not surprisingly, the interdependence has reinforced the tendency to downplay negative news and cast everything that happens during a game or season in the best possible light.

Television stations that have paid for the right to broadcast sporting events have a vested interest in presenting the event in the best possible light. This includes the telecast of the event itself, the pre- and post-game shows that wrap around the game, and the halftime show. All of these elements became integral parts of the broadcast, not only to serve a journalistic function of bringing the accounts and descriptions to the viewer, but also to inspire the interest and adulation of the viewing public. The codification of production values for coverage of sporting events evolved over the first three decades of television; however, the main tenets were articulated by ABC's Roone Arledge shortly before ABC began its coverage of NCAA college football in 1960. Arledge wanted to bring the viewing audience to the game by making viewers familiar with the host campus, by providing impact shots of the coaches, players, cheerleaders and people in the stands, and by supplying human drama—bringing the players to the audience in up close and personal ways. These "delightful adornments," as Arledge referred to them, were complemented by using "video tape recorders to enable us to replay the decisive plays of the first half during the half-time break."[80]

Thanks to videotaped highlights, halftime for the television viewers included much more than the pageantry of marching bands. In fact, halftime highlights became significantly more important in 1970 when ABC re-introduced a sports program into the prime-time flow with *Monday Night Football* (MNF). The six- to seven-minute package of the NFL's best games combined highlights into a montage that utilized both the technology of videotape and filmed footage shot by NFL Films crews the previous day. The edited film was shipped directly to the host city for MNF, and Howard Cosell narrated the package, working from only a "bare-bones play sheet."[81] Cosell unquestionably elevated the commentary provided by newsreel sports announcers and the early television announcers who reported sports in local newscasts. The halftime highlights segment became an important component of MNF, even when the game itself lacked interest and marks another important step in the development and deployment of highlights, one that placed a premium on affect in the attempt to keep the audience entertained when no on-field action was available.[82]

With increased use of highlights to entertain the audience tuned into live telecasts, to report on completed games and events, and to promote upcoming games, a gradual re-orientation occurred in the level of sports news self-promotion among competing networks. Increasingly, both networks and local stations presented news reports of, and promotions for, those events to which they held the rights and access. The larger the event and the costlier the rights to telecast the event, the more pronounced co-promotion was utilized to maximize viewership. For example, the networks signed exclusive contracts with several boxers who had won gold medals at the 1976 Montreal Olympics. Owning the rights to telecast the fights of these boxers, the network never bothered to inform audiences that the fighters were contractual employees of the network.[83] Networks not only routinely used name athletes to promote events they would be telecasting, but they often employed expert commentators (e.g., Dick Button, Donald Dell) who also owned production companies for the sports which they promoted and then commented on. What strains the ethical fabric was not the use of these promoters as commentators per se, but the network's failure to inform audiences about possible conflicts of interest during the telecast.[84]

In the two decades following the introduction of videotape and the proliferation of highlights, television sports journalism rarely investigated, critiqued or reported on the increasingly important role that sponsors and other commercial interests exerted on mediated sport presentations. Both televised event coverage and sports reporting struggled to attract and maintain an audience to deliver to advertisers. Under these conditions, the networks often deferred to sports stars and the organizations to which they were commercially beholden. As the commercial dimensions of the industry grew substantially in the next two decades, television's view of sports remained unchanged. The complexity of the relationships between sports organizations, media and sponsors remained largely beyond the public's reach by broadcasters who increasingly abdicated journalistic integrity in the name of entertainment, protecting their financial investment and those of sponsors by portraying sports in a way that avoided controversy and maintained self-serving sporting and social values. In short, television's approach was to become even more commercialized in its presentation of sports and athletes.

The Ecstasy of Communication

Television used sports to cultivate its audience in the years following World War II within the neighborhood tavern. In 1946 only 8,000 television sets had been sold to people in the New York City area. The following year, sales of television sets increased to 14,000 units, and then jumped to 172,000 sets in 1948 as more and more stations cropped up west of the Mississippi River. By the mid–1950s over seven and one-half million television sets were in use, and some television shows were receiving higher ratings than radio's top-rated program, *Lux Radio Theatre*.[85] The path to home viewing of television traveled through the neighborhood tavern, evidenced by a 1947 survey that showed most viewers watched from the tavern rather than from home.[86] According to *Business Week*, tavern patrons preferred sports and news to other types of programs. When bar owners began to advertise that sports were available for viewing, baseball owners threatened to prohibit baseball telecasting in the future. First motion picture exhibitors and later local liquor boards considered initiatives to curtail the use of televisions in taverns. Bar owners quickly realized the opportunities that mediated sports programming afforded them, including raising prices, imposing drink minimums, and suspending draft beer sales in favor of more expensive bottled beer during important sports telecasts.[87]

Televised sports also changed the social dynamic within the bar, since more often than not people came to the bar to watch television and not for the social drinking experience; these viewers also drank more slowly, tended to leave as soon as the game was over, and made regulars feel unwelcome. In 1948, the *New York Times* reported, "Thanks to the intrusion of a garrulous pictorial contraption called television, the thirsty talker has had his forum shot out from under him. As a business bait, television may offer momentary rewards; as a curb on freedom and continuity of speech, it can only breed resentment."[88] From its very beginning then, televised sports programming clearly impacted the social sphere of the bar, providing a venue for spectatorship instead of a space of interpersonal communication.

As viewing habits shifted from the social sphere to the home, audiences readily came to expect sports programming to be entertaining. Invoking participation from the viewer was largely achieved through familiarity with production values related to visual and auditory techniques and effects that elicited emotional identification with specific players and teams. That participation is largely anti-mediatory, not allowing the viewer to communicate or change aspects of the presentation. The viewer's choice is limited to observe and consume or reject the presentation. As television production values became more sophisticated, rendering viewers passive was largely accomplished by overwhelming them with sensations that were both related and unrelated to the game or event. Camera angles, close-ups, slow motion, instant replays, game summaries, and highlights all became pieces of a production model that emphasized immediacy, pace and action.

While attempting to recoup the soaring costs of rights fees and production, the television networks emphasized entertainment values and attenuated the traditional sporting experience. Scholars have argued that television sacrificed sport's inherent drama to the requirements of an entertainment ethos governed by a technologically driven power to magnify and distort images. By interrupting its telecast with advertisements, special reports, replays, pre-recorded interviews, statistical graphics, and the ubiquitous "stay tuned" teasers for upcoming segments (e.g., halftime show, post-game show, other events), the narrative was undercut by fragmentation. Despite producing programs within a realist frame that purported to present accounts and description, sports broadcasters undercut their reportorial function by leading viewers to believe the telecast represented the only acceptable version of sport. Ultimately, this has compromised the sports journalists' ability to pursue important stories. Aggressive and contentious sports announcers or reporters often are vilified by an audience conditioned to sports programming that no longer confronts living in the drama of alienation, as defined by Marx, but instead leaves viewers entranced within the ecstasy of communication, as set forth by Baudrillard.[89]

Conclusion

Television presentation of sports was impacted by two key technological innovations, videotape and satellite communications. In 1951, five years before the advent of videotape, CBS provided a program featuring highlights with "live" commentary of college football games as a way of getting around the limited broadcast schedule of NCAA games on NBC that fall. Videotape's impact was immediate in that it allowed stations not on the coaxial cable to present a much improved version of programs. Not only did videotape allow for easier time shifting of programs, but it also spurred the development of omnibus-format sports programs like CBS's *Sports Spectacular* in 1960 and ABC's *Wide World of Sports* in 1961 that were shot live and edited to fit the program's time slot.

Satellite technology offered television networks the means to share programming with stations in Europe and Japan. Presented with an opportunity to televise the 1964 Tokyo Olympics live from Japan, NBC offered only the Opening Ceremonies to viewers in the Eastern Time Zone and tape-delayed the telecast for the West Coast. The issue brought into focus the conflict over use of television as a means of fostering cooperation and communication in the national interest and the use of television to satisfy the commercial interests of the networks. Significantly, *New York Times* reporters like Val Adams, Jack Gould, Orrin Dunlap, Jr., and Richard Witkin covered the emerging importance of television and its relationship with sports with considerable insight, offering incisive criticism.

Videotape was also used to provide instant replay during live coverage of sporting events and to facilitate the use of highlights during the sports segment of newscasts. Instant replay not only changed what viewers saw in a sports telecast, but it also eventually changed the way several sports were officiated on the field. With more effects at their disposal, network presentations of sports and sports news became more entertaining in order to cultivate and maintain an audience to present to advertisers. The interdependency between broadcasters and advertisers resulted in less criticism of contractual partners. Sports journalists increasingly reported on those events being covered by the television station. As the commercial dimension of the sports industry became more substantial, television's view of sport did not significantly change.

The reporting of sports scores and the presentation of highlights during newscasts arguably suffered from the same sense of routine that plagued newsreel coverage of sports. Part of the problem stemmed from the very same issue that impacted live reporting of the accounts and descriptions; namely, television stations were dependent on the teams they covered for access to the games, coaches and players. Although never stated explicitly, sports journalists traditionally avoided controversy in their coverage of the local team and its players, believing that to expose wrong-doing or ineptitude would result in a loss of the broadcasting rights, sponsorship support, and access to highlights. One of the results of this relationship was that sports newscasters took the lead in focusing more on celebrities and the sporting celebrity culture. Highlights have the power through repetition to elevate the status of certain athletes into iconic figures. In this way, not only does the *who* often determine which highlights make the newscast, but the athlete's celebrity status also steers the newscast away from controversy. Not surprisingly, sports journalists have argued that politics should be kept out of sport. As the links between sports and television outlets, both national and local, grew closer, a vested interest in promoting and presenting sport in a positive light became part of the sports journalist's routine. Significantly, television's refusal to change its view of sports in light of the changing cultural, economic and ideological forces mirrored the same stubborn approach the newsreels had employed. That approach, of course, doomed the newsreels.

The model used to cultivate an audience for sports on television remained anti-mediatory, wherein viewers were led to believe that what was presented to them constituted the natural and universally accepted version of sport. The many enhanced production techniques—music amplification of noises on the sport field, collages, superimposed graphics, rapid cuts, computer simulations, color arrangements, shocking images—are used to capture and maintain the audience's attention. Mediated sports presentations revolve around the production of affect through a flow of images, commentary and music that stimulates consumption but often effaces history.

That sports telecasts' enhanced production values have the capacity to distort a viewer's perception of what is being watched is evidenced in the findings of a study conducted in 1983. According to the *Miller Lite Report on American Attitude Toward Sports*, almost half of all adult Americans, and 64 percent of those who regularly view televised games, "feel that given the right training they could at least sometimes perform as well as the athletes in their favorite sport."[90] For those under 35 years of age, the proportions were even higher. Two in five believe they could do at least as well, if not better, than coaches and referees, despite the lack of specialized training. Rather than being drawn to sporting events by their respect for and appreciation for athletic prowess, viewers are drawn "by the belief that anyone can play and there is nothing special about those who do, at least nothing special enough to discourage active emulation."[91] In other words, the very scientificity that characterizes effects like slow-motion action replays can be employed to deny differences in ability and competence, even in professional sports where talent levels are clearly discernable.[92] This paradoxical situation occurs as a result of mediated sport becoming a victim of its own popular appeal. As viewers become more attentive to style than substance, the criteria for measuring worth lurch toward the more sensational and less nuanced aspects of the sport. As presentations of sporting events depend on support of a mass audience, the need to entertain an audience that is more interested in spectacle than achievement leads to enhancements that divert attention with those sensations divorced from the athletic performance.

CHAPTER 6

Sports Junkies, Junk Journalism and Cathode Ray Sterilization

Sports highlights received a tremendous boost when cable television expanded the sports broadcasting menu. Arguably, the most important development was the creation of the Entertainment and Sports Programming Network (ESPN) by William Rasmussen and his son Scott. Until May 27, 1978, Rasmussen served as communications director for the New England Whalers of the World Hockey Association (WHA) and executive director of Howe Enterprises. On that late May day, Rasmussen received a phone call from Colleen Howe, who informed Rasmussen that she was terminating his relationship with Howe Enterprises and that Howard Baldwin, managing general partner of the Whalers, was firing him from his position with the Whalers. As Rasmussen related in his book, *Sports Junkies Rejoice! The Birth of ESPN*, that call from Colleen Howe "sparked a series of events that no scriptwriter worth his salt would concoct."[1] Over the next few weeks, Rasmussen, his son Scott, Ed Eagan and Bob Beyus hatched the idea for a cable network that ultimately changed how electronic sports journalism was done. Until Rasmussen received the fortuitous phone call, he had almost no experience with the world of domestic satellite communications and very little practical experience with cable television. While satellite communication's impact on television had been realized throughout much of the 1960s, cable television's genesis was anything but spectacular. Started in the late 1940s in Pennsylvania by John Walson, cable television was Walson's pragmatic response to poor reception caused by the area's geographic topography. Walson decided to put up a much higher antenna and to provide television signals to people in the mountains who bought sets from his appliance store in Mahanoy City, charging $100 per hookup and $2 per month.[2] Known for most of its first twenty-five years as Community Access Television (CATV), cable television literally took off with the launching of the RCA Americom communications satellite in December 1975. Until the launching of the RCA Americom satellite, programming was not the concern of the fledgling CATV industry; rather, reception of existing television programming was its only concern. Even after its launch, the RCA Americom satellite was greatly underutilized because there were only two earth receiving stations—one in Jackson, Mississippi, and one in Fort Pierce, Florida. As a result, in 1976 there were fewer than twelve million households receiving cable television, which represented less than 20 percent of the total number of television households in America. By 1980, the number of receiving stations exceeded 3,000 and more than 18 million households, or one quarter of all television households, were receiving cable.[3]

Within five years from the day ESPN launched its programming, the television schedule was saturated with sports, fragmenting the audience, driving ratings down, and creating Friday afternoon "fire sales" for advertisers.[4] The result was predictable: by the mid–1980s no station, cable or broadcast, was making money telecasting sports. Competitive bidding invariably drove up the rights to major sporting events. For example, almost two years before the 1984 Los Angeles Olympic Games were held, cable television executives pitched the idea to representatives of the Seoul Olympics Organizing Committee that the exclusive rights to the 1988 Seoul Olympics would be worth $750 million and that a "pay TV package offering 19 straight days and 24 hours of Olympic activity at $200 a household might generate as much as $1.8 billion just from the United States."[5] Even though these predictions proved to be more than twice the actual amount paid by NBC, cable television drove up the rights fees for sporting events until the market was saturated and prices decreased.

Further complicating the television landscape were several legal decisions that wreaked havoc on an already teetering empire. In 1981 after two universities challenged the National Collegiate Athletic Association's (NCAA) right to control television contracts, a federal judge ruled that the NCAA could no longer negotiate television contracts with the networks for coverage of football games. Ruling that the NCAA had engaged in unlawful restraint of trade under the Sherman Antitrust Act, the judge created a veritable free-for-all in allowing all broadcasters a share of the television pie. Other decisions directly impacted the regulation of cable television. One ruling by the Federal Communications Commission (FCC) in 1980 allowed cable television systems to broadcast as many distant signals from commercial networks and local stations as they wished. That decision reversed a 1972 FCC ruling that had limited the number of distant signals that local cable systems could pick up.[6] Almost immediately, the NFL contested the 1980 FCC ruling because cable systems were then able to telecast several professional football games to a given city each Sunday. The NFL challenged the FCC in court and was joined in the suit by the three major professional leagues and the three broadcast networks. The 1976 Copyright Act had provided cable systems with considerable leverage in being able to import signals into their systems. The act also fixed compensation rates, further compromising the rights holder's ability to make a profit on the distribution of the signal.[7]

Cable television's use of sports highlights changed not only the way events were telecast, but also changed the stadium and arena experiences, long regarded as the last bastion from television's encroachment on the sporting spectacle. In 1982, the *New York Times* reported, "the public's fascination with replays is one reason why many arenas and stadiums have installed large scoreboards equipped with slow-motion and [instant] rerun capabilities."[8] Other improvements included the use of blimps in live coverage of the 1983 America's Cup race, which earned ESPN its first Emmy. That production values increasingly became a critical aspect of how viewers perceived a sportscast was evidenced by the fact that as early as 1982 communication research was cited in newspaper reports about cable television.[9]

The proliferation of sports programming stemmed in part from the creation of more regional sports enterprises, further fragmenting the audience and dispersing advertising revenues. As coverage of sporting events became more segmented, sports audiences became more specialized in the same way as readers of magazines. This forced networks like ESPN to broaden its programming in 1983 by adding a non-sports program to its morning line-up and scheduling morning fitness shows for women.[10] Despite the addition of those programs, women's sports were rarely covered, and women sports journalists were underrepresented in the broadcast booths and production studios.[11] Because of increased competition, both the over-the-air and cable networks offered live sports coverage at all hours of the day and manipulated playoff schedules and starting times to maximize exposure.[12] For example, ESPN offered live coverage of the 1980 NFL draft at 9:30 a.m. on a Sunday, and both NBC and ABC provided live coverage of select events during morning hours. Cable networks like ESPN also enjoyed the advantage of being able to show an early event live and then re-broadcast the event again later that evening and perhaps even a third or fourth time over the next day.

By the mid–1980s, increased competition and the proliferation of programming led to a drop in ratings for televised sports programming. For example, in 1983 ABC's *Monday Night Football* earned its lowest ratings for the telecasts of its 16 games that fall. Not only did the loss of rating points hurt ABC in terms of its battle for prime time supremacy, but it also meant the network had to compensate advertisers with free commercial spots during other sports telecasts.[13] Cable television also wrestled with ratings, although for distinctly different reasons. For one, it took several years before cable networks reached enough homes for Nielsen to gather data. Additionally, the cable networks had to sell advertisers on the idea of reaching a target rather than a heterogeneous audience. Advertisers did not readily adopt this concept since the size of the audience remained their controlling factor. Cable networks such as MTV and ESPN employed complementary measurement strategies tailored to reflect cable's strengths.

The proliferation of sports programming created more problems for sports journalists, despite the advances that videotape technology had afforded them. In a *New York Times* article titled "Highlights Aren't Enough," Michael Goodwin decried the lack of depth and "the bland menu of scores, taped highlights and tame interviews"[14] that dominated local televised sports news. Local stations were not alone in questionable journalistic practices. In a separate article, Goodwin noted that the news served up by the broadcast networks during the news segments of their pre-game shows (e.g., CBS's *NFL Today*) "reveal themselves better at self-promotion than journalism."[15] Additionally, the presence of women journalists in the press boxes, announcing booths and locker rooms changed the dynamic of the sports-media relationship. Women sportswriters and broadcasters were subjected to intimidation and sexual harassment by players, coaches and co-workers. Only after two much-publicized lawsuits brought by women sports journalists did the leagues and networks enforce policies intended to punish blatant sexism and allow access to locker rooms to both genders. Despite the publicity related to these cases, women remained underrepresented in sports journalism broadcasting and management positions.

By the time ESPN celebrated its 15th year of broadcasting in 1994, the line between sports and entertainment had been blurred beyond recognition. That ESPN had successfully "invaded the broader culture beyond sports"[16] was evidenced in the many times *SportsCenter* was cited in popular movies and television shows like ABC's fictionalized *Sports Night*. Having adopted the self-proclaimed mantle of "the worldwide leader in sports," ESPN fostered a discourse that played on being hip, witty and non-threatening while inviting the audience to "crave" its ever-expanding stream of messages, highlights, and top-ten plays. The 1990s advertising campaign, titled "This Is *SportsCenter*," was not merely an advertisement's tag-line; rather, it "induced viewers to crave more ESPN,"[17] to indulge their addiction and to never be satisfied. The sports junkie's loyalty was largely predicated upon an operational aesthetic in which the highlights in ever increasing numbers became the network's *sui generis*.

Liftoff

Domestic satellite communication operations began in the spring of 1974 with the launch of the Western Union Corporation's Westar satellite. It was equipped with 24 transponders, each capable of receiving and transmitting one color television channel or 600 two-way voice signals at one time, as well as "telephone calls, data transmission, communications between land point and offshore points, television shows, movies and visual presentations."[18] Although the Communications Satellite Corporation (COMSAT) had served as the official representative of the United States in the international satellite field throughout the 1960s, it was not until 1970 when the FCC rejected COMSAT's argument that its charter entitled it to run the domestic satellite business and adopted an "open skies" policy advocated by the Office of Telecommunications that the domestic satellite industry took shape.[19] The FCC adopted the stance that satellite communications should be "open to any applicant qualified and financially able to handle the expenses."[20]

In addition to the monthly cost of leasing a transponder, companies wanting to utilize satellite capability also had to factor in the cost of a ground station, which, the *New York Times* reported in a September 1975 article, would run from $1 million to $4 million each, depending on size.[21] The *Times* also reported that the number of applications to construct earth stations had increased from 14 to 68 during the preceding year. In response to increased demand, the FCC streamlined the regulatory procedures regarding earth stations by consolidating into one application the requirements for obtaining one permit to purchase earth-station equipment and another to construct the station.

Significantly, satellite technology and cable television were first used to transmit a boxing match. On September 30, 1975, Home Box Office (HBO) became the first television network to deliver signals via the Westar satellite when it showed the boxing match between Muhammad Ali and Joe Frazier. In this brutal fight, the third and deciding fight between the two boxers, Ali earned a technical knockout when Frazier did not answer the bell for round 15. Billed as "The Thrilla in Manila," the fight was produced by Don King and broadcast to many countries worldwide via HBO's signal. The fight also garnered tremendous media attention, thanks in large part to Ali's taunting of Frazier in the lead-up to the fight. In fact, Ali played up the fight's billing in news conferences by punching a rubber gorilla meant to represent Frazier while saying, "It's gonna be a chilla, and a killa, and a thrilla, when I get the Gorilla in Manila."[22] In 1999, ESPN's *SportsCentury* listed the fight as the fifth greatest sporting event of the 20th Century.[23]

On December 12, 1975, the RCA Global Communications Corporation, a subsidiary of RCA, launched the Satcom 1 satellite from Cape Canaveral, becoming the second domestic communications satellite to be launched. Equipped with 24 transponders, Satcom I was originally designed to provide long distance services between Alaska and the lower 48 states, as well as to offer competition with Western Union's Westar satellite and one proposed by AT&T and the General Telephone and Electronics Corporation (GTE), scheduled for launch in the summer of 1976. Built at a cost of $50 million, Satcom I had transponders available in 1978 when Al Parinello, an RCA salesman, pitched the satellite's capabilities to Scott and Bill Rasmussen in a conference room leased for $20 from United Cable because the Rasmussens did not want anyone to see the "very low-budget offices" of what was called ESP-TV.[24] Parinello described the leasing rates for a transponder on Satcom I, depending on the time requested, which in 1978 RCA was offering from one occasional hour to five hours nightly. Before leaving, Parinello mentioned one rate not on the card: a preemptable 24-hour transponder for $35,000 a month with an increase after 12 months over the course of a five-year lease with termination liability.

Despite not having financing, the Rasmussens determined that it was less expensive to lease a transponder for $35,000 a month than it would be to pay the daily fee of $1,250 for five hours seven days a week. Within days, ESP-TV had a 24-hour transponder with no money down and no payment due until 90 days after the contract was signed. That ended up being the last transponder RCA leased under those terms. When the *Wall Street Journal* published a story predicting that the cable television industry was on the threshold of considerable growth and expansion because of the availability of satellite communications technology, media companies like Time, Inc., Walt Disney Co., 20th Century–Fox, and Warner Brothers Communication began applying for transponders. Having beaten these media giants to the punch, ESP-TV was not only guaranteed a transponder, but did so before the fees to lease transponders increased dramatically. Despite the fact that satellite communications technology was far from perfect—Satcom II lost control and pitched position and Satcom III was lost—its impact on cable television was profound. Writing for the *New York Times*, John Noble Wilford noted, "Cable television in this country is proliferating in large part because of the revolution in satellite communications."[25]

Loosening the Cultural Glue

Even before ESPN went on the air for the first time on September 7, 1979, several occurrences provided indications that the network would impact sports broadcasting. In addition to leasing a transponder on RCA's Satcom I, Rasmussen acquired $75,000 in funding from the K.S. Sweet investment firm, enough to keep ESP-TV afloat and produce a test telecast on November 17, 1978. That telecast featured taped coverage of a University of Connecticut (UConn) men's soccer game, followed by live coverage of a men's basketball game. The telecast was viewed by 850,000 households across 26 states, including several UConn alumni who contacted athletic director John Toner "to express how happy they were to see Connecticut sports on television."[26]

Building on the interest that telecast generated, Rasmussen and J.B. Doherty, representing the Sweet investment firm, pitched the idea of a sports cable channel to Stuart Evey, who was in charge of Getty Oil's non-oil ventures. Over the course of 45 days, Rasmussen shuttled between Getty's headquarters in Los Angeles and NCAA headquarters in Shawnee Mission, Kansas, attempting to secure funding from Getty, which, in turn, would satisfy the NCAA enough to grant ESP-TV the rights to NCAA contests. Throughout December 1978, ESP-TV, having used up all of the K.S. Sweet investment money, was on the verge of demise. Yet, at times, fortune smiled on them: On the day Scott Rasmussen was supposed to pay $18,000 for a plot of land in Bristol, Connecticut, on which the cable network's facilities were to be built (money they did not have), a snowstorm forced the meeting to be rescheduled for February.[27] Although Rasmussen ultimately had to sell off 85 percent of ESP-TV to secure the $10 million investment money from Getty, he leveraged that security into a two-year contract telecasting a plethora of NCAA events, some live and some taped.

The trajectory from statewide cable channel to national all-sports network was as improbable as it was daring. ESP-TV's original stated purpose was "to complement rather than compete with current NCAA television contractual arrangements … [to] televise nationally a minimum of five hundred (500) NCAA Division

I, II, III men's and women's athletic events."[28] Not only were events broadcast several times to maximize exposure, but "highlight packages, commercial network action segments, and extensive NCAA and member institution promotion [were] to be an integral part of ESP-TV's effort."[29] That modest proposal was enough to land in May 1979, almost four months before going on the air, a $1.38 million contract with Anheuser-Busch, which, the *New York Times* noted, constituted "a record in the annals of cable television."[30] The deal's importance cannot be overstated. ESPN made frequent use of the relationship in an advertising campaign over the next year. For example, one display ad states: "Bud and ESPN. It's a natural. Anheuser-Busch is the king of TV sports advertisers. ESPN, the 24-hour total sports cable network, is the future of TV sports."[31] The ad mentions several other advertisers, including American Express, Michelin, Noxzema, Magnavox, and Hilton. That the hotel chain became another major advertiser of ESPN is understandable given Evey's vision that ESPN would become what he called a "'lift network,' part of a basic package that cable operators could use to … entice viewers with the pay-movie channels like HBO and Cinemax, where the real profits were."[32] Several weeks after the cable channel went on the air, its list of advertisers also included national companies like Pontiac, Hertz, *The Wall Street Journal*, Sony and Getty.

On July 13, 1979, ESP-TV became ESPN, and five days later, Evey signed Chester R. Simmons, former president of NBC Sports, to assume control of the new cable network. Almost immediately, Simmons began to enlist the help of many NBC colleagues. Once again, a struggling television entity pilfered the older network's treasure trove of talent, signing producers like Scotty Connal and announcers like Jim Simpson, who provided much-needed sports broadcasting experience both in front of and behind the cameras. In a *New York Times* article, Simmons added salt to the older network's wound, noting that while the three broadcast networks combined to provide more than 1,200 hours of sports programming, ESPN, "when it reached maximum programming, would have 8,700 hours … and the seven mobile units now under construction would make ESPN the best equipped network for covering sports."[33] To punctuate the cable network's brashness, Simmons could have mentioned that the center of the sports cable television landscape had moved from New York City to Bristol, Connecticut, a fact that was noted in a *Times* article soon after ESPN began broadcasting on September 7, 1979.[34]

When Lee Leonard said the very first words uttered from the ESPN studio, "If you love sports … if you REALLY love sports, you'll think you've died and gone to sports heaven…."[35] it is doubtful that many viewers residing in the 16 million households equipped to receive a cable signal took Leonard's words literally. In part, that was attributable to the sports programming ESPN provided during the first year—rugby, hurling from Ireland, Australian-rules football, karate, table tennis, as well as NCAA football, basketball, soccer, and hockey games—constituted events that the three networks had little interest in broadcasting. Although a Nielsen study of subscribers to 400 television systems that carried ESPN showed subscribers tended to be more upscale than network television viewers, both Simmons and Rasmussen described viewers of ESPN in separate *New York Times* articles as "sports junkies," a description Red Smith echoed in a column about cable television that was given the headline "Cable TV for Sports Junkies."[36] After describing a typical weekend of sports programming on ESPN, Smith created a brief exchange in which one man complained that ESPN posed a threat to the country's social fabric. In response, the other corrects him. "No, it is ESPN, the Entertainment and Sports Programming Network for sports junkies who have to have a fix everytime [sic] they touch the dial."[37]

In Smith's column and in other articles, Chet Simmons explained that ESPN did indeed attract the sports junkies, as well as insomniacs and workers coming off the night shift. Simmons explained the phenomenon by using the concept of narrow-casting:

> Cable subscribers have about 18 channels to choose from. There are 24 hours of news, 24 hours of religion, 24 hours of movies, etcetera. We offer 24 hours of sports, so we can repeat a lot of shows in different time slots for people who can't tune in the first time.[38]

By February 1980, television critics were describing cable as "an electronic magazine rack" with channels devoted to almost every interest, as well as programming for children, the elderly and minorities. People's willingness to pay for what they wanted to watch on television marked a significant cultural change that was as important as the technological revolution. This was evidenced by the fact that consumers were not so much interested in the technology as what programming it provided. In this way, Les Brown noted, "[C]able is not only breaking up the mass market of television but also is loosening the cultural glue that has bound the country for three decades with the three-network system of commercial television."[39]

Challenging Big Daddy

If the cultural glue was loosening, cable was also loosening viewers' purse strings, as well as those of major advertisers and, more importantly, sports organizations and professional leagues. *Television Digest* estimated that in 1979 cable revenues reached $1.87 billion, and predicted that at the current rate of growth, revenues would exceed $6 billion by the mid–1980s with a third of the revenues generated by pay-cable.[40] Because the broadcast networks were barred under FCC rules from owning cable systems, they were forced to track cable's growth from a distance, knowing that it was only a matter of time before cable impacted their control. In a *New York Times* article, Kevin O'Malley, the vice president of program planning for CBS, noted that cable, even though it was only available in 30 percent of the country, was already competing for showcase sporting events. He predicted that when cable was available in half of the country, the industry would become more competitive.

If, as the *New York Times* opined, television had become "America's Big Daddy of sports during the 1970s … building its own games and names … and tantalizing viewers with sophisticated space-age toys like mini-cameras and videotape machines,"[41] then the 1980s marked the beginning of the decentralization of television broadcasting dominated by the networks for three decades. ESPN made inroads into that domination with a two-pronged strategy. The first strategy was to secure live events that the networks did not telecast. For example, in March 1980 ESPN aired over 400 hours of NCAA men's college basketball or related programming, especially the early rounds of the tournament, which were completely ignored by the networks.[42] In April 1980, ESPN began a weekly boxing series to which a Saturday night series was added in the fall of 1982 to counter a college football game-of-the-week deal signed by Turner Broadcasting System (TBS). Beginning in July 1982, ESPN began airing its 16-game schedule of the Canadian Football League (CFL), which, the *Times* reported, drew no official comment from the NFL regarding what impact that might have if it proved successful.[43] Also that summer, ESPN and The Spanish International Network between them offered every game of the World Cup for home television, the first time in Cup's history the entire tournament was shown in America.[44]

The second prong of its strategy was to increase news programming with its first highlight show, *Sports Recap*, eventually dropped in favor of *SportsCenter*, with which ESPN began its weeknight broadcast schedule. The most significant hurdle faced by the show's producer was securing highlights. Seeking permission to use network highlights, Simmons approached his network contacts. NBC, tired of losing employees to the cable network, offered its highlights with the condition that Simmons stop hiring away NBC employees.[45] ABC also agreed to share its highlights, believing that the cable station posed no serious threat to its sports programming. When CBS balked at his numerous requests, Simmons decided to take highlights without permission. Despite complaints, Simmons continued using CBS highlights until the network relented, believing that contesting Simmons with legal action would be a waste of time.

In addition to securing network highlights to complement its own footage, ESPN borrowed from reliable sources like NFL Films, with which it signed an agreement in the fall of 1980 at a significantly lower rate than its owner, Steve Sabol, normally charged.[46] Sabol hosted the program himself during early morning hours; however, the program became such a viewer favorite that the show's producer requested use of Sabol's films during its Monday night football show, *NFL Prime Monday*, which preceded ABC's telecast. The strategy proved fruitful, and viewers migrated to the cable show from the network telecast. That would be but the first of many ESPN news programs related to the NFL, which came to include *NFL Gameday, NFL Matchup, NFL Live, Sunday NFL Countdown,* and *NFL Primetime*. In fact, the very first NFL gem ESPN secured was the rights to the NFL Draft, which it broadcast for the first time on April 29, 1980, after convincing the NFL to shift the date from a Tuesday to a Sunday. ESPN advertised the event, emphasizing that the draft was "*LIVE* ONLY ON ESPN."[47] Although few could have imagined that the show would attract much of an audience, over time it became one of the events ESPN became known for covering.

While the decision to secure the rights to the NFL Draft was consciously taken, coverage of other events was prompted by viewers. For example, in September 1983, viewers requested nonstop coverage of the seventh and deciding race of the America's Cup being contested by *Australia II* and *Liberty*. As Peter Alfano noted in his review of the overall poor coverage by both the networks and cable channels, ESPN had passed up the opportunity to acquire exclusive rights to the races, believing "that sailing was too specialized to appeal to a sport-oriented audience."[48] It was only when the Australian challengers tied the series at 3–3 after having fallen behind by deficits of 0–2 and then 1–3 that the network sports divisions decided that the event was newsworthy, which should have been obvious given the New York Yacht Club had successfully defended the America's Cup since 1851, a run of 132 years. Alfano decried the networks' coverage, relegating race results to morning news shows (i.e., *Today*, *Good Morning America*). While admitting that it was unrealistic to believe that the networks would devote five to six hours televising the races live, Alfano argued that "a nightly 15-minute or half-hour recap following the 11 p.m. news would have been nice. And more elaborate coverage on the weekend anthology shows [*Wide World of Sports*, *Sports Spectacular*] would not have been asking too much."[49] Although ABC's Jim McKay provided a brief segment during *Wide World of Sports*, he offered nothing more than setting and atmosphere since light winds had forced the race to be rescheduled until the following Monday.

Significantly, if only by default, ESPN provided the most complete coverage. Having planned to provide occasional updates beginning at noon, ESPN made the decision to offer live race coverage in its entirety. ESPN aired WJAR's feed, which included aerial views that Alfano described as breathtaking. He noted, "The America's Cup might not make for action-packed viewing, but it is one of the more esthetically pleasing sports events. And because this was the deciding race, all the elements of excitement, drama and urgency were present. If nothing else, it was different and more interesting than two-minute drills."[50] In responding to the demands of its viewers, ESPN learned an important lesson about broadcasting special events. The next time ESPN had the opportunity to secure the exclusive rights to the America's Cup in 1987, it would not need prompting from viewers. In fact, it showed Big Daddy how to produce an esoteric event like the America's Cup into a full-fledged sport media spectacle.

End of a Classic Cartel

Even though long-range optimism for cable's prospects remained high—buoyed by promising numbers that showed the industry in the final months of 1982 was adding 1,000 jobs, 250,000 subscribers and one satellite service monthly—warning signs that all was not well with sports programming were becoming clearly visible.[51] The most telling development occurred in September 1982 when U.S. District Judge Juan Burciaga struck down the NCAA's college football television contracts with CBS and ABC after two college football powers, the University of Georgia and the Oklahoma University, brought an antitrust suit in 1981, contending that the NCAA, acting like a classic cartel, "has unreasonably restrained trade in the televising of college football games."[52] Judge Burciaga's decision was upheld by the United States Court of Appeals for the 10th Circuit in May 1983. The NCAA and the networks were able to operate under the terms of the old contract for the 1983 college football season only after U.S. Supreme Court Justice Byron R. White, a former University of Colorado football standout, issued in July a stay of the appeals court's decision so that the U.S. Supreme Court could consider the case.

The following year, in a 7–2 decision, the U.S. Supreme Court upheld the rulings of Judge Burciaga and the Court of Appeals that the NCAA's power to negotiate television contracts and to set limitations on the number of appearances a school's team could make constituted an unreasonable restraint of trade that violated Section I of the Sherman Antitrust Act. Associate Justice John Paul Stevens wrote the majority opinion, in which he agreed with the District Court's findings that "competition in the relevant market had been restrained in three ways."[53] In addition to fixing the price for particular telecasts, the NCAA's exclusive network contracts "were tantamount to a group boycott of all other potential broadcasters ... and placed an artificial limit on the production of televised college football."[54] These anticompetitive practices resulted in individual competitors losing their ability to compete in the marketplace. Justice Stevens argued, "Price is higher and output lower than they would otherwise be, and both are unresponsive to consumer preference. The latter point is perhaps the most significant."[55]

The Court rejected the NCAA's arguments that it had no market power, "no ability to alter the interaction of supply and demand in the market."[56] It also rejected the argument the NCAA had used since 1950 that its television plan was necessary to protect live attendance, holding that argument "is not based on a desire to maintain the integrity of college football as a distinct and attractive produce, but rather on a fear that the product will not prove sufficiently attractive to draw live attendance when faced with competition from televised games."[57] In effect, the NCAA's television plan protected ticket sales by limiting output, "just as any monopolist increases revenues by reducing output."[58] While noting that the NCAA needed ample latitude "in the maintenance of a revered tradition of amateurism in college sports," Justice Stephens concluded that "rules that restrict output are hardly consistent with this role."[59]

Issued on the day Division I schools were meeting in Chicago to consider intercollegiate legislation, the ruling sent the members in search of a direction to follow for the coming football season, scheduled to begin within two months. Until the NCAA received clearance as to what role it could play from the federal court in Oklahoma City where the antitrust suit had originated, schools were reportedly "eager to avert a circumstance in which each would negotiate separately with over-the-air and cable networks."[60] Coincidentally, at the very same meeting, representatives from the 105 schools in Division I-A rejected a proposal for a post-season championship game, despite the fact that it was the only sport in the NCAA that did not have a national championship game, until various playoff formats evolved into the Bowl Championship Series, based, in part, on a ranking system that had the veneer of objectivity in order to protect the vested interests of the bowl promoters.[61]

The ruling's impact on the networks was mixed. On the one hand, as Peter Kaplan reported in the *New York Times*, the Supreme Court's affirmation of Judge Burciaga's decision to strip the NCAA of its power to negotiate contracts for college football telecasts "will most likely save the big networks money and give them better games to broadcast."[62] Removing the limitation on the number of games that could be televised greatly expanded the number of games available, driving down the price for rights fees. For example, shortly before the 1984 season began, the *Times* reported that CBS was paying $10 million for 14 games involving the Big Ten and Pac-10 conferences over ten Saturdays. ABC offered $12 million for a package of 20 College Football Association (CFA) games over 13 Saturdays while ESPN paid $9.2 million to televise 15 CFA games, primarily on Saturday nights.[63] That meant the price for nationally televised games ranged between $525,000 and $575,000 while the maximum price for a regional telecast was $400,000.[64] The lower price was directly attributable to the coverage by "two major networks, two national cable networks [TBS and ESPN], five syndicators, countless local cable or pay-per-view systems and even the Public Broadcasting Service."[65] With almost 200 games being broadcast in 1984, a number that more than doubled the previous year's total of 89, coverage of college football was certainly lurching toward saturation, and invariably producing lower television ratings, especially for the broadcast networks.

Packaged Reality

Not only did the emergence of sports on cable television engender a plethora of social, legal and economic changes, but the cable networks also altered the texture, perceptions and images of sports for both stadium fans and television viewers. Decreased advertising revenues and slumping ratings precipitated by a saturated market did not forestall the advance of ever-increasing "refinements in editing, replays from a variety of camera positions, slick graphics and lighter, more mobile cameras."[66] In late 1982, Neil Amdur of the *New York Times*, cited Dr. Jennings Bryant of the University of Evansville in Indiana, who described what the viewer actually sees on television as "packaged reality." Bryant defined package reality as "not the reality of the stadium or arena. It's what the producer and director, by their shot selection and pictures and the addition of commentary, create."[67] Not only did television's technical innovations result in changes at arenas and stadiums with the addition of scoreboards equipped to show slow-motion instant replays, but television also fostered other changes including "more attractive, tighter-fitting uniforms, the liberalizing of rules in many sports and the focusing on Olga Korbut and Nadia Comaneci in Olympic gymnastics, a relatively obscure sport, as further examples of television's ability to rearrange reality."[68]

That television had become totally enamored with technology was evidenced in such innovations as use of blimps for overhead shots, installation of cameras in stock cars, and the use of wireless microphones on football and basketball coaches, runners and outriders at thoroughbred race tracks. Further, in the 1984 Super Bowl, CBS provided over 100 replays in little more than one quarter of play.[69] The following year, the USFL introduced the use of a television instant-replay system to review on-field decisions by officials during a pre-season game. While instant replay was being used "to eliminate the second-guessing that surrounds crucial calls in many games,"[70] it was also being used to entertain viewers. In his column, Amdur cited Dr. John Ledingham, an associate professor at the University of Houston, who said, "For many people, watching Dr. J [Julius Erving of the Philadelphia 76ers] flying through the air for a dunk is not as exciting as watching the rerun of the dunk. And the athletes have caught on to the theory that they're show-business people."[71]

Packaged reality also depended on an increase in dramatic rather than descriptive commentary. Bryant's seminal study of the impact commentary can have on viewers' perception of a sporting event was cited in Amdur's column. In Bryant's study, 100 college students listened to dubbed commentary of a routine tennis match between two veteran players. One third of the group listened to commentary in which the players were reported to be good friends; one third heard commentary describing the players as bitter enemies, and the last group heard commentary in which the relationship was not specified. The study's results suggested that "viewers who perceived the competitors as hostile found the telecast more interesting, exciting and enjoyable."[72] Integrating more drama into a telecast, then, was shown to elicit more involvement from viewers. This resulted in a trend toward more commentary emphasizing player-versus-player conflict. Amdur's column included one of Dr. Bryant's conclusions about the difference between the stadium experience and the television experience that remained for many years unchallenged: "Viewers expectations of sporting events have changed because of television. Because TV has to rely on dramatic elements that often have to do with high risk, giving all and violence, the event on television is different from what is unfolding on the field."[73]

Other technological innovations included the use of a computer software program to count punches thrown and those landed by boxing contestants. HBO Fight-stat, a program developed by Sports Information Data Base of Hasbrouck Heights, New Jersey, was first used in February 1985 during the televised rematch between

Livingstone Bramble and Ray Mancini. The software program required that two counters, one for each fighter, feed the statistics into a computer that was available to HBO's boxing analysts, one of whom, Larry Merchant, told the *New York Times'* Michael Katz that he was looking forward to using it. "You can't break down a fight punch by punch any more than you can an opera note by note or a painting stroke by stroke. But I'll be looking forward to having some fun using it in a discreet-enough way so that it supplements what our eyes tell us."[74] The pay-channel had a distinct advantage for using the Fightstat information in not breaking for commercial spots between rounds. HBO's producer for the fight, Ross Greenburg, explained that he would not use the computer's data during rounds, noting, "Those three minutes are intense enough. And in the wrong hands, it can be the stupidest statistics in the world."[75]

When the cable and broadcast networks attempted to enhance their live boxing coverage by keeping viewers apprised of the judges' official scoring for a fight in progress, the innovation was "doomed by ostrich-like commissions that were worried about the effect on 'gaming'—whatever that means—and partly as protection for the judges from second-guessers on television."[76] Katz's sarcasm is well-employed here in that the term "gaming" was doubtlessly used as a euphemism for gambling, although it is unclear why knowing exactly how each judge had scored a round could have an effect on "gaming" interests while a fight was in progress. Each judge's round-by-round scoring was made available to the press following a fight, and second-guessing by reporters, both in print and broadcasting, had always been a part of boxing coverage. Katz quoted Bob Lee, the acting commissioner of New Jersey's State Athletic Commission, as saying, "Not knowing who's winning, that's part of the suspense."[77] Katz decried such reasoning, explaining that the only problem with open scoring occurred "when the arena crowd can immediately second-guess the judges. But when only the television audience is involved, there is no reason [not to use it]."[78] In not providing television announcers the judges' scores immediately after a round, the state boxing commissions' desire to protect judges only obfuscated what should have been a transparent process.

Junk Journalism

Even though Katz lamented the failure of state boxing commissions to embrace open scoring, he took exception over what he considered a cheap shot directed at boxing by ESPN *SportsCenter* anchor Tom Mees. In reporting on a nationally televised fight between Meldrick Taylor and a fighter named Roberto Medina, who was, in actuality, John E. Garcia, an escaped convict from a Colorado state penitentiary, Mees said, among other things, "only in boxing."[79] Noting that boxing was an easy target for "the Tom Meeses of broadcasting," Katz sarcastically decried the cryptic remark as "the kind of in-depth commentary one expects from television sports news.... There are a lot of escaped convicts; for all we know, some may be working on television."[80] What fueled Katz's ire was the lack of serious television reporting on boxing, such as that provided for a time by Howard Cosell, who, although he had enhanced his journalistic stature covering boxing, became an outspoken critic of the sport and covered his last fight in December 1982. Cosell provided quality investigative reporting on the award-winning program *Sports Beat*, regrettably canceled by ABC in 1985 after Cosell published his autobiography, *I Never Played the Game*, in which he criticized colleagues at ABC Sports.

In the same column, Katz criticized CBS's omnibus program, *Sports Sunday*, for its coverage of the Tour de France by implying at the top of the taped show that the final leg Sunday down the *Champs-Élysées* would decide the overall winner. "What nonsense. CBS knew very well, as it explained graphically later, that Bernard Hinault of France was going to win his fifth Tour and that Greg LeMond, his American teammate who finished second, was not allowed to even try to beat Hinault. In boxing, they call this a fix."[81] Claiming that boxing was a lot cleaner than bicycle racing, Katz parenthetically remarked that drug use was rampant and that one should never "bet against the chalk in the Tour de France."[82] He saved his most stinging criticism for reporter John Tesh, who "deserves a purple jersey for his prose," when Tesh compared the leader's yellow jersey in mythological terms: "The golden fleece was up for grabs where Pyrenees and mist had fashioned this bizarre battleground."[83]

Katz was not the only *New York Times* columnist who offered criticism of television sports reporters. In a piece titled "Highlights Aren't Enough," Michael Goodwin used the occasion of two New York stations' search for sports anchors as a vehicle to comment on the sorry state of local television sports news. Goodwin began the piece with his own classified ad that delineated the requisite qualifications: "Good teeth and nice hair essential.... Must believe in the divine right of athletes."[84] While admitting that there were indeed good television journalists in New York, Goodwin added that none covered sports, and he doubted the new hires would "provide any major relief to the bland menu of scores, taped highlights and tame interviews that dominate local sports news."[85] In addition to his criticism of sports journalists' reverential attitude toward the athletes they cover, Goodwin allowed the outgoing reporters to point out the failure of the sports report to provide anything more than a headline approach that prevented serious investigative journalism. The lack of pressure to do investigative journalism stemmed from the absence of competition between stations, all being equally comfortable with what was done and not done to entertain viewers, many of whom cared little about sports. Goodwin concluded by debunking the idea that if the sports reporter were given more time, more serious journalism would be presented. "If more sports time would only be wasted on more headlines, let's hope extra time at channel 9 goes to the weatherman. Better yet, why not give him the sports job?"[86]

Goodwin's criticisms were not limited to the sports reporting on local television stations. In "The Perils of Slapdash Journalism," Goodwin attacked the networks' pre-game shows before coverage of the NFL. Despite aspiring to be more than fun by providing a news segment, these pre-game shows (i.e., CBS's *NFL Today* and NBC's *NFL '86*) were better at self-promotion than journalism. As evidence, Goodwin cited examples in which NBC announced the teams playing in that year's Fiesta Bowl and CBS announced it had retained the rights to the men's college basketball championship. "Neither network included an important aspect of such 'news'—the price the network paid for these events. And neither generally finds such items newsworthy at all if it means mentioning a rival network."[87] Goodwin offered a more blatant example of slapdash journalism in which NBC's Bob Costas reported that "informed sources" had intimated that Miami University football coach Jimmy Johnson might be headed for the University of Texas. Even though Costas denied asserting that Johnson was going to Texas, his cleverly worded statement that "speculation may have him headed for the vacancy" constituted, for Goodwin, little more than a sleight-of-hand, "intended to give that impression while not exactly saying so.... Knowing that, and seeing how they constructed their report, it is hard to believe NBC didn't want viewers to think they meant to say Johnson was going to Texas. Call it junk journalism."[88]

ABC's coverage of the 1988 Calgary Games also drew criticisms, although not for spreading rumors. Rather, the criticisms were directed at ABC's team of analysts covering the Olympic Winter Games in Calgary, many of whom were former athletes. These athletes-turned-announcers were most comfortable providing detailed analysis of a performance, especially during highlights; however, as Gerald Eskenazi noted, "when it came to fleshing out an interview, it was a different story."[89] For Eskenazi, the general coziness between athletes-turned-analysts and competing athletes was symbolized "by Peggy Fleming's impulsively hugging Debi Thomas in an interview after Thomas's missteps cost her the figure-skating gold medal."[90] Eskenazi also noted that ABC had been beaten to the punch by newspaper reporters in covering controversies surrounding the bobsled and speed-skating teams. In fairness, Eskenazi posed the question as to what a televised Olympics was supposed to be—showcase for tough journalism or television event—and then provided the answer with which most television critics would agree. "The lines have always been blurred and always will be."[91] As a sports journalist working for a print medium, Eskenazi readily criticized television's failure to offer hard-hitting reports while pointing out how newspaper reporters covered controversies more effectively; however, in overlooking newspaper reporters' often cozy relationship with athletes, Eskenazi demonstrated a bias for the work of print journalists.

That the lines had become permanently blurred was evidenced not only in weak interviews by analysts who, for the most part, had little or no journalistic training, but also in questionable journalistic practices that at times turned a blind eye to issues of violence and sexism in order to achieve sufficient ratings within a highly competitive, saturated marketplace. With the increased access provided by cable and satellite dish technology, viewers watched more sports on the airwaves. Even though broadcasters did not completely ignore violence that went above and beyond what is allowed in the rules, the message being provided by sports reporters was often overwhelmed by the pictures on the screen. Richard Horrow, a Florida-based attorney who wrote a book about law and sports violence, said, "I really think that exposure with a disclaimer is as significant as exposure with nothing said. As for kids, the trickle-down effect is that they're learning about elbowing, sliding with spikes high and jabbing with hockey sticks."[92]

Local sports broadcasters inadvertently contributed to increased exposure of violence by showing more highlights gleaned from games all over the country. This concentration on violence in sportscast highlights led to charges and counter charges by league and media executives. Warner Wolf of WCBS in New York said, "It's not that I condone it. It's a journalistic issue. If I don't show them, I'd be censoring the news. I'll stop when they stop fighting."[93] Wolf's assertion illustrates the tendency of broadcasters to sidestep the issue of whether or not a fight or a violent hit actually merits consideration as a sportscast highlight. More germane to the issue was Horrow's argument that whether or not fighting and other violence actually increased was not as important as the perception that it had, fueled by media's concentration on violent plays as highlights.

Offensive Interference

More disturbing than the conflicting signals television broadcasters sent out about violence were those issues related to women's role as sports journalists and control of the sports broadcasting discourse by corporations. Not only were women's sports largely underreported, but when women's sports were covered, they were often covered without women in the broadcasting booth. NBC's coverage of the 1983 French Open women's final included Dick Enberg and Bud Collins in the booth with Donald Dell and Bjorn Borg at courtside. In his review Neil Amdur noted that Borg was too reticent and Dell did not belong because of a conflict of interest stemming from his role as a lawyer who represented players and tournaments. Amdur added:

> More conspicuous during the final two days, however, was the absence of a woman announcer during the taped telecast of the women's singles final on Saturday between Chris Evert Lloyd and Mima Jausovec. Any number of current or former players … could have contributed more about the players and the women's tour than Dell or Borg.[94]

Women sports journalists' struggle to gain equal access to broadcast booths, press boxes, locker rooms and production facilities made headlines in the 1970s. On January 21, 1975, the NHL became the first professional sports league in America to allow women sports journalists to enter the players' dressing room for interviews after its All-Star game.[95] Shortly thereafter, the NBA instituted a rule opening the locker room to all reporters until 45 minutes before the start of a game and after the first ten minutes following a game. Despite that progress, in late 1977 Melissa

Ludtke, a reporter for *Sports Illustrated*, brought suit against the commissioner of Major League Baseball, the New York Yankees, the mayor of New York and other city officials for barring her from Yankee Stadium's locker rooms during baseball's playoffs and World Series. Ludtke and TIME Inc., the parent company of *Sports Illustrated*, sought "an injunction enjoining defendants from denying Miss Ludtke and other accredited representatives of *TIME* access to professional baseball clubhouses on the basis of their sex."[96]

MLB Commissioner Bowie Kuhn's prepared response stated that he would allow "female sportswriters" into locker rooms if they "could satisfy us that we have violated any law" with current policy. Kuhn considered the policy of "providing female reporters with interview facilities adjacent to the teams' dressing quarters completely appropriate and consistent with the views and interests of the press in general, the players and our fans."[97] By invoking the interests of the media, players and fans, Kuhn subtly shifted the issue from one of access to "standards of decency." The implication was that allowing women access to locker rooms where ballplayers wander "naked and semi-naked" near their lockers "would be offensive" to those standards.[98] Ludtke decried the way MLB successfully made "equal access appear as a moral and not a political problem and as a sexy, but not a sexist issue that it is."[99]

Baseball was not alone in questioning women's pursuit of equal access. In January 1978, ABC *Sports Magazine* aired a segment exploring the issue, and two *New York Times* columnists, Roger Kahn and Red Smith, employed variations on the modesty rationale in addressing the issue. Kahn compared the restrictions imposed on Ludtke with those imposed on him: "Covering the Yankees, she cannot catch Thurman Munson in the shower. I remain slightly restricted. Covering Wimbledon, I cannot catch Chris Evert in the tub."[100] Noting that the women's basketball team from Immaculate had not invited a *New York Times* reporter into their changing room, Smith framed the issue dichotomously—press freedom vs. indecent exposure, right to know vs. right to privacy, and "the equal rights movement vs. the manly modesty of Catfish Hunter."[101] Absent from Kahn's column was any mention about the importance of allowing women the access needed to function on a level playing field with their male colleagues.

On September 27, 1978, Judge Constance Baker Motley ruled that all reporters, regardless of sex, should have equal access to athletes, even if such access included the locker room. What followed was, in Ludtke Lincoln's own words, "a three-ring news circus" that bombarded the public with reports of the plight of women in the Yankee locker room. In a column she wrote for the *New York Times* shortly after the beginning of the 1979 season, Ludtke Lincoln lamented that "not one reporter chose to address the issue of why women need access to the athletes to do their job. Instead, some newspapers and television stations assigned women to report on how their presence affected the ballplayers."[102] Later in her piece, Ludtke Lincoln explained the dilemma facing women sports journalists. She and other women journalists were being portrayed "as women who wanted nothing more than to wander aimlessly around a locker room, to stare endlessly at naked athletes and to invade the privacy of individuals whose privacy had been disrupted for years by our male colleagues."[103]

Unfortunately, the accusation that women sports journalists used their access to male locker rooms to engage in voyeurism again surfaced in September 1990 when *Boston Herald* reporter Lisa Olson was accosted by several naked members of the New England Patriots as she conducted a practice-day interview in their locker room. According to the NFL's official investigation, which produced a 108-page report, Zeke Mowatt, standing naked at an arm's length from Olson, made an accusation: "You are not writing; you are looking." Mowatt and four other teammates then began fondling themselves, asking Olson, "Is this what you want?"[104] After the story broke, Olson received obscene phone calls and hate mail, and her car and apartment were vandalized. As a result of the investigation, Mowatt and two teammates were fined by the NFL. Victor Kiam, Patriots owner, publicly called her "a classic bitch," and at a Stamford Old-Timers Athletic Association dinner, he told a joke that asked: "What do the Iraqis have in common with Lisa Olson? They've both seen Patriot missiles up close."[105] Kiam was fined $50,000 by the NFL on November 27 and publicly apologized to Olson for his comments. Olson filed a sexual harassment suit against the Patriots, Kiam and several members of the team in April 1991 and eventually settled out of court. Although the NFL strengthened its policies regarding equal access to the locker room, Commissioner Paul Tagliabue showed a lack of resolve when it came to collecting the players' fines. Speaking to the Association for Women in Sports Media, Tagliabue said that he might not be able to collect the fines, citing the threat of a lawsuit from the players' union, even though the league regularly instituted policies involving players without the union's blessing.[106] Significantly, by calling her a "looker," the players attempted to curtail Olson's publicly recognized role to criticize male performance as part of a profession that gave her access into the locker room.[107]

The New Economy

By the time the NFL signed a new $1.428 billion television contract in March 1987, cable's impact on the television sports broadcasting was undeniable. For the first time, a cable network, ESPN, was included in the package, paying $153 million for three years' rights to eight Sunday night games, four preseason games and the Pro Bowl game, which ended the NFL season. The new contract marked the first time rights fees for NFL games actually decreased—by 3.3 percent—and the amount paid remained flat at $476 million for each of the three years.[108] Many factors contributed to the decrease, including lower ratings and network losses (i.e., production and increased rights fees) for NFL telecasts over the previous two seasons with losses in 1986 alone reaching a combined $75 million. Additionally, escalating player salaries, which had doubled over the course of the last television contract as a result of competition from the USFL, meant that television revenues, which had risen only 50 percent, were not keeping pace with other expenditures.[109]

One of the first indications that the market for professional football was softening occurred in the fall of 1983, the same year in which the USFL played a spring schedule, when ABC's *Monday Night Football* finished its 14th year on the air with the lowest ratings in its history.[110] The 18.1 rating and 31 share marked a decrease of 2.5 rating points from the previous year, the lowest since its first season in 1970. The other networks' telecasts on Sunday afternoons also slipped in 1983, although by a smaller percentage. While different reasons were offered for the decreased ratings, including an unappealing schedule of games assembled for Monday night, some industry executives said they believed that "the glory days of professional football in prime time may have passed."[111]

One direct result of the decreased ratings was an accompanying drop in the cost of advertising. This drop in cost was directly attributable to the saturation of sports programming on television, which overwhelmed viewer interest and fractured the audience. These conditions created a situation in which broadcasters were unable to sell commercial time on many sports programs at full or nearly full price. For example, in 1985, selling was so difficult that "50 percent price reductions were not uncommon, even for major [sporting] events."[112] Instead of leaving slots unsold, the networks were selling them for prices that were below 1984 prices, and in some cases, below those of 1983. What had once been an industry that earned profit margins that regularly reached 10 to 15 percent suddenly found itself losing considerable amounts of money. Goodwin reported that in 1985, ABC Sports lost upward of $40 million, with both of its major attractions, baseball and football, believed to have suffered considerable losses.

With so much more sports programming being televised, traditional sports advertisers became more strategic in evaluating alternative advertising vehicles. While automobile makers and beer companies continued to advertise on sports programs, they also decided "to no longer focus their marketing efforts exclusively on the male audience that an athletic event provides."[113] For example, Chevrolet reduced its emphasis on sports by 25 percent when studies showed that women bought 35 percent of all cars, an increase of 10 percent from the mid–1970s. Not only did Chevrolet move its ad money to prime-time shows, but what money it allocated to commercial time on sports programs was largely diversified. Rather than placing a package with one network, Chevrolet bought commercial time on college football broadcasts with CBS and ABC and purchased halftime coverage of ESPN's Saturday night broadcast, as well as sponsoring its own post-game show on the cable network.[114] Even though beer companies did not spend less, they also diversified, reducing the concentration on network sports programming and focusing more on cable options. Over the next two decades, however, sports sponsorship, the process of allocating resources for the production of sports events to achieve organizational objectives,[115] increased dramatically. The total amount of money spent on global sports sponsorship trebled in the 1990s alone, with 37.8 per cent of that being allocated for events in North America, 36.4 percent for Europe, and 20.8 per cent for Asia. Sport sponsorship and advertising rose from $500,000 in 1970 to $20 billion in 2000.[116]

The networks accepted the loss in advertising revenues because they were paying less for rights fees. The reduced payments the networks paid for rights to the NFL in 1987 was an extension of what had begun in 1984 after the NCAA lost its antitrust case. Further evidence was provided by the bidding for the 1988 Seoul Olympic Games. Because ABC had generated $450 million in revenues after paying $225 million for the rights to the 1984 Los Angeles Olympic Games, many industry experts believed the rights would surpass $500 million and perhaps reach $1 billion.[117] All three networks bid considerably less than that, with NBC ultimately paying $300 million. Organizers of smaller events saw their payments decrease from the networks by as much as 70 percent.[118]

Cable networks like ESPN actually thrived in the new sports economy. Despite losses that exceeded $100 million in its first six years, ESPN showed a $10 million profit in the final quarter of 1984, and earned more than $35 million the following year.[119] Several factors contributed to the upturn, including the decision to charge cable stations ten cents per subscriber rather than to depend solely on advertising revenues. Before ESPN landed its part of the NFL contract in 1987, the price was 26 cents per subscriber. After the contract, ESPN promptly increased the price to 36 cents per subscriber.[120] Those increases were accepted by the cable systems largely as a result of the 1984 Cable Communications Policy Act, which provided for full deregulation of fees,[121] meaning cable operators could charge whatever they wanted for a basic package of channels, which invariably included ESPN. Profits continued to soar, in part because non-union labor reduced ESPN's operating and production costs in comparison to network expenditures. Finally, in January 1989 ESPN was available in more than 50 million homes, becoming the first cable station to surpass 50 percent penetration of households in the United States.[122] By the time the Walt Disney Company bought ABC and ESPN in the summer of 1995 for $19.08 billion, ESPN was deemed by Michael Eisner, chairman of Disney's board, as "the crown jewel" of the purchase.[123]

Conclusion

Cable television proved to be a Pandora's Box for television sports. On the one hand, it decentralized sports programming, gradually forcing the networks to give up precious pieces of the sports pie to cable networks like ESPN and TBS. On the other hand, cable networks saturated television with live coverage and news programming that made up with quantity what was lacking in quality. Because the cable networks could not afford to compete with the networks for major sporting events, they showed sports that previously had not been seen on television. Cable networks helped to popularize sports like gymnastics, figure skating and ice hockey while the networks played it safe with traditional sports like football, basketball and baseball. The metaphor of the electronic magazine rack was an appropriate one for cable television in its first two decades.

Television critics and communication scholars contended technological innovations continued to transform sports viewing into a mediated spectacle. Underpinning such assertions were the mass-mediated sport entertainment spectacles that represent the primary motor of sport's cultural economy, and a significant element of the broader cultural economy. That sports have become commercialized and transformed into a spectacle is one of the characteristic features of contemporary society, one that took shape with cable television's saturation of sports programming. Arguably, a cable network became the prototypical purveyor of mass-mediated sport entertainment spectacle, namely ESPN.

Bryant's assertion that what happens on the field and what happens on television are different gradually has, to a great extent, lost some of its significance. While fundamental differences between the stadium experience and the television experience still exist, what unfolds on the field and in the stadiums and arenas has been directly impacted by television. Examples include television timeouts, rules changes to enhance action, and instant replay to challenge on-field officiating decisions. Moreover, the addition of scoreboards with replay capabilities and enhanced audio technologies has significantly narrowed the differences between stadium and television experiences. In fact, players and stadium fans routinely watch scoreboard replays, and their reactions are often picked up by the telecast.

The proliferation of sports programming has done little to improve the quality of broadcast sports journalism. Many of the analysts are former athletes, and many have struggled with the mechanics and techniques of fundamental journalistic practices like researching and interviewing. At this time, many sports announcers received little formal training or support from their organizations. Without appropriate journalistic training, these broadcasters struggle to identify, develop, and contextualize a story, or anticipate an audience's state of knowledge and understanding about sports issues.[124]

That women sports journalists struggled to gain equal access into the press boxes, broadcast booths, locker rooms, and production facilities provides compelling evidence that "professional athletics participates in the construction of gender as an asymmetrical relation between two mutually exclusive but complementary categories and establishes that social construction as a fact of nature."[125] Despite significant progress made by women sports journalists, producers and announcers, we have not yet, as a society, reached a point where we totally devote our attention to their accounts of sporting events and not to who happens to be reporting the story, but it is a goal worth pursuing. The presence of women sports journalists in the broadcasts booths, press boxes and production facilities of national media is important because these journalists serve as models for local stations and shape perceptions about women athletes within the larger culture.[126]

As cable television has emerged, the many references to television's sports junkies that continuously need a fix from an unending stream of sports programming raises disturbing questions about the relationship between programmer/pusher and viewer/junkie. That a woman named ESPN as a codefendant in a divorce case during the summer of 1982, charging "that the network was instrumental in ruining her marriage by providing too much sports coverage,"[127] is perhaps indicative of a deeper, more pervasive distortion of values. As Richard Sandomir explains, "ESPN exists in a self-created wonderland, one that took root innocuously, then grew into a force so potent that it treats itself as a producer of events and studio shows as well as a newsmaker on par with the leagues it buys games from."[128] The wonderland of highlights reflects tendencies of postmodernist thought in which the world becomes highly fragmented and meaning becomes elusive and slippery. Ultimately, however many highlights are shown during live coverage or on *SportsCenter*, the sports junkie is never satisfied, instead being fixated on a perpetual present of constantly changing texts—game recaps subsumed within pastiches of spectacular plays removed from game context followed by random images not tethered to any overarching narrative. By utilizing a discourse of addiction to rationalize its form of junk journalism, broadcasters demean viewers and trivialize the product they purport to celebrate.

Chapter 7

The Little Shop of Highlights

ESPN's role in the proliferation and deployment of sportscast highlights should not be underestimated. Since its initial broadcast on September 7, 1979, ESPN has grown "from a curiosity to the level of Kleenex, Coke or Band-Aids—brand names signifying products...."[1] Before ESPN, television viewers relied on the three broadcast networks and their affiliates to receive sports broadcasts. Except for major events like the Olympics, sports were televised primarily on weekends. The television sportscast landscape changed dramatically as ESPN's nightly newscast grew from 15 minutes to 60 minutes.[2] Occupying a ubiquitous place in our culture in reaching 82 percent of the 108 million homes in the United States, ESPN estimates that an average of 94 million Americans spend 50 minutes per day or almost six hours per week engaged with ESPN media.[3]

In addition to coverage of live sporting events, however, ESPN drastically altered the landscape of television sports news with the program that launched the cable network, *SportsCenter*, which the *Times'* Richard Sandomir described as the heart of ESPN, "a news show with a hummable theme song, enormous breadth and creativity, stars like [Dan] Patrick and [Bob] Ley (backed by lesser-knowns plucked from stations nationwide or raised on a highlight-rich regimen on the ESPNEWS ranch), and others who believe a sports report cannot be justified without attempting a joke or snide allusion every 30 seconds."[4] Sandomir's description aptly captures some of the elements that have made *SportsCenter* the premiere (and only) nationally televised daily newscast.

The "hummable" theme song was composed by Annie Roboff for the Satellite News Channel, which quickly went out of business and sold the theme to ESPN. In an interview, Roboff explained, "I love that so many guys know that theme.... I never saw a penny from the everyday play, because it had been sold to the Satellite News Service as a buyout (it was the very early days of cable when no 'rules' had been established)."[5] The theme became so well known to viewers and athletes that the final two bars—da-da-da da-da-da—have become synonymous with highlights, so that having made a great play and knowing the play will make that night's *SportsCenter*, players hum the final two bars in a process of unabashed co-promotion.

SportsCenter's breadth and creativity are both a blessing and a curse. Having broadcast its 30,000th program on February 11, 2007, passing the *CBS Evening News* for most broadcasts, *SportsCenter* has provided a breadth of coverage that no three-to five-minute local sportscast could ever duplicate. Not only did it spawn the network fictional series *Sports Night*, but it also engendered clones on other networks, including most notably CNN/SI's *Sports Tonight* (1980–2001). *SportsCenter* also gave birth to 11 nation-specific namesakes that belong to its ESPN International division, including *SportsCenter Asia*, *SportsCenter Brasil*, and *SportsCentre*, the Canadian version of the program.[6] Each of these originates in the country it serves except for the one that is available on pay television in Australia and other Pacific Rim countries. That particular *SportsCenter* was produced and anchored by Australian journalists and personalities at ESPN headquarters in Bristol, Connecticut, to make use of the "state-of-the-art digital production facilities and a ready-made staff of editors, technicians and other experts."[7] In addition to the nation-specific *SportsCenter*, the program served as the template for spin-offs like *SportsNight*, which debuted on ESPN2 in 1993; *X Center*, a news program specifically created to accompany X Games broadcasts; *SportsCenterU*, which provides news and highlights from men's and women's intercollegiate athletics; and *BassCenter*, which aired on Saturday mornings from 2003 to 2006 within ESPN2's "Outdoors" lineup.

SportsCenter's most defining characteristic has been its personality, brought to life by its anchors. The long line of anchors—George Grande, Chris Berman, Tom Mees, Dan Patrick, Keith Olbermann, Kenny Mayne, Linda Cohn and Stuart Scott—changed the dynamics of how sports news was delivered. Rather than focusing on scores and statistics, *SportsCenter* changed the discourse to one emphasizing popular culture. The banter-filled exchanges between anchors reshaped *SportsCenter* from a three-minute segment focusing on local sports to one in which sports were no longer positioned in relation to other news. Rather, the program was completely devoted to every aspect of sports in a style that emphasized personality and drama thanks to highly developed production values. That repertoire included specific catchphrases that each anchor used over and over again. By repeating their own trademark phrases, *SportsCenter* anchors not only patented and claimed their expressions, but they also distanced themselves from these articulations, offering them to a growing allegiance of fans who perpetuated them in the public sphere, enhancing the anchors' reputations.[8] So prevalent has the *SportsCenter* discourse become that many fan Web sites are devoted to the program. One, the "*SportsCenter* Altar," was created with the expressed goal "to catalog and index all the popular catch phrases uttered by the sports anchors and trace them back to their origins."[9]

Although the hip catchphrases, banter, and self-referential exchanges that characterize the anchors' performance have certainly contributed to setting *SportsCenter* apart from all other sportscasts, the use of highlights serves as arguably the program's single most important element. It was not until ESPN secured access to the broadcast networks' highlights that *SportsCenter* became a viable entity. In fact, the very first *SportsCenter* included no highlights since the first half-hour show of highlights was called *Sports Recap* and aired at 11:30 p.m. By the time ESPN began broadcasting 24 hours a day in 1980, *SportsCenter* had become the most important vehicle of the cable network's sports news programming, thanks in large part to having begged (ABC), bartered (NBC) and stolen (CBS) from the networks to secure access to their highlights. As Chris Berman explained in the introduction to the *Ultimate Highlight Reel*, "The presentation of highlights has been the backbone of ESPN from our very start in 1979."[10]

Significantly, with the publication of *ESPN Ultimate Highlight Reel* in November 2006 through ESPN Books, ESPN has positioned itself as the foremost deliverer of sportscast highlights. This cross-media morphing of a highlight reel into a book purports to present "The 365 Wildest, Weirdest, Most Unforgettable *SportsCenter* Moments of All Time" by selecting each calendar day's most spectacular highlight over the first 25 years of *SportsCenter*. The book also marked ESPN's second publishing venture devoted to its presentation of highlights, following the 2004 publication of *ESPN25: 25 Mind-Bending, Eye-Popping, Culture-Morphing Years of Highlights* by Charles Hirshberg. In his book, Hirshberg asserts that ESPN impacted the television sports landscape "by adopting, and perfecting, an underutilized, unappreciated method of communication: the sports highlight…. ESPN has made highlights the primary means by which the patterns and stories of sports are revealed. It's a perfect medium for modern America…."[11] While these books are clearly promotional vehicles for *SportsCenter*, they also establish the program's use of highlights as the primary news frame for its brand of sports journalism. These books capitalize on one's familiarity with the ESPN brand and style of commentary to at once dissolve the boundary of one medium (television screen) and invoke participation through another medium (book) in creating a canon of "the all-time favorite highlights."[12] Moreover, ESPN's attempt to stamp its imprimatur on sportscast highlights raises basic questions about how culture becomes commodified, produced and reproduced under transnational corporatized modes of acculturation.

ESPN's appropriation and commodification of highlights greatly expanded as *SportsCenter* became the network's flagship program. While *SportsCenter* doubtlessly made highlights its primary means of communication, the contention that it is "a perfect medium for modern America" raises questions about what impact the spectacularization of sport has had on viewers, journalists and athletes within a late-capitalist economy, what values are being promoted through these highlights, and whose stories are being told. *SportsCenter*'s ubiquitous place in American sports journalism can be considered in terms of its formation and development, its constitutive elements, one of its offshoots—namely the "This is *SportsCenter*" advertising campaign and a reality show that offered a self-reflexive view of the program, *Dream Job*.

Lastly, ESPN's distinct position among the producers of mediated sport is predicated on the fact that *SportsCenter* develops content within a cultural economy in which information, images and ideas are exchanged. Because audiences often know the outcome of games before they watch *SportsCenter*, they must be maintained as an audience. As a result, both event coverage and the news programs have changed from being primarily information-oriented to being primarily entertainment-oriented by producing increasingly affective highlights and witty commentary. Hirshberg contends, "A good highlight is at once a poetic distillation of athleticism and a carnival barker's holler for your attention, a shameless effort to keep you from pressing that damned remote."[13] In turn, this "shameless effort" to maintain the audience dictates both quantitatively and qualitatively which highlights are presented and how commodification is achieved. Producers of mediated sports texts have the capacity to shape social value and culture since value lies in the ephemeral nature of symbolic products. In this sense, value is manifested in the design and appearance of the text, its sign-value, and in the ability to connect disparate economic processes. Sports highlights, with their high levels of sign-value, are prototypes of an affective economy in which value is largely symbolic.

The entertainment ethos has only increased as media sport producers such as ESPN attempt to recoup the money spent on rights fees and production costs. Those costs have motivated producers to not only enhance broadcast production values that utilize the latest technologies to attract and maintain viewer loyalty, but also to make sure that every segment of every production is fully sponsored and branded. No longer is it sufficient to broadcast game highlights that convey information about who won, who lost and what star led the way to victory. In today's highlight culture, each segment of ESPN's *SportsCenter* is invested with corporate sponsorship that results in considerable profits for the cable network and is used to seduce and fascinate viewers by bringing together ideology and consumer behavior within a proliferating system of late-capitalism.[14]

SportsCenter's use of the highlights, which serves as the vehicle for an unending stream of encoded texts that emphasize the spectacle and the star, has enabled it to emerge as an important purveyor of cultural expression. As Sandomir explains, nobody knew in 1979 that ESPN would become a "wide world all its own with a manifest destiny to devour all sports and all manner of media. ESPN has become Microsoft, Wal-Mart and Audrey II—the carnivorous plant of 'Little Shop of Horrors'"—demanding all to "Watch me."[15]

A Menu Without a Main Course

That *SportsCenter* was not always the heart and soul of ESPN was evidenced in 1983 when for a brief time after the departure of Chet Simmons *SportsCenter* was cut from 30 minutes to 15. Additionally, on March 1, 1983, the network began offering a two-hour program on weekday mornings between 6 and 8 a.m., *Business Times*, hoping, as Frank J. Prial of the *New York Times* reported, to "attract former viewers who have drifted to the networks rather than watch reruns of old football games."[16] The addition of a non-sports program was precipitated by intense competition, lagging advertising sales, escalating rights fees and increased production costs. William Grimes, who succeeded Simmons upon his departure for the short-lived United States Football League, told the *Times* that while the network was committed to sports in prime time, "we have to look at daytime more closely. We have to look for opportunities to get more female-oriented advertising."[17] The article reported that ESPN's advertising was 30 percent behind projections for the year. Several fitness and exercise shows were already scheduled during early morning hours, but Grimes intimated that more would be needed because women were an important demographic that constituted "a large part of ESPN's audience."[18]

Reaction to the cutting of *SportsCenter* by half was swift and decisive. Viewers were not alone in criticizing the move, as media critics joined in the chorus of complaints. ESPN staff lobbied Grimes and Stuart Evey to reinstate the 30-minute time show. The executive agreed and a month later, *SportsCenter* was back to a 30-minute schedule. Having lost $20 million in 1982 and expecting $10 million more in losses the following year, ESPN doubtlessly believed something had to be done, including the decision to charge cable operators ten cents per subscriber instead of four cents as a means of making up for lagging advertising revenues.[19] However, cutting a studio show that offered exactly what viewers could not get on over-the-air and other cable networks was not the right direction to take. The decision to return *SportsCenter* to its regular 30 minutes and even lengthen it during special events proved to be decisive in ESPN's ascension as the most available and reliable source for sports news.

Expanding *SportsCenter*'s schedule was attempted the following summer during the 1984 Los Angeles Olympic Games. Despite the limitations imposed by the International Olympic Committee (IOC) of no more than three minutes of highlights three times a day after ABC completed its coverage at 2 a.m., ESPN increased the early evening *SportsCenter* to a full hour. Unable to show highlights, the network hired noted Olympic cinematographer Bud Greenspan to offer expert commentary for a feature series during *SportsCenter*. Titled "Olympic Digest," the segments offered "profiles of the best-known athletes on the days they are competing."[20] In creatively overcoming the limitation of not being able to show Olympics highlights, ESPN enhanced the program to which viewers came for news by offering someone with Olympic credentials to narrate its profiles.

The following summer ESPN televised Major League Baseball's Hall of Fame induction ceremony at Cooperstown, New York, providing three hours of live coverage. Even though the acceptance speeches of inductees did not, as Michael Katz noted, necessarily make for compelling television, the cable network's coverage "was a public service, something ESPN does best. No major network was about to devote three hours to Cooperstown."[21] In the same review, Katz also complimented ESPN for its weekly series on horse racing, *Down the Stretch*, as well as its host Sharon Smith. Katz explained, "Those are the kinds of programs ESPN should concentrate on, rather than filling its considerable time with replays ad nauseum of three-hour events it has already telecast."[22] Those single-sport weekly wrap-ups on auto racing, baseball, basketball, hockey and eventually professional and college football became some of the network's most popular programs, natural extensions of what it was beginning to do on *SportsCenter.*

ESPN showed exactly how far it could stretch its creative programming even when it did not have the rights to an event when it broadcast over 15 hours of football-related programs before Super Bowl XX in January 1986. As Steven Schneider reported, "Faced with having a menu without a main course, the sports channel has chosen to address this shortcoming with an avalanche of supportive programming...."[23] The menu began at 2:30 a.m. with a special *SportsCenter* devoted primarily to last-minute developments related to the Super Bowl, followed by a team-by-team review of the 1985 season, then highlights from NFL Films of the first 17 Super Bowls before a noon broadcast of *SportsCenter* with live reports from New Orleans, site of the game. While NBC aired its telecast, beginning at 3 p.m., ESPN offered counter-programming that featured nontraditional sports. At 9 p.m. it televised "the second theatrical offering it has ever presented,"[24] titled *Lombardi—I Am Not a Legend*, a 90-minute drama that had been staged in several Canadian cities and at the Edinburgh Festival in Scotland. After another round of NFL Films' football follies, the menu concluded with another *SportsCenter*, including live cut-ins from New Orleans, as well as game highlights, analysis and interviews with players and coaches. Whether or not this menu sated viewers was not as important as its creation, and within a few years, even the networks began offering their own day-long Super Bowl smorgasbords, gradually increasing pre-game shows from three to six hours.

Seminal Seventeen

By the late 1980s *SportsCenter* had established itself as ESPN's most popular program, and as ratings grew, more resources and personnel were devoted to its production. By this time athletes had become an integral part of the viewing audience. Not only could they hum the final bars to the program's theme song, but they doubtlessly tuned in knowing they might see themselves in the highlights or being interviewed. Even though the program was increasing in popularity with viewers, it was the hiring of John Walsh as executive editor that turned *SportsCenter* into something much more than the newspaper sports section. Walsh, who had honed his journalistic skills at magazines like *Inside Sports* and *Rolling Stone*, demanded and received more resources, reshaping *SportsCenter* around the belief that viewers could never get enough highlights, statistics and inside information.

Before Walsh's arrival, *SportsCenter* typically began with a report on the day's big game, followed by all the scores and highlights from that same sport, in the process burying stories with greater news value. Walsh jettisoned that singular approach, making sure that stories with the greatest news values led the broadcast and lobbying to push commercials even later into the show. Wanting to give the program more punch, Walsh overhauled graphics and increased the length and number of highlights. In addition to putting more reporters in the field to provide more in-depth coverage, Walsh insisted on more extensive research, a tighter format and better organization in all aspects of production. Those changes extended beyond *SportsCenter* into the single sport wrap-up programs as well. A show like *NFL Primetime* increased its highlight packages from 15 minutes to more than 30 minutes.[25] Not surprisingly, ratings increased dramatically.

In the early 1990s, the codification of highlights began at ESPN when highlight coordinator Dan Steir created a list of the various ways game highlights could be packaged to tell a story. Steir's list, which was known as "The Seminal Seventeen,"[26] became one of teaching tools used by Barry Sacks to instruct production assistants in the art of story-telling. While admitting that an infinite number of ways to report these stories existed, Steir estimated that 90 percent of the highlights seen on ESPN fell into one of the 17 categories. These categories ranged from narrative-based like "The 'Who Won' Highlight" and "The Turning Point Highlight" to non-action-based like "The Cutaway Highlight," which focused "on fans or mascots, or something in between like Hogettes" when the game "is just plain boring or bad."[27]

In effect, everything directly or indirectly related to an actual sporting event has the potential to be (re)presented as a highlight, and this condition produces a mediascape in which everything contributes to the creation of the spectacle, moving from the lived experience to a state of representation.[28] Instead of sports news as part of a larger narrative ground in real events, ESPN presents a discourse that relies on the production of the spectacle it creates. Significantly, the highlight as spectacle becomes a space of meaning generation and communication that merges the objective forms of consumer consumption with subjective feeling states into a shared culture. Rather than interpreting messages according to the viewer's own code and end, the viewer is positioned within a model that does not allow for communication and in which the viewer can only consume or reject the sport spectacle. With its discourse of straightforward news reporting, irreverent commentary, frat-house gags, trivia and nostalgia,[29] ESPN's *SportsCenter* has turned the highlight form into a cultural commodity.

SportsCenter Set, Format and Video Conventions

The *SportsCenter* set and format have changed on a regular basis to reflect advances in technology, as well as changes in management and ownership. Typically, during the week the program airs for 60 minutes at various times in the morning and evening. Designed by Walt Disney Imagineering, the current set was first used on June 7, 2004, the date *SportsCenter* first broadcast in High Definition. Shows typically begin with a graphic, showing the following: "Available on ESPNHD" (this animation precedes all high-definition broadcasts of ESPN or ESPN2). This is followed by a short *SportsCenter* animation before the screen comes alive with a montage of highlights accompanied with canned music, not necessarily specific to that show's news. As soon as the anchors are shown, the *SportsCenter* "Rundown" is stacked vertically along the screen's left hand side, listing the stories in the order they will be presented, and the "BottomLine" ticker begins its crawl at the bottom of the screen. At other times, after the introductory graphics and animation, the show begins with a shot of one anchor standing in the studio. The program's anchor typically introduces the top story, as a loop of video clips (with canned music) matching the script is played on screen. This is followed by another montage of video clips without commentary but with the *SportsCenter* theme, and then another *SportsCenter* animation loop.

Following this, a medium shot of the two anchors is presented, and an on-screen graphic displays the anchors' names. The anchors introduce themselves, and one will begin the top story. In most cases, the broadcast begins with the most important (e.g., NCAA men's basketball), most unusual (e.g., NAIA quadruple overtime), or most celebrity-infused (e.g., Kobe Bryant or Lebron James) game recap of the day. Before going to commercial break, the anchor provides voice-over for a montage of highlights (e.g., "Still to Come") that will follow the advertisements. Another montage of unaccompanied highlights leads into an animation that ends the sequence and cuts to the commercial break.

Following the break, a graphic with the brand name and logo of a specific sponsor leads into the next segment. On-screen graphics flash the brand name and logo as the camera pans across the studio in the background. Halfway through the show, the anchors reprise or reset the day's top stories in a segment titled either "*SportsCenter* Reset" or "*SportsCenter* Xpress." There is no noticeable difference in the format of either of these segments, other than the names and graphics.

Toward the end of the hour-long broadcast, the "Top Ten Plays" (Monday through Thursday) or "Top Ten 'Brilliant' Plays" (when Guinness was the sponsor), "Top Ten Plays of the Week" (on Sunday), or "Hardly the Usual Top Ten" (Friday) segment is introduced by an anchor. Each play is separated by an animation graphic of the play's respective number in the ranking. The anchors alternate plays, with each anchor providing commentary, which typically includes one or more of their pet phrases (e.g., "Cool as the other side of the pillow," "Representin'," etc.). Otherwise, the final segment of the show, "What 2 Watch 4," promotes broadcasts of games or events either later in the day or in the coming days on the ESPN and ABC networks. The show ends with a final shot of the anchors at the desk, who typically sign off by reminding viewers that "ESPNEWS is always on." If there is extra time, the anchors fill the time with improvised attempts at humorous banter. This time can range from 20 seconds to more than a minute.

Segments

SportsCenter segments refer to titled, often sponsored, parts of a SportsCenter broadcast that flesh out each story of the "Rundown." A segment usually lasts from one to several minutes; several segments are usually included in a given sequence of six to eight minutes before another sequence begins or the program breaks for a commercial advertisement. While every SportsCenter program is unique and includes different segments, some segments have become regular features of the broadcast and can be classified into at least three primary groups—those sponsored by corporate entities, those featuring expert analysts, and those featuring specialty highlights. For example, corporate-sponsored segments include the "AT&T SportsCenter Minute," which provides a focused discussion of day's top story; "Budweiser Hot Seat," in which a personality (sports or non-sports) will be asked to take sides on issues, teams, etc.; and "Coors Light Cold Hard Facts," in which a six-pack of questions about a certain sport is directed to an analyst.

Expert analysts factor into many SportsCenter segments, depending on the season. "Fact or Fiction," asks analysts to debate whether or not something is likely to happen (e.g., will the Boston Red Sox repeat as World Champions, or will the University of Tennessee women's basketball team repeat as NCAA champions). "On the Clock" is part of ESPN's never-ending NFL news programming in which every team's strengths and weaknesses are explored to frame the team's needs in anticipation of the late–April NFL draft. The segment features NFL draft expert Mel Kiper, analysts Ron Jaworski and Chris Mortensen, and host Mike Tirico. To a large extent, ESPN's SportsCenter has become the most highly rated national sports news program because of its ability to hire and feature the leading experts of the major professional and collegiate sports. "Barry's Best" features NHL analyst Barry Melrose, who figured prominently as the primary analyst for NHL 2Night on ESPN2 when ESPN had the rights to the NHL. In this segment, Melrose picks his top hockey highlights of the night, which are divided into the top goals, saves, and hits.

While the individual stories, game summaries, previews or profiles that comprise a SportsCenter broadcast each utilize a highlight package, an audio component and a graphics component, the program also includes segments that feature specialty highlights. These segments typically serve as teasers (e.g., "Still to Come" and "Inside SportsCenter") to whet the viewer's appetite before commercial breaks. These action-packed montages string together a sampling of the best highlights (e.g., home runs, touchdowns, knockouts, dunks and goals) to follow by showing only the most intense images to produce affect. Montages are unquestionably the most frequently used editing technique to lead into and out of commercial breaks. Another specialty highlight used on SportsCenter combines a visual highlight clip with the radio broadcast of that particular play. "Pump Up the Volume" brings together the drama and narrativity of radio announcing with the affect and immediacy of video. Most often, the radio portion is gleaned from the broadcast of the team that scored and won the game since the segment's goal is to ratchet up the intensity. Interestingly, this conjunction of two different media characterized some of the first live televised sports broadcasts by the BBC in 1938, often with disastrous results.[30] The BBC discontinued the pairing of a radio broadcast with television coverage because it quickly realized the effect produced was overkill, the very effect *SportsCenter* seeks to achieve with this particular segment.

One segment that garnered considerable criticism from bloggers and media critics was called "The Ultimate Highlight," shown during the 11 p.m. *SportsCenter* on Sunday evenings. Sponsored by Gatorade, the segment set a week's worth of highlights into a music video format, featuring popular music artists that clearly appeal to younger viewers. As a postmodernist text, the music video de-centers the viewer by presenting a flow of images and words without recognized boundaries or a contextualized past and present. The music video form is characterized by a disavowal to contextualize its images to communicate a clear signified message, allowing textual elements like narrative and meaning to be undercut by the editing process. The resulting pastiche creates a two-dimensional effect that leaves the viewer without a point of reference.[31] The music video's constantly changing texts provide only "the promise of a plenitude forever deferred."[32] A plenitude that never satisfies and rarely contextualizes does more to efface history than enrich it. The idea that highlights efface history is counterintuitive to an appreciation of sport based on knowing and understanding its history. In fact, an understanding of sports within an historical context is one of the primary tenets that characterizes modern sports.[33] Despite such pointed criticism, ESPN used the "Ultimate Highlight Reel" as the title for its 2007 calendar book.

"Top 10 Plays" has remained one of *SportsCenter's* most popular segments. During the week, the top plays will be counted down in one segment. On the Sunday evening program, the segment is cut into two parts, the first counting down the top plays from ten through six and the second part presenting plays five through one. "Top 10 Plays" does on a daily basis what the *Ultimate Highlight Reel* book did for highlights as they happened across a calendar year and what other special highlight programs like "Greatest Highlight with Chris Berman," "100 Greatest *SportsCenter* Moments," "100 Greatest (North American) Athletes of the 20th Century," and "Greatest Games of the 20th Century" have done to establish an ESPN canon of the most important games, athletes and highlights for ESPN viewers. In establishing these lists, comprised of sports highlights and athletes, ESPN uses its gate-keeping function to codify what historic achievements, displays of brilliance and athletic renown are worthy of consideration. As Chris Berman explained in the introduction to the *Ultimate Highlight Reel*, "It's our job to *show you* the who, the what, and the why of the wins and losses that make your world—and ours—go around."[34]

Berman's contention that ESPN's job is to show viewers which highlights are the "Top 10 Plays" of the day, the year, or the century establishes the preferred position assumed by the media giant. Although Berman admits that viewers certainly have their own favorites, he could assert with certainty that many of the viewers' choices would be found in the book because codification works by reducing personal preference to a list with which one can either only agree or disagree. Since the ESPN panel that selected the greatest athletes was comprised of sports journalists, celebrity sportscasters, and newspaper columnists, groups who play an integral role in publicizing athletic events within the commercial media structure, it is likely that status, connotations and cultural ideals play a role in the selection criteria.[35]

During the summer of 2004, ESPN counted down the top "100 *SportsCenter* Moments" of the previous 25 years, which of course coincided with its broadcast history, 1979–2004. Hosted by David Overton Wilson III, "ESPN25" consisted of 30-second segments shown during the 6 p.m. *SportsCenter* each day from May 31, 2004, until it reached the ultimate moment on September 7, 2004. That moment featured the U.S. victory in men's hockey over the Soviet Union in the semifinals of the 1980 Lake Placid Olympics. When ESPN created its own fan-based tournament, "Greatest Highlights with Chris Berman," the very same event was selected by the fans. This is arguably not coincidence.

Audio Conventions

That audio conventions, especially the prominence of anchor catchphrases, constitute a key component of *SportsCenter* production values was evidenced in a brief story in the March 18, 1997, issue of *Sports Business Daily* that reported ESPN had signed a licensing deal with Pro Player to capitalize on ESPN brands in apparel products. The line of outerwear, polo shirts, T-shirts, knits, sweatshirts and fleece items were to feature ESPN and ESPN2 logos, as well as clothing "incorporating ad slogans and signature catch-phrases used by ESPN sportscasters."[36] In a memo addressed to ESPN, ESPN2 and ESPNEWS on-air staff, *SportsCenter* anchor Keith Olbermann expressed concern about "whether we have any voice in how our own words are used" and "that many of the catchphrases in question could hardly be considered either our individual, or ESPN's, intellectual property."[37] Olbermann encouraged other on-air staff to seek legal protection since ESPN's desire to profit on their popularity might land them in trouble. Although nothing more came of the appropriation of anchor catchphrases, the incident illustrates the importance of anchor catchphrases to the production of *SportsCenter* highlight packages.

Anchor commentary within the newscast ranges from explicit news reading to implicit ideological values. Explicit on-camera commentary is used to frame specific events being covered, introduce segments, and provide context and continuity for the highlight and graphics packages that convey both information and affect. Having provided the narrative framework to set up the highlight, the anchor can then more creatively add voice-over to the visual components. It is within this aspect that

SportsCenter anchors have created their own stylistic and linguistic flourishes. An anchor's identity is contained in the catchphrases, which draw attention to sports talk in general and to a particular way of talking about sports in public. By utilizing a highly stylized discourse that reaches beyond a traditional sports lexicon and borrows liberally from various cultural flows, the *SportsCenter* anchor's use of catchphrases offers a dynamic relationship between the familiar and unfamiliar. As a result of their ubiquity, *SportsCenter*'s glib, witty catchphrases leak into the larger, non-sport lexicon.

Another important *SportsCenter* audio convention is the interview, conducted either in-studio with the anchor, from another off-site studio with the anchor, or with a reporter from the site of event. As already noted, interviews can also be formatted into specific segments like the "Budweiser Hot Seat." Getting interviews is predicated upon access, and access to players in locker rooms and on the playing fields is crucial to personalizing an athlete's performance. Viewers want more than scores and statistics because the practice of sports journalism has always been to frame narrative around combatants—winner and losers, favorites and underdogs, heroes and villains. Because ESPN is the largest sports news organization, it enjoys considerable leverage in getting interviews with the players because players understand that in talking with ESPN reporters, they get greater exposure. Leonard Shapiro, who covers golf for the *Washington Post*, expressed frustration in not being able to get an interview with Tiger Woods because Woods' handlers deny him access. Shapiro explained, "Then I pick up *ESPN The Magazine* and this *SportsCenter* anchor has a one-on-one Q & A with him that runs for six pages."[38] Gaining exclusive one-on-one interviews with athletes like Tiger Woods enhances ESPN's stature, and, thanks in part to the treatment they get from ESPN, the athletes are often fans of the network.

In addition to anchor commentary and interviews, *SportsCenter* utilizes a full range of expert analysts, including former players, coaches and practicing journalists. *SportsCenter*'s use of expert opinion, or punditry, can be structured in different ways. One involves a single analyst providing commentary over a highlight or statistical graphic or in split-screen shot with the visual component. A second option involves a pre-recorded segment in which two analysts face off and make predictions or play "Fact or Fiction." Lastly, several analysts can be brought together for a panel discussion in studio or at a remote site. Expert opinion only has relevance when based on insider information that beat reporters cannot acquire, so again, as with interviews, ESPN's experts enjoy a distinct advantage of having sources that are willing to provide the kind of information that allows ESPN to break stories. Few question or complain when sports experts offer insider information from unnamed or anonymous sources. Providing information that experts glean from insider sources enhances ESPN's standing with viewers because it fosters the perception that the network has a better grasp of what is going on than other sportscasts. With the use of expert opinion, television newscasts can more easily set the agenda about what are the important issues, as well as dispensing praise and criticism without consequence.[39]

Audio conventions constitute an important part of the discourse presented on *SportsCenter*. Catchphrases, expert opinion and interviews with athletes provide a discursive space within which sporting events and athletes can be framed to promote cultural values and further an ideological agenda. If highlights form the backbone of *SportsCenter*, then catchphrases are its lifeblood.

This Is SportsCenter?

ESPN leveraged the popularity of *SportsCenter* by promoting it in an advertising campaign titled "This Is *SportsCenter*." Originally a 30-spot campaign created by Wieden & Kennedy of Portland, Oregon, the campaign revolves around what happens behind the scenes of the program. In an early review, *Advertising Age* praised the campaign's spots for capturing the network's unique combination of highly passionate dedication to, and irreverent disposition about, the world of sports. The reviewer noted that the campaign works in large part because of its "tongue-in-cheek … straight-faced parody of behind-the-scenes looks—but the insight is nonetheless there."[40]

Written by Hank Perlman and directed by the team of Bryan Buckley and Frank Todaro of Radical Media, the campaign incorporates "off the wall situations, absurd comic asides, hysterical cameos of athletes and team mascots…."[41] Anthony Vagnoni reported that Buckley and Todaro referred to the style of the shoot "as strictly run and gun,"[42] which itself utilizes a sports simile associated with an up-tempo basketball offense. Vagnoni explained that while some spots were tightly scripted, others worked from a one-line idea, often related to the anchors' work ethic, their relationship with each other and the athletes, and the dynamics of the *SportsCenter* newsroom. For example, one spot plays on the idea that the *SportsCenter* catchphrases are made up on the spot, so the ad takes the viewer into an editing room where anchor Kenny Mayne tries out various catchphrases that he is known for—"I am the most popular player in the land!" "Yahtzee!" "That must be a Homer, Simpson, cuz the pitcher just said, 'D'oh!'"—to accompany a highlight of Ken Griffey hitting a home run.[43] The spot and the catchphrase both play on the viewer's knowledge of sports and popular culture—in another spot anchor Charley Steiner is "traded" to *Melrose Place* in exchange for Andrew Shue—while also debunking the notion that being a *SportsCenter* anchor involves creativity and spontaneity, which in reality, are required.

The "This Is *SportsCenter*" campaign was judged *Advertising Age*'s Best of Show for television spots in 1995. The campaign garnered not only industry awards, but also earned for the network "continuous ratings growth, unprecedented brand recall and … a positive buzz among sports' elite," according to Allan Broce, ESPN ad director. Additionally, the campaign was adapted for print, and ran during late night sports and entertainment programming on both broadcast and cable.[44] Judy Fearing, senior vice president of consumer marketing at ESPN, explained that the campaign was designed to solidify the ESPN brand image "as not just a TV network but as a huge sports fan itself."[45] The campaign's success was certainly related to its ability to naturalize the perception that ESPN is a huge fan of sports just as the athletes that the network covers are equally loyal fans of *SportsCenter*. Garfield reported that after the campaign began athletes like Dennis Rodman called *SportsCenter* anchor Dan Patrick to offer several suggestions for "This is *SportsCenter*" spots.

Athletes, of course, figure prominently in many of the spots. The athletes' presence has come under criticism from journalistic scholars and media critics who question how ESPN can run "delightful commercials praising ESPN that feature the very star athletes that ESPN covers."[46] ESPN managing editor Bob Eaton responded to those criticisms by pointing out that the athletes are not paid for their appearance or given preferential treatment. Al Thompkins, who teaches broadcast news ethics at The Poynter Institute, asked, "How would it be if you appear in a promo with an athlete, and then the next day you have to do a difficult story about their cocaine use? It would be difficult."[47]

Other spots involving athletes tend to downplay their athletic abilities, perhaps to blunt criticism. One features NBA star Grant Hill's piano-playing ability to soothe anchor Dan Patrick's bruised ego after a difficult show by playing the chords for the "Charge!" riff that ballpark organists often play to rally a team. When ESPN conducted a poll at its *SportsNation* Web site to select the fans' favorite "This is SportsCenter" commercial, it offered this tongue-in-cheek introduction: "Here at ESPN, we don't just cover athletes—we employ them, often in thankless and low-paying tasks. We figure, hey, we give them enough recognition on the field. It's about time they contribute off of [sic] it, as well."[48] One of the most successful spots capitalized on the fame of Tiger Woods, who is shown strolling through the *SportsCenter* newsroom when he encounters Stuart Scott, who asks about meeting for lunch. The punch line is visual, for as Woods walks away, he is followed by a gallery, similar to those that follow him on the golf course.

The ESPN-as-fan-of-sports-and-athletes-as-fans-of-ESPN concept was utilized in other advertising campaigns, including the 1999 seven-spot "Old School" campaign for ESPN Classic, formerly the Classic Sports Network, which ESPN acquired in October 1997. The "Old School" campaign employed the use of young celebrities to pay homage to athletes of years past, putting "a contemporary spin on a network that telecasts old sporting events."[49] For example, in one spot Chamique Holdsclaw celebrates basketball star Julius Erving, and in another actor Michael Rappaport waxes nostalgic about tennis champion John McEnroe. In 2001, ESPN launched the "Which *SportsCenter* do you watch?" campaign, featuring sports stars out of uniform and watching the network's premiere news program. The ads for this campaign were augmented with a ticker streaming scores and news that had been recently introduced on various programs. Also in 2001, ESPN launched campaigns with displays that featured the ticker—one on New York City taxis and another on phone kiosks. David Goetzl reported that the "displays are less about providing up-to-the-minute scores and more about serving as a marketing vehicle to impress fans with shock value and the network's commitment to reach them in innovative ways."[50]

The "This is *SportsCenter*" campaign was lauded as one of the most influential campaigns of the 1990s and credited with triggering a wave of "mockumentary"-style copycats. Despite the proliferation of imitators, Wieden & Kennedy and ESPN have continued to use the behind-the-scenes format in updated versions of the campaign developed over the past several years. Walter Berger reported in *Advertising Age's Creativity* that the campaign has been updated by introducing more topicality.[51] That has allowed ESPN to capitalize on specific events, like Mark McGwire hitting a then record 62nd home run, the Y2K hysteria, and the launching of *SportsCenter* in High Definition (HD). While that means the spots may not have a long shelf life and may require frequent productions, Fearing noted that "as long as we touch on what's topical in the world of sports and do it in unexpected ways, then I think this campaign can evolve for years."[52] The campaign continues to run.

Significantly, the "This is *SportsCenter*" campaign reflects a subtle but important shift in ESPN's overall mission. According to Lee Ann Daly, executive vice president of marketing, the company's mission statement, written in 1993, was about risk taking, creativity and integrity in being the self-proclaimed "worldwide leader in sports." Daly noted:

> But our brand positioning was that we're not an entertainment company, we're the world's biggest sports fan. And that's really driven where we've extended the brand over time. We chose that position because a human position is more accessible than the "worldwide leader in sports." We wanted a conversational role with the fans.[53]

Part of the "This is *SportCenter*" campaign's success was predicated on the eccentricities, quirks and foibles of *SportsCenter* anchors and anchor wannabes. None of the spots uses the "worldwide leader of sports" claim, although it continues to be used to introduce live event coverage and other promotional spots. For example, in one spot Dan Patrick and Keith Olbermann are shown applying make-up while discussing the violence in hockey, revealing that even though they deal with the tougher side of sports, they retain an effeminate side concerned with rouge and foundation.

Humor has proved to be a key ingredient in all the campaigns because, in part, *SportsCenter* has become a cultural icon for sports news broadcasting that spawned a network television series, *SportsNight*, which aired on ABC for two seasons beginning in 1998. Lastly, one spot played on the idea of a young anchor, who, like his athlete counterparts, comes to the "big leagues" too early and cannot quite handle the pressure of being a *SportsCenter* anchor. Interestingly, that spot suggested that becoming an anchor, like becoming a professional athlete, requires more than a love of sports. Nonetheless, ESPN spun that spot's premise into a reality series in 2004 that was anything but a laughing matter, especially to some of those occupying the *SportsCenter* anchor desk.

Dream Job

Prompted by its mission statement to be the world's biggest sports fan, ESPN literally offered one sports fan the opportunity to become an anchor on its most popular and prestigious program, *SportsCenter*. Titled *Dream Job*, the program marked ESPN's second attempt at a reality series, following *Beg, Borrow & Deal*, which featured two teams of four racing against each other to get a specified destination by performing sports related tasks, a format similar to CBS's Emmy Award–winning reality show, *The Amazing Race*.

ESPN aired *Dream Job* on Sunday evenings starting in February 2004. One significant difference that separated *Dream Job* from other reality shows was that the winner was offered a one-year contract to work for ESPN, sitting at the *SportsCenter* anchor desk. Like other reality shows, *Dream Job* had no difficulty attracting applicants, more than 10,000 of whom went through the initial auditioning process that had its own sponsor in Labatt's Beer.[54] From the auditions, ten contestants and one alternate won invitations to vie for the *Dream Job*, and a Wendy's promotion involving soda cups at franchises provided the 12th candidate, called the "wild card" like the NFL and MLB teams that qualify for the playoffs despite not having won division races.[55] Shortly before the series aired, producers allowed the alternate to become the 12th contestant.

The first season's contestants ranged in age from 21 to 40, and came from diverse occupational backgrounds, including several college students, a computer programmer, a retail manager, an attorney, an executive recruiter, an auto parts salesman, a comedian and an actor singer. Both finalists were college students who had had some broadcasting experience. As Wade Paulsen noted, "Their biggest edge, though, was being very young on a network trying to maintain its cachet with youth so that it can continue to raise its sky-high subscriber rates to cable systems (at the time $2.61 per subscriber per month just for basic ESPN)."[56] In the show's final hour, viewers selected Aaron Levine to be cut, leaving Mike Hall as the first *Dream Job* winner. In addition to winning a new Mazda-3 and a one-year ESPN contract, Hall appeared on *SportsCenter* later that night to take a sports quiz in which each correct answer added $5,000 to the value of his contract. Before officially joining *SportsCenter*, Hall was to be given on-air work for ESPNEWS.

The program garnered respectable cable ratings that averaged slightly more than one million households, triple the number from the previous year's ratings for NHL games that ran in the 10 p.m. time slot on comparable Sundays. Sandomir explained that the show capitalized "on the worship of wisecracking anchors and highlights massaged into a hyperbolic reality separate from actual games."[57] *Dream Job* was something of a nightmare for others, including anchor Dan Patrick, who expressed incredulity on his radio show that the winner was being hired to serve as a *SportsCenter* anchor, asking, "Would you give the punt, pass and kick winner a contract to punt for the Bengals?"[58] Patrick's rhetorical question brings into focus the mission statement and brand positioning that ESPN is the world's biggest sports fan and that all sports fans share equally in its gestalt. As Sandomir pointed out in a review of the program, "It [*SportsCenter*] is a mystical place for fans, an Emerald City where the Wizard of Oz is Dan Patrick; it is a comfort zone where an hour's worth of news, highlights and Top 10's fulfills a craving that regenerates nightly."[59] Pointing out that live television combined with on-air inexperience hardly made for compelling viewing, Sandomir also explained that *Dream Job* at least dispelled the notion that anchoring *SportsCenter* could be mastered by wannabes without "skills and personas honed delivering three-and-a-half-minute nightly reports in smaller markets."[60]

After briefly sharing the anchor desk with Linda Cohn in July 2004, Hall was assigned to ESPNEWS. The following year Hall became, according to Burke Magnus, ESPN vice president, "the guy, the face and voice of ESPNU,"[61] the ESPN network devoted to college sports that was launched in March 2005. Given the long-term planning that invariably went into the decision to launch ESPNU, it is reasonable to conjecture that finding a young talent to host ESPNU was the ultimate, though unstated, goal of *Dream Job*.

Conclusion

In a mediascape dominated by the proliferation and consumption of images, all forms of production, including sportscast highlights, are impacted by the presence of spectacle. This has occurred, paradoxically, out of the desire to establish a world of leisure unencumbered by the demands of work and politics. One reason why mediated sport has been unable to resist the encroachment of politics lies in *SportsCenter*'s proven capacity to attract and deliver the most attractive consumer demographic to the marketplace in volume with regularity. The male demographic of 18 to 34 year olds has been shown to have an insatiable appetite for not only mediated sports texts, but also for the consumer products that are advertised on those programs. ESPN has certainly assumed a leading position in acculturating its viewers to not only its own brand, but also those of its sponsors. In the process it has become ABC's *de facto* sports division and having raised its own profile as well as the profiles of ABC's other properties.

The success of ESPN's *SportsCenter* within the political and cultural economy stems from its ability to harness power by controlling the production, distribution and consumption of mediated sport resources. Because political economy tends to concentrate on a specific set of social relations organized around the power to control other people, processes and objects, ESPN must continually create circuits of communication products that link a chain of primary producers to wholesalers, retailers and consumers whose purchases, rentals and attention are fed back into new processes of production. What becomes critical for this circuit is control of the code—the visual and audio conventions that go into ESPN's programming. In the transmission of these codes, all types of consumer products and services from sports equipment to alcohol to travel destinations are associated with mediated sport events or serve as sponsors for specific *SportsCenter* segments (e.g., "Budweiser Hot Seat," "Gatorade Ultimate Highlight," "Top Ten 'Brilliant' Plays"). Corporate growth and production are designed to produce both the needs and need satisfaction for consumers.

Viewers of ESPN's *SportsCenter* are promised the exhilaration of athletic achievement and seduced into completing their part as consumers in a reproductive social order. Both producers and consumers, those behind and in front of the screen, are involved in a continuous (co)production of the promotional culture.[62] The self-proclaimed mantle of "Worldwide Leader in Sports," with all the brand recognition and prestige that such purported leadership entails, gives ESPN an important competitive advantage in the sport-media-commercial complex. Arguably, the power employed to captivate and move consumers through *SportsCenter*'s constellation of signs and images resides in its highlights and glib catchphrases. In the process television personalities and sport stars serve as surrogate friends and neighbors for viewers in an electronic simulation of friends and community. *SportsCenter* segments are branded so that a constant stream of product names and icons act as lead-ins before the viewer gets to the actual highlight, commentary or interview. Arguably, these segments can be seen as examples of postmodern art that bring together advertisement imagery, ideological codes and symbols of consumer capitalism.[63] Viewers are implicated in consumerism based on affect. Rather than allowing people to satisfy real human needs, the market culture constrains individuals to satisfy their needs in consumer products and prescribed behaviors.

In ESPN's "Little Shop of Highlights," *SportsCenter* constantly demands that viewers watch its "Top 10 Plays," its "Ultimate Highlight Reel," its "100 Greatest Athletes of the 20th Century," its "This is *SportsCenter*" commercials. In doing so, it has codified the highlight news frame and selected which sports moments, achievements, and athletes deserve to be in the canon. In this Disney-owned company's culture of promotion, all signifying gestures are swallowed up, continually proffered and deferred, creating a maze in which there is no take-away meaning, no end point, no ultimate reward for watching other than being a fan of ESPN.

CHAPTER 8

The Real Virtuality for an Audience of One

Developments in new media have provided additional vehicles for deploying sports highlights. Over the past two decades, sports broadcasters, fans, athletes and the leagues have all been impacted by technological changes, especially those precipitated by developments in delivery systems (e.g., World Wide Web and mobile devices). However, because the integration of new media with coverage of major sporting events involved not only changes in technology, but also social and cultural practices, it is important not to fall prey to what Henry Jenkins calls the Black Box Fallacy,[1] a form of technological determinism that reduces changes in media systems to technological change, casting aside changes to the cultural milieu in which the changes occur, namely those associated with market economics, law, genres and audiences.

The relationships between existing media and markets, genres and audiences underwent considerable change as a result of the Telecommunications Act of 1996, which called for all restrictions on cable rates to be lifted in March 1999. The prospect of complete deregulation of cable rates, which were already growing at a pace four times that of overall consumer prices raised concerns among consumer groups and members of Congress.[2] Despite new types of direct-broadcast satellite service (e.g., DirecTV), cable still controlled 87 percent of the market share. Increases in subscription prices were as constant as the changes in basic packages as cable systems moved to a fiber optic network capable of delivering expanded channel capacity, high-speed Internet connections, video on demand, and residential phone service.[3] The Telecommunications Act also called for a change in the broadcasting standard from analog to digital, ensuring that programming, whether standard or high definition (HDTV), would be "picture perfect, free of ghosts and snow."[4]

In addition to these changes, new media spawned even more delivery systems, genres and audiences, further complicating the sports media market. On the one hand, as delivery systems changed rapidly in the 1990s, their utilization was anything but smooth, as evidenced by International Business Machines' (IBM) disastrous attempt to employ its computer network to facilitate media coverage at the 1996 Atlanta Olympic Games. Only two years later, however, the Internet provided soccer fans of World Cup '98 not only highlights of all the tournament's goals but also live broadcast of matches as well as updates, complete rosters, schedules and souvenirs.[5] On the other hand, cultural protocols and practices related to media were dynamic for both producers and consumers. To comprehend the dynamics of the new sports media landscape, it is necessary to consider the changed context of sports broadcasting and the changed model of consumer behavior, dominated by a model of affective economics—the bedrock of emotions driving consumption decisions.[6]

Before the end of the twentieth century, a media giant like CBS found itself in competition with Internet media companies to provide the latest sports news and highlights. Not surprisingly, in March 1997, CBS announced that it had acquired a 22 percent stake in Sportsline USA Inc., a company specializing in providing sports information to various Web sites, as a necessary first step in the network's Internet strategy.[7] At almost the same time, ABC News began its venture online jointly with Starwave Corporation, "a 300-person collection of software programmers and journalists behind a series of popular Web sites, led by ESPNet Sportszone, an on-line sports service."[8] At the time, Sportszone was the most heavily trafficked new-media service on the Internet apart from the major search engines like Yahoo and computer sites like CNET and ZD Net.

Professional sports leagues and organizations also embraced the new technology. By 2001, the National Football League (NFL), which had the most valuable television contract in sports, signed the largest league Internet rights package, worth more than $300 million in cash and non-cash value with a consortium of America On Line (AOL) Time Warner, Sportsline.com and Viacom, which had purchased CBS in September 1999.[9] Although the NFL had an $18 billion reason why its Web site should not draw viewers away from the coverage of football telecasts, the league quickly learned how to make its Web site and online shop a virtual parking lot, "where the fans can get close to the players as they make their way out of the stadium."[10] That closeness was also manifested in sales of NFL team apparel and merchandise.

If the Internet was helping to create new alliances by producers in the dissemination of sportscasts, then so too was it changing the way consumers accessed sportscasts and sports news. Television may have spawned the Couch Potato, and he was eventually joined by his online counterpart, the "Web Potato."[11] Even though data showed that for many people the Web had already become an electronic routine and companies were employing software programs (e.g., Little Brother) to rein in employees' "digital dalliances,"[12] television traditionalists at the 1999 National Association of Television Executives' NAPTE convention predicted that people would never use their computers to watch favorite television programs.

The final phase in the deployment of sports highlights can be understood within the contexts within which new media, despite enhancing access to the coverage of sportscasts, only further fragmented the audience for mediated sports, saturated an already soggy sports market and guaranteed staggering losses for the television and cable networks that continued to pay exorbitant rights fees that even Rupert Murdoch believed "have gone beyond an economic level."[13] Unfortunately for the networks, the difficulty of attracting a mass audience for sports telecasts drove the cost of securing the rights for premium events higher. Although no one was quite certain why, television ratings for the major sports continued a decade-long decline. During this time, sports ratings had been eroded by cable television, home video and satellite dishes, a trend that continued with the Internet, TiVo and DVR recorders. Most importantly, for a generation nurtured on highlights, instant replays, and more cable versions of ESPN than there were broadcast networks for the generation that preceded it, sports were being watched in a far different way than they had been during the three-network era.[14] As Richard Sandomir explained, "The bonds of loyalty to a nationally televised sport can be broken more easily because there is so much else to do and perhaps less patience."[15] Viewers constantly searching for marquee match-ups more readily passed over games and events in which star attractions were not competing.

New alliances between broadcast and cable networks, technology companies, and wireless mobile phone providers helped to build a new fan base for sports by offering Internet pay packages, enhancing production values for live coverage of major events, and providing more infotainment, especially highlights. As broadband connections became more available, sports programming providers offered more online pay packages. For example, Major League Baseball (MLB) teamed up with Sun Microsystems to create MLB Advanced Media (MLBAM) in 2000. Through its Web site, MLB.com, the league began offering pay-packages that enabled visitors to "listen to and watch live games and highlights, check scores, buy game tickets, purchase team merchandise and even manage a virtual team."[16] With an average of 6 million visitors daily, 10 million page views per day and no application downtime in a two-year period of operation, MLB.com became the Internet's most successful broadband Web portal devoted to professional sports.[17] In 2005, ESPN introduced viewers to ESPN 360 and its "Full Circle" coverage for the presentation of a men's college basketball game, in which each of its networks presented a different angle of the game being broadcast. Wireless companies like Verizon utilized second- and third-generation systems like VCAST, which included more than 300 daily video clips from channels and shows like CNN, NBC Sports and ESPN.

Lastly, at the same time the professional leagues were offering coverage of their games, highlights and previews to consumers willing to subscribe to pay packages, they were also seeking to expand control of their intellectual property rights. This desire to expand control of intellectual property rights pitted the professional leagues against the First Amendment rights of the news media, especially traditional print media and independent media seeking to cover "a public news event which ought to be in the public domain."[18] While the root of the issue can be traced back to the International Olympic Committee's creation of Rule 49 to its *Charter* in 1956, which set strict limitations on news media coverage of the events, the newest battle was precipitated by the creation of the Internet and alternate ways of distributing news.

A Technological Spoilsport

The strategy for the twenty-first-century sports mediascape was established before the end of the twentieth century: In order to maintain and add to its customer base, entities like the International Olympic Committee and NBC wanted the consumer's attention, as well as the consumer's time and money, at every possible moment. Harnessing and utilizing the technology proved to be far more difficult in practice than it was in theory. In 1996, organizers for Atlanta's Olympic Games promised "the most technologically sophisticated Games ever."[19] However, by the second day, IBM's $80 million information system, "Info 96," was missing "large blocks of data, including any warnings about the continuing troubles to the Olympic transportation systems."[20] Although IBM's goal was to provide results in real time from the 29 venues to its mainframe computers and then on to the rest of the world, Olympic technology officials were reduced to transmitting results by facsimile machines from the outlying venues to a central office and distributing them by runners. News agencies, promised an electronic results system fed directly from Olympic computers, were reduced to having employees "watch the competitions on television and then type results into their systems."[21]

Despite the problems with its communications systems, the Atlanta Olympic Games were indeed the first Olympics that offered access through the Internet. Promises exceeded what was delivered, especially at the two largest sites, both of which were collaborative efforts—the IBM-Atlanta Committee for the Olympic Games site and the NBC-IOC site. Arguably, the best way to get information about specific sports was to access sport-specific sites like Velonews Interactive. For example, Ken Brown of the *New York Times* reported that although the IBM site promised "a continuous flow of digital images from nearly every venue," what they got were delays and "relentless commercialism; the home page is like an infomercial for Olympic junk."[22] Similarly, NBC planned to integrate its television broadcasts with its Web pages. However, NBC's plan to use new Intercast technology developed by Intel was mostly for show because few possessed the equipment needed to use Intercast technology.

With a little more digging at sport-specific sites, however, computer users at sites like Velonews Interactive were provided "details only a fanatic could love, including pictures of Super Bike 2, which American riders will use in the Olympics … [and] expanded pages that show even the smallest details of a competition, noting that the winner of the 3-meter springboard diving competition nailed a forward 11/2 somersault in pike position on his fourth dive."[23] Rather than enduring NBC's 171.5 hours of coverage devoted primarily to the most popular events and name athletes, serious fans of a less popular sport no longer had to waste hours "wearing a hole in the living room carpet waiting for a fleeting glimpse of a triumph or failure."[24] Even those opposed to Olympic commercialism found information to reinforce their beliefs. At the interactive sports magazine, *Competitor Online*, visitors found a feature article about how the Olympic Games were displacing Atlanta's homeless. Brown added, "The highlight here is Spoilsport, the anti-mascot of the Olympics."[25]

By the time of the next major world sporting event, World Cup '98 held in France, many of technological problems plaguing the integration of new and old media during the Atlanta Olympic Games had been solved. Not only were all 64 games of World Cup broadcast live in the United States by ABC, ESPN, ESPN2 and Univision, the Spanish-language network, but a plethora of Web sites were available to satisfy diehard soccer fans. Because of the six-hour difference between France and the Eastern time zone of the United States, live coverage ended before most people had completed work. Nonetheless, several Internet sites offered live Webcasts of the matches, including one that offered highlights of every goal scored during the tournament. One magazine's Web site featured the work of 35 photographers stationed in 22 countries around the globe "to chronicle how the world watches and reacts to the World Cup."[26] Matchday.com still operates and provides links to many other sites, including Rugby USA and Team USA.

Time difference proved to be a major handicap for NBC's coverage of the 2000 Sydney Olympic Games, resulting in ratings that were the worst in television history for the event.[27] The precipitous ratings drop was directly attributable to not only NBC's decision to delay broadcasting events in the United States until many hours after they had been contested in Australia, but also to "a flood of information about the Games … on the Internet and on sports cable channels and sports talk radio stations, some of which did not exist four and eight years ago."[28] Because the Sydney Olympic Games were scheduled in late September, NBC's broadcasts faced competition from the other networks' coverage of National Football League games, pennant races of Major League Baseball, and college football games. Having invested more than $3 billion in rights fees for the next five Olympics, NBC sought to improve ways to keep viewers informed about Olympic athletes between Games.[29] The most important way, according to NBC president Bob Wright, was the Internet, and at its Web site NBC offered features especially directed toward young fans. Bonnie Rothman Morris of the *New York Times* noted that most of the educational content for children on the NBC site was provided by Scholastic, as well as plenty of interactive games that came courtesy of sponsors, such as the IBM Basketball One on One game, the Visa Long Jump game and the Budweiser Boxing Battle.[30] Not surprisingly, NBC was criticized for its overt commercialism during its coverage of the 2000 Sydney Olympic Games, just as it was for its patriotic jingoism during the 2002 Salt Lake City Olympic Games, despite claims that it would not overemphasize patriotic elements in the wake of September 11, 2001, promising to carry celebrations by athletes and fans from various countries.[31]

Niche Players

Given the ability to promote their Web sites with almost limitless amounts of television advertising, the major television networks were presumed to have distinct advantages in attracting traffic to their sites. Despite brand depth and consumer loyalty to their television offerings, as well as millions of dollars in promotions, the networks, more accustomed to being "mighty media monoliths than niche players scrounging for audiences," experienced a humbling reminder that it needed to compete with Internet portals like Yahoo, American On Line and Microsoft's MSN.[32] In part, the networks' problems stemmed from an overestimation of their own strengths. Although promotions helped attract users, a lack of depth and sophisticated features at the sites failed to turn the curious into steady visitors. Once they waded in, the networks discovered they needed to build online necessities and protocols related to directories and retail services that were foreign to existing media expertise.[33]

One area of expertise that the networks transferred to their Internet sites was in providing sports news. When CBS acquired a stake in Sportsline, a leading Internet sports service, it used the partnership to gain a foothold online to disseminate its sports content. The $100 million deal, which included an option to increase ownership to 33 percent in the following five years, was part of an overall strategy predicated on backing independent, specialized Web services like Sportsline and MarketWatch rather than trying to create a network-scale portal.[34] Successful integration occurred when CBS Sports used its sports broadcasts to encourage viewers to visit CBS Sportsline.com for updates and highlights of ongoing events (e.g., Masters golf, U.S. Open tennis) in the same way CBS News cited financial reports on CBS MarketWatch.com. CBS maintained the relationship with Sportsline for more than a decade. Finally, in August 2007, CBS SportsLine.com renamed the site CBSSports.com to unify the CBS Sports brand across its multiple delivery systems.

Unlike Disney's launch of Go.com, which failed to muster much of a challenge to the major search engines, ABC found a measure of success for its Internet venture by collaborating with an innovative new-media company. In Starwave Corporation, ABC aligned itself with Paul Allen, co-founder of Microsoft Corporation, as well as a team of programmers and journalists who had already succeeded in developing a series of popular Web sites, including ESPNet SportsZone. By the time the Walt Disney Company purchased Starwave, the ESPNet Sportszone had already established itself as the most successful Internet site focused on a mainstream topic, namely sports.[35] In 1997, the Sportszone, heavily promoted during ABC and ESPN sportscasts, received 600,000 visitors and almost 7 million page views daily, and brought in roughly $7 million a year in advertising revenues.[36] Additional revenues came from the 60,000 subscribers who paid a monthly fee for premium services, called ESPN Insider, including special columns and fantasy baseball games. In 1999, Disney named Steve Bornstein, former head of ESPN, as president of the Web portal

Go.com. Michael Eisner, Disney's chairman, pointed out that Bornstein, who joined ESPN "when cable was a nascent industry—much like the Internet today—was instrumental in building ESPN into the undisputed market leader."[37] While ESPN maintained its position as market leader in delivering online sports information, Disney pulled back from the portal business in 2000 under Bornstein's direction and focused on its mainstays—travel and entertainment.

While the networks struggled to find their niche on the Internet, the transition was considerably easier for the professional sports leagues, despite the seasonal nature of their operations. Like the networks, the major professional leagues depended on a collaborative effort to host and produce their Web sites. For example, in 1998, the NFL signed a $10 million, three-year deal with ESPN.com for its Web site, NFL.com; and Venator Inc., which owned the Foot Locker and Champs' sporting goods chains; for NFLShop section of its Web site and catalog operations.[38] At that time, the site offered scores of games in progress, text-based play-by-play descriptions and post-game articles. Even though it attracted an average of almost half a million individual visitors to its site, its vice president for broadcasting, Dennis Lewin, downplayed the site's significance. "We don't believe anybody really wants to sit at their computers and watch a game in text."[39] Lewin's comment is understandably understated in light of the $18 billion television rights package the league had signed with the networks in January 1997, and he added that the NFL Web site would not be enhanced "in any way, shape or form that will ultimately draw people away from the game,"[40] by which he doubtlessly meant away from watching the game on television.

Two years later, the NFL.com Web site surpassed CBS Sportsline.com with 6.1 million users and moved behind only ESPN.com, still the most visited sports site on the Web. Users of NFL.com spent almost $40 million at the Web site, representing approximately one-third of the roughly $125 million in yearly revenues generated through licensing agreements with makers of team apparel and merchandise.[41] Given its ubiquitous brand, more than 600 free advertisements for NFL.com and NFLShop on network television broadcasts and CBS/WestwoodOne radio network broadcasts, and the minor role online commerce played in the NFL's business, the Web site was a guaranteed success. Commissioner Paul Tagliabue also pointed to the Web's importance in reaching younger fans. "If you look at it in terms of who's using the Internet now, it's the technology optimists, the young people. And we do want to connect them to the game."[42]

Internet analysts were not at all surprised when the NFL signed a new five-year deal worth $110 million in cash and at least $200 million in non-cash value with a consortium of AOL Time Warner, Sportsline.com and Viacom in July 2001.[43] Sportsline.com replaced ESPN.com as the host of NFL.com, and AOL coordinated the site's marketing, cross-promoted it with programming on Viacom networks (i.e., CBS, MTV and Nickelodeon), and offered a limited number of NFL video highlights. This last point had been the deal-breaker for ESPN.com, which was in the process of expanding its own NFL-only site and wanted more video rights than the NFL was offering.[44] Significantly, as the number of visitors to its Web site increased, the NFL became increasingly vigilant in controlling the dissemination of video highlights, not posting them to NFL.com until after the ESPN Sunday night game. Why the NFL only posted game highlights after Sunday's final game is not completely clear, since this enabled local television stations to use the highlights in their late night sportscasts before they became available at NFL.com. Perhaps not posting game highlights on its Web site earlier was a concession to the networks. This self-imposed embargo on its own site was not the last time the NFL imposed limitations on the use of highlights.

Convergence

If the networks were not quite certain how to use the Internet as a delivery system, few knew how consumers would use the Internet. Even though the expression "surfing the Web" had become part of everyday parlance by the mid–1990s, the Web's democracy of opportunity did not necessarily translate into a democracy of equal outcomes. In fact, as more people spent more time online, they did so at a smaller number of sites.[45] As the *New York Times'* Amy Harmon posited, "That America's infatuation with the Web as a haven for cybersurfing adventures has morphed into a more mundane fondness for a useful information tool is in many ways testament to how quickly it has become a part of everyday life for so many."[46] A Jupiter Media Matrix study showed that in 2000 about 60 percent of Internet users visited more than 20 Web sites in a month, but by the following year the proportion had been halved, even though the study revealed that the time spent online was rising.

This concentration of longer visits at fewer sites arguably sheds light on the public's lack of interest in diversification, but it was also attributable to strategies employed by the site developers. For example, in 1998 ESPN launched an advertising campaign for its ESPN SportsZone built around Netboy, "a sports-crazed, cyber-savvy twentysomething, interacting with athletes and ESPN on-air talent."[47] The ads sought to legitimize ESPN's online service with the television network's credibility in the same self-deprecating tone used in the "This is *SportsCenter*" campaign. Significantly, the ads positioned visiting the SportsZone Web site "as an everyday ritual."[48] Not only did Netboy become such an iconic figure that he was employed in promotions for upcoming television programming, but *SportsCenter* also ran segments that directed viewers to learn more about a story at the SportsZone. Additionally, SportsZone visitors were encouraged to find "Insider" information by subscribing to the site's ESPN Insider service.[49] That ESPN's SportsZone, eventually renamed ESPN.com, became the Web's most-visited sports only site was not surprising given the marketing and advertising budgets for campaigns on ESPN-owned television, print and radio to drive consumers to its site. Large sites like ESPN.com and Yahoo quickly learned how to utilize features like Yahoo's "Buzz Index," which listed the most-searched stories and photos of the day.

Only national, international and business news ranked higher than sports news among those who used the Internet as their primary source of news, a 1998 study revealed. These news consumers, who regularly signed on at work where connections tended to be faster, did not take the time to play video clips of news events. This may have been attributable to employers' attempts "to rein in such digital dalliances" by utilizing software programs like "Little Brother" that allowed managers to track which sites employees visited on the Web.[50] Of course, such measures gave rise to countermeasures like "Stealth Surfing," software designed to avoid management computer monitoring. If employees were engaged in cyber-surfing, their digital dalliance stemmed, in part, from the proliferation of sports webcasts that were readily available from ESPN SportsZone, CBS Sportsline and several smaller operations presenting simulations of games as they happened by using text updates and animation relayed from the events.[51]

In April 1998, ESPN's SportsZone launched its first full season of Web-based baseball coverage while CBS Sportsline was in its second, both having also provided Webcasts of football games the previous fall. As Matt Richtel noted in a 1998 *New York Times* article, "Baseball Live" was CBS Sportsline's most popular online offering, attracting hundreds of thousands of viewers each game. Although the experience of a Webcast was far inferior to a television broadcast, it allowed displaced fans to follow their favorite teams via the Internet. Richtel also explained that Webcasts were a harbinger of "what is called convergence, the melding of television hardware and content with home computer hardware and content."[52] This form of convergence allowed visitors to the site to use a single screen to access the broadcasts, as well as all available statistics. Interestingly, these simulated Webcasts harkened back to the first decades of the twentieth century when baseball games were "shown" on large display boards that recreated the action forwarded over telegraph wires. Just as radio rendered these crude animations obsolete, so, too, would Webcasts eventually give way to newer technology. Audio-Net, a Dallas-based Internet broadcaster, was already offering play-by-play for events broadcast exclusively for the Internet, particularly those at small universities.[53] Although CBS Sportsline's executive producer predicted that Web simulcasts would begin incorporating streaming video and still shots to create a much richer experience, video streaming of live sporting events did not occur for several more years.[54] Before Web simulcasts were made available, licensing issues related to rights fees had to be sorted out. A necessary first step on the road to live video Web simulcasts was the addition of streaming video highlights.

At the 1999 television trade show, called NAPTE, sponsored by the National Association of Television Executives, the importance of streaming audio and video was preached by, among others, Mark Cuban, co-founder and president of Broadcast.com Incorporated, who told a ballroom full of television executives "that any day now people will use their computers to watch television, buy merchandise from their favorite shows and even send feedback to producers or advertisers."[55] That Cuban accurately envisioned consumers' changing computer protocols and practices was evidenced not only in the fortune his company made, but also in the increasing number of people who used their computers to date, shop and watch sports. Whereas a seminar about how to sell advertising on a Web site had drawn ten people at the previous year's NAPTE, that year it drew over 100, and more than a third of all the seminars were devoted to new media issues.[56] Despite the growing importance of streaming audio and video, one television executive boldly predicted that "people will never use a computer to watch 'E.R.' or 'Everybody Loves Raymond,' or any other hit show, movie, or sports event, for that matter."[57]

Motion Sickness

Such a prediction defied logic given the assortment of technological gadgetry already available to consumers. For example, exercising had been enhanced with the first virtual-reality bike, the Tectrix VR bike, which took users "through simulated adventures projected by a CD-Rom on a computer screen."[58] Golf and ski enthusiasts used multimedia technology to take video tours of courses or ski areas, get instructions or equipment reviews, talk with famous golfers or skiers and even play a free virtual game at GolfWeb.[59] While the golf and ski sites presented photographs of scenic vistas and perilous plunges, they often lacked much objective content, reading as if they had been written by a publicist. For hard news, there were sites like the Professional Golfers Association (PGA) Tour site, which offered live, hole-by-hole scoring updates during its events, as well as links to other tours (e.g., Senior, European and Nationwide).[60]

All sports seemingly utilized the Web to attract fans. With the development of Virtual Spectator, yachting enthusiasts enjoyed coverage of the 1999 and 2003 America's Cup races online. Thanks to telemetry data emitted directly from each race boat, subscribers to the service followed the competing boats' positions on the course marked with an illustrated snail trail.[61] Significantly, that new technology was employed to bring America's Cup races to sports fans in general—an occurrence that had occurred in 1897 with film, 1930 with newsreels, and 1983 with cable television—attests to the importance of aesthetics in the appreciation of a sporting event, especially one not often considered visually compelling. The point has added significance when cast in the light of the sport's purported elitist appeal.

Those more interested in playing video games had several choices from ESPN Digital Games from which to choose: National Hockey Night, NBA Tonight and X-Games Pro Boarder. Not only did these games play like other video games for the personal computer Xbox or PlayStation, but they also included features similar to an ESPN television broadcast—shots from the goal-cam, color commentary from ESPN announcers, and "instant replays from multiple points of view to cap the moment. On the PC version, you can see those replays on the Jumbotron...."[62] After playing for a week, the computer created "a 30-second 'Plays of the Week' segment, a cross-section of highlights from the league, including a few of your most spectacular plays."[63] That a television segment featuring top plays and a montage of highlights was adapted and incorporated into a sports video game provides compelling evidence of the highlight form's importance. Additionally, the intertextuality between a game and a real television program (i.e., *SportsCenter*) illustrated the ESPN-Disney reliance on synergy and cross-promotion.

ESPN was also quick to enhance its use of video highlights at its Web site with a technology called ESPN Motion. While most Web sites were offering video clips of news segments, sports highlights or music videos, the clips appeared in a separate window apart from the main body of the site.[64] ESPN's approach involved a program that activated the graphic box in the center of the ESPN.com home page to play a video clip of game highlights associated with its lead story. The program allowed the video to start more quickly and have greater quality than streaming video, which downloaded only after initiated by users.[65] Additionally, the video remained an integral part of the home page rather than an appendage. Even though users had to download the ESPN Motion program and watch the ads that accompanied the video highlights, the technology marked for G.M. O'Connell, chairman of Modem Media, a significant "tour de force" for users, and for the marketing community "it's a kind of tour de interesting possibility."[66] O'Connell added that attracting advertisers who had previously been ambivalent about the Web was predicated on utilizing the Internet's own technological advantages rather than duplicating what older media already did. The ESPN viewer performed well enough that ESPN began selling it regularly to its television advertisers, signing Gatorade and Lexus, among others. ESPN charged advertisers up to $25 per 1,000 people who watched its Web commercials, CNET reported. While some criticized ESPN for shifting its focus from sports information to cross-marketing their television shows, magazine and the ESPN brand, ESPN Motion was only the first of several advancements in new media. These included ESPN 360, the short-lived ESPN Mobile, and ESPN High Definition (HD). All of these delivery systems were developed to accomplish the network's goal of shaping its brand reputation as the worldwide leader in sports or the world's biggest sports fan, securing consumer loyalty across the entire range of media touch points rather than through individual transactions.[67]

Broadband

Even though a segment of the 18–34 male demographic abandoned appointment television for the Internet, the group did not completely forsake sportscasts. In fact, sports sites ranked third among the Internet content sites with the highest concentration of male visitors, trailing only pornographic and music sites.[68] According to figures from comScore Media Metrix, young men tend to gravitate toward sites frequented by other young men. For example, they were 36 percent more likely to spend time at Web sites devoted to computer games than the general Internet population, and nearly 50 percent more likely to visit sport sites.[69] While many enjoyed playing sports video games, others paid for a subscription to stream audio and video sports Webcasts. In 2002, more than 200,000 people paid $14.95 for the complete season to listen to online radio broadcasts of baseball games and watch video of game highlights, making baseball the most popular paid Webcasting service.[70] The following year, baseball became the first major league sport to broadcast live video feeds online for a major portion of its games.

As new computers were loaded with the latest software and connected to high-speed broadband, the quality of video clips improved considerably. The use of free basketball highlights on NBA.com increased 500 percent in the 2002–2003 season, prompting the league to offer game highlights and other programming from its new NBA television network as part of a $9.95 monthly service.[71] The major sports were not alone in offering subscription packages. RealNetworks offered "Surfing Live," a service that showed classic surfing videos and live Webcasts of the waves at Banzai Pipeline and other beaches in Hawaii.[72] Other services complemented network broadcasts of events. NASCAR's "TrackPass" offered a service through RealNetworks that provided subscribers with instrument readings and radio transmissions between a driver and crew chief, and its "PitCommand" used Global Positioning System (GPS) to follow cars on the track.[73]

In April 2004, EarthLink, a leading Internet Service Provider, launched its EarthLink Premium Sports package, the most comprehensive sports premium product offered on the Internet. The new service bundled sports video and audio, including content from NASCAR, MLB, the NHL and college sports, along with fantasy sports games and information. Powered by Synacor's existing relationships with a variety of popular fee-based online services, the platform enabled all the content that made up EarthLink Premium Sports to be fully integrated and available through a single sign-in and interface.[74] Among the bundled content was "NHL Highlight Machine," which allowed subscribers to create their own video portfolio of players to track, create and store their own ultimate highlight reel and keep track of fantasy teams by watching them in action and tracking their statistics.[75]

MLB Advanced Media, the interactive media and Internet company of MLB, was established in 2000 through a strategic technology alliance with Sun Microsystems. At MLB.com, visitors were offered more than 1 billion minutes of streaming media and over 2,430 full-length games per season to over 1 billion visitors.[76] By providing every out-of-market game live, as well as game highlights, previews, scores and statistics, MLB's site became the Internet's most successful broadband Web portal devoted to professional sports. The site averaged 6 million daily visitors and 10 million daily page views, with a record-breaking 90 million views delivered during Game Seven of the 2004 American League Championship Series between the New York Yankees and Boston Red Sox.[77] While most of the other major leagues offered streaming video highlights and live coverage of games with streaming audio, MLB's video pay packages set the standard in terms of accessibility.

ESPN began offering online Webcasts of sporting events as premium Internet programming in January 2005 with an all-access weekend for the *Winter X Games*. ESPN 360 was marketed as "an always-on application that provides sports content directly to your computer, including live sportscasts, on-demand video, interactive games, event coverage, news analysis and more."[78] Rather than offering it directly to consumers, however, ESPN offered it through Internet providers, who had to pay special fees for the right to carry it in the same way that cable operators pay the Disney company to carry ESPN's various television channels (e.g., ESPN, ESPN2, ESPNEWS, ESPN Classic). Consumer groups expressed concern that the adoption of a cable television model, which forced Internet providers to pay for the service, would lead to higher prices for consumers, who invariably pay for premium services they do not necessarily want.[79]

In March 2005, ESPN 360 broadcast 22 live events over a 22-day span, including college basketball games, college hockey games, two wrestling matches, plus a dual-screen presentation of an IndyCar Series race, taken from ESPN's linear networks, and a SuperCross event. The veritable blitz came at the exact time when operators were "in a dog fight with digital subscriber line providers for high-speed customers."[80] It also meant that ESPN had to go back to the NCAA to renegotiate online rights. Securing those rights engendered reasons for creating new and different advertising models, including the use of hot spots inside video wherein consumers could click on that hot spot and connect to that product at the advertiser's site.[81]

By April 2006, ESPN 360 was available in 8 million homes and had already built up a library of 5,000 videos. It was incorporated into what ESPN called its "full circle" coverage of certain sportscasts. First employed for the Duke–North Carolina men's basketball game in March and again for the first game of the 2006 NBA playoff series between the Miami Heat and the Chicago Bulls, "full circle coverage" involved traditional cable television coverage with live commentators on ESPN. ESPN2 carried the same game from an above-the-rim perspective with commentary provided by ESPN's NBA analysts in a New York studio. ESPN 360 provided a live stream of ESPN's coverage, and ESPN Radio and ESPNEWS offered frequent updates.[82] Such overkill for a first-round playoff game between a 2-seed and a 7-seed served as an indication of what ESPN was planning for its coverage of *Monday Night Football* later that fall. John Skipper, head of content, said at a presentation that ESPN "will take over the host city. We want fans to think about [the game] all day across all of our platforms."[83]

Wireless

Wireless cell phone companies began providing sports content in 2002 when Verizon and FOXSports.com joined with ActiveSky to present live sporting events, news and highlights to Internet-enabled cell phones for a monthly fee.[84] ActiveSky created the program that integrated visual action, sound, text and low-tech graphics in a facsimile of a live sports broadcast, enabling live coverage of baseball-game broadcasts in which tiny icons move around a color diamond while a box score and running text provide real-time updates on the game.[85] The service, available to Verizon's "Get It Now" customers for $3.99 a month, also provided gamecasts of football and basketball games, as well as text updates for NASCAR races. As the *New York Times'* Marc Weingarten noted, "While the service may be useful only to full-fledged sports fanatics, it's at least a baby step toward the integration of wireless technology with entertainment content."[86]

The full integration of wireless technology with entertainment content was realized with the development of so-called third generation, or 3G, networks that doubled the capacity from 150 kilobits to 300 kilobits of data per second.[87] Handsets had to have an add-on called EV-DO to run the service, which Verizon called VCAST, that included "more than 300 daily video clips from channels and shows like CNN, NBC, ESPN and *Sesame Street*."[88] Carriers like Verizon, Cingular, and Sprint also offered pay packages that allowed subscribers to receive music, television and mobile Web access. Verizon's VCAST included the ESPN MVP service, which provided live gamecasts, the latest highlights on demand, real-time game updates, fantasy team updates and exclusive ESPN programming, including programming like *SportsCenter, Pardon the Interruption*, and *Around the Horn*.[89]

Verizon also offered premium sports programming from Setanta Sports North America, the only dedicated European sports and rugby channel in North America. In 2007, Verizon and Setanta offered a pay-package of the Rugby World Cup highlight footage to VCAST video customers. Even though live gamecasts were not available, subscribers received up to eight highlight clips from each televised match, "including the hardest hits and final scores,"[90] as well as pre-show video clips that highlighted classic matches from the tournament's inception to the latest championship. Additionally, in November 2007, Verizon and the NHL announced the launch of NHL game video alerts, "enabling hockey fans to receive video messages of game highlights on their mobile phones, moments after they happen on the ice."[91] In what was marketed as a first for all professional sports leagues, the NHL teamed with Verizon to capitalize on the concept of immediacy by providing subscribers to the $2.99 per month/per team package with the latest scores and highlights, totally by-passing news organizations.[92] Spokespersons for both Verizon and the NHL emphasized immediacy in the news release announcing the deal. Significantly, these deals clearly illustrate the altered mediascape in which providers of sports content attempt to reach fans whenever they can and wherever the fans happen to be. Only by offering customers sports gamecasts and highlight packages on every device can they compete in the marketplace while demonstrating how highlights have become a saleable commodity to attract customers.

High Definition

Although the professional sports leagues diversified their delivery systems, they were still largely dependent on the rights fees from broadcast and cable networks as a main source of revenue. Television still provided the largest segment of the audience that in turn attracted the most lucrative advertisers and sponsors. That reality forced the networks to enhance production values of sports programming coverage in an attempt to forestall dwindling ratings. Some refined existing technologies, others added to the production repertoire. For example, in 1998 ESPN debuted Sportsvision Incorporated's yellow electronic first-down line on its *Sunday Night Football* telecasts, and each of the networks offered a similar technology the following year.[93]

Such an innovation pales in comparison to the network's deployment of high definition television (HDTV). Since the technology's introduction in 2003, ESPN HD and ESPN2 HD certainly became the crown jewels of ESPN's technological initiatives. Although some analysts forecasted that HDTV would be a terribly expensive flop, those predictions echoed similar warnings before radio boomed in the 1920s and television took hold in the 1940s, sports programming helping to attract buyers of the sets.[94] Sports action was perfectly suited for what digital does best: namely, provide video and audio that together offer a sharper, clearer and larger than life quality. The Consumer Electronics Association accurately predicted that the number of high definition television sets sold in 2006 would match or exceed that of standard definition television sets, clearly indicating that HDTV was on its way to public acceptance.

ESPN built its HD repertoire around a triad of programming—most notably, a considerable number of remote events launched on March 30, 2003, with a *Sunday Night Baseball* telecast. The numbers grew steadily from 144 events in the first 12 months to 184 events in 2004 to over 400 events plus more than 2,000 programs representing more than 6,000 hours in 2005, bolstered by the addition of ESPN 2 HD, which broadcast its first program on January 5, 2005.[95] The second component of ESPN's triad evolved from studio programming at its Digital Center in Bristol, Connecticut. This state-of-the-art facility opened June 7, 2004, with the first telecast of *SportsCenter* in HD. With over 6 million feet of cable and three HDTV studios totaling 17,000 square feet, the Digital Center facilitated the network's transition of its most popular programs to high definition, including *NFL Countdown*, *NFL Primetime*, *Baseball Tonight* and *NFL Live* as well as the news and information programming built around game coverage. Programs from ESPN Original Entertainment (EOE) such as *Playmakers* and *TILT* constituted the third tributary to the flow of

HD programs. These offerings have spearheaded ESPN's initiative to become the self-proclaimed "Worldwide Leader in HDTV."[96]

The Digital Center was designed to provide employees across all ESPN entities access to footage from any company computer in the world. This tapeless concept, or Liquid Edit, provided the ability to select and edit high or standard definition video, eliminating the time-consuming process of searching for tapes. As noted at its Web site, "For the first time in ESPN's history, events can be simultaneously recorded while at the same time the content can be annotated, edited and taken to air without handling video tape."[97] ESPN's coverage of all 64 games of the 2006 World Cup Soccer tournament was broadcast in HD. With five times more detail than analog, with a film-like 16:9 ratio perspective instead of 4:3 of standard definition, and with six-channel surround sound, HD not only eliminated ghosts, static, snow and poor quality video, but it was perfectly suited to the wide-angle perspective of most field sports. Given the propensity of its news shows for showing game highlights, ESPN has already begun the process of embossing its imprimatur on what the HD sportscast is supposed to look and sound like.

ESPN was not alone in enhancing production values. CBS's telecast of the 2001 Super Bowl introduced EyeVision, a new instant-replay technology developed by the Robotics Institute at Carnegie Mellon University that utilized 33 robotic cameras, DVD technical backup and 90,000 feet of fiber-optic cable that could offer rotating 270-degree views of players with stop-action shots from simultaneous angles.[98] A camera operator panned and focused the cameras at the same point on the field to produce rotating three-dimensional-like pictures that offered purportedly conclusive evidence about on-field decisions. Although CBS planned to lease the robotics replay system to other networks for $50,000–$75,000 an event, the technology proved too expensive for regular use.[99] The networks' continued reliance on action replays was evidenced in coverage of NFL playoff games, which in 2004 were used for almost 70 percent of the plays (i.e., 161 plays, 111 replays), a figure which does not include lead-in and cut-away montages or promotional messages.[100] So prevalent have replays become that they constitute an entity unto themselves, a form of remediated content. In a *New York Times* article about the amount of action during the telecast of a football game, Richard Sandomir noted, "One could argue that replays constitute an alternate form of action because they show what you just saw but this time at slower speeds or from different angles. So if one figures that each replay takes 5 seconds, the amount of action in Indianapolis's triumph would soar by 11 minutes."[101]

Control

In attempting to maintain control of sports content, the professional sports leagues enacted a series of legal barriers impeding the transmission and use of play-by-play coverage of games, as well as the use of still and moving images. In 1997, a federal appeals court ruled "that the National Basketball Association could not block Motorola and a paging company from sending real-time scores and plays to subscribers."[102] In 2001, MLB attempted to impose restrictions on the number of pictures that sports journalists sent out "while the game was in progress and how those photographs can be used after the initial news coverage."[103] Those restrictions were contained in the credentials reporters and photographers signed and carried to get access to ballparks. When several newspapers balked at the restrictions, preferring not to cover the games rather than accept the restrictions, MLB backed off by allowing reporters to transmit "historic" information, meaning "the progress of a quest for a significant record"[104] as it happened. In addition, news organizations were allowed to post up to seven photographs on their Web sites while a game was in progress.

More significantly, in 2006 the NFL banned local television cameras from sidelines during games in order "to protect one of the leagues' greatest assets—highlights of game action."[105] The NFL claimed that the policy was consistent with what other sports leagues and organizations were doing and that banning local television stations would not impact viewers because the stations retained access to all footage shot by the national network telecasting the game. The stations countered that the ban limited their ability to capture "the local flavor of games, such as low-level camera shots, isolated film on players for feature stories, or pictures of the crowd."[106] The issue has economic implications, for tighter control of the rights to highlights ultimately makes them more valuable. Directly related to the issue was the tremendous economic potential of video highlights as content for the Web and mobile devices. After considerable criticism, the NFL relented and allowed coverage by one "pool" crew to shoot footage, and the following year the NFL changed the policy so that up to five local camera crews from each team's market were granted sideline access.[107]

That video highlights constituted content with direct economic value became evident the following year when the NFL imposed a restriction of 45 seconds of video and audio clips per day of team personnel at team facilities on Web sites of news organizations not affiliated with the NFL. Having seized control of its Web site from CBS Sportsline in 2006, the NFL re-launched the site offering the one thing that other websites could not: "highlights from games that can be tailored to focus on each fan's favorite players and teams."[108] As USA TODAY's Michael McCarthy reported, before the restriction of 45 seconds, Web sites were free to post a reasonable amount of video highlights and streaming video from a team's facilities. McCarthy explained that the change in policy reflected the NFL's belief that the presence of NFL video highlights was a way to attract advertisers to a Web site. Organizations like the American Society of Newspaper Editors (ASNE) and the Radio-Television News Directors Association decried the restriction as a way of diverting people from their Web sites to NFL.com. They argued that press restrictions were part of an overall strategy by the NFL to control its image by controlling the media's access.

The strategy has also been employed by individual teams like the Washington Redskins, whose owner Daniel Snyder has created "his own news coverage of the Redskins and team-produced programming,"[109] which is sold to local television stations. The team has also denied local newspapers such as the *Washington Post* the right to run online video clips. By creating their own broadcasting and Webcasting entities (e.g., NFL Network, NBA TV, MLB Channel), professional sports leagues have entered into direct competition with the media for advertising revenue. The leagues' media push also raises important questions about unbiased coverage. As McCarthy noted, "Such league-owned outlets can give fans access to players and teams that traditional media aren't granted—while casting news, and controversies, on the league's terms."[110]

At the other end of the spectrum, local television stations have begun soliciting viewers to send them highlights of games they are unable to cover, which are then posted at the station's Web site. With the proliferation of digital cameras, almost anyone can capture game highlights that can then be uploaded onto a computer and disseminated to news organizations' Web sites or to YouTube, the great clearinghouse for every kind of sports highlight imaginable. Many of the professional leagues' daily highlight packages like the NBA's *The Daily Zap* end up on YouTube. Few news organizations bother to prohibit content from ending up on YouTube, since the site provides additional exposure for the leagues and broadcasters.

Conclusion

"Any pipe. Any device."[111] That was the mantra voiced by then ESPN and ABC Sports president George Bodenheimer when discussing the network's philosophy about the development of new media technologies. Speaking at the UBS Global Media Conference, Bodenheimer articulated what has become clear to industry insiders, media critics and scholars over the past decade: that when it comes to sportscasting, neither the broadcast networks nor the cable networks can afford to operate in television alone. Any network involved in sportscasting necessarily must present itself as a total sports media entity, which includes utilizing radio, television, game players, Internet and mobile phone technologies to send out both the accounts and descriptions of live event coverage and infotainment packages that include scores, highlights, interviews and other features related to actual and fantasy sports teams and leagues.

Recent initiatives by broadcasters, mobile phone companies and the professional sports leagues certainly bear this out. For example, in January 2008, *Advertising Age* reported that on several days in the fall of 2007 ESPN "had more visits to the NFL content on its mobile-phone website than it did to the same area on its PC [personal computer] website."[112] The same trend was documented in Europe by M:Metrics, a mobile-measurement firm, that conducted a study over the previous two years showing "the mobile audience looking up sports information on mobile devices increased significantly around major events,"[113] the most significant of which was England's Football Association (FA) Premier League.

The only way to do that was, in sports parlance, through a "Full Court" press, which, coincidentally, happened to be the name of an early ESPN pay-per-view packages. By providing content on home television, on the radio, on the computer, on mobile phones, on video game players, and even at their own restaurants, networks like ESPN have created a type of total sport saturation, which removes the impediments of space and time, although this same freeing can become disruptive.[114] Accessing ESPN, FOX, CBS or the NFL anytime and anywhere has provided the sports fan with an ever-expanding potential for self-expression and an increasing repertoire of sports discourse, yet total saturation in attending to sports leads to total desire. While the technology of social saturation removes the impediments of space and time, this same freeing "ironically leads to a form of enslavement."[115] ESPN's foray into new delivery systems led *Fortune* senior writer Marc Gunther to conjecture that soon to come will be "a tiny ESPN alarm clock, to be implanted in a fan's ear, so that he or she can be awakened each morning with scores and highlights of late games from the night before."[116]

Perhaps total saturation is not as far away as one would think. Despite the growth of broadband connections in homes, usage still spikes during the workday, or, put another way, as soon as the diehard sport fan leaves the television and can get to a computer.[117] What new and traditional media have created with the technological innovations and new consumer protocols is a communication system that generates what Manual Castells calls the culture of real virtuality. Castells defines that system as one in which "all messages of all kinds become enclosed in the medium, because the medium has become so comprehensive, so diversified, so malleable, that it absorbs in the same multimedia text the whole of human experience, past, present, and future."[118] One of the features of this multimedia culture is that the communication of all kinds of messages in the same system induces an integration of all messages in a common cognitive pattern. Today's communication system captures, in this case, sport reality in its entirety so that the user, an audience of one, becomes fully immersed in a virtual image setting in which appearances are not just images on the screen through which experience is communicated, but they become the experience itself.[119]

CHAPTER 9

Replay and the Façade of Certitude

Pitana's Dance

In the first half of the 2018 FIFA World Cup final match between France and Croatia, referee Néstor Pitana drew a rectangle with his hands signaling for replay, after having been alerted via headset by the video assistant referee (VAR), who is charged with advising the match referee. In the moments leading to Pitana's decision to invoke replay, several French players pointed to Croatian winger Ivan Perisic, who appeared to have touched the ball with his hand in the penalty area deflecting it out of play. Given this momentary break, Pitana did not immediately acknowledge an infraction and seemed instead to point for a corner kick, despite French players pleading for a handball (as only *les Bleus* can). A handball infraction in the penalty area may result in a penalty kick, if the handball is ruled to be deliberate, so the call was crucial. Did the defender deliberately move his hand or was he hit on the hand with an "unexpected ball" from a point-blank shot with little distance between opponents?[1] By invoking replay, Pitana chose to utilize VAR protocols to make his decision, marking the first time VAR was utilized in a World Cup final match. Coincidentally, Pitana had invoked replay for the very first time in a World Cup tournament during the opening match between 2018 host Russia and Saudi Arabia. The referee can use technology to determine a decision only if one of two eventualities occurred: (a) a clear and obvious error and (b) a serious missed incident. Here was an application of replay to determine whether a penalty had occurred, the HD visual evidence slowed down to be crystal clear.

Pitana followed recommended protocols by first waving off French players, who, by rule, should not attempt to influence or interfere with the review process, and then by drawing the rectangle symbolizing a television screen.[2] After reviewing two different replays at the monitor, Pitana communicated his final decision by pointing decisively to the penalty box for a penalty kick. Replay provided Pitana with the answer about whether a handball had occurred; the ball definitely hit Perisic's hand. As to whether Perisic's hand had moved toward the ball, which, according to the rule, makes it deliberate, the video evidence confirmed movement. Pitana determined the movement was indeed intentional because Perisic's hand moved in a direction counter to his body's movement. After the successful PK, France held a 2–1 lead, both goals indirectly the result of referee decisions.

At halftime, BBC commentator Alan Shearer decried the "ridiculous decision"[3] that ultimately turned the match into a foregone conclusion when France scored two quick goals in the second half. The reviews from sportscasters, analysts, and especially fans of the Croatian side were quite clear; Pitana, the former actor, was panned as inept, and VAR failed in FIFA's most important game, reigniting debate regarding its use. Not surprisingly, at its annual general meeting in March 2019, the International Football Association Board (IFAB) proposed changes "to provide a more precise and detailed definition for what constitutes handball, in particular with regard to the occasions when a nondeliberate/accidental handball will be penalized."[4]

Replay is supposed to provide visual representation to explain a written rule, which, because of its linguistic nature, is necessarily subject to interpretation. Pitana's dash to the sideline and his two-step shuffle in the review area set in motion a discursive chain that connects ontological authority and the pursuit of transparency, certitude, and integrity within a set of communicative logics articulated in today's high-definition sport media commercial complex.[5] Replay, unfortunately, is no panacea for solving vexing questions regarding player intent, regardless of the technology's specificity in showing clear images. Nor can it repair the self-inflicted damage done by FIFA's Executive Committee in awarding World Cups to Russia and Qatar at that fateful convention when the hopes of England and the United States were dashed by Sepp Blatter's band of merry men and the infamous stuffed brown envelopes.[6]

This chapter contextualizes replay within the discourse of sport media, unpacking how it functions as part of sport adjudication, a specialized discourse that constitutes arguably the most compelling yet contentious aspect of the live sportscast. Considerable scholarship has explicated how replay impacts perceptual-cognitive functions, how technologies have been used to enhance sport presentations, and how scientificity and rationality were applied to analytics to change athletic training and specialization. Far less has been done to contextualize replay as constituted by and constitutive of sport media discourse, due in part to its relatively recent deployment by sport leagues and organizations. That deployment, however, supports the values underpinning scientificity, authority, objectivity, and certainty, first realized through the development of sophisticated cameras and timing devices.[7] As sportscasts included more in-game, slow-motion replays that showed obvious officiating errors, a tsunami of criticism inundated officials, leagues, and organizations, precipitating calls for adoption of more technology to remedy obvious errors. Technology remedies invariably arrive with potential problems related to unanticipated consequences, discursive breakdowns, and coded bias in algorithms.

Generally, replay has rule-bound, affective, and informational dimensions, aligned with the disparate ways it is deployed and repurposed throughout the sportscast. Given sport media's key locus within the entertainment industry, the use of replay is a key technological innovation that has brought even more consolidation and coordination between sport media, sport leagues and organizations, as well as gambling/gaming operators. Replay is media's contribution to maintaining the veneer of integrity, promulgating "presumptive justice,"[8] the notion that the outcomes are fair, that justice has been served, and that the outcome was not fixed. Although scholarship has focused on the history of replay in sportscasts dating back to the last decade of the nineteenth century, it is important to analyze how that discourse has evolved into the highly charged narratives that dominate within a culture attuned to highlights. Analysis of replay provides an opportunity to interrogate whose interests are being served and consolidated in the mobilization of this technology within affective economics that satisfy a twenty-first-century neoliberal sensibility. However, these logics existed under both capitalist and communist economic systems with accompanying ideological messaging about how to develop and train world class athletes.[9]

The area in which replay has had the greatest impact is officiating. Replay resides at the intersection of the jurisprudence of sport and sport media production, challenging the ontological authority of field officials who cede part of their epistemological privileges—superior view and specialist skills—to VAR officials, who use technology to slow the action and get a clearer view.[10] Replay not only shifts part of the responsibility for adjudication from the field to a video operations room, but it also requires officials to be trained in reviewing and analyzing video, to use replay as an evaluation tool, and to instruct players and coaches about rule changes. Lastly, replay has become an important option for sport media to protect their vested financial interests in owning the rights to broadcast by providing the façade of certitude. By imagining that media can guarantee the integrity of the game, replay has become "a false idol of error-free measurement, and its counterpart, false transparency."[11] Photography was used to settle disputes, born of the idea that the camera is truer than the eye, had no interest in the content it revealed, and took neither side in any dispute. This led to a tacit acceptance of media determinism, which holds that the viewing public of sport demands clarity and virtuousness to right wrongs and impose justice. Once the temple has been erected, it becomes increasingly difficult to take down. As the ubiquity of technology sends us deeper into an interactive mediascape whose circuitry of entertainment, advertising, and surveillance relies on affect and algorithms as part of its infrastructure, replay can be seen as sport media's latest attempt to maintain the integrity of the game in light of its primary motive, profit. Little wonder that FIFA, like the IOC, has credibility issues when denying charges of corruption, especially after the U.S. Department of Justice indicted nine members of FIFA and five corporate executives, charging them with racketeering, wire fraud and money laundering conspiracies, among other offenses.[12]

Replay and Remediation

The foundation of remediation is rooted in poststructuralist literary theory that argues all interpretation is reinterpretation; any act of mediation is dependent on previous acts of mediation.[13] As a significant part of a live sportscast, replay functions within and beyond that liveness, a concept that remains part of the theoretical scaffolding of sport media.[14] On the one hand, the primary function that defines replay is its use in the appellate process of adjudication within a sporting event. A more generic function of replay is the decontextualized representation of a play, the sportscast highlight form, also referred to as "the highlight reel,"[15] the "action replay,"[16] and most commonly "instant replay."[17] Essentially, a highlight is created in the editing process of interrupting the flow of a live sportscast to interject or replay a previous part of the sportscast. Of course, there is nothing instantaneous about replay, and though editors can find, isolate, decontextualize, and recontextualize replays very quickly, narrative continuity is necessarily interrupted for commentary and analysis.[18] In-game replays are repurposed and redeployed for use as montages to transition into and out of commercial breaks or as packages that analysts can break down and discuss by translating the visual images into descriptions of technique, strategy, and context. Of course, not every replay contains action, evidenced by the importance of the reaction shot. Although the term highlight has gained foothold in popular culture and is used in a range of non-sport broadcasts from reality programs to cooking contests, every highlight does not necessarily live up to its dictionary or technical definitions: "an outstanding part of an event or period of time" or "aesthetics of the instant."[19]

Repurposing is arguably the most important component of remediation, based on the principle that media must constantly be developing and disseminating content in order to gather data through its many convergent platforms.[20] Sport media in particular must supplement what is available from the live broadcast, and the greatest part of that is generated by in-studio and on-location analysis and prepackaged video sequences featuring the athletes, the coaches, the stadium, elements that constitute a sport spectacle.[21] To maintain popular acceptance, and therefore economic success, sport media must convince consumers that their sportscast "improves on the experience of older ones."[22] Similarly, the entertainment industry's understanding and application of remediation as repurposing reveals the inseparability of the economic from the social and cultural context.[23] In both functions of replay—as adjudication and as decontextualized replay—the repurposing of edited content is an act of remediation, not only identifying that which is needed to represent the meaning of a rule/law, but also decontextualizing it from spatial and temporal orientation in the broadcast flow for use in another context.

In terms of adjudication, replay is invoked when either the match referee or the VAR decide that a play must be reviewed, setting in motion established protocols. Significantly, at least in the case of FIFA matches, VAR has independent access to, and replay control of, television broadcast footage.[24] Independent access and control does not, however, keep the media from showing the same content to fans in the stadium/arena on liquid crystal display (LCD) screens, as well as to viewers watching or streaming the sportscast via television, personal computer, or mobile device.

Replay is the visual representation of a verbal representation and as such, an actualization of remediation. On- and off-field officials look at segments of the high-definition television digitally captured representation from one or more camera angles; the referee must then interpret what that representation reveals in the context of a written rule or determine with complete exactness a boundary issue and weigh that against what the assistant officials experienced—what they saw. Usually by the time the referee's decision is rendered, those in the stadium or accessing the sportscast/stream have already seen the play from every available angle and have made their own assessment of what the replay shows. Only when the referee provides the decision by giving the signal of goal, penalty, or red card is the replay fully constituted and immediately reenters the sportscast's discursive flow as decisive information. In effect, it becomes what is next analyzed, discussed, re-replayed through many different iterations, depending on the direct impact the decision has on the outcome of the contest.[25]

As an example of remediation's potential to exert undue influence and to make field officials temporarily redundant, replay functions to not only resolve disputes and provide justice, but also to satisfy the need for transparent justice.[26] The media and the sport leagues have reaffirmed a contractual dependency for their cultural significance. The rule may be in print, yet it is the visual representation that establishes the legitimacy of the referee's call. FIFA's referees must translate the decision into a signal to communicate the decision, comparable with the set of hand gestures used by major league baseball umpires. Referees in the National Football League and National Hockey League render their verdicts over the arena's public address system and enter the sportscast directly, breaking through the fifth wall and adding dramatic effect. That signal or oral explanation is an appeal to authenticity, bringing the logics of immediacy and transparency together.[27] In addition to its discursive function of providing a definitive interpretation of a rule, replay creates a multidimensional temporality as a specialized fragment that reconstitutes the sportscast flow, superimposed onto the liveness, which must be recharacterized as a result the referee's on-field decision.

As an example of remediation, replay is charged with providing a technological exactness to ensure that sporting event outcomes can be fairly enacted, the result of the players' actions and not a referee's error. Sport's quest for certitude certainly predates HDTV, but as the presence of cameras increased and more visuals were shown that the importance of technology only increased. Because of the exorbitant costs to stage these sport spectacles, sport organizations and sport media agreed to incorporate replay into the adjudication process to protect their vested interests in creating a spectacular event with integrity and fair play. The magnitude of the spectacle demands accountability, which must be at once precise, efficient, and trustworthy. As *New York Times* sports journalist Dave Anderson noted, "In any sport, nothing is as important as the correct call."[28] The quest for the correct call is fundamental to sport media's mandate to deliver authenticity, the concept that "the experience of the medium is itself the experience of the real."[29]

The appeal to authenticity of experience is what brings the aspects of immediacy and opacity together in the logic of remediation. That is not to say, however, that all viewers experience replays in the same way. Obviously, with any controversial call and the resulting decision, fans of the team/player negatively impacted by replay draw, at times, a completely different conclusion from those whom the replay benefited. Replay does not completely blot out bias, injustice, and ill will, and losing fans are often quick to blame technology. As Mark Andrejevic aptly notes, "There is nothing particularly new about people dismissing evidence that does not accord with their commitments and beliefs—or finding ways of rationalizing and explaining the discrepancy through recourse to the very logics they have discredited."[30] Arguably, fans can blame their own dissatisfaction with officiating errors for replay's deployment. Sport media and the sporting organizations attempted to forestall criticism of game officials with limited replay after a generation of fans, nurtured on a plenitude of slow-motion sport highlights, demanded change. The attempt to create an aura of infallibility came with unexpected conditions that complicated the decision making, akin to mathematical monsters like the Mandelbrot set and Koch's curve, with their endless iterations of fractal geometry revealing infinite variations.[31]

Replay, Affective Economies, and the Highlight Culture

As an aesthetic principle, replay has historically been utilized in film, radio, and television, enabling producers to create the representation of a live event for presentation to an audience at another time. To capture an event required cameras equipped with enough film to record not merely a moment in time as in a still image but some part of an ongoing event. Limitations forced newsreel camera operators to routinize what constituted information that could be packaged as infotainment. To provide the viewer atomized bits of important sporting events, newsreels relied on synecdoche—in which a part represents the whole—to create a sporting discourse that reached a wider audience than any other sport media. Newsreels dominated from 1911 to 1967, when the last newsreel gave way to television.[32] Accomplishing the goal of time shifting to create highlights required technological developments and a set of normative practices to make them comprehensible and meaningful to viewers.

The change from magnetic wire to magnetic tape with its distinct improvements in sound quality and increased playing time was the breakthrough that ultimately engendered the in-game sport highlight. Developed by engineers at *Allgemeine Elektricitats Gesellschaft*, the German division of General Electric, magnetic tape technology became one of most lucrative spoils of war that U.S. military personnel brought back from Europe after World War II.[33] Popular American singer Bing Crosby is credited with being the first entertainer to record his radio show and to play the recording for broadcast in the western time zones of the United States.[34] Time shifting gave new meaning to liveness, the most prominent characteristic of early radio programming. A decade later engineers developed a machine that used magnetic tape to capture dual audio and video tracks of a live television program. When the Ampex Corporation developed the Mark IV videotape machine in 1956, CBS became the first U.S. television network to time shift its nightly newscast, *Douglas Edwards and the CBS News*, for West Coast audiences. However, the singular event that established videotape's importance in television's ascendency as the public's medium for news was the murder of Lee Harvey Oswald, broadcast live on the Sunday following the assassination of John F. Kennedy on November 22, 1963, in Dallas, Texas.

> The incessant replaying of this shocking event attests to the pervasiveness of magnetic technologies in news broadcasting as early as 1963. Moreover, the fact that this event is roughly concurrent with one of the earlier sports-broadcast uses of replay indicates that the instant replay resonated culturally far beyond the sports arena.[35]

That event was the Army–Navy college football game, which was scheduled for November 23 but delayed until December 7 because of the assassination. The ability to capture live images for immediate replay drastically altered perceptions of time and space, but viewers adapted to the fragmentation of linear narrative forms within live broadcasting, accustomed to such manipulation in popular fictional films.

Replay's impact on sportscasts was significant, resulting in considerable deformation.[36] Not only is the overall geometry of the game altered in the camera's myopic gaze, but the television screen becomes a canvas on which multiple, fragmented images are displayed. No longer subject to the restraints of time or place, highlights from an event generate an endless supply of decontextualized images to promote brand image, upcoming programming events, and fodder for analysis, gaming, and betting. As Rowe argues, "A single sports 'live' TV broadcast can be shown in 'real time' and endlessly afterwards, and can be cut up and packaged in myriad ways, with its soundtrack separated from its visual images, so that both can be continually manipulated and reproduced."[37] Repurposing provides sport media with an almost endless supply of content to disseminate across an assemblage of digital platforms.

The hyper-marketing of an event to which a broadcaster owns the rights is part of the strategy to guarantee that it can provide a large audience to warrant high advertising fees. In this sense, highlights harness the power of emotions in stimulating and sustaining viewer interest around spectacular athletic achievement. The surfeit of highlights allows media producers to generate not only the master narratives that underpin representational models of reality, but also visceral shortcuts that distill the agony and ecstasy of sport into shared emotions. As Sarah Ahmed notes, within affective economics, "emotions do things, and they align individuals with communities—or bodily space with social space—through the very intensity of their attachments. Rather than seeing emotions as psychological dispositions, we need to consider how they work, in concrete and particular ways, to mediate the relationship between the psychic and the social, and between the individual and the collective."[38] Sportscast discourses fuse the mundane recitation of facts with hyperbolic celebrations of exceptionality, guile, strength, courage, timing, and so on, to produce a symbiosis of high-performance sport and its mediatization as reality entertainment by attempting to steer clear of ideological, political, and cultural disconnects.

In-game replays allow for the analysis and appreciation of complicated choreography, the nuances of which were normally inaccessible to view. In-game replays also present the commentator(s), coaches, and physiologists with ample data to analyze individual performance. This capacity to harvest analytic data has justifiably lent special effects innovations and the accompanying discourse an aura of scientificity. Sportscasts added the expert commentator whose role is based upon demonstrated expertise in the game, most often an ex-player or ex-manager who has experiential knowledge not obvious to nonparticipants. Having a panel of experts became a standard feature for pregame prognostications and the postgame dissections. Invariably, with more slow-motion replays came more disputes related to officiating. The 2018 World Cup final match was no different in that regard.

Not only did the emergence of cable television engender a plethora of social, legal, and economic changes to the sport media commercial complex, but the cable networks also altered the texture, perceptions, and images of sports for both stadium fans and television viewers by providing a plethora of special effects and CGI. With more technology at their disposal, broadcast, cable, league, and sport-specific networks presented live sportscasts and sport news programming as entertainment to satisfy an audience that played digital versions of the sport, created fantasy leagues, and ultimately helped legitimate sport betting in the United States. The interdependency between broadcasters and advertisers resulted in less criticism of contractual partners. Sports journalists increasingly reported on those events being covered by the team's or organization's television station. As the commercial dimension of the sports industry became more substantial, television's view of sport did not significantly change, despite an array of ongoing social problems related to racial justice, gender identity, political ideology, economic equality, and performance-enhancing drugs.[39]

Camera angles, close-ups, slow motion, in-game replays, game summaries, and highlight packages all became pieces of a production model that emphasized immediacy, pace, and affect. Viewers are led to believe that what is presented to them constitutes the natural and universally accepted version of sport. This paradoxical situation occurs as a result of mediated sport becoming a victim of its own appeal. Viewers are implicated in consumerism based on affect. This affective investment "anchors people in particular experiences, practices, identities, meanings and pleasures."[40] Rather than allowing people to satisfy real human needs, the market culture constrains individuals to realize their needs in "mass-produced material packages and professionally approved behavioral scripts."[41]

Sport media's need for the sensational and the spectacular within sporting events attenuates its principles of journalistic authoritativeness by exaggerating the importance of those events, their seriousness, and their dramatic character.[42] The converse is also true. Overwhelming the viewer with sensations extrinsic to the games leads the viewer to expect only the most sensational, in the process bleeding the traditional sporting experience of its capacity "to release people from the ennui of daily life, to inculcate values, or to bind people together."[43] Removed from the context of the actual sporting event, spectacular replays become the means to instant gratification, transferring the excitement from the event to a continual, concentrated sense of exhilaration. By the time the actual sporting event is reproduced as cultural iconography, the principal values associated with the nature and purpose of competition—such as hard work, innovation, cooperation and teamwork, self-determination, self-sacrifice, and an emphasis on sportsmanship—become distorted in the pastiche of imagery and discourses that have no meta-narrative or unified grand theory.

Ultimately, the economics of sport media are aligned with the questions of cultural politics. Because of the exhilaration that accompanies the viewing of a sports spectacle, it is easy to disregard the notion that sporting myths hybridize culture and advertising into new nodes of power.[44] Such power is essentially seductive in motivating viewers to not only consume the images, but also more importantly to satisfy emotional needs. The constant barrage of highlights—before, during, and after—fuels the rush of emotions for viewers who, in turn, use social media platforms to comment about what they are watching, critique sportscasters, and serve as the ultimate arbiters of the officiating. These supra-textual interpretations articulate a digital version of "Kill the umpire!"

Replays and analytical commentary evoke the emotional responses of fans and spectators whose evolving expectations of the game result in greater demand for an authentic experience. In this sense, affect does not reside in the replay, but serves as the by-product of the circulation between image and discourse. The more replays circulate, "the more affective they become, and the more they appear to 'contain' affect."[45] When controversial decisions are made, officials come under intense extensive scrutiny by fans and commentators who have the luxury of replay technologies and who use it to offer harsh criticism on social media. Even though participatory forms of interactivity empower agency in a digital sphere by sharing information through their own social media pages largely do not translate to political and material validation.[46] In point of fact, agency is further undermined by the data being collected and sold. The surveillance society's ultimate goal is data harvesting.

Replay, Officiating, and Ontological Authority

Replay has had an indelible impact on referees, officials, umpires, and judges as well as the ways sporting events are adjudicated. Replay is constituted within the sportscast in phrases like "clear and obvious error" and "serious missed incident" and "incontrovertible visual evidence." Considerable research has established how replay is also used to evaluate the performance of officials,[47] to train officials in decision-making processes,[48] and to provide coaches and players with visual examples of rules and their application.[49] Although sports like tennis, fencing, and swimming rely on technological means to determine touches without human input, FIFA's replay requires interrupting an event's progress to retrieve a representation of what happened.[50] Significantly, in the FIFA final, Pitana looked at the replay once, started to leave the referee review area, and then was prompted to take a second look, to see a different angle of the handball, slowed down enough to show movement in the defender's jump, attempted header, and deflection with his hand. It was only after this second review that Pitana left the referee review area, blew his whistle, and pointed to the penalty box. One journalist suggested that when Pitana took a second look, he was purportedly relying on his acting experience. "Even when he appeared to come to a decision, he quickly spun on the spot and returned to the screen for one quick look, with every second of all that acting experience coming into use as he built the tension to a fever-pitch level."[51] Pitana's dance at the replay video monitor arguably undermined whatever decision he then had "to sell," which is how IFAB describes the protocol of informing a decision. Although VAR-generated replays are to be used for factual decisions, on-field review "can be used for a factual decision if it will help manage the players/match or 'sell' the decision."[52] Pitana's back-and-forth two-step was probably precipitated by what he was hearing in his headset. If he had asked for a second replay, Pitana would have stayed at the monitor. Pitana would only have left the monitor the first time if he had made his decision. Before he could give the signal, however, he stopped and returned to watch something else. In doing so, he immediately left himself open to the criticism that he had waffled, a clear example of the way technology is not supposed to be used. However, viewers voting at the ESPN FC Twitter Poll approved the referee's awarding of a penalty kick by a 53–47 margin.

Wrapped within the sportscast discourse, Pitana's encounter demonstrates how replay momentarily shifts ontological authority—the vested power to make decisions and interpret rules—from the on-field referees and assistants to replay officials, fans, sportscasters, and commentators.[53] Replays shown to viewers rarely provide an accompanying explanation of the rule or how that language is translated into video representation, let alone how the technology works. Considerable scholarship about the use of technological decision-making aids has shown that systems like Hawk-Eye, Close-Call, etc., which show computer-generated graphic representations have a margin of error.[54] The widespread assumption that technology is capable of unerring exactitude can easily lead to false transparency, which creates the impression that "a kind of justice is being done when it is not being done."[55] Regardless of whether replay corrects an officiating mistake or creates a new one, every replay conceivably makes sporting events less entertaining, reduces the pleasure and satisfaction of the spectators, and forces sportscasters into the unnatural role of attorney.[56] Because replay serves as an aid to decision making, and invariably impacts the outcome or perceived justice, scholarship has shown how replays are used in coordination with basic perceptual and cognitive functions.[57]

Replay offers a visual tool to assist officials in learning to manage a game to a high standard with greater economy of effort.[58] To optimize officials' decision-making skills, training is conducted using laboratory settings in which replays of specific game situations are presented. Although the goal is to improve the ways in which visual information is generally registered and processed, and improve perceptual performance in particular, simulations can provide opportunities to complement experience that must be gained in real-time situations. In a similar way, video replays can be shown by league officials to instruct players and coaches how a specific rule will be adjudicated. Instruction around rule changes can assist players' and coaches' understanding of the refereeing philosophy. Referees, coaches, and players benefit by identifying complex rules and their interpretation with video examples from different perspectives, together with an expert's detailed decisions and the reasons underpinning them.[59] Such systematic training not only speeds up development of officials, but also increases player and coach understanding, which may lead to a reduction in controversial incidents. Moreover, coach and player education in the application of the rules can potentially "reduce the number of infringements and lead to more flowing and attractive games."[60]

Replay is used as an evaluation tool for officials and players following contests. Officials are not immune from criticism, and sport media exercise considerable power when it comes to assessment. Research suggests that officials must balance the accountability that comes with large audiences, television critics, and replays of critical incidents.[61] Officials reported that they attend to opinions after the game, distinguishing between justified and unjustified criticism. The evaluation systems available to elite-level officials through mentors, referee inspectors, and match replays enable officials to debrief after games and learn from their own performance. By providing a performance measure the referees respect, the evaluation helps referees to externalize abuse and criticism from other sources. Unfortunately, such resource-intensive evaluation cannot be made available to all referees.[62]

Complementing replay analysis is personal reflection, which enhances a confidence that comes with insight, understanding, and purpose. Scholars argue that officials "can consciously recalibrate techniques to align with rule implementation and other goals (such as safety, order, fairness, prevention, proportion), and review aspects of context and interpersonal interactions that complicate or support the attainment of these goals."[63] Reflection assists officials with "subtleties of context," and should deliberately bring to the surface what is often submerged in discursive exchanges with players and coaches.[64] Post-match disciplinary procedures based on video replays have been introduced in several sports for player fouls that may have gone undetected during the contest. Hearings are conducted in league offices, and based on evidence gleaned from replay, retrospective punishment involving fines and/or suspensions are levied.[65] Moreover, for officials, it should be noted that replay serves to adjudicate beyond the playing field.

When it comes to on-field officiating, the impact of replay on decisional accuracy depends on the type of decision and the type of situations under review. For more objective assessments, such as spatial or temporal issues, replay can arguably increase decisional accuracy. Indeed, as Berman notes, "the fact that referees reverse their own initial calls is further evidence that officials want to get calls right and are not overly sensitive about being reversed."[66] In judging intentionality, however, replay may not be as effective, given previous research investigating the way replay speed affects human judgment in the courtroom. Viewing a situation in slow motion, compared with regular speed, increased the perceived intent of a violent action.[67] That is one reason why some critics of replay decry its use involving matters of interpretation, including the Perisic handball in the WC final. As Peter Walton, general manager of the Professional Referee Organization, explained, "Looking at a slow motion replay should be for point of contact only, context is in full speed."[68] This is the key point: intentionality is not something that slow-motion replay can determine, given its psychological rather than physiological point of fact. The issue of perception is not easily mitigated. Two people watching the same thing can arrive at distinctly different conclusions. The standard of proof for overturning an on-field decision, clear and obvious error, is extremely difficult to meet because the referee is more likely to be right than is the reviewing official: "the referee (or jury) is most likely to get the call right because he has seen the actual evidence firsthand, while the reviewing official (or appellate court) is limited to seeing what was captured on camera (or the court transcript)."[69] The intended consequence of entrenchment is to drastically minimize the number of times a correct initial call is reversed.[70] Was there enough evidence to reverse his call on the field? Critics of Pitana's decision after VAR point to the idea that his initial call of corner kick was correct; to the naked eye, there was contact, but it was inadvertent. In slow motion, Perisic moves his hand toward the ball. It is ironic that the technology employed to increase the likelihood of certainty is ill-equipped to settle matters of interpretation. Despite having more information at its disposal, VAR must recognize when to relent in such matters.

Referees are asked to adjudicate games by exercising the rules and accounting for the spirit of the rules.[71] Crucially, referees are increasingly encouraged to establish a "feel for the game," where the aim is to be realistic rather than literal in applying the rules. Game management represents the art rather than the science of refereeing, the confidence and focus to stay in the flow. Pitana never seemed to have the final in any kind of flow, especially when Marlo Mandzukic headed in an own goal in the eighteenth minute after a free kick was given to France on a questionable foul-flop play against Griezmann that many analysts argued was unwarranted. Perhaps the Croatian mishap on the own goal was lodged in Pitana's mind, given that in live officiating the referee must judge an almost instantaneous sequence of events that requires processing at the unconscious level and the conscious level. This takes the experience and practice required to grasp a situation rather than to assemble a decision out of discrete observations.[72] Within this naturalistic setting, a referee must remain fully integrated into the flow of the game. Referees and officials are most appreciated when unnoticed. That equipoise had no opportunity to take hold as Pitana's overzealous management of the game injected an air of controversy that halftime sportscast analysts exacerbated thanks in large part to the "historic and controversial"[73] first ever goal in a WC final awarded after replay. The VAR's instruction for Pitana to take a second look resulted in changing his mind about what he had seen; doubtlessly, that second look in slow motion created false transparency about Perisic's intent to touch the ball. For whatever reason, Pitana did not consider the quickness with which the ball hit Perisic's hand. The problem of interpretation was compounded by the ambiguity of the rules articulating intent.

Replay forces discursive attention onto the referee. Sportscasters analyze the evidence in the context of the rule and the game. They anticipate what the replay ruling will be and what the resulting situation will involve. Replay's focus on the immediate past interrupting the present and precipitating the future speaks to its discursive flexibility, signifying its importance beyond more generic in-game replays and subject to far greater scrutiny at online websites like Close Call Sports (https://www.closecallsports.com/), which catalogues controversial calls in baseball and other professional sports.[74] When an official announcement is made, the final verdict is given verbally or signaled, producing a collective cheer or groan.

When controversial decisions are made, referees and officials are scrutinized by fans, spectators, and sportscasters who access technologies capable of showing 3D representations of the playing field.[75] As a result, the application of specialist skills from a naturalistic setting becomes "a widely distributed ability, making judgments about what happened on the field a ubiquitous expertise rather than a specialist expertise."[76] Even though referees occasionally reverse their own initial calls, correcting mistakes does not mitigate the criticism levied by sportscasters, viewers, and spectators. Moreover, people will come to disrespect the officials if, as in Pitana's case, the clear and obvious error suggests to viewers that the officials are doing a bad job. As Berman notes, "If that is how it appears, the fact that the calls are rarely reversed will not protect the officials' reputation; and if that is not how it appears, then more frequent reversals will not imperil it."[77] Uncritical acceptance of the capabilities of technology to achieve error-free officiating has worrisome consequences, and given the proclivity for cheating and corruption that undermine sport governance and notions of fairness, it is a short journey to allegations of fixing, doping, and organized criminality.[78] Despite its deployment of VAR, FIFA has become the poster child of corruption in sport.

Replay, Certitude, and Mediatization

In utilizing replay, sport leagues and organizations responded to a mandate to create a means to correct obvious officiating blunders and turned to the media, which face their own challenges related to audience fragmentation. Soaring costs of broadcast rights, production, and marketing budgets can only be recouped by delivering a mass audience to advertisers and to its other programming.[79] That audience brings high expectations and a sophisticated understanding of sport media institutional practices. To interrogate the complex hybridity that replay constitutes within sportscast discourse, it is "more useful to think in terms of conflicting tensions between attempts to achieve transparency and desire to build in entertainment values."[80] Every time an event is stopped for replay, the audience waits and argues about the call. Fans become frustrated by the seemingly interminable breaks, then further irked by goals reversed after celebrations, or decisions going against home teams—though the decisions are technically correct. As one sports journalist noted, "Video reviews are black holes into which all the excitement and spontaneity of live sports is sucked."[81] Because of the clarity of HDTV's digital image, replay shares with other technologies the ability to reveal what is not visible to the naked eye, part of what the revelationist tradition associates with the optical unconscious.[82] By providing a perspective not in an official's direct line of sight, replay technology brings focus to a spatial-temporal moment that can be manipulated. The dynamic forces of human energy are rendered in slow motion to reveal the minutiae, atomizing the action, and impacting consciousness. Each replay forces viewers to recalibrate what is known. "When a replay occurs, our experience and consciousness are certainly not a constant: each iterative experience of a replay affects our experience and perceptual understanding of the world—the replay effectively recursively redefines our consciousness."[83] Our capacity to function ontologically with an overwhelming number of external stimuli and memories has been interpreted as a product of selective retention. Affiliation, identity, and history contribute to shaping how fans process any replay's outcomes, especially as it impacts the result. That is why spectators and sportscast viewers watch the event—to know with certainty the outcome. Television has brought "old instances of presumptive justice into the realm of transparent justice."[84] If justice can be seen to be done, then there is in the very least certitude. It is primarily in a match's ultimate outcome that fans experience the cathartic moment of truth. Our obsession with knowing is a blessing and a curse. Having experienced the ultimate outcome, we become sagacious of a natural harmony in knowing with certainty what the fates have destined, even though it's really only data.

Replay is purportedly the means of providing a moment of revelation, but it comes with costs. On the one hand, most of the professional sport leagues appear willing to expand the use of replay, finding new aspects to review while slowing the game, but on the other hand, there is a tolerance of murkiness, evidenced in FIFA's decision to clarify what constitutes a handball infraction and how matters of intentionality are to be decided. Even if replay can deliver on the promise of greater overall accuracy, indisputable visual evidence can be manipulated. Artificial Intelligence can create almost anything from next to nothing; a new system can take a still image of a person and an audio clip and create a video of the person speaking the audio.[85] As Collins has warned, "The day is arriving when computer-generated television images will be indistinguishable from real-time television photography and, unless the public is well-trained and vigilant, this could put the ability to create what appears to be truth in the hands of the powerful."[86] No one knows to what extent computer-generated graphics that overlay the live action can be further enhanced, framed, and digitized. The present system allows for false transparency, suggesting the possibility that the image shown is not what it appears to be.

Another cost comes from entrenchment; we have become enamored with technology and its ethos of infallibility, directing us away from human error to a purportedly more reliable device, despite its random errors. Unfortunately, television networks are in the business of attracting advertisers, which is accomplished by keeping viewers watching. Networks are unlikely to include disclaimers regarding the accuracy of decision-aid technologies like Hawk-Eye or explain in an aside that the graphic shown is merely a reproduction of algorithms based on data points not excluding margins of error. Sporting entities have welcomed the use of media technology to aid in on-field decisions, but in doing so they have adopted an uncritical acceptance of a surfeit of data, algorithms, and artificial intelligence, an approach that does not foster a better public understanding of the limits and the possibilities of technology or of the value of human performance. This surfeit of information has also resulted in an increased skepticism about the objectivity of news organizations.

> An era of information overload coincides, in other words, with the reflexive recognition of the constructed and partial nature of representation.... If it is impossible to be fully informed, in the sense of knowing all of the available accounts of the world (and accounts of the accounts), it is also necessarily impossible for any particular account to be complete and anything other than partial—in both senses of the word.[87]

Because replay now occupies a pivotal place within the televisual experience, understanding replay to adjudicate sporting events must be contextualized within sport media's ability to advance a neoliberal political agenda by coopting "popular cultural practices, including sport, and render them sites for the expressive reenactment of normalized, highly politicized, affective investments."[88] Ultimately, despite having a facade of certitude and scientificity, replays carry discursive messages about whose stories and what values are worth communicating while dismissing or obscuring others.

Last Dance

The deployment of media technology in the quest for scientific certitude has changed sport. Some argue that replay has improved sport by eliminating blunders by on-field referees; others argue that the attempt to eliminate human error has created a false sense of certitude, added unnecessary delays, and resulted in an abdication of responsibility by the games' arbiters. Striking the right balance of using replay to review spatial-temporal disputes and to review decisive, game-changing calls is critical for the success of any replay program. Eliminating all controversies is admittedly impossible but minimizing blatant injustices should not be. The most prominent problem that replay or any mechanical objectivity does not seem capable of eradicating is a referee's interpretation of a rule written in language to represent contingencies like intent.

Replay has a rich history in terms of enhancing sport media live broadcasts and sport news programming such as pregame and postgame shows, which invariably rely on providing highlights of game action for analysis and to create data and to stimulate emotional responses within affective economics. In this sense, the repurposing of replays to create new texts about athletes, sport, and human aspiration facilitates the media's tendency to empower ideological assumptions with which they are inextricably bound. Sport media routinely expropriate elite athletes as the prototypical avatars of the self. Their celebrity status is embodied in neoliberalism's emphasis on individualism, and they are idolized as exemplars of success born of traditional values.

As the pendulum swung in the direction of technology, replay's resulting overzealousness, evidenced in controversies involving fans of golf calling in rule infractions, led to calls for a reassessment of technology's role. Calling in rule infractions represents a case study of "ubiquitous expertise,"[89] viewers' self-appointed right to adjudicate the rules. Standing opposed to specialist expertise, fans watch replays and make their own interpretations of what the replay shows. As Pitana's dance at the VAR monitor shows, the epistemological privilege of the referee's superior view and specialist skills must also pass the test of digitally-enhanced, slow-motion technology. By removing decision making from the field, FIFA has created an overdependency on the relative certitude that imagery is supposed to provide. The mediatization of current culture is characterized by the visual superimposing itself over the linguistic media.[90] The rule may be in print, yet it is the visual representation that serves to establish the legitimacy of the referee's interpretation. What is most needed is recognition of the discursive construct of any representation, including replay.

CHAPTER 10

Dead Reckoning and the Discourse of Deviation

Beyond the immediacy of replay as an illustration of how media repurposes content, the aesthetic principles of distillation have been applied to other types of sport media, most notably the sport documentary. More than a decade has passed since Ian McDonald argued that the sport documentary warranted "rigorous and systematic analysis of its defining features, politics, aesthetics, and the genre's modes of production" from cultural critics, sociologists, and historians in sport studies, who have heretofore given it "scant regard."[1] One might posit that given its position, floating between disciplinary fields, sport documentary scholarship figuratively languished in the doldrums. However, the publication of books like *From Networks to Netflix* (2018) and *Sporting Realities: Critical Readings of the Sports Documentary* (2020) suggests that scholars have attempted to answer the call for more engagement with the sport documentary by considering "the industrial and commercial elements informing the sports documentary's ideologically loaded depictions [...]."[2] Given its visible and powerful position in contemporary culture, the sport documentary remains ripe for critical contextualization.

Casting Off: Dead Reckoning

Borrowing from sailing parlance, this chapter establishes a dead reckoning of one specific (sub)genre of the sport documentary, the Endurance Ocean Sailing (EOS) documentary, by estimating without the aid of landmarks, celestial navigation, or electronic global positioning systems (GPS), the directions and distances travelled in representations of women sailors from 1951 to 2021. Dead reckoning provides a way to fix where the EOS documentaries have taken positions, where they have travelled from, and where they are likely headed. Through cinematic practices and discursive tropes, the EOS documentaries provide viewers with a transcendent experience that emphasizes the performative aspects of the sailor, who faces death and danger to resist the existential angst of postmodern life. The performative aspects of sailing, like those of the alpinist, become a means for viewers to vicariously embrace risk, danger, and death. Viewers share the thrill and terror of mountainous waves crashing over the sailboat or the deafening roar of a gale, knowing they face neither actual danger nor imminent death. Like other sport adventure documentaries, the EOS documentary utilizes an "economy of death"[3] to create its tension by making death manifest, by redeeming the past, and by celebrating the sailors for exhibiting courage and independence.

In the documentaries under consideration—*Maiden* (2018, dir. A. Holmes); *210 Ten Days: Around the World with Jessica Watson* (2010, prod. A. Fraser); *Maidentrip* (2013, dir. J. Schlesinger); *Kay Cottee: First Lady* (1990, dir. P. Sutton); and *Ellen MacArthur: Taking on the World* (2001, prod. Richard Simmonds)—I analyze cinematic techniques and tropes, unpack the discourse of deviation, and question representations related to gender, class, and race. Covering a period of more than sixty years, the EOS (sub)genre reflects the changing attitudes about women's participation in a sporting culture dominated by men accomplishing "amazing feats and personal journeys."[4] Given the dearth of attention to women athletes and the recent political and U.S. judicial assault on women's constitutional right to self-determination (i.e., SCOTUS overturning *Roe v. Wade*), critical engagement is warranted. Particularly relevant to these documentaries is their connection with sailing's past, an intertextual referencing that binds them together. As Susan Birrell notes, narratives constructed to recreate the past are vested with special interests, blending meanings that can be re-produced and re-mobilized to further larger ideological aims and to reinforce the shared sense of achievement concentrated in values that maintain the status quo and enhance commercial gain.[5] Despite being saddled with what Tracy Edwards has called sailing's anachronistic attitudes about women, "male, pale, and stale,"[6] most of these women have devoted themselves to raising awareness and advocating for improvements in educational and career opportunities for girls and young women, as well as for innovative stewardship of the environment.

Hull and Ballast: The Compelling Narrative

Essentially, the EOS film, television program, or digital stream is created in the editing process of repurposing audio and video, as well as primary source data gathered from a sailor's logs, transcripts of radio, voice, and text messages, media interviews, a soundtrack, and computer-generated imagery. As a documentary, it functions as journalistic record-keeping buoyed with cinematic license to create a compelling narrative. Works that fit within a genre exhibit similar themes, features, and modes of production, as well as specific systems of expectations and repertoires that audiences bring to the viewing. The repetitive nature of production and consumption creates "generic verisimilitude,"[7] the idea that works within a genre are so defined as they conform to the rules of the genre. As more films are produced and disseminated, audience expectations tend to hybridize around known repertoires, which involve understanding characteristics from one film to another, while reinforcing the historical identity of the genre.

These routinized media production practices and audience expectations illustrate the main tenets of remediation.[8] As sport media has transitioned from early film and newsreels to television's live broadcasting to on-demand streaming providers, producers disseminate content across an assemblage of platforms integrated within a corporatized system's infrastructure. Sport content readily turns news into advertising into brand recognition. To maintain popular acceptance, and therefore economic success, the EOS documentary must convince consumers that a newly released film "improves on the experience of older ones."[9]

The EOS documentary must do more than set forth a record of the accomplishment, as the Internet has radically changed how to track a sailboat's progress, thanks largely to satellite technology and the ability of GPS to position a sailboat at all times. As advertised on Jessica Watson's DVD, the documentary provides "never before seen footage ... [and] allows viewers unprecedented access into her journey and the battles she fought along the way."[10] The EOS documentary's emphasis on providing access to the sailor's most intimate moments during the voyage overshadows the fact that the outcome may be already known. The EOS documentary delivers a coherent message that moves beyond end results to inspiration and motivation. As *Outside Magazine*'s review of *Maidentrip* made clear, "It's impossible to watch *Maidentrip* and not want to immediately start scheming your own audacious adventure."[11] Lastly, the sport media industry's utilization of remediation as repurposing illustrates the inseparability of the economic from the social and cultural.

Considerable scholarship analyzing sport documentaries as well as studies of women's presence in competitive-adventure sports and in the media inform this chapter. The participation of an all-women team in the 1995 America's Cup is a particularly instructive case study of how both the social construction of sport and perceptions about women athletes impede their entrance into top-level competitions.[12] This perspective, also articulated in a study of women golfers, conceptualizes gender as a social structure that organizes society into different and unequal categories based on sex and as an ideology that promotes inequities between the socially constructed categories of women and men.[13] Additionally, a study on the competitive sailing subculture in Australia explores how gender and power are conjoined in competitive sailing through a complex and contradictory bricolage of subjectivities (defined as bodies of feelings), social practices, and social structures. How to place subjectivities into the center of analysis without essentialism or reductionism lies at the heart of considering conceptual frameworks.[14] Other analyses focused attention on women's sailing from a recreational/cruising context and how the sailing lifestyle can become a means to foster greater or lesser agency for women.[15] The idea that women have been inhibited and excluded from sailing culture was also explored from a marketing context, by considering key discourses surrounding the history of women that affect their role in the sailing community.[16]

Questions about women and the expression of femininity in the sailing discourse focus attention on the visibility and performativity of femininity itself. Women who use their bodies to play sport, an institution largely constructed and dominated by media's representations of men, often experience contradictions, ambiguities, and conflicts. Many of these experiences will be associated with having transgressed normative gender boundaries, while "at the same time being involved in the conservative practices surrounding traditionally male sport."[17] Lastly, academics have analyzed the intersection of life stories, cultural politics, and self-understanding, all key components of the EOS documentary genre. They argue that stories people tell about themselves are interesting not only for the events and characters they describe but also in the construction of the stories themselves—what is emphasized and what is omitted. That becomes an important part of this analysis, given the multiple sources bringing events into focus.[18]

Rigging: Producing Women's Sport History

Sport documentaries focusing on women's accomplishments in sailing constitute a source of sport media discourse that warrants critical analysis, not only because sport media coverage of women's accomplishments historically upheld an ideology of hegemonic masculinity in which sports were almost exclusively a male preserve, but more importantly because several of these documentaries were produced, directed, edited, or photographed by women. That the EOS documentaries chronicle record-setting achievements by women serves not only to illustrate the way history is socially constructed around abstractions like greatness and heroism, but also to reinforce values that connote strength, courage, and perseverance.

The genealogy of sport documentary cinematic modes of production can be attributed to the convergence of fiction and nonfiction forms in which real-life events are told through sophisticated filming and editing techniques to create a verisimilitude in which death is vanquished, the "first" is achieved by the "youngest" or "oldest," and redemption through self-sacrifice and overcoming deprivation leads to a deeper understanding of self and the natural world.[19] Production values allow viewers the opportunity to share in what has been called the post-adventure experience, a type of ecstatic transcendence achieved through a mediated simulacrum, shaped by production techniques and reception protocols subsumed within postmodern aesthetics.[20] All aspects of the documentary film infrastructure are driven by the interrelated processes of commercialization, commodification, and spectacularization, subject to the logics of a highly technologized capitalist economy and propagated by mediated spectacles and circuitry.[21]

The idea of a woman or an all-women crew circumnavigating the globe in a sailboat to do something no one had done before served as the key selling point to attract sponsors, producers, and media attention. As Tim Madge, co-author with Edwards for the book, explained in *Maiden*, "Selling the idea of an all-woman crew was easy. Of all the great sporting adventure stories left in 1986 there were a few not yet achieved by women. There was Mount Everest, the North and South Poles, and the Whitbread. In the years that followed, as it turned out, all the others were conquered by all-women teams. By 1989 only the Whitbread was left, for those few who studied such things, the Whitbread remained the biggest challenge of them all."[22]

Media representations of women's achievements in sports took shape in newsreel coverage of Gertrude Ederle's English Channel swim, was rigidly standardized in early television, reached a crescendo with spectacles like the 1973 tennis match between Billie Jean King and Bobby Riggs, and expanded as women explored sporting adventures previously denied. This is not to aver that Ederle was the first woman athlete of note, but rather that Ederle's swim was constructed into a mediatized spectacle of woman's sporting history and resonated much more forcefully in King's victory over Riggs. The idea of women's ascendancy in "a man's world" had already been popularized and in the post–World War II popular Irving Berlin song from *Annie Get Your Gun*, "Anything You Can Do I Can Do Better." Women's progress was later commodified into the tobacco advertising slogan, "You've Come a Long Way, Baby..." which was grafted onto the Virginia Slims women's tennis tour. More important than a mere battle of the sexes, however, King's victory legitimated a women's professional tennis tour, which persevered thanks to the Women's Tennis Association, an organization that fought for parity in not only prize money and playing conditions, but also access to greater representation in umpiring, administration, and coaching.

For skipper Edwards and the all-women crew of *Maiden*, achieving many firsts in completing the Whitbread Round the World Race was only part of the significance. As Edwards explained, it was not about beating or being like men.

> When I first thought of entering the Whitbread with an all-female crew it was because I wanted to give other women the chance I had craved so much. It was a dream, too, to achieve what so many had dubbed 'impossible.' I did not get into all this to prove to others as much as I—and all the crew—wanted to prove to ourselves. We certainly did not want to be male clones.
> We are women; we love sailing. That's all. That's it.[23]

Edwards' summation illustrates the paradigmatic nature of women's activism to achieve both personal realization in the pursuit of larger economic and cultural capital. Competing with and beating men to win two legs of the race was not going to mean much if women failed to consolidate advances on fronts beyond sports—especially in acquiring the means to access media and acquire control over representations of women athletes.

Another production characteristic of the EOS documentary is its use of the past and sailing's history. The many references to the past and the exploits of other sailors brings into focus a "practical nostalgia," which is a means to provide an enduring sense of continuity while enough distance for the development of a cultural critique of the contemporary scene.[24] Reading books from "The Mariners Library"[25] about the accomplishments of Joshua Slocum (1899), Bernard Moitessier (1971), Sir Francis Chichester (1971), and Robin Knox-Johnston (1969) became a rite of passage for many of these sailors. However, that list must also include works by women documenting their own sailing adventures, beginning with Ann Davison's *Last Voyage* (1951), her account of the wrecking of *Reliance* and the death of her husband Frank. The book's Epilogue captures the moment Davison awoke on a float and realized she was going to survive the ordeal, but not escape the accusations and suspicions that accompanied her entry into the sailing establishment.

> I saw the headlines ripping out—and vultures picking over the bones of our beliefs. Heard the speculations of armchair sages, wise to another's troubles, not to truth. Heard the baying of the wolves.... And listened to rumours, whispers and suspicions.... They say.... You ran away. You purposefully wrecked the ship. You dare not face your responsibilities. You could not face what was coming. You killed yourselves. Shirked.... Ran.... Suicide.... They say....[26]

Davison faced considerable criticism for purportedly cashing in on Frank's death by writing the book; however, she persisted and eventually proved her sailing expertise, achieving a woman's "first" solo, transatlantic crossing in a 23-foot sailboat, chronicled in *My Ship Is So Small*, published in 1956. That was followed by a series of other sailing achievements and books, including Naomi James' solo circumnavigation, documented in *At One with the Sea* (1979); Kay Cottee's first solo, nonstop circumnavigation in *First Lady: A History-Making Solo Voyage Around the World* (1989); and Lisa Clayton's *At the Mercy of the Sea* (1996), documenting her attempt to better the IYRU/World Sailing Speed Record Council world record for a non-stop, solo circumnavigation. Notably, after each's accomplishment, James, Clayton, and Edwards were featured in segments of the BBC-produced program, *This Is Your Life*.

All of the films analyzed are based largely, but not exclusively, on these women's autobiographies, which established a definite bonding with past sailing accomplishments and the ideological meanings they empower, as the vessels and sailors were invested with symbolic meanings around nature, heroism, and greatness. The EOS documentary is tethered to sailing's rich library, much in the same way alpinist literature grounds mountain film documentaries. As Madge noted, "Cape Horn is to sailors what Mount Everest is to mountain climbers. Both are inaccessible, wild, treacherous killers, places peopled by heroes and ghosts. Both are the settings where history is made."[27] This analogy to alpinism is apt, and James even quoted climber Chris Bonington to explain why she was "staking one's life on one's judgment, playing the calculated risk" to answer the basic question about why she attempted to do what no other woman had done. "[P]erhaps a ton of threatening, crashing water on a rolling foredeck would horrify him [Bonnington] as much as looking down a vertical wall of ice would mortify me. It was, of course, the survival element which was

common to both ventures, and it was this which gave even the more routine things like sail handling a different flavour—something very different from the sort of danger encountered while crossing a street in central London."[28] The possibility of being swept off the boat with no chance of rescue is the sailor's parallel to a climber's risk of falling.

Because sailing requires the same type of self-reliance and measured risks as other adventure sports, the EOS documentary makes use of the "marginal situation"[29] to create the impression that while all of these sailors returned, many others have perished. Characterized as a bodily state in which individual confronts death, the marginal situation "radically challenges all social objectivated definitions of reality—of the world, of others, and of self."[30] However, while a sense of death is always lurking, the filmmakers show that sailing is rooted in minimizing risk, as Watson explained in footage showing her certificate for having fulfilled maritime training. "So, sorry to spoil all those dramatic ideas about me heroically battling with sails on the foredeck in monster seas and high winds, but this particular voyage is more about cutting down on risks, lots of preparation, and sticking it out for a (very!) long time rather that edge-of-your-seat action sailing. That comes later!"[31] This balancing of white-knuckle action with the tedium of expedition preparation and planning gives the EOS documentary a means to chart human performativity in the face of danger and death and to cultivate the heroic protagonist overcoming physical and psychological obstacles.[32]

The EOS documentary utilizes a commercial-industrial infrastructure that provides a distribution network tied to advertisers of sailing products, destinations, and services. All are necessary to reach and motivate participation by consumers, often referred to as the "market of a captive audience."[33] Sailing media, boat shows, marinas, and expositions provide venues for building awareness about sailing consumerism, a way to sell lifestyle and cultural commodities, and to create messaging for and about the worldwide sailing community. This specific market was utilized as a vehicle to disseminate these films, much in the same way alpine adventure films are marketed to mountain film festivals. Because these particular films are about women, they have the capacity to engender interest in non-sailing and non-sporting women beyond the captive audience of sailing enthusiasts.

The logics of branded sponsorship revolve around a circuitry of private capital to finance desired commodities that reinforce connections between products and practitioners. The sailboats in these EOS documentaries had many corporate sponsors, whose vested interests were primarily aimed to be a part of sailing history and enhance their brands. Advertising posters, PR media kits, and DVDs prominently display sponsors' logos and every effort is made to reinforce the link between the sailboat and the adventure. Not surprisingly, Cottee's sailboat was named *Blackmoor's First Lady*, the sponsor occupying primary position. James named her sailboat after acquiring sponsorship from the *Daily Express* newspaper, whose editor Derek Jameson "didn't seem to think it at all unusual that a woman should want to sail round the world on her own."[34] The ship's name was then changed to *Express Crusader*—a crusader became the logo/motif which appeared under the newspaper's banner; the sponsorship entailed James' filming and writing articles for the *Express*, which would be collected at prearranged rendezvous points as well as short radio reports every week or so. *Maiden*'s name was originally *Maiden Great Britain*, after Edwards approached members of the British royal family to assist in launching the sailboat and secured not only the support of Princess Sarah Ferguson and Prince Andrew, but also landed the sailboat's launching ceremony in newspapers across the globe. When Royal Emirates took over *Maiden*'s primary sponsorship, the name was shortened. Lastly, Watson described how her sailboat acquired a naming sponsor.

> Ella Baché, the oldest family-owned skin-care company in the world, had offered to become my major naming sponsor for the trip. … When I heard that Ella Baché's mission is to inspire you to be the best you can be, something that I also strongly believe in, I could see it was going to be a great partnership. So *Pink Lady* was proudly renamed. She became *Ella's Pink Lady*.[35]

These examples clearly illustrate the importance of how corporate sponsorships provided not only financing, but also ideological messaging about sailing's capacity to bring out "the best you can be" and other traditional values worth emulating. Ultimately, the filmmakers distill the voyage into visual representations of what achievement means within a mythology of independent heroes.

Sails and Battens: EOS Documentary Characteristics

While EOS documentary films may share certain characteristic elements such as an identifiable plot, identifiable filming techniques, a relationship to a similar genre in other media, and an audience that recognizes these elements, it should not be presumed that all of these elements are found in every film.[36] Filming a documentary about sailboat voyages, whether chronicling a race or the attempt to set a circumnavigating record, presents logistical, technical, and production problems not easily overcome. Exactly what actions are recorded—either for live transmission via computer-satellite hookup or as b-roll for recontextualization—is often determined by the sailor responding to weather conditions or passing landmarks. When not determined by the sailor, footage was filmed by professional camera operators before or after the actual voyage from land, boat, plane, drone, or helicopter (the favorite choice of directors under consideration).

Because of a circumnavigation's length, emphasis is given to visually compelling sequences, specifically, the beginnings and ends. Accompanied by a flotilla of boats, EOS racers or circumnavigators are literally swarmed with attention, creating a din that serves as a stark contrast to what these sailors have experienced during the intervening time, namely extreme isolation. These parade-like spectacles serve as the metaphoric bookends that hold together long periods of solitude on a seemingly unchanging seascape. And that is when the film's focus necessarily turns to the performative nature of the sailors, who guide viewers through the voyage and its obstacles. The length of time required to race around the globe is a major part of the story, and how a sailor copes within the confines of solitude adds one structural dimension to the narrative. For example, the Watson documentary makes use of its title, *210 Days: Around the World with Jessica Watson*, harkening back to Jules Verne's *Around the World in 80 Days*.

The narrative structure of the EOS documentary follows the plot of the adventurer's quest to survive a battle against the forces of nature. This focus on real people putting themselves into life-death struggles gives the story its dramatic appeal, generated by delving intimately into the heroine's reasons for undertaking the struggle, her background, character, and experiences with sailing. To establish immediacy and context, different openings are employed. For example, in *Taking On the World*, the opening sequence shows MacArthur in heavy seas attaching a line to the foresail while being sprayed by waves hitting the boat. She narrates the moment in a muffled VO, as if the statement had been given after duress, in deep solemnity.

> You have to think you're going to come back. Even if you have problems … you're in a storm. That's in the back of your mind … you think you might never come back. But you can't afford to think that.[37]

Bringing the possibility of not returning into the opening sequence establishes the gravity of the situation. Facing one's fears and forging onwards becomes a dominant discursive trope. This moment-of-truth distillation crystalizes for the viewer what the stakes are. This is not merely a documentation of MacArthur's attempt to win the 2001 Vendée Globe yacht race; rather, it is couched within an existential struggle for survival.

A more straightforward exposition can be seen in *First Lady*, which chronicles Cottee's solo, nonstop circumnavigation. Cottee is shown sailing while the narration is delivered by an off-screen Voice-of-God narrator. "In the [Australian] bicentennial year, 1988, one such story unfolded. It is a story of a girl, a mountain that had not been climbed. It is the story of a dream. It is the story of courage and determination that lives within us all. It is the story of a dream that came true."[38] Utilizing this more historical context allows the filmmaker to paint with broad strokes to establish the quest by referring to the analogous alpinist adventure.

EOS documentaries consistently follow a lineal story structure. By distilling moments of high drama, whether leaving loved ones behind or confronting the ominous forces of wind and water, the filmmakers create tension and build empathy for the individual battling nature. As Barnard explains, "The universality of the hero quest manages to span the gap between the viewer and the practitioner even if the protagonist is on a quest way beyond the realm of the viewing audience."[39] Doubtlessly, sailing the world's oceans is beyond the skill level, desire, and financial means of most viewers, yet it provides a vicarious fantasy scenario for imaginings of personal triumph. Once the protagonist has been established, the goal defined, the context of boat and water clearly measured, the challenges posed by having to live aboard a sailboat while managing, operating, and repairing all its systems provide the narrative with oppositional forces needed to maintain interest.

The EOS documentary's narrative climax logically focuses on the sailor's return to port, celebrated by a raucous flotilla of boats, cheering crowds, and punctuated with a boom of the cannon to mark the voyage's completion. And it is at this moment of success that the EOS documentary historicizes the magnitude of the accomplishment, defines what constitutes greatness, and articulates the meaning of women's ability to fulfill her dreams within a socially constructed paradigm.

In addition to a common story structure, recognizable practical elements are deployed to create cinematic effect, including, but not limited to, special effects, specialized camera equipment for filming on a sailboat, use of the protagonist as "talent" who can perform for the camera and is aware of the viewers' needs, use of GPS navigational imagery and computer-generated simulations of the sailboat's movement on a course captured from navigational data, and *mise en scene* to edit the sailing experience into an long-form film.

Part of the filmmaker's goal is to convey the vastness of the seascape against the smallness of the individual in this environment. Often accomplished with a helicopter tracking shot showing the sailboat as it approaches a landmark like Cape Horn, the solitary sailboat faces a seemingly endless horizon and the unknown. At some point during the voyage, the sailors all confess how small they feel, how utterly alone they are, and how precarious is their condition. For example, Dekker described it as a love-hate relationship with sailing. "Ninety per cent of the time it's nothing special, but the remaining 10 per cent makes it all worthwhile. Especially the thrill of arriving somewhere and the attraction of what is waiting just beyond the horizon; these factors continue to drive me westwards."[40] This sense of smallness is also conveyed through hand-held camera shots of the cramped quarters of the cabin below deck, creating a sense of the claustrophobia and the starkness of confinement. Finally, the constant presence of water heightens the tension. Edwards described the deleterious effects of salt water. "Although we are in the fresh air, it is not necessarily healthy. Wounds don't heal easily. Our skins suffer terribly from boils and sores—partly not changing clothes for weeks at a time, partly the salt and the accumulated dirt. Curiously, your hair doesn't seem to suffer from not being washed."[41]

In addition to the tracking shot, the most commonly used filming techniques include fixed camera shots, which are pointed forward/backward or upward/downward to capture the sailor performing tasks; the hand-held camera shots, which the sailor uses to reveal conditions on the sailboat, on the water, or in the air; to-camera interviews, in which the sailor speaks directly to the camera or shows herself either communicating with others or explaining some process or feeling; time-lapse shots are used to show renovations, repairs, and any progression; and lastly, computer-generated images are created to show the sailboat's position at a specific moment in time, movement across the water, or performance in relation to the other racers.

Of these defining characteristics the most important is having the adventurer film herself, which has become a staple of the modern adventure documentary, made possible with the development of lightweight digital cameras that can easily be affixed to something stationary like a mast or helmet.[42] Showing the sailor in action framed by ocean waves only increases the intensity. One film scholar argues that even though key moments might be missed due to the extreme conditions, the proximity of the filmmaker-sailor to the elements carries inherent strength.

> The fact of the matter is that this kind of film can actually achieve a more or less successful compromise between the exigencies of the action and the demands of reporting. A cinematographic witness to an event is what a [wo]man can seize of it on film while at the same time being a part of it.[43]

In EOS documentaries, turning on the camera is a purposeful decision, and the sailor must balance the demands of documentary filmmaking with the materiality experienced at any given moment. Several of the sailors were under contract to provide footage, write newspaper articles, or do publicity during the trip via radio or Internet. Clayton even received training with the camera by BBC technicians who accompanied her on practice sails.

Decisions about what to film could be planned around landmarks and calendar events, like crossing the Equator or celebrating a holiday. Dekker, Watson, MacArthur, and Cottee all narrated footage of them paying homage to Neptune as they crossed from one hemisphere to another by offering up gifts of wine and food. This symbolic ritual provides a link to the traditions passed down among sailors. Footage of the sailors celebrating Christmas in their decorated cabins is another example of a planned event, one with visual cues of presents and messages of missing family. These planned events comprise one part of the narrative that elicit an affective response in viewers who readily understand the importance of missing loved ones at Christmas.

Capturing dramatic events constitutes another source of footage. For example, MacArthur, standing in the cockpit, points her camera to show icebergs in the Southern Ocean only a few hundred meters from her boat. Visibly shaken, she expresses frustration for having navigated herself in the vicinity of them, which was extremely dangerous, never mind having to sail through them at night in complete darkness. In the next shot, darkness fills the camera's frame as she confesses to praying that she would make it through. After viewing that segment of the ITV documentary, MacArthur explained her rationale for turning the camera on when she was distraught, emotionally drained, or injured.

> The first thing which hit me was the level of emotion. I knew that of all the original twenty-four hours of footage perhaps only ten minutes of it was emotional. But the reality of TV is that, when the programme is made, all of the most moving emotional footage will be shown. Perhaps I would have seemed much more of a "hero" if I'd come back without

the footage of the bad bits. It would certainly have been a much easier task if I hadn't filmed those parts of the journey; but I chose to share the downs just as much as the ups, and though I didn't need to film myself in a totally exhausted state, in doing so I was being honest about what really happens out there.[44]

ITV emphasized MacArthur's struggles by highlighting her vulnerabilities. On at least three occasions MacArthur is shown tending to an injury or weeping at a point of exhaustion because of sleep deprivation. That she understood why ITV chose to use most of this footage to arouse affect is clear. In attempting to be honest about her experiences, MacArthur provided footage that was contextualized around vulnerabilities brought on by exhaustion, injury, or distress.

Conversely, as Edwards recounted, *Maiden*'s progress around the world was characterized by good humor and laughter, to the point where the television producer editing the on-board footage asked if he could have a bit more grim-faced action, "if only to convince viewers it wasn't such a holiday."[45] Doubtlessly, part of the difference between these two can be traced to sailing solo as opposed to being part of a crew, as well as the ordeal of nonstop circumnavigation as opposed to a circumnavigation comprised of legs. However, the goal of ramping up the emotional content was explicitly conveyed to *Maiden*'s crew, which certainly confirms the filmmaker's intent.

The need for "grim-faced action" is most easily realized by showing storms at sea. In *First Lady*, Cottee provides a VO to b-roll footage that includes radio exchanges heard in the background. She describes experiencing a violent storm just a few days before approaching Cape Horn. As the winds increased, the waves became bigger and bigger. "I felt real fear. It's hard to estimate, but the waves were up to 60-feet high…. Turquoise, aqua-color, how beautiful. Then I snapped out of it and realized it was going to break over us."[46] The scene immediately cuts to images from the film titled *1927* showing a violent storm south of Cape Horn. The VO then shows Cottee tackling Cape Horn alone, handicapped with a cracked boom, which she is then shown repairing, using time-lapse filming.

Being at a point of physical exhaustion was plotted as the key psychological obstacle to overcome. For example, in *210 Days*, Watson explained that she never felt alone until confronted with a sense of isolation brought on by fatigue and a series of storms. "It was weird, because most of the time I was fine and loved being by myself and then, boom, out of nowhere I'd just want someone there to give me a hug and look after me. At one point in that week there were things I absolutely had to do and I had to force myself to keep going when all I wanted to do was get into my bunk and sleep for days."[47] Similarly, MacArthur took footage of her bunk area and explained why the sailboat's constant movement made sleeping almost impossible as she slid back and forth with the wave action. She could close her eyes, but she could never relax.

Sleep deprivation is not like torture, it *is* a form of torture. I was running on empty, and for the first time in my sailing career I was learning what that really meant. I was on the brink of despair, my actions went beyond the realms of logic, and I was reduced to functioning like a robot to stay alive. It was intense; more intense than anything I had been through before, and physical and mental exhaustion in this extreme form was new to me. I had found a place inside me which I have no wish to visit again, but a place that I am grateful to have seen and returned from.[48]

In addition to self-filmed footage, EOS documentaries also made use of footage gleaned from news media. Reasons for involving the mainstream media varied with the sailors, depending on how much autonomy each was willing to accede to them. For example, Cottee related that she had to be reminded by her manager and film producer, Peter Sutton, about fulfilling media requests for interviews. "I am a private person and dislike being interviewed. He displayed great tolerance in reminding me I had sponsorship commitments to fulfil and explained that so many people, both young and old, were gaining pleasure from sharing in my adventure. The only way to satisfactorily involve them was via the media."[49] Clayton explained that she felt like an actor, performing for the cameras. "It was the sort of challenge [sailing downwind] I didn't need in front of so many onlookers, and with so many boats around. I tried to quell my nervousness as I smiled at the TV cameras and floating crowds. I felt rather like an actor on a stage, and tried to play my part as was expected of me."[50]

Dekker's experiences with reporters and documentary production team were often confrontational, made clear in a scene between Dekker and a reporter. Despondent, impatient, and uncooperative, Dekker was fulfilling an obligation that clearly irked her. Part of the reasoning can be found in her book. After a scheduling snafu with the Dutch national public broadcaster, VARA, Dekker refused to reschedule.

> I'm afraid my opinion of the media isn't improving. Sometimes it's all a bit too much. Too many friendly people who unintentionally demand attention and can't stop talking…. Do I always have to be cheerful and put on a smile? Both at sea and on land, I have these "it's all a little too much" moments…. The attitude of the cameraman who's doing a documentary on me doesn't improve matters either. I see him peering at me through his lens almost every morning when I wake up and look through my porthole. Why is he always there so early, and why does he need to see me get out of bed every day? For the umpteenth time I tell him that it's not appreciated, but he just doesn't listen.[51]

These filming techniques, intrusive to the point of being voyeuristic, provide the raw material for repurposing and recontextualization during the editing process.

Deviation: Keeping Women Within Boundaries

> It was not done for women's lib or to prove that anything man can do woman can do better. It was undertaken for that indefinable reason that makes men climb mountains and soar into the sky and fight the elements. It was achieved by a special lady.[52]

Written by sailor Chay Blyth, this statement illustrates a discourse of deviation that can be read in EOS documentaries and sources. In navigation manuals, magnetic deviation refers to compass error caused by magnetized iron within a ship or aircraft.

This iron has a mixture of permanent and temporary magnetization induced by the Earth's magnetic field. EOS documentaries manifest errors in deviation and errors of omission magnetized by cinematic, sporting, and historical alloys that attempt to keep women within cultural, commoditized, and ideological boundaries.

Blyth essentially disclaims women's agency to forge personal achievement into ideological power by defining what her accomplishment did not mean. By disassociating James from the women's liberation movement of the late 1970s, her accomplishment could be expropriated and couched within values that typify male adventures. Accomplishment for accomplishment's sake, however, is an anachronism from the gentleman's code of respectability that governed sporting enterprises, governing bodies, and media representations over the past two centuries, until women, people of color, and people with disabilities challenged and sued for equal access.

The degree to which EOS documentaries show deviation in taking ideological standpoints can be traced in part to their chronology, with the different eras' larger social, political, and economic currents shaping individual discourses. A number of scholars have argued that media's representations of extreme adventure have served as a basis for subversive politics centered on individuals' challenges to limitations.[53] At the beginning of the nineteenth century, body movement came to signify a weapon of resistance, a fundamental expression of agency. Even though sailors are literally bound within the confines of a rather small vessel, endurance sailing becomes a performance of human embodied agency, "a kind of corporeal subversive politics ripe with possibility for renewal that feeds back into private social life, inflecting it with new horizons…."[54] Discourse about being alone at sea and independent is offered as the counterpoint to societally-enforced loneliness, and though this creates a false dichotomy, the filmmakers distinctly do not challenge this idea, carefully navigating those straits.

The earliest iteration appears in Davison's explanation about why people detested conditions in post–World War II Great Britain. "People unable to settle into peacetime niches; people tired of the bonds of socialism; people tired of the bonds of any civilization, all turning their eyes to distant lands across the sea, but thwarted because shipping space was so short after the war and waiting-lists were long. […] Private ventures as a whole were in bad odour in a socialist State and private sailing ventures simply stank to high heaven."[55] James also explored this idea in an interview in which she answered a question about her voyage being an escape. "I didn't care; the world and its inhabitants were too remote for their opinions to be considered, and since I hadn't yet reached the stage of answering myself back during these deliberations, I also wasn't likely to be contradicted."[56] Clearly, James and Davison embraced the idea that sailing was a means to assert one's self-determination and independence.

The next sailors in the timeline—Cottee, Edwards, and Clayton—were empowered by the women who had preceded them as well as societal changes for women. For example, when questioned by media about how it felt to have conquered a man's world, Cottee responded: "I was brought up believing there is no such thing as a man's world or a woman's world. It's everyone's world."[57] With a marina in the background and holding a copy of James' book, Cottee narrates how even before deciding to attempt a solo, non-stop circumnavigation, she had started a charter sailboat business that was dominated by men. Having succeeded in her business venture, Cottee knew how to organize and promote. Once she had acquired enough sailing experience to feel competent, she began putting together plans for her circumnavigation. In the documentary Cottee confesses that she did not want someone else to become the first woman to solo circumnavigate nonstop. "And always in the back of my mind, I feared another woman would beat me to it."[58] Clayton began by merely wanting to circumnavigate and ended with the idea of challenging Cottee's record. For Tracy Edwards and the crew of *Maiden*, their achievement of being the first all-female crew to complete the Whitbread race meant that they were extraordinary. "We are special," Edwards told the U.S. media when the race reached Florida. "It's not just our being first, it's being who we are."[59] When Edwards learnt of another all-female crew taking on the Whitbread challenge, she knew that the stakes would be a lot higher. Again, following in another's footsteps, overcoming what others could not overcome serves as an historical reference point of achievement or disaster in trying—vanquisher or vanquished. Creating myths around sporting legends has long been a part of the sport discourse. Determining what constitutes greatness is a social construction which "employs a collection of techniques that stress scientific rigor"[60] involving assessment, survey, simulation, and archive. Only by meeting strict guidelines can a sailor enter the record book and have the accomplishment certified and recognized.

For the twenty-first-century sailors—MacArthur, Watson, and Dekker—breaking records and barriers provided only a small part of their motivation. Dekker had to prevail in court against Dutch authorities attempting to keep her from making her journey—first by challenging parental custody of her and then not issuing her Yachtmaster's Offshore Certificate license despite having successfully passed the exam: "I didn't set out to break a record [for being the youngest], or to seek recognition. I simply wanted to do it; it was a dream, a great adventure through which I wanted to explore my boundaries, and get to know nature and myself."[61] Watson explained that she had been hoping to increase awareness about the work of OceansWatch, which works closely with the world's yachting community to undertake marine conservation projects and to deliver humanitarian aid to developing countries. When Watson was de-masted by a cargo ship shortly after her initial departure, attacks by news media on her parents reached a frenzy, and the Queensland government considered stopping her venture.

MacArthur used her sailing achievements to focus attention on climate change and the need for responsible action. When MacArthur announced that she would not seek to regain her solo nonstop circumnavigation record after it had been taken by Francis Joyon in 2008, she surprised many by focusing instead on developing a foundation that could promote sustainability. MacArthur explained that having sailing accolades meant little in navigating other cultural discourses. "In my heart of hearts, I knew that this new journey on which I was embarking was not about using sailing as a vehicle, it was about heading into an unknown territory which would have its own storms, challenges, nightmares and victories, but, unlike the others, I didn't know where I was going to find the start line, let alone the finish line."[62] MacArthur's honesty in separating herself from sailing to navigate existential uncertainties shows her advocating for alternatives to give meaning to life's voyages. In this sense, MacArthur's political engagement implies that a means-end orientation must coexist with meaningful reflection and deliberately take us beyond our own limits.[63]

In addition to emphasizing the physical and psychological barriers that must be overcome, deviation is also the result of omission. For example, while the documentaries explore gender issues, issues related to race and class are not critically engaged. Edwards and Madge recount in her book that Edwards' first house was called IBNA, which, as Madge explained, stands for the "International Boat Niggers Association (now, rather lamely but more politely, called the International Boat Workers Association). Because we live in hypersensitive times the very phrase 'boat nigger' conjures up something unpleasant, even racialist. But boat niggers call themselves that because they perceive themselves as the hardworking element in a luxury trade—yachts. They are the workers; the owners, the charterers and the guests are the 'nobs.'"[64]

This rationale equates hard-working, paid employees in a luxury trade with a term historically used in institutional slavery to dehumanize individuals and rob them of identity. By claiming the term conjures racialist ideas in the politically correct or woke, Madge shifts responsibility, defending bad judgment by implicating his critics. Using this term might have seemed less dubious at the time, but it shows a considerable lack of understanding, because slavery has nothing to do with the element of demeaning work, but everything to do with power over others, a manifestation of white privilege. In this regard, sailing has yet to own its part in the slave trade and the importation of imperialism. When Edwards revised the book for Kindle in 2016, she clearly accounted for the use of racist language. "[Forty] years ago, the use of misogynistic and racist language was widespread in the world of sailing. I do not agree with the use of that language in the [1990] book. Battling against that demeaning language and those harmful attitudes is a key part of all that I have strived to achieve during my career. There is still work to be done, but I am committed to contributing to the process of removing such attitudes and language from sailing."[65] Edwards also addressed the topic in interviews, but director Alex Holmes chose not to address the fact that Edwards had changed her views about boat workers and more recently recruited women of color for the MaidenFactor foundation's mission.

In several interviews publicizing *Maiden*'s release, Edwards admitted her views on the importance of *Maiden*'s accomplishments for women had evolved into a greater appreciation for women's empowerment. Greater recognition brought a deeper understanding of what the crew's achievements mean for women today. As Rosenwald and Ochberg explain: "Stories people tell about themselves are interesting not only for the events and characters they describe but also for something in the construction of the stories themselves … what they emphasize and omit, their stance as protagonists or victims, the relationship the story establishes between teller and audience—all shape what individuals can claim about their own lives."[66] More than a recitation of events, then, EOS documentaries are an organization of experiences through which viewers learn about what constitutes legitimate sailing experiences, as well as what achievements are historically worthy of being enjoined with other sailing heroes.

Knots and Tell-Tails: Conclusions on the Hard

Taken together, these EOS documentaries clearly established a significant trove of sailing history that chronicles many exploits, and the source material for these films constitute a wellspring of sport media history. While encompassing more than sixty years of sailing, the selection of analyzed films was certainly not exhaustive. Other important achievements were not analyzed, for example, Krystyna Chojnowska-Liskiewicz's first solo circumnavigation in 1978, Shirley Robertson's Olympic sailing gold medals in 2000 and 2004, and Jeanne Socrates' solo non-stop circumnavigation at age 77, to name only a few. The sailing exploits of such figures as Grace O'Malley, Jeanne Barat, and Skipper Thuridur from the seventeenth and eighteenth centuries were also not discussed.

Rather, this chapter unpacks modes of production, genre filmic characteristics, and discursive tropes that celebrate women's sailing accomplishments within a social construct of gender, greatness, and heroism, a commodified circuitry that reinforces the larger cultural and ideological establishment. Finding correspondences among any genre's films does not necessarily establish truth, but similarities do reflect a collection of preferred and partial truths that serve to commemorate people and events, "a strategy for memorializing—a communal sense of the important issues that require capturing for posterity, that might be venerated in the ritual process of narrative. … Resolving the discrepancies among accounts through intertextual strategies is not the primary aim: locating these discrepancies within the context of their production and consumption and within their specific historical contexts is."[67] The idea that deviation in feminist agency can be traced through these mediatized representations should not be surprising, given the time periods in which they occurred, as well as specific set of skills and practices employed in endurance sailing. The messages and meanings communicated about what should be venerated as historically significant reflects an aspect of sports myth-making that warrants critical engagement.

Deviation affects historiography and offers counter narratives against the dominant imagery and symbolism of EOS documentaries. For example, in the film's climactic scene, Watson openly contradicts Australian prime minister Rudd's pronouncement that she was a hero for all Australians. "I told Mr. Rudd that I wasn't a hero, I was just an ordinary girl who believed in a dream. I hope I didn't seem cheeky or ungrateful. I spoke up only because I feel so strongly that you don't have to be someone special to achieve something. And I was definitely not a hero."[68] Watson explained that she was lucky enough to have the perseverance and support to achieve her goal, which in turn afforded her and the other sailors a platform to advocate for causes beyond sailing.

EOS documentaries play a significant role in shaping how sailing histories are manufactured, produced, and consumed. Elevating sailors' accomplishments to greatness fits squarely into affective economies that anchor people in particular experiences, identities, and pleasure. Given its reliance on the marginal situation, which has the ability via its dance with danger and death to explore human capabilities and limitations, then arguably it is time, as Lewis suggests, "to conjoin the pursuit of happiness, the search for personal well-being, with various forms of politically motivated behaviour"[69] to advance women's social, economic, and cultural empowerment. While the sailing community now finally has its first female commodore and has fostered numerous adaptive programs and scholarships to encourage greater participation by people of all abilities, races, and cultures, Edwards believes more needs to be done. "Enough has not changed, and it's been too long a battle. Men need to stand up with women."[70] Perhaps, too, it's time for media representations to move beyond the predictable, the voyeuristic, the affective, and the economy of death.

CHAPTER 11

Big Data and the Gamblification of Sport (Media)

Convergence

Over the first two decades of the twenty-first century, the sport-media ecology has changed rapidly, spurred by the processes of digitalization, globalization, and commodification, and by the convergence of these processes with datafication and hyperscale networks. No longer merely used as a marketing buzzword, big data can be understood as the digitization of information that now involves a range of applications and services that consolidate the space of communication into one network constituted by telecommunications, the Internet, and mass media.[1] The tremendous advancements in networked computing has reconfigured how media companies operate, as well as intensifying the merging of Internet networks and communication networks, creating new centers of power. In short, media depend on big data to understand not only what content it should develop by providing predictive analytics, but also how best to reach its audience. By further conflating production, distribution, and marketing functions, media use content to amass data "to know who will consume what, on what platform, when, and for how much."[2]

The convergent advancements in media, technology, and athletics are no accident, as media and datafication have become integral to all phases of athletic training, coaching, and performance enhancement. By having visual representations of movement in action, technique became easier to teach and master. This standardization of practice routines through visual imaging was further enhanced by technology's facilitation in the accumulation and analysis of statistical data, advanced biokinetics, nutrition, and psychology. This homogenization and quantification of athletic performance laid the foundation for today's data-driven, technology-enriched, vibrant sport commodity perfectly suited to the needs of the gambling industry. For example, while fantasy sport games were conceived and developed before the advent of the Internet, it was only with the proliferation of personal computers and the World Wide Web that mass dissemination was possible and convergence with other games of chance led invariably to interest by the gambling industry. As one scholar noted, technology's process of digitization facilitated integration of sports-themed products into the larger gambling market.

Sport content delivered by the media serves multiple journalistic and cultural functions related to record-keeping and legitimating the importance of sport as a marketable commodity that can be trusted.[3] Researchers argue that trust between betting operators and consumers evolved as the transmission platforms became more capable of presenting spectators with visual proof of the contests, as articulated in Chapter 9. Another implication is the familiarity with the dissemination of sporting events via media. As more and more sport content became available across media platforms, greater accessibility and greater familiarity with personal communication devices (i.e., mobile phones) led to increased interest in that content. Unable to forestall the popularity of fantasy sports, the U.S. major sports leagues did not hesitate to embrace them, realizing those games enhanced popularity to the leagues. Because fantasy sports brought with them an image of clean fun, any negative implications of sports betting quietly faded, advancing a message that fantasy sports are a kind of Disney-like land of endless fascination apart from reality.

Arguably, a predictable ramification of the complex commodification process traversing sport today is the proliferation of online betting on not only sporting events, but also free-to-play fantasy games and its ultimate manifestation, Daily Fantasy Sports (DFS). When the U.S. Supreme Court ruled in *Murphy v. NCAA* that certain provisions of the Professional and Amateur Sports Protection Act of 1992 (PASPA) violated the anti-commandeering doctrine, which relates to the unconstitutionality of federal statutes compelling states to enforce federal law, it opened the door to legalized betting, and more than thirty states have enacted legislation that legalized betting on sports and fantasy games. As one scholar observed, "With PASPA upended, a myriad of legal issues now surrounds almost every facet of the sports industry with everyone from state legislatures to the leagues to gaming companies attempting to figure out the appropriate way forward."[4] Sports media and the major U.S. sports leagues campaigned to make sure sports betting legislation included structures to guarantee the integrity of their sports, an "integrity tax" for example, which would function as an insurance premium to compensate the leagues for increased risk to their products. Failure by the state legislatures to incorporate some form of protection may lead to litigation over intellectual property—the real-time statistical data—which constitutes the basis of much gambling activity. What exactly constitutes sport intellectual property remains open to interpretation, especially in relation to systems of data collected during those events. In short, Big Data is now Big Daddy.

Syncronicity

Not surprisingly, two months after the Murphy decision, NBA Commissioner Adam Silver announced that the league and MGM Resorts International had reached an historic agreement making MGM the official gaming partner of the NBA, and marking a new era of the interrelationship between professional sports and professional gambling, as well as the resulting proliferation of sport media programming and promotional materials around gambling. The resulting changes have been described by scholars as the gamblification of sport and its synchronous relative, the sportification of gambling. The relationship between these disparate entities is the result of the convergence and application of gambling's logics to something which, previously, it had only tangential relations, and those were uncomfortable at best. As Lopez-Gonzalez and Griffiths explain:

> By gamblificating sport, neighbouring industries have incorporated gambling opportunities into their business models and have connected their interests to those of the gambling operators. Correspondingly, sportification is the process of incorporating the logics of sport to non-sporting contexts.[5]

This idea of sportification is made manifest when non-sport industries capitalize on the socially redeeming attributes of athleticism (e.g., health consciousness, teamwork, leadership, and purposefulness), while attempting to maximize the entertainment and playability of their products and generate its affective values.

The process of sportification has significant similarities with the application of game-design characteristics to non-game environments. Cultural acceptance of gambling on sports has only accelerated as non-sport programming featuring contests of all kinds—from singing and dancing to cooking to forging weapons—and has proved to be a viable reality television genre. In terms of marketing ploys, nothing involves an audience more than being able to pick winners. The process of sportifying reality television involves borrowing sports-world elements, particularly a live audience, a "Kitchen Stadium" setting, brand-name sponsors, a trophy, and competition with temporal and spatial obstacles. That these broadcasts usually include sport media aesthetics like instant replay, official judges, expert commentators, and roaming reporters add to the sport-motif dramatization. Getting up close and personal and editing in backstories are used in the same ways that canned segments were introduced into the live sportscast. Audience participation is encouraged in person and online. Audiences reveal their preferences in different ways, including fan websites and betting communities. Not surprisingly, betting odds have become increasingly featured as the field is ultimately whittled down to favorites and upstarts and pairings take shape along sporting mythologies. Sport discourse around favorites and underdogs, game plans and strategy, creativity and technique dominate the presentation.

In the same way, the gamblification of sport is premised on the idea that people, in their behaviors, give meaning to sporting events as cultural and economic capital distinguishable from other phenomena. Identification with a team, players, and spaces (i.e., home field), is often manifested in financial support for a team in season tickets, merchandise, and betting. By demonstrating commitment to that team and/or activity, fans engage in transactions in which they control how much they are willing to spend, and how much they are willing to risk in a betting situation. To lend greater significance to the event, sport media create narratives around which team-fan emotional links are commercially exploited. That exploitation is sustainable only if the event retains its veneer of legitimacy, played according to the rules and adjudicated by an objective, fair, and impartial party—the camera never lies—and affirmed with finality. In much the same way, sports betting relies on the confidence of consumers that the transaction is legitimate, regulated, has reliable payment systems, and remains private. What has been transpiring in this interrelationship between technology, markets, culture, and consumer transactions around sport-mediated gambling is worth unpacking in greater detail.

Fantasy Sports

According to the Fantasy Sports Trade Association (FSTA) website, more than 60 million Americans are now participants in some form of fantasy sports and have spent more than $8 billion on fantasy sports since inception.[6] It certainly did not start out that way when in 1962 two sportswriters at the *Oakland Tribune*—Scotty Sterling and George Ross—teamed with Bill Winkenback, a limited owner of the NFL's Oakland Raiders, to form the Greater Oakland Professional Pigskin Prognosticators League (GOPPPL).[7] Not surprisingly, interest in fantasy football has remained the most popular U.S. fantasy sport with 78 percent of fantasy participants playing. In terms of fantasy players, three-quarters of them also bet on some type of sport in 2018, and three-quarters of all sports bettors play fantasy football.[8] Even though the Pigskin Prognosticators League never generated significant national attention, it set the stage for what came to be known as MLB's Rotisserie League.

Founded in the 1979–1980 offseason by Daniel Okrent, Glen Waggoner, and others, the Rotisserie League took its name from a popular Manhattan restaurant, *La Rotisserie Française*, where the rules for rotisserie baseball were purportedly generated in its creation story. Okrent had been a student at the University of Michigan at the same time Bill Gamson was developing his Baseball Seminar as an academic diversion from his work on game theory. The Baseball Seminar established rules for an auction of MLB players using four statistics: batting average, RBI's, ERA's and wins. Gamson related that statistics were not nearly as available and varied as they are now.[9] Despite the dearth of statistical data, baseball harbored the kind of quantitative scaffolding that lent itself to comparison, debate, and conjecture that could be repurposed for games. A decade later, Okrent published his ground-breaking book, *The Ultimate Baseball Book*, and began collaborating with Bill James, a statistician who loved the sport.[10] Thanks to the conjunction of these gamers and statisticians, rotisserie baseball acquired the impetus and expertise needed to develop into a popular pastime.

The next important historical event was the development of computer software programs that could be encoded to simulate actual game play, compile and analyze statistical data, and facilitate access to team and player information. When the Internet exploded onto the fantasy sports scene, rotisserie leagues proliferated at a much greater rate. In addition to providing abundant information instantaneously, the Internet provided a virtual space that accommodated both rotisseries and pool leagues whose results can be based on current actual play as well as single-season leagues from keeper leagues.[11] Technology not only facilitated rapid growth and ease of communication, but it also provided its own metadata about those gamers, with their demographic and psychographic profiles emerging over time.

Thus, the typical participant fantasy sport participant has been characterized as a young, well-educated, White male, who is financially stable, occupying a highly privileged position in the social hierarchy.[12] Displaying sports knowledge offers the prototypical fantasy sports participant the opportunity to assert one's superior knowledge in businesslike ventures in which "masculinity is fortified by accepting and exercising social power over players as well as by challenging other participants to trade athletes to create the best team possible."[13] This assertion of masculinity by displaying sports knowledge provides opportunities to reclaim superiority within a highly competitive environment. Given that eighty percent of fantasy sports participants are male, efforts to increase women's participation in fantasy games remain stunted despite tactical marketing ploys that emphasize women's management acumen, incentivize participation, and promise acceptance.[14] One indication of women's reluctance can be traced to television media's dearth of coverage of women's sports and women athletes, reinforced by the fact that fantasy sports leagues also neglect and largely ignore women's sports.[15] And similar to how women's participation in sports is not considered threatening until women assert equality (e.g., tennis prize money, compensation for representing the nation), women's participation in fantasy sports is not considered threatening as long as it reaffirms male superiority reflected in superior sports knowledge.

Despite being a mostly male preserve, research has shown that motivations for participation in fantasy sports differ depending on a variety of demographics beyond gender, especially age, as "younger participants are more likely to pursue entertainment, enjoyment, and surveillance desires while passing time was key for older participants."[16] This makes sense in the context of superior sports knowledge as well. Development and application of that knowledge—accumulated across years of attending to sports—is highly correlated with one's composition of a roster, experienced by fantasy team owners. Nonetheless, there is no significant relationship between the amount of money spent on fantasy games and overall sport media consumption, but there is a relationship between the amount of money spent on fantasy games and overall fantasy sport consumption.[17] Clearly, investing in fantasy sports and overall consumption of fantasy sports increase together. As asserted by Ipsos Public Affairs, fantasy sports participants outspend the general population in major product and service categories, but also outspend the average sports fan with regard to spending habits.[18] The increase in participation, consumption, and spending related to fantasy sports can be attributed to the emergence of Daily Fantasy Sports (DFS). Not surprisingly, people with the highest levels of sports knowledge are also the ones who more readily migrate to DFS or integrate DFS into their fantasy sports repertoire.

Daily Fantasy Sports

In DFS, fantasy owners/GMs pay a daily or weekly entry fee to compete for payouts, which are based on that day's (or week's) standings within one particular pool of contestants.[19] Unlike season-long fantasy sports, which plays out over the course of several months and allows more agency to fine-tune a team's roster, DFS requires more instinctive maneuvering, whereby the DFS contestant drafts a new team each day and pays a set buy-in or ante. Sports betting pools require contestants to pick whom they believe will be the winners of each game for that week's schedule. It only holds to reason that the players to draft are on teams that are likeliest to win, so trying to pick different or sleeper teams would not be considered a "safe bet," even though the legal interpretation is that playing DFS does not cross the threshold into legal gambling.[20] The Supreme Court's reasoning that chance and random luck have a greater impact than skill in these games would appear to be borne out in how the game is structured. Nonetheless, the objective for players is to win money based on one's superior sports knowledge. Contestants may bet on as many teams, and in as many and varied ways, as they want without having to plan for the next week. As one legal scholar has concluded, "Gambling, not camaraderie, competition, or the thrill of victory against friends, appears to be the main purpose of playing DFS."[21]

Another area in which DFS has come to resemble gambling is that the chance to win or lose money is much greater for DFS than for season-long leagues. Industry-sponsored data verifies that while the average amount spent is approximately $500 per year, DFS participants spend considerably more and have to play significantly more often in order to make the Return-on-Investment lucrative enough to sustain a high level of engagement.[22] Additionally, DFS players not only gamble, but also experience significantly higher rates of comorbid substance and mental health problems than the average gambler.[23] Taken together, these findings suggest that DFS players likely share etiological characteristics with a subgroup of "problem gamblers who are motivated by a desire to escape aversive mood states or who utilize gambling as an additional form of sensation-seeking and an outlet for impulsivity."[24] Previous research into fantasy sports gambling had suggested that the elements of fun, excitement, competition played a bigger role than winning money when compared with traditional gamblers. However, more recent studies—especially those conducted in countries that have had legalized gambling for a longer time—suggest that marketing strategies in which sports betting products and sports bettors are associated with the positive values of sport actually improve the public perception of sports betting. That there is a growing overlap between DFS participants and sports bettors can be understood in terms of the marketing strategies directed to consumers of fantasy sports. Included are product placements, cross-promotions, and traffic-drivers established either by fantasy providers in conjunction with their marketing partners or with brands seeking to independently buzz the market through fantasy sports.

Gamblification

The road from participation in fantasy sports to sports gambling has been and continues to be carefully constituted so as not to blur the distinctions mandated in the SCOTUS legal opinion. The Unlawful Internet Gambling Enforcement Act did not legalize fantasy sports, but did provide an exemption from federal prosecution if fantasy sports operators followed the statutory requirements. For example, the First Amendment freedom to use player statistics and other information trumps any major league player or owner right to publicity of that information.[25] Despite this exemption for fantasy sports, the number of sports betting marketing techniques embedded into sportscasts has only proliferated, providing opportunities to engage sports viewers with sponsors' brands, including online gambling sites. Sponsors enhance brand recognition by embedding promotional messages within live sports broadcasts, as well as pre- and post-game programming. Included among the various techniques employed are gambling sponsored segments, on-screen displays of betting odds, celebrity endorsement of gambling brands, discussions of betting by match commentators, studio cross-overs to wagering operator reps to discuss bet types, specials and odds, as well as paid advertisements in commercial breaks.[26]

The proliferation and diversity of sports betting marketing strategies has signaled for the public the rapid growth of the sports betting market, the ubiquity of which has led some researchers to refer to it as "the gamblification of sport."[27] As a cultural category, sport lends symbolic value to sports betting which, in turn, is transferred down to consumers of betting products, ultimately becoming associated with the positive aspects of sport and an improvement of the public perception that sports betting is fun. Fantasy sports participation and sports betting are predicated on team identification as a point of demarcation, meaning that financial investment in a team—real or fantasy—is an important way of demonstrating commitment to that team.

The purpose of marketing strategies is to transform team loyalty into sports betting brand loyalty, which commercially exploits the team-fan affective link.[28] What is transferred from sport to sports betting are the very meanings that constitute the sports narrative built around the idea that outcomes that can be controlled and properly managed. In other words, winning in betting is not so different than winning in a sports meritocracy that rewards hard work, effort, preparation, etc., and failure to succeed is a direct result of inexperience, insufficient skill, or faulty preparation in training or coaching. Blaming external factors such as injuries, weather conditions, or referee bias has its counterpart in blaming bookmakers' odds, structural bias, and situational factors. Little wonder then that sports betting marketing strategies focus on promoting chance-minimizing, skill-maximizing scenarios in which sports knowledge can supposedly beat the book.[29] Knowing exactly what the bet is and what scenarios are involved are main parts of demonstrated betting fluency and competency. That these two parallel success narratives largely omit those who do not make it to the Show like those who veer into problem gambling confirms these narratives' inherent survival bias.[30]

The gamblification of sport media has surged thanks to the embedding of sports-betting related commodities into sports programming, like the FOX Bet Super 6 contest during the 2022 NFL Super Bowl and MLB World Series. This free-to-play prediction app features former players like former Pittsburgh Steeler Terry Bradshaw and Boston Red Sox star David "Big Papi" Ortiz, who provide the money for the contest. Overseen by the FOX Bet umbrella, which is a division of Flutter Entertainment, no betting or wagering of any kind is made on the FOX Bet Super 6 platform, as averred in promotional material.[31] That said, clearly the free-to-play constitutes an incentive to try other online and mobile sportsbook commodities developed through a first-of-its kind national media and sports wagering partnership in the United States. Other national and regional sports media have followed this path: Being aligned with a sportsbook gambling operation is now routine, and incorporating gaming and gambling incentives into the sportscast continues to proliferate.

Unwilling to turn down a lucrative revenue stream from the purchasing of advertising rights by wagering operators, sport media has gone "all in" with them, accompanied by an expectation that sport journalists will assume an added role of betting experts.[32] For example, betting odds increasingly feature in sports "news" segments on television, radio, and daily podcasts. Given the fact that data companies deliver information to both media outlets and betting companies makes it more probable that the published data sets are at the same time conveniently shaped for betting purposes, manufacturing a discursive thread intimating a probable outcome without explicitly encouraging a bet on it.[33] A variety of statistical measures of player productivity are regularly featured at websites like NFL.com's "Stats Lab," with comparisons and graphics updated regularly. Additionally, anyone watching live sportscasts today can't help but notice the number of sports betting brand names prominently displayed ubiquitously in stadiums/arenas across the United

States. Research has shown that brand recognition plays a role in cueing consumer engagement in addictive behaviors, including gambling.[34]

In addition to stadium/area signage, sports fans are deluged with advertising within the televised or streamed sportscast for the latest promotions aimed at specific consumption communities that gamble on sports. These promotions have an almost immediate impact, based on the constant availability of gambling commodities through online websites which second-screen users easily access. Not surprisingly, Internet sports bettors with higher problem gambling proclivities responded more positively to gambling promotions during televised sport.[35] Moreover, results indicated that young male Internet sports bettors remain vulnerable to problem gambling, particularly if they hold positive attitudes to gambling sponsors who embed promotions into sports broadcasts and to the promotional techniques employed therein. The extent to which promotions embedded within sportscasts are fueling this increase is generally not well understood. Gambling promotions have more effect on maintaining or increasing gambling patterns, but they have little impact on converting non-gamblers into gamblers.[36] While unable to provide demonstrated causality, results are consistent with research that found a relationship between increased exposure to sports betting advertising and greater sports betting intention and behavior.[37]

In the same way that the Internet greatly advanced the reach of fantasy sports, it has also become the "cyberplace"[38] for sports gambling participation, illustrating the interrelationships between technology, markets, ideology, culture, and social assimilation in today's hyperscale network society. Success of the gambling industry's sustainable business model is predicated on consumer confidence in the platform, privacy concerns, government regulations on market access, and reliability of payment systems. With these factors being satisfactorily navigated, the realization of a new sport meta-sphere constituted around the Internet, media, gaming, and gambling becomes more entrenched. Experts predict that by 2025 the Internet will connect consumers to 64 billion commodities (i.e., things and services), more than six times the number available in 2018.[39] Additionally, digitization has not only made statistical data readily available, but algorithms also enable websites to track user preferences to increase engagement, keep users on the site, and match advertisements to profiles. The problems with algorithms and facial-recognition technologies have been detailed in books such as *The Weapons of Math Destruction* by Cathy O'Neil and *Algorithms of Oppression* by Safiya Umoja Noble. Unsurprisingly, digital ad purchases surpassed legacy media ad spending by 2019, with the largest revenue shares going to Google, Facebook, and Amazon, major nodes in what is referred to as the hyperscale network.[40]

The proliferation of online sports gambling has resulted in the convergence of several independent, non-sporting processes related to the globalization of sport markets, the datafication-quantification of sport performance, the commodification of sport media, and the ubiquitous presence of technology through personal mobile devices. Temporal and spatial boundaries have long since dissipated, so while distinct seasons exist nominally, the idea of off-seasons no longer constrains participation in or betting on fantasy sports, electronic sport-related videogames, virtual sports, non-sport videogames, and real-world sporting events. It is literally possible for bettors to gamble around the clock, in the same way that investors trade in worldwide financial stock markets.[41]

Atomization

The atomization of sports content, having evolved from the aesthetic principles of the highlight form is key to understanding how digital integration of that content through an assemblage of platforms converts action into data that is repurposed functionally to serve in the commodification process. The quantification of sport performance has assumed a position of priority in the twenty-first century with data-driven technologies utilizing hyperscale networks to transmit content and gather users' data left behind along a trail of social media interaction, website navigation, and consumer behavior that can then be sold for profit.[42] In terms of gambling operators, any and every element can become a bet operationally defined within unequivocal boundaries of win or lose. That sport content is disseminated by sophisticated media technologies plays a vital role in lending assurances to bettors and betting operators that the result is legitimate and trustworthy. That trust predictably became a foundation for the proliferation of mobile betting apps.

It should be no surprise that online sports betting is an off-shoot of the complex commodification process defining sport today. Mobile betting reflects a change in not only how but also how often bettors can engage in the activity. Betting operators report generating approximately three-quarters of their revenue from mobile apps.[43] Even more significant than removing barriers to betting, mobile apps provide opportunities for live in-play betting, furthering the interactions between mediated sport consumption and betting—a portrait of the fan who bets on sports while watching or streaming the sportscast. While mobile betting apps have facilitated betting accessibility, they have not completely extinguished traditional off-line betting venues, which continue to provide a retail setting in which bettors feel at home in the company of like-minded consumers, in a similar way the sports bar accommodates patrons who want to watch sports in a communal setting. Both venues integrate online betting through digital access. Stadiums and arenas of professional teams have also provided their customers with access to free Wi-Fi systems that enable fans to bet online while watching the game in person. A recent article in *USA Today* explained that the new arena for the NBA's Phoenix Suns franchise will partner with FanDuel® to open a 7,400-square-foot retail sportsbook with sports gaming machines, live betting windows, 40 television screens, a full-service bar, and a complimentary VIP room for high-stakes bettors.[44] More than a half-dozen other professional franchises have similar plans to provide retail betting locations in their venues. Despite not knowing the full implications of how online betting affects other at-risk behaviors, sporting organizations, leagues, betting operators, and the media are heavily invested in capitalizing on sport betting commodities that have dramatically altered from a discontinuous, one-off form to a continuous form of gambling, characterized by increased access and betting options.

Surveillance

Sport media's role in legitimating sports gambling has a rich history in which cultural representations (d)evolve from film narratives about the bookie, the card or pool shark, the crooked horse trainer, all cut from the cloth of the misfit-savant lingering on the fringes of society, hustling to make enough money to retain autonomy from the bounds of acceptable society. These cautionary tales about the seamier underbelly of dark money and questionable morals reinforced the negative stereotypes of those willing to play just one more hand, one more rack, one last race to free them from falling deeper into trouble with some more menacing underworld mob figure like Arnold Rothstein, portrayed in John Sayles' *Eight Men Out* as having fixed the 1919 World Series. Gambling's rehabilitation, spurred by the growth and diversification of Las Vegas as a tourist and convention destination mecca, took root within televised sport media in 1976, when CBS introduced Jimmy "the Greek" Snyder to its pre-game programming, *The NFL Today*. Snyder served as resident prognosticator who offered a discourse of dispassionate, analytic assessment and evaluation of players, coaches, general managers, and owners. That discourse constituted sporting entities as commodities to be carefully measured before committing to any financial support. Having drawn nationwide attention with his Las Vegas–based syndicated newspaper column, "Wizard of Odds," Snyder brought to mainstream sports media a perspective that celebrated the culture of calculated risk-taking.[45] At the same time CBS Sports introduced Snyder's position as resident odds-maker, it was also attempting to push boundaries by making former Miss America Phyllis George a co-host in order to reflect the changing societal dynamics, and by hiring Irv Cross as a reporter, the first African American former player to transition into a broadcasting career. CBS chose this moment of deliberate inclusiveness to overhaul its pre-game format from packaged segments to live programming largely to enhance its own brand, as well as the NFL's identity as entertainment for everyone. This change repositioned both the NFL and CBS "in ways that reflected an emerging and dominant set of political priorities that demanded new kinds of citizens: self-interested, calculating, and savvy enough to provide for a future with minimal state assistance."[46] This reinforcement of neoliberal ideology about controlling and minimizing risk through reasoned, informed calculation has come to characterize sport as any other investment strategy.

Snyder ultimately fell from favor when he answered a reporter's question about the progress of African American coaches that offended many. "If they [African Americans] take over coaching like everyone wants them to, there's not going to be anything left for the white people.... I mean, all the players are black; I mean, the only thing the whites control is the coaching jobs."[47] This raced-based trope of eugenics around "natural" advantages was nothing particularly new in racialized sports discourse, but it justifiably led to his firing. What remained largely unexamined, however, were the attempts to frame examples of explicit racism as isolated instances of individual beliefs that did not necessarily reflect institutional, structural articulations within which white ideologies and assumptions of privilege are manifested. As Thomas Oates explains, the current iteration of NFL fandom marketed through the media represents the triumph of Snyder's worldview. "Encouraged by forces beyond sport, the perspective he helped bring into the mainstream has reframed the most popular sport in the United States, nurturing a market-oriented, risk-averse sensibility, reinforcing the desirability of racial integration and color-blindness, while naturalizing a surveillance-based system of racial control directed at a mostly black population."[48] The idea that sport media perpetuate this surveillance-based system is best illustrated in the collection, analysis, and dissemination of data that is commoditized and sold for profit.

Big Data

The traditional model of sport media is structured around media providing coverage of third-party contests to sufficiently large audiences that will attract advertisers who want to invest in, or sponsor, aspects of that coverage to enhance its market-share. This model defines the sport game/contest/event as content-programming used to attract audience share, yet it no longer adequately explains the connectivity and interdependencies between the Internet and media communication networks that have resulted in two significant trends—the datafication of media and the application of big data services.[49] The need to harness the power of big data has only intensified the interdependencies between the Internet and media communication networks, facilitating the digital realization of data as an emerging global format and creating new centers of power, based more on control of data than on control of content.

The turning point in this digital revolution occurred in 2007 when Hadoop, an open-source software that allows for the sharing of data processing across computers, was introduced.[50] The greater computer processing power enabled a tremendous surge in collecting data. By November 2011 when Accel Partners announced the launch of its $100 million Big Data Fund Hadoop World, datafication became the means to acquiring control. Not only did other venture capital funds already investing in big data start-ups expand greatly, but the hype brought focused attention to the importance of big data and the attenuating services related to analytics, cloud storage, and content monetization.[51] Not surprisingly, most media companies have begun utilizing big data services, precipitating changes in all aspects of production, dissemination, and routinization. The introduction and testing of new metrics has allowed media companies to interconnect with other media organizations that make up the global network. No longer governed by the logics of content, market share, and audience demographics, media organizations are now driven by data-collection enterprises that package and sell data to advertisers and marketers.

No better instance of how big data works can be illustrated than the collusion between media organizations, betting operators, and sport entities as embodied in the wearing of betting organizations' logos on FIFA team jerseys, which are shown during coverage by television cameras that, in effect, provide maximum exposure for those brands and blur the lines between entertainment, advertising, and data harvesting. As Andrejevic argues, in an affective economy, "The more emotions are expressed and circulated, the more behavior is tracked and aggregated, the greater the ability of marketers to attempt to channel and fix affect in ways that translate into increased consumption."[52] In this regard, big data has ushered in an era of emergent social sorting, the ability to identify persistent patterns, however unanticipated, that can be employed to influence the life chances of individuals and groups. The data flowing through hyperscale networks represents the digital actualization of the interdependence between the Internet and media networks, a cultural as well as technological normalization of the convergence of legacy and digital media networks.

Despite concerns raised by professionals in the behavioral sciences about the media's promoting sports betting during live sportscasts, which contain betting operators' logos, signage, websites, and betting odds, there is little impeding this interrelationship. Even though U.S. networks are limited for the time being to six wagering promotions during live sportscasts, little is being done to challenge the kind of messaging that fosters the notion that participation in, and betting on, sports "leads to power, wealth, male bonding, and social and sexual success."[53] The media, of course, are under no federal regulation to provide public service announcements that encourage self-appraisal of betting behavior or provide information in very small print about sources that offer help with gambling. High stakes wagers are celebrated within a culture in which the acceptance of risk has come to characterize sports entertainment. We have arrived at that juncture where the processes of gamblification and sportification are synchronous, with little research about the long-term implications for how society conceptualizes such activities and how much oversight might be needed.

Any review of sports programming available at websites for the teams and leagues reveals how prevalent are the promotions for gaming and betting operators. Visit any professional stadium or arena and you'd be hard-pressed to miss the dynamic or fixed banners for betting operators, as well as billboards in every direction, every public staircase, restroom, and work station. The net effect remains sport media's complicity in mining data for what Jenkins calls affect, defined as that ambient sentiment that can be productively modulated and manipulated in ways that impact upon the desires, emotions, or preferences of individual viewers and consumers.

Of course, no one has to bet on any sports event. It's just out there. Like playing a game of chance. Heads or tails. Can't miss. "Play with David Ortiz's money," says the promotional ad.[54] Guaranteed cash prizes. Contest winners. It's all very seductive and legal. States in which gambling is legal regularly report collecting millions of dollars of tax revenues, without having to detail how much of the revenue went for treating problem gambling.[55] In this space, sport media compete in a global marketplace in which getting likes is the most important measure. In this TikTok world, if you are not being liked, you are not being, you are not now. Such is the new ontology. Every little thing is mere data within an algorithm.

CHAPTER 12

Highlights and History

What happens when sporting events captured in highlights become history? This book has shown how, in their ability to distill, commodify and essentialize sporting events, sportscast highlights have served to popularize and nationalize sports and their stars, providing remediated narratives that have brought and continue to bring the drama and spectacle of sport into the everyday lives of people. As such, sportscast highlights can be seen as both content and discursive frame. As content, highlights take on a life of their own, encapsulating events into singular moments of achievement or futility that are imprinted on the collective consciousness. As a discursive frame, highlights are a journalistic tool as ubiquitous as a headline, a caption or a lead, guided by an underlying aesthetic and rhetorical principle in which a part represents the whole. If journalism is indeed the first draft of history, then highlights are a kind of shorthand used to distill that history into something memorable. Memory built with sports highlights offers a shared past, constituted in time and space, that facilitates an ability to establish identity for not only the individual, but also, more importantly, for the collective. Armed with the knowledge of what constitutes the most important sports achievements, sports journalists and consumers can more easily attend to those representations of sports and athletes that fit within the mythology and collective memory, validating themselves as well as the memories they invoke.

Sportscast highlights took shape in the early days of film, became standardized in newsreels, then commodified on network and cable television, and deployed ubiquitously across new delivery systems. While the delivery systems have changed, the utilization of highlights in both live sports coverage and news programming has followed key principles that bridge the modern and postmodern, illustrating important issues related to culture and media. Although sportscast highlights have been utilized for over a century now, little scholarship has been devoted to them and how they shape our collective memory and sports history.

The Rhetoric of Highlights

The highlight became the most important electronic sports journalism news frame because capturing a part of an event and presenting it as a representation of the whole allowed broadcasters the most efficient means available to communicate a story. Even before sportscasts, companies selling the fight sequences staged in Edison's Black Maria studio realized the importance of packaging and selling these fights by rounds. Not surprisingly the knockout round was the most profitable. Customers often skipped the first five rounds, wanting to watch only the round with the knockout. Rather than pay sixty cents to see an entire fight, customers paid ten cents to watch only the knockout round. Packaging and technological limitations pointed producers in the direction of profits and viewers in the direction of instant gratification.

Equally important to the development of sports highlights was the formula Edison's cameramen used to capture an event—whether the event's duration lasted two minutes (e.g., horse race) or four to five hours (e.g., America's Cup race)—in 50 or 150 feet of film. In coverage of the 1897 Suburban Handicap and the 1899 America's Cup races, Edison's cameramen captured key moments of these two distinctly different races. In the former, the shots included a three-shot sequence: the parade, the start and the finish. In the latter, which included several races, Edison's titles provided the key components, including *"Shamrock" and "Columbia" Jockeying for a Start*, *"Shamrock" and "Columbia" Rounding the Outer Stake Boat*, and *"Columbia" Winning the Cup*. Not only do the titles serve as indexical markers for the larger event, but these films also capture essential action that conveys meaning. In sports, essential action is delineated in the outcome—what is of most interest to most people is who won. Even though results are not the only stories that comprise a sportscast or a newspaper sports section, they are the lead stories or the front-page stories above the fold. Significantly, this concept of essential action changed as production values were enhanced by technology—who won eventually became subsumed within spectacular feats of star athletes.

Even as newsreels standardized their sports segments, capturing memorable moments remained the key production convention. Faced with economic, technical and time limitations, newsreel cameramen developed the sequencing of shots that served to distill and essentialize sporting events. The highlight was comprised of an establishing shot (i.e., place and time), followed by a field-level shot, then by a crowd shot (e.g., cheering), a moment-of-truth shot (e.g., touchdown), a close-up shot of the victor, and the celebration shot.

To give the newsreel a sense of historical continuity, the event was condensed into a few shots that displaced actual time and space considerations in order to create a self-contained narrative. As this point in time, capturing a highlight was still very dependent upon the artistry of the cameraman. Because newsreel sports segments were composed of representations of multiple events, the production of a highlight reel gradually became more dependent on the artistry of the editor. Ultimately, production became so formulaic that newsreel sports segments did not change significantly between 1927, when sound was first introduced, and 1967, when the last newsreels were shown. In those 40 years, the newsreels captured the pageantry and spectacle of major sporting events in a highly formulaic manner.

The introduction of videotape in 1956 allowed television, and later cable, networks far greater flexibility in deploying the highlight for maximum affective impact. The role of announcers in guiding viewers to a correct interpretation of the images in their new context changed after the introduction of instant replay from one that added "color commentary" to one that provided detailed analysis of why plays worked and how athletes succeeded or failed. Sports news anchors on programs like ESPN's *SportsCenter* provided commentary that traded on both literary allusions and hip-hop vernacular. It is not the highlight image alone that conveys the event's meaning, but a combination of recontextualized images with narrative accompaniment that generates the meaning context.

Limitations

Economic and technical limitations played a key role in how sports highlights came to occupy such a prominent position in live broadcasts and news programming. For example, early film was limited by the camera's film storage capacity, which restricted sequences to 50 feet and 150 feet. Even after cameras were able to hold larger spools of film, the cost precluded shooting extended sequences. The early film's sensitivity to light also restricted shooting to outdoor subject matter or well-lit interiors. Edison's Black Maria studio utilized a type of retractable roof and was constructed on a track that rotated to maximize exposure to the sun. The development of indoor lighting allowed fights to be filmed indoors, although the heat had a debilitating effect on the boxers.

Early television cameras were limited in terms of what they captured. For this reason, television relied on coverage of boxing and wrestling because the participants remained close in proximity to each other, the ring's space was easily framed, and the duration of a boxing round was fixed at three minutes. Early coverage of sports like baseball and hockey suffered because of the difficulty of tracking a fast-moving baseball or hockey puck. Only after producers utilized a number of cameras located in strategic positions did the quality of the pictures improve. It should also be noted that television set's screen was relatively small, compounding the problem for viewing fast-paced sports. Other limitations were related to reception in that the broadcast signal was transmitted via a network of coaxial cable. Since the first coast-to-coast live broadcast did not occur until 1951 and outlying areas were not connected to the network, many stations were limited to broadcasting kinescopes that filmed what was being shown on television screens.

Because new media delivery systems were limited by the modem connection's capacity to deliver quality video, early Webcasts relied on animation and streaming audio. Only after broadband increased storage and transmission capacities were Web sites able to utilize streaming video to attract visitors. Wireless mobile service technology followed a similar trajectory in that the first two generations delivered half of the amount of digital information (i.e., 150 kilobits) that the next generation was able to deliver, and only then were able to transmit high-resolution content. Significantly, discourse about technology is often couched around advancement, yet the technology's limitations most often determine its utilization and deployment.

Cultural Hegemony

The proliferation of sportscast highlights led to a hegemony that glorified the dominant white culture and often marginalized women and non-white athletes. For example, in the 1904 St. Louis Olympic Games, George Poage, an African American, won two bronze medals, one for the 200-meter hurdle and the other for the 400-meter hurdle. However, an integrated audience was not allowed at either the Olympics or the World's Fair since organizers had built segregated facilities for the spectators. Almost as soon as Jack Johnson became boxing's heavyweight champion in 1908, legislators and civic leaders attempted to ban the distribution of fight films. This ultimately led to passage of the Sims Act of 1912, barring the interstate transportation of fight films for commercial exhibition. This legislative intervention was linked to a moral concern over the effect both of prizefights in general and the effect of images of Johnson's victories in particular. A racial ideology that demonized Johnson was draped in a discourse purporting to protect women and children.

Newsreel and television presentations of America's black and Indian athletes were characterized by a discourse that sought to avoid controversy by presenting individual achievement within a framework of the U.S. team, as in the 1932 Los Angeles Olympic Games in which Ralph Metcalf and Eddie Tolan won multiple gold medals in track and field. Those representations finally gave way after many years to reporting that often focused on race only with stories involving sensational, often criminal, activity (e.g., O.J. Simpson's arrest and trial, Darryl Strawberry's drug use, Michael Vick's dog fighting, and Ray Leonard's spousal abuse). When the contributions of blacks and American Indians in Olympiads could not be avoided (e.g., Jim Thorpe in 1912, Jesse Owens in 1936), they were explained under the "melting pot" paradigm that celebrated these victories as evidence of the democratic ideal of inclusiveness. Often, the presentations employed a dialectic in which white athletic prowess was aligned from superior intellect, will power, and scientific training while black and Indian athletic prowess was aligned with natural ability, closeness to nature, and physical attributes peculiar to their race. Highlights equipped the mainstream media with a vehicle to frame the achievements of black and Indian athletes without having to explain the total absence of minorities from national organizations and federations, as well as the absence of non-white owners, coaches, and managers.

Sportscasts highlights were also used to marginalize the athletic achievements of women. Women's sports were covered within a context of gendered power relationships, meaning women's sports have been almost entirely produced by men and edited by men with commentary written and provided by male sports journalists. That images of women were almost entirely produced through the male gaze to accommodate male interests and desires was evidenced in the *Pathé Weekly* newsreel directive in the 1920s that cameramen should get shots of only the most beautiful women athletes. Newsreel and television coverage of women's sports marginalized athletic achievement for a discourse that highlighted the athlete's femininity and her role as wife or mother.

Women's sports have remained largely underrepresented in sportscasts, comprising no more than five to seven percent, according to recent studies of national media like CNN, *USA TODAY* and ESPN's *SportsCenter*. Although in 1948 NBC broadcast a television news program devoted to women, *Sportswoman of the Week*, it lasted only four months. Even though more women than men have graduated from journalism schools ever since 1977, women sports journalists constituted less than 15 percent of sports journalists, and an even smaller percentage of editors, managers and owners in that same period of time. Moreover, women sports journalists have faced considerable obstacles in gaining equal access to broadcast booths, press boxes, locker rooms and production facilities. Judicial intervention was needed before women sports journalists were granted equal access. Sports organizations attempted to use moral concerns and issues of privacy to deny them access. When women sports journalists did gain access, they were sexually harassed by athletes and co-workers, evidenced by the case of Lisa Olson of the *Boston Herald*. In the twenty-first century, women athletes continue to be marginalized, largely absent in Fantasy League Sports gaming.

Positioning

Not only did highlights constitute the main technique used in the production of newsreel and television sports segments, but they also became the primary element around which pre- and post-game programs were developed in the early 1950s and greatly refined with the addition of videotape. The fact that sports constituted its own segment, apart from news and weather, offers an important clue about our culture and a direct bearing on the relationship between sport, race, gender, ethnicity and national identity. This positioning of sports within electronic news media reflects the general place of sports in our culture as a well-defined enclave that bears little or no relation to the rest of the news.

With the arrival of sports news programs like ESPN's *SportsCenter* in 1979 and CNN's *Sports Tonight* in 1980, televised sports journalism truly set itself apart from the rest of the news. These programs had an immediate impact on local stations and the way they covered sports, leading some stations to conclude that there would not be much of a future in local television sports. At that time, sports ranked at or near the bottom in most research polls of why people watch local television news. A 1998 poll conducted by the Radio and Television News Directors Foundation found that the percentage of people (2 percent) who watched local news because of sports matched those that said they watched because there were no other choices on television.

Even before the development of videotape, the television networks developed wrap-around programs to complement live coverage of sporting events. Pre-game shows, which used highlights gleaned from kinescopes, were introduced in 1950. Although existing technology did not allow the use of highlights during post-game shows until the 1960s, the networks offered programs such as the *Philco Touchdown* show as early as 1948, featuring kinescope films of the season's outstanding collegiate football games. Pre- and post-game programs are still utilized in the production of local, regional, and national sportscasts. ESPN has offered weekly sport-specific wrap-up shows like *Baseball Tonight* and *NFL Live* since the 1980s, and many of these programs are offered nightly. Since the development of the Internet, the professional leagues have utilized their Web sites to offer previews and summaries of every league game, and highlights figure prominently in all of them. These pay packages have allowed fans who no longer reside in the vicinity of their favorite team to watch a Webcast of every game.

Media organizations have contributed to and maintained the widely held belief that broadcast sports are entertainment, staged to attract an audience to whom sponsors and advertisers can sell their products and services, and glean data. This belief has had lasting implications in terms of how sports journalism's institutional values and practices were formed. As the costs to broadcast rights for sporting events have escalated, these privately controlled sports teams and leagues became immune to the usual intrusions of journalists into topics that surround sports other than what takes place on the playing field.

Commercialization

The commercial imperative governing sports programming is predicated on attracting the largest audience to present to advertisers and sponsors. In order to attract the largest audience, broadcasters utilize production values that enhance an event's pageantry and spectacle. Sports leagues and associations, television, and advertising work together to create a single promotional entity. The increased pressures to create ever more dramatic and entertaining forms of sports spectacles are the result of the appropriation by this sport-media-commercial complex. The 1980s saw greater state support for economic development of sports facilities, international events, and the showcasing of world-class athletes. Gambling and gaming have become the 2020s most lucrative sporting commodities, betting sportsbook machines now as ubiquitous as a 1960s jukebox or an ATM.

Arguably, this entertainment model is largely anti-mediatory, wherein viewers are led to believe that what is presented to them constitutes the natural and universally accepted version of sports. Many enhanced production techniques—music amplification of noises on the sport field, collages, superimposed graphics, rapid cuts, computer simulations, color arrangements, shocking images—are used to capture and sustain the audience's gaze. Montages of highlights and commentary constitute the most effective means to achieve the desired end of maintaining viewer interest. The viewer's participation is invoked through a familiarity with the form and style of highlights while affective identification with specific players and teams dissolves the boundary of the television screen. So powerful has that dissolution become that many viewers believe with proper training and coaching, they could do as well as the athletes they are watching. In other words, the highly technical analysis that often characterizes effects like slow-motion action replays are employed by viewers to deny differences in ability and competence.

As the links between sports and media outlets grew closer, a vested interest in promoting and presenting sport in a positive light becomes part of the sports journalist's routine. The interdependency between broadcasters and advertisers has resulted in less criticism of contractual partners. Sports journalists increasingly report on events being covered by the television station. As the commercial dimension of the sports industry became more substantial, television's view of sport has not significantly changed. Stations are dependent on the teams they cover for access to the games, coaches and players. Although never stated explicitly, sports broadcasters have avoided controversy in their coverage of the local team and its players, perhaps fearing that to expose wrong-doing or ineptitude would result in a loss of the broadcasting rights, sponsorship support, and access to highlights.

The commercial imperative is also reflected in not only the corporatized branding of almost every segment of a broadcast, but also in the tightening of control over the dissemination of highlights. That the professional leagues have imposed restrictions on the use of highlights and still images of a game in progress speaks to their value in attracting fans and viewers to media.

Constructing Canons

Codifying what constitutes the most important sports highlights can be traced to producers' need to create programming to satisfy the 24-hour news cycle and the propensity of news organizations like ESPN to produce increasingly affective highlights to satisfy the insatiable sports junkie. By the 1990s ESPN had developed its own typology of highlights, referred to as "The Seminal Seventeen," which became a tool for training production assistants. Finding the "Top Ten Plays" on a nightly basis invariably leads to a daily canon in which only the most spectacular dunks, the most vicious hits, the most spectacular shots, saves, and goals by the most recognizable athletes make the list. In this way, the gate-keeping process is biased by endorsements and name-recognition rather than actual achievement to create a skewed rank order. Not surprisingly, the quest for the nightly "Top Ten" invariably spawns "Top Ten Plays of the Week," which spawns a weekly version of "The Ultimate Highlight," which spawned a book, *The Ultimate Highlight Reel*, which presents a calendar of the greatest highlights that happened to occur on a given date. The process regenerates itself, providing an unending stream of only the spectacular, based on a known quantity's ability to shock and awe.

ESPN's production of shows based upon a ranking have included: "Greatest Highlights with Chris Berman," "Who's Now," "The 100 Greatest (North American) Athletes of the Twentieth Century," "Greatest *SportsCenter* Moments," "Top Ten Greatest Games," and "Top Ten Greatest Coaches." In creating these monuments to greatness, ESPN appropriates athletic achievement in the service of brand recall and ratings, and enhances its aura of authoritativeness. As expressed in the introduction to *The Ultimate Highlight Reel* book, while everyone has his or her own favorite highlights, the "ultimate" decision of what highlights make the canon resides with ESPN. Of course, the first criterion is that they appear on *SportsCenter*. The unfortunate side effect of such listings is a narrowing of the sports discourse. One can agree or disagree with ESPN's lists, but few alternatives are produced, none that has the reach or marketing to create an impact. In this way, codification produces a canon of the "Greatest Highlight," absent the contributions of many of the world's athletes and sports not particular popular with the self-proclaimed worldwide leader in sports.

Viewer Protocols

The protocols associated with viewing sportscast highlights have changed considerably. Watching film in a Kinetoscope parlor was largely a solitary experience, though other customers were doubtlessly in the same parlor at the same time. Nonetheless, until the development of projection, reception occurred one person at a time. With film projection, the experience became communal, and viewers interacted with the commentator, the figures represented on screen and each other. Cheers, boos, foot-stomping and wild cries of joy were observed in newsreel audiences, and the evocation of a communal response testified to the medium's power to reduce individuality.

Before television sets became readily affordable in the early 1950s, sports fans often watched games from the bar or tavern rather than from the living room. Bar owners realized the opportunities that sportscasts afforded them and enacted rules to govern behaviors. Televised sports changed the social dynamic within the bar since people often came to the bar to watch television and not for social interaction. Televised sportscasts impacted the social sphere of the bar as a venue for spectatorship and as a space of interpersonal communication.

When home viewing became the norm, a new set of behaviors entered the lexicon. Watching sportscasts was not only pleasurable, but an addiction that had to be continually fed. Terms such as "sports junkie" and "couch potato" were used to describe the excessive viewing habits. While cable acted like an electronic magazine rack providing programming for women, children and minorities, advertisers for sportscasts appealed to a predominantly male audience.

While fundamental differences between the stadium experience and the television experience still exist, what unfolds on the field has been directly impacted by television. However, the addition of large screen video display units with replay capabilities and enhanced audio technologies has significantly narrowed the differences between the stadium and television experiences. In fact, players and stadium fans routinely watch scoreboard replays, and their reactions are often picked up by the telecast. Finally, when highlights captured errors in officiating, professional sports leagues eventually adopted the use of technology to adjudicate their sports by allowing coaches and managers to challenge calls or by creating the video assistant referee or VAR, who can alert the match referee and call for replay. Creating this veneer of certitude became an intrinsic part of protecting the integrity of a sport, as drug use and other forms of cheating threatened consumer confidence. Scandals related to buying hosting rights for the Olympics or World Cups also marred organizations' veneer.

Viewers of sportscast highlights come to the experience with specific affiliations and expectations, meaning they may already have seen the sportscast and often know the outcome. As a result, they may come to the experience with a fixed emotional attitude. Another important consideration is that highlight segments most often feature opponents, whether in the form of teams or individuals. Viewers come to the viewing experience from a number of different perspectives—those who identify with team or individual A, those who identify with team or individual B, and those who have no particular vested interest in either team. Granted, the strength of a viewer's identification will vary along an emotional spectrum from strong to weak, as it will for those viewers who are without a vested interest in either team since few viewers are so completely neutral that the highlight will arouse no emotional stimulation about either A or B. Similarly, the way a highlight and its commentary are structured relative to the teams and individuals affect how viewers will be disposed to the highlight.

By ESPN's own admission, *SportsCenter* highlights do not all focus on a game's outcome or narrative. These segments are comprised of paradigmatic images, decontextualized highlights that do not recount a specific game or event. Removed from the context of the actual events, these highlights are relatively fluid, fractal texts that do little more than entertain but also contribute to an effacing of history. Typically, these highlights serve as promotional vehicles to generate enthusiasm for ongoing events, to remind viewers "This is *SportsCenter*," and to serve as lead-ins for upcoming segments or commercial breaks. For the viewer, these highlights do not focus on specific games and teams but depend on rapid-fire displays of athleticism. Having no game context and no team identification, the viewer can only watch this overproduction of imagery. "The Ultimate Highlight" is an example of paradigmatic imagery that often evokes affect, but also boredom, emptiness, and loss. These highlights are designed to engage the viewer on a very visceral level. Often, they showcase a series of games or a series of plays, as in *SportsCenter*'s "Web Gems," "Buzzer Beaters," and "Jack U Up." Their significance emerges by escaping from context and producing its own effect. Viewers actively (co)produce their pleasure by providing the meaning, which lies beyond any narrative context. The viewer experiences a transgressive pleasure, a momentary loss of self, a conjunction of text and self that seeks to escape social control but ultimately cannot elude the ideological underpinnings that ESPN's *SportsCenter* invariably attaches to the images.

For the past two decades, new delivery systems have provided individuals considerably more access to sportscast content. Ironically, these delivery systems, especially computers and wireless mobile devices, reach an audience of one, bringing the viewing experience full circle to the days of peep shows. That more sports fans are using devices like mobile cell phones to access sportscast highlights was evidenced in a report by the mobile-marketing industry that showed on at least three different occasions in the fall of 2007 more people accessed ESPN's NFL highlights with their phones than with personal computers. Additionally, in March 2008 CBS presented every game of the NCAA men's basketball championships on the Web for free, marking the first time a major U.S. sporting event has been made available online for free. Significantly, according to data from CBS and TNS, a research firm, the network made $4.83 in advertising for each of its almost 5 million online viewers compared with $4.12 in advertising for each of its 132 million television viewers. As more people consume sportscasts online, generating more advertising revenue, the protocols for watching sportscasts will continue to evolve.

Spectacle

Technological, economic, legal and social developments in film, newsreels, television and new media contributed to the prevalence of sportscast highlights by shaping production techniques and reception protocols. Sportscast highlights evolved out of the operational aesthetics of each medium's particular style, mode of production and intertextualities that attracted audiences. As the rights fees for broadcasting the major sporting events increased, network and cable broadcasters increasingly made their broadcasts more appealing by focusing on the spectacular. Court rulings and legislative regulations stripped organizations like the NCAA of their control over broadcast rights, facilitating a saturation of the market place that eventually led to lower television ratings and an increasingly commercial presentation.

Sportscasts, arguably one of the most important culture industries, have progressed through pre-commercial and commercial phases to their current iteration in which all aspects of the sports sector (i.e., goods, services, and experiences) are now transformed into commodities to be hawked within the commercial marketplace. As a result, virtually all aspects of the global sports infrastructure—governing bodies, leagues, events, teams, and individual athletes—are now driven and defined by the inter-related processes of commercialization (the exploitation of an object or practice for capital gain); corporatization (the rational structuring and management of sporting entities according to profit motives); and spectacularization (the production of entertainment-driven experiences). Contemporary sport has become subject to the logics of a high-technology capitalist economy, propelled by commercially mediated spectacles and circuitry that moves seamlessly across digital platforms interconnected within hyperscale networks.

The commercial entertainment ethos has only increased as networks attempt to recoup the money spent on rights fees and production costs by collecting and selling data. These costs have motivated broadcasters to not only develop video and audio technologies to nuance their coverage in ways that maintain viewer attention, but also to make sure that the production is fully commodified. In today's integrated spectacle, almost every segment of a sportscast is invested with corporate sponsorship that results in considerable profits for the network and is used to seduce and fascinate viewers. Segments are branded, so that a constant stream of product names and icons act as lead-ins before the viewer gets to the actual highlights, commentary, or interview. Arguably, these segments can be seen as examples of postmodern art that bring together advertisement imagery, ideological codes and symbols of consumer capitalism. Not surprisingly, ESPN has accomplished with highlights what MTV did with the music video and YouTube and TikTok do with streams.

Sportscast highlights have facilitated an overproduction of images that are recontextualized by producers to serve their own and their sponsors' interests. This proliferation of information has led to a decrease in meaning, which is literally imploded when decontextualized and then reformulated by the media to produce affect. Affective economics anchor people in particular experiences, identities, and pleasures that invariably promote and consensualize the dominant ideology's view of reality. Such power is essentially seductive in motivating viewers to not only consume the images, but also to manifest their emotional needs in conspicuous consumption. As Roland Barthes has noted, it is not when ideology hovers close to the surface and is easily recognizable that it is most powerful, but when it is strongly present but apparently absent, allowing myths to do their affective work on the emotions.

Rapid cuts, music, superimposed graphics, and computer simulations contribute to capture and sustain viewer attention and interest. Slow-motion instant replays and edited highlight packages, which are based on the principles of film montage, manipulate and atomize both time and space and result in a fragmentation of reality. In addition to contextualizing sporting events by offering analysis and critical insight, sportscasters have deployed highlights to intervene in events, recasting them as something devoid of their original meaning and adding to the effacing of history. By the time actual sporting events are reproduced as highlight images, the principal values associated with the nature and purpose of competition—such as hard work, innovation, cooperation and teamwork, self-determination, self-sacrifice and an emphasis on sportsmanship—become distorted in the pastiche of imagery and discourse permeated with metrics. Removed from the context of the actual sporting event, spectacular dunks, towering home runs and golden goals become the means to instant gratification, transferring the excitement from the athletic contests into a continual, concentrated sense of exhilaration meant to maintain only that which is of commercial value.

Chapter Notes

Introduction

1. Daniel Dayan and Elihu Katz, *Media Events: The Live Broadcasting of History* (Cambridge: Harvard University Press, 1992), 6.

2. Martin J. Medhurst, "Propaganda Techniques in Documentary Film and Television: AIM vs. PBS," in *Television Studies: Textual Analysis*, ed. Gary Burns and Robert J. Thompson (New York: Praeger, 1989), 186.

3. For a detailed explanation of the development and importance of these technical achievements, see Arledge; Schultz; and Verna.

4. Bill Rasmussen, *Sports Junkies Rejoice! The Birth of ESPN* (Hartsdale, NY: QV Publishing, 1983).

5. Paddy Scannell, "History, Media and Communication," in *A Handbook of Media and Communication Research: Qualitative and Quantitative Methodologies*, ed. Klaus B. Jensen (London: Routledge, 2002), 194.

6. David Rowe, *Sport, Culture and the Media* (Buckingham: Open University Press, 1999), 70.

7. Rudy Martzke and Reid Cherner, "Channeling How to View Sports," *USA Today*, August 17, 2004, D2.

8. Charles Hirshberg, *ESPN 25: 25 Mind-Bending, Eye-Popping, Culture-Morphing Years of Highlights* (New York: ESPN Books, 2004), 12.

9. *Ibid.*

10. Robert Stam, "Television News and Its Spectator," in *Regarding Television: Critical Approaches—An Anthology*, ed. E. Ann Kaplan (Frederick, MD: University Publications of America, 1983).

11. Hirshberg, ESPN 25, 12.

12. Streible, *A History of the Prizefight Film, 1894–1915* (PhD diss., University of Texas, 1994), 94–98.

13. Henry Jenkins, *Convergence Culture: Where Old and New Media Collide* (New York: New York University Press, 2006), 60–61.

Chapter 1

1. Elliott J. Gorn, *The Manly Art: Bare-Knuckle Prize Fighting in America* (Ithaca: Cornell University Press, 1986), 221.

2. Charles Musser, *Edison Motion Pictures, 1890–1900: An Annotated Filmography* (Washington, D.C.: Smithsonian Institution Press, 1997), 27.

3. Pierre Bourdieu, "The Forms of Capital," in *Handbook for Theory and Research for the Sociology of Education*, ed. J.G. Richardson (Westport, CT: Greenwood Press, 1986).

4. See Gordon Hendricks, *The Kinetoscope: America's First Commercially Successful Motion Picture Exhibitor* (New York: Theodore Gaus' Sons, 1966), 99.

5. Tom Gunning, "The Cinema of Attractions: Early Film, Its Spectator and the Avant-Garde," *Wide Angle* 8.3–4 (1986): 64.

6. Quoted in John Rickards Betts, *America's Sporting Heritage: 1850–1950* (Reading, MA: Addison-Wesley, 1974), 62.

7. *Ibid.*, 61–62.

8. Musser, *Edison Motion Pictures*, 105.

9. *Ibid.*, 69.

10. "The Kinetograph," *New York Sun*, May 28, 1891, 1–2.

11. Gorn, *Manly*, 237.

12. Quoted in *ibid.*, 236.

13. *Ibid.*, 238.

14. *Ibid.*, 241.

15. See *ibid.*, 242. The New Orleans athletic clubs helped systematize boxing, and Richard Kyle Fox recognized six weight classifications, providing championship belts for each.

16. Quoted in *ibid.*, 243.

17. Quoted in Betts, *Heritage,* 77.

18. Quoted in Gorn, *Manly*, 244.

19. *Ibid.*, 245.

20. "The Kinetograph—A New Industry Heralded," *The Phonogram*, October 1892, 217–218.

21. W.K.L. Dickson and Antonia Dickson, *History of the Kinetograph Kinetoscope and Kineto-Phonograph* (New York: Arno Press & The New York Times, 1970), 19.

22. Hendricks, *Kinetoscope*, 27.

23. Quoted in *ibid.*, 37.

24. Dickson and Dickson, *History*, 34.

25. The Kinetoscope Exhibition Company, the Latham-Rector-Tilden venture, should not be confused with the Kinetoscope Company, belonging to Raff & Gammon.

26. Musser, *Edison Motion Pictures*, 102.

27. See footnote 18 in Hendricks, *Kinetoscope*, 96.

28. *Ibid.*

29. Streible, *Prizefight*, 53.

30. Quoted in Hendricks, *Kinetoscope*, 92–93.

31. *Ibid.*, 94.

32. "Knocked out by Corbett," *New York Sun*, September 8, 1894, 1.

33. Because of the newspaper articles that appeared, September 7, 1894, has become the accepted date for the staged fight, despite some confusion in Hendricks' using a different date in his first reference to the fight, although he later corrects himself. Brady's autobiography also lent to the confusion in dating the event incorrectly.

34. See note 33 in Streible, *Prizefight*, 76.

35. "Knocked out by Corbett," *New York Sun*, September 8, 1894, 1.

36. *Ibid.*

37. *Ibid.*

38. "Charged the Grand Jury. Judge Depue Wants the Corbett Fight Investigated," *Newark Daily Advertiser*, September 11, 1894, 1.

39. "Not Regarded as a Fight. Edison's Idea of the Corbett-Courtney Mill," *Newark Daily Advertiser*, September 12, 1894, 1.

40. Charles Musser, *The Emergence of Cinema: The American Screen to 1907* (New York: Scribner's, 1990), 84.

41. *Ibid.*, 91–92.

42. "Magic Lantern Kinetoscope," *New York Sun*, April 21, 1895, 2.

43. Musser, *The Emergence of Cinema*, 98.

44. Quoted in *ibid.*, 96.

45. *Ibid.*, 97.

46. Quoted in *ibid.*, 116.

47. Musser, *Edison Motion Pictures*, 213.

48. "Keith's New Theatre," *Boston Herald*, September 22, 1896, 4B.

49. "The Suburban," *New York Herald*, June 24, 1896, 8.

50. See "Note" for Suburban Handicap, 1897, in Musser, *Edison Motion Pictures*, 313.

51. Medhurst, "Propaganda Techniques," 186.

52. Quoted in Musser, *The Emergence of Cinema*, 196.

53. See Streible's discussion, *Prizefight*, 94–98.

54. Quoted in Musser, *The Emergence of Cinema*, 198.

55. *Ibid.*

56. Streible, *Prizefight*, 122.

57. Erik Barnouw, *A Tower in Babel: A History of Broadcasting in the United States to 1933* (New York: Oxford University Press, 1966), 23. Although he discusses the 1901 America's Cup races and the attempt to use wireless to document the race's progress, Barnouw makes no mention of Marconi's demonstration at the 1899 America's Cup races.

58. See note 12 in Streible, *Prizefight*, 196.

59. Sam C. Austin, "Lively Bidding for the Jeffries-Sharkey Fight," *Police Gazette*, July 29, 1899, 11.

60. "The Films That Failed," *The Phonoscope*, May 1899, 14.

61. *Ibid.*

62. Quoted in Musser, *Edison Motion Pictures*, 508.

63. "Jeffries Cries 'Foul,'" *New York Herald*, November 4, 1899, 4.

64. Musser, *The Emergence of Cinema*, 206.

65. *Ibid.*

66. *Ibid.*, 320.

67. "Around the Bulletin Boards," *New York Times*, October 21, 1899, 1.

68. United States Naval Institute, Proceedings of the United States Naval Institute (The Institute, 1899), 857.

69. Edison Films, March 1900, 6.

70. Musser, *Edison Motion Pictures*, 554.

71. Edison Films, July 1901, 32.

72. Musser, *The Emergence of Cinema*, 208.

73. Streible, *Prizefight*, 258.

74. "Pictures and Pugilism," *Motion Picture World*, December 18, 1909, 871.

75. "Almost a Lynching Over Gans's Victory," *New York Times*, September 5, 1906, 16.

76. Streible, *Prizefight*, 341.

77. Uncle Rod Kees, "Johnson Shows Physical Powers of the Negro," *Freeman*, November 6, 1909, 7.

78. See Streible, *Prizefight*, 341.

79. "Rickard Explains 'Secret' Session," *New York Times*, December 5, 1909, S1.

80. Streible, *Prizefight*, 351.

81. "Bar Fight Pictures to Avoid Race Riots," *New York Times*, July 6, 1910, 3.

82. Article 1, No Title, *New York Times*, July 6, 1910, 3.

83. See Streible's and Musser's discussions of the audience and women's access to prize fights.

84. Allen Sinclair Will, *Life of Cardinal Gibbons* (New York: E.P. Dutton and Sons, 1922), 802.

85. Robert J. Handy, *A Christian America: Protestant Hopes and Historical Realities* (New York: Oxford University Press, 1971), 126.

86. "Barred in San Francisco," *New York Times*, July 7, 1910, 3.

87. "Picture Men to Fight," *New York Times*, July 7, 1910, 3.

88. "The Johnson-Jeffries Fight," *St. Paul Appeal*, July 16, 1910, 2.

89. "At Stag Houses Only," *New York Tribune*, July 11, 1910, 3.

90. Congressional Record, July 19, 1912, 9305.

91. Musser, *The Emergence of Cinema*, 184.

Chapter 2

1. Raymond Fielding, *The American Newsreel: A Complete History, 1911–1967* (Jefferson, NC: McFarland, 2006), 47.

2. Luke McKernan, "Witnessing the Past," in *Researcher's Guide to British Newsreels, Volume III*, ed. J. Ballentyne (London: BUFVC, 1993).

3. Nicholas Pronay, "The Newsreel: The Illusion of Actuality," in *The Historian and Film*, ed. P. Smith (Cambridge: Cambridge University Press, 1976), 98.

4. *Ibid.*, 96.

5. See Mark Dyreson, "Aggressive America: Media Nationalism and the 'War' Over Olympic Pictures in Sports 'Golden Age,'" *The International Journal of the History of Sport* 22.6 (November 2005): 974.

6. See Pronay, "Illusion," 96–98.

7. Peter Baechlin and Maurice Muller-Strauss, *Newsreels Across the World* (Paris: UNESCO, 1952), 18.

8. Michael Oriard, *King Football* (Chapel Hill: University of North Carolina Press, 2001), 51.

9. McKernan, "Witnessing," 4.

10. Pronay, "Illusion," 104.

11. Oriard, *King*, 50–51.

12. "Jones Wins U.S. Open for the Fourth Time as 10,000 Look On," *New York Times*, July 13, 1930, 127.

13. *Ibid.*

14. For a discussion of McGeehan, see Mark Dyreson, "The Emergence of Consumer Culture and the Transformation of Physical Culture: American Sport in the 1920s," *Journal of Sport History* 6.3 (Winter 1989): 270; for the most complete discussion of ballyhoo and its impact on the newspaper industry, see Silas Bent, *Ballyhoo: The Voice of the Press* (New York: Boni and Liveright, 1927).

15. Baechlin and Muller-Strauss, Newsreels, 29. The study on newsreels was published by UNESCO in fulfillment of its constitutional obligation to promote "the free flow of ideas by word and image" in order to further "mutual understanding among peoples."

16. See Fielding, *Newsreel*, 89.

17. *Ibid.*

18. "Zev, Champion Colt, Injures His Hoof," *New York Times*, September 11, 1923, 11, 23.

19. "Mitchell Demands Zev Race My Own," *New York Times*, October 1, 1923, 1.

20. *Ibid.*

21. *Ibid.*, 8.

22. *Ibid.*

23. "Zev Is Selected to Meet Papyrus in Match Race," *New York Times*, October 6, 1923, 1.

24. "My Own Is Coming by Special Train," *New York Times*, October 19, 1923, 23.

25. "May the Better Horse Win," *New York Times*, October 20, 1923, 14.

26. "Fights Race Film with Smoke and Sun," *New York Times*, October 21, 1923, 1.

27. *Ibid.*

28. *Ibid.*, 5.

29. *Ibid.*

30. *Ibid.*

31. "The Screen," *New York Times*, October 22, 1923, 17.

32. Fielding, *Newsreel*, 89.

33. "London Is Shocked by Decisive Defeat," *New York Times*, October 21, 1923, 1.

34. "Race No Fair Test, Say London Critics," *New York Times*, October 22, 1923, 22.

35. "Picture Rights Let for Olympic Games," *New York Times*, November 28, 1923, 11.

36. *Ibid.*

37. "Pro Charge Annoys U.S. Rugby Players," *New York Times*, May 8, 1924, 15.

38. "French to Admit U.S. Camera Men," *New York Times*, May 10, 1924, 11.

39. *Ibid.*

40. "Protest UFA Monopoly," *New York Times*, January 24, 1928, 5.

41. "Plan to Charge $60,000 for Olympic Rights Draws U.S. Protest and May Bar Films Here," *New York Times*, May 16, 1928, 30.

42. "Detectives to Aid Olympic Photo Ban," *New York Times*, May 27, 1928, 14.

Chapter 3

1. Mark Inabinett, *Grantland Rice and His Heroes: The Sportswriter as Mythmaker in the 1920s* (Knoxville: University of Tennessee Press, 1994), 7.

2. Jennings Bryant and Andrea M. Holt, "A Historical Overview of Sports and Media in the United States," in *Handbook of Sports and Media*, ed. A. Raney and J. Bryant (Mahwah, NJ: Lawrence Erlbaum Associates, 2006), 29–30.

3. Steven W. Pope, "American Muscles and Minds: Public Discourse and the Shaping of National Identity During Early Olympiads, 1896–1920," *The Journal of American Culture* 15.4 (1992): 109.

4. "Americans Ahead," *New York Times*, April 8, 1896, 3.

5. See Mark Dyreson, "Melting-Pot Victories: Racial Ideas and the Olympic Games in American Culture During the Progressive Era," International Journal of the History of Sport 6.1 (1989): 53.

6. Quoted in Pope, "American," 112.

7. *Ibid.*, 109.

8. "Our Athletes in Paris," *New York Times*, July 12, 1900, 9.

9. "American Athletes Win," *New York Times*, July 15, 1900, 4.

10. *Ibid.*

11. Quoted in Pope, "American," 117.

12. *Ibid.*, 116.

13. *Ibid.*, 112.

14. "About Carlisle Athletics," *Carlisle Arrow*, September 8, 1908, 3.

15. See Ray Gamache, "Sport as Cultural Assimilation: Representations of American Indian Athletes in the Carlisle School Newspaper," *American Journalism* 26.2 (Spring 2009): 7–37.

16. "Olympic Prizes Lost; Thorpe No Amateur," *New York Times*, January 28, 1913, 9.

17. Raymond W. Wheeler, *Jim Thorpe: The World's Greatest Athlete* (Norman: University of Oklahoma Press, 1975), vii–viii.

18. Mark Dyreson, "Aggressive America," 983.

19. Mark Dyreson, "Marketing National Identity: The Olympic Games of 1932 and American Culture," *OLYMPIKA: The International Journal of Olympic Studies IV* (1995): 24.

20. Quoted in Dyreson, "Marketing," 26.

21. Universal News, February 4, 1932.

22. *Ibid.*, February 11, 1932.

23. *Ibid.*, February 9, 1932.

24. *Ibid.*, August 4, 1932.

25. *Ibid.*, August 8, 1932.

26. *Ibid.*, August 11, 1932.

27. John Slater, "Changing Partners: The Relationship Between the Mass Media and the Olympic Games," Fourth International Symposium for Olympic Research, University of Western Ontario, London, Ontario, Canada (October 1998): 51.

28. Universal News, February 2, 1948.

29. *Ibid.*

30. *Ibid.*, August 12, 1948.

31. *Ibid.*, July 21, 1952.

32. *Ibid.*

33. *Ibid.*, July 31, 1952.

34. Mike Huggins, "'And Now, Something for the Ladies': Representations of Women's Sport in Cinema Newsreels 1918–1939," *Women's Historical Review* 16.5 (November 2007): 686.

35. Quoted in *ibid.*

36. Universal News, February 9, 1948.

37. Quoted in David B. Welky, "Viking Girls, Mermaids and Little Brown Men: U.S. Journalism and the 1932 Olympics," *Journal of Sport History* 24.1 (Spring 1997): 31.

38. Huggins, "Something," 685.

39. Universal News, August 9, 1948.

40. *Ibid.*, April 25, 1935.

41. *Ibid.*, August 9, 1948.

42. *Ibid.*, February 25, 1952.

43. Gina Daddario, *Women's Sport and Spectacle: Gendered Television Coverage and the Olympic Games* (Westport, CT: Praeger, 1998), 24.

44. Mark Dyreson, "Icons of Liberty or Objects of Desire? American Women Olympians and the Politics of Consumption," *Journal of Contemporary History* 38.3 (Autumn 2003): 438.

45. "No Women Olympians for American Team," *New York Times*, March 31, 1914, 9.

46. "Baby Swimmers Will Show the World!" *Pittsburgh Press*, August 15, 1920, sporting section, 3. See Dyreson, "Icons," 442–443.

47. "American Swimmers Shatter World's Record in Olympics," *Atlanta Constitution*, July 21, 1924, 6. Quoted in Dyreson, "Icons," 450.

48. J.P. Abramson, "U.S. Athletes Fail 4 Times at Olympics," *New York Herald Tribune*, August 3, 1928, 1, 18.

49. Paul Gallico, *Farewell to Sport* (1938; repr., Freeport, NY: Books for Libraries Press, 1970), 233–244.

50. Huggins, "Something," 691.

51. Daddario, *Sport and Spectacle*, 26.

52. Quoted in Welky, "Viking Girls," 32.

53. *Ibid.*

54. *Ibid.*

55. Melissa A. Johnson, "Pre-Television Stereotypes: Mexicans in U.S. Newsreels, 1919, 1932," *Critical Studies in Mass Communication* 16 (1999): 418.

56. Oriard, *King*, 296.

57. Mark Dyreson, "American Ideas about Race and Olympic Races from the 1890s to the 1950s: Shattering Myths or Reinforcing Scientific Racism?" *Journal of Sport History* 28.2 (Summer 2001): 186.

58. Quoted in Oriard, *King*, 296.

59. *Ibid.*

60. Huggins, "Something," 695.

61. Pronay, "Illusion," 99.

Chapter 4

1. James Von Schilling, *The Magic Window: American Television, 1939–1953* (New York: The Haworth Press, 2003), 1.

2. For a discussion on the importance of baseball in the development of television, see James A. Walker and Robert V. Bellamy, "Baseball on Television: The Formative Years 1939–1951," *Nine: A Journal of Baseball and Culture* 11.2 (2002).

3. Dale L. Cressman and Lisa Swenson, "The Pigskin and the Picture Tube: The National Football League's First Full Season on the CBS Television Network," *Journal of Broadcasting & Electronic Media* 51.3 (Fall 2007): 479.

4. Benjamin Rader, *In Its Own Image: How Television Has Transformed Sports* (New York: Free Press, 1984), 27.

5. Jeff Neal-Lunsford, "Sport in the Land of Television: The Use of Sport in Network Prime-Time Schedules 1946–1950," *Journal of Sport History* 19.1 (Spring 1992): 75.

6. David A. Klatell and Norman Marcus, *Sports for Sale: Television, Money and the Fans* (New York: Oxford University Press, 1988), 220.

7. Jack Gould, "Television, in Big Strides, Advances Across the Nation," *New York Times*, April 24, 1949, XX1.

8. Arthur Daley, "When the Ringside Becomes the Fireside," *New York Times*, March 27, 1949, SM17.

9. *Ibid.*

10. "NBC-TV Provides Weekly Sports Reel for Stations," NBC-New York, Press Release, September 25, 1951, 1.

11. See Klatell and Marcus, *Sports*, 212.

12. "First Television of Baseball Seen," *New York Times*, May 18, 1939, 29.

13. *Ibid.*

14. *Ibid.*

15. "Watching a Televised Baseball Game," *New York Times*, September 3, 1939, X10.

16. Orrin E. Dunlap, Jr., "Watching a Battle," *New York Times*, June 4, 1939, X10.

17. *Ibid.*

18. *Ibid.*

19. *Ibid.*

20. *Ibid.*

21. *Ibid.*

22. *Ibid.*

23. *Ibid.*

24. See Neal-Lunsford, "In the Land," 60.

25. *Ibid.*, 59.

26. "TV Names Gobel Best Newcomer," *New York Times*, March 8, 1955, 33.

27. "Graziano Slugfest on WJZ Tonight," Display Ad 100, *New York Times*, January 18, 1946, 27.

28. *Ibid.*

29. Neal-Lunsford, "In the Land," 61.

30. Jack Gould, "Radio News," *New York Times*, March 11, 1948, 54.

31. Jack Gould, "The News of Radio," *New York Times*, August 25, 1947, 34.

32. Gould, "Radio News," 54.

33. "Video Status Confused, Agency Finds," *Broadcasting*, August 12, 1946, 32.

34. "Louis vs. Walcott," Display Ad 39, *New York Times*, June 23, 1948, 35.

35. *Ibid.*

36. *Ibid.*

37. "News of Radio," *New York Times*, June 23, 1948, 54.

38. Margaret Moen, "Broadcast Bomber," *Air & Space*. Retrieved from http://www.airspacemag.com/issues/2007/august/oldies_and_oddities.php.

39. "No Moaning for Loser," *New York Times*, June 26, 1948, 11.

40. Jack Gould, "Television, in Big Strides," *New York Times*, April 24, 1949, XX1.

41. *Ibid.*

42. *Ibid.*

43. See Neal-Lunsford, "In the Land," 72.

44. Sidney Lohman, "Coverage of Sports," *New York Times*, April 24, 1949, XX10.

45. Sidney Lohman, "News of TV and Radio," New York Times, September 17, 1950, 119.

46. Rader, *Image*, 70.

47. *Ibid.*

48. "Top Football Games Will Be Telecast by NBC in Fall; More Than 50 Stations to Carry NCAA Events," NBC Television News, August 10, 1951.

49. Rader, *Image*, 71.

50. *Ibid.*

51. "'American Forum' to Debate What's Wrong with College Football, on Oct. 7," NBC News, October 2, 1951.

52. "Lindsey Nelson Appointed Assistant Sports Director for NBC," NBC-TV News, July 23, 1952.

53. "NBC's Football Staff Plans for Complete Schedule of College Games to Be Televised by Network," NBC-TV News, July 29, 1952.

54. *Ibid.*

55. "General Motors to Sponsor Coast-to-Coast Telecasts of College Football Games on NBC," NBC-TV News, August 25, 1952.

56. *Ibid.*

57. Ron Powers, *Supertube: The Rise of Television Sports* (New York: Coward-McCann, 1984), 224.

58. Jack Gould, "Football on Video," *New York Times*, November 15, 1953, X11.

59. *Ibid.*

60. *Ibid.*

61. *Ibid.*

62. *Ibid.*

63. *Ibid.*

64. See Powers, Supertube, 68–79.

65. Michael MacCambridge, *America's Game: The Epic Story of How Pro Football Captured a Nation* (New York: Random House, 2004), 69.

66. "Pro Football Seeks Dismissal of TV Suit," *New York Times*, October 30, 1951, 25.

67. "Court Limits Pro Football's Control of Television to the Area of Home Games," *New York Times*, November 13, 1953, 30.

68. *Ibid.*

69. *Ibid.*

70. The reserve clause reserved the right of Major League Baseball team owner to do with a player's contract as he so desired. It limited the player from negotiating with other teams or selling his services to the highest bidder.

71. "Court Limits Control," 30.

72. Arthur Daley, "Sports of the Times," *New York Times*, November 13, 1953, 31.

73. *Ibid.*

74. *Ibid.*

75. *Ibid.*

76. For a full discussion of television's impact on minor league baseball, see Powers, *Supertube*, 59.

77. MacCambridge, *America's Game*, 105.

78. *Ibid.*

79. Walter Byers, *Unsportsmanlike Conduct: Exploiting College Athletes* (Ann Arbor: University of Michigan Press, 1995), 79–80.

80. Tim Brooks and Earle Marsh, *The Complete Directory to Prime Time TV Shows, 1946–Present* (New York: Ballantine, 1981), 965.

81. *Ibid.*, 1036.

82. *Ibid.*, 365.

83. Rob Turnock, "The Arrival of Videotape." Retrieved from http://www.birth-of-tv.org/birth/assetView.do?asset=123173128_1117789877.

84. For a detailed discussion of the growth of NFL Films, see MacCambridge, *America's Game*, 182–184.

85. Curt Smith, *Voices of the Game: The First Full-Scale Overview of Baseball Broadcasting, 1921 to the Present* (South Bend, IN: Diamond Communications, 1987), 296–297, 303–304.

86. "'Football Kickoff, 1951': Lou Little, Charles Caldwell, Jack Lavelle and Others to Preview Season on Special NBC-TV Program," NBC Television, WNBT New York, News Release, September 11, 1951, 1.

87. "Ted Husing to Give Pre-Game Warmup of College Football Telecasts on Saturdays," NBC-New York, NBC-TV News Release, September 27, 1951, 1.

88. "Special Pre-Game and Post-Game Football Programs To Complement NBC-TV's Gridiron Coverage," NBC-New York, NBC-TV News Release, September 10, 1951, 1.

89. *Ibid.*

Chapter 5

1. Jeff Martin, "The Dawn of Tape: Transmission Device as Preservation Medium," *The Moving Image* 5.1 (2005): 48.

2. Michael Biel, "Time Shifting by the Networks." Retrieved from http://members.aol.com/jeff560/am2.html.

3. *Ibid.*

4. Val Adams, "TV Network on Film," *New York Times*, May 27, 1951, 8.

5. *Ibid.*

6. Stewart Wolpin, "The Race to Video," *Invention and Technology* (Fall 1994), 52.

7. Adams, "TV Network," 8.

8. *Ibid.*

9. Val Adams, "Television Film Men Question Scope of New Tape Recorder," *New York Times*, April 16, 1956, 51.

10. See Roone Arledge, *Roone: A Memoir* (New York: HarperCollins, 2003), 58, and Rob Turnock, "The Arrival of Videotape." http://www.birth-of-tv.org/birth/assetView.do?asset=123173128_111778977.

11. *Ibid.*

12. Neal-Lunsford, "In the Land," 76.

13. Brad Schultz, *Sports Broadcasting* (Boston: Focal Press, 2002), 15.

14. *Ibid.*, 16.

15. See Powers, *Supertube*, 144.

16. *Ibid.*, 146.

17. Arledge, *Memoir*, 58.

18. Anna McCarthy, "'The Front Row Is Reserved for Scotch Drinkers': Early Television's Tavern Audience," *Cinema Journal* 34.4 (Summer 1995): 36.

19. *Ibid.*, 40.

20. Raymond Boyle, *Sports Journalism: Context and Issues* (London: Sage, 2006), 67.

21. Charles P. Ginsburg, "The Birth of Video Recording," Paper first delivered at the 82nd Convention of the Society of Motion Picture and Television Engineers on October 5, 1957. http://www.labguysworld.com/VTR_BirthOf.htm.

22. *Ibid.*, 1.

23. *Ibid.*, 6.

24. *Ibid.*

25. Martin, "The Dawn," 51.

26. Wolpin, "The Race," 52.

27. Quoted in Martin, "The Dawn," 53.

28. Val Adams, "TV Is Put on Tape by New Recorder," *New York Times*, April 15, 1956, 1.

29. *Ibid.*

30. Adams, "Men Question," 51.

31. Jack Gould, "TV: Color Film on Tape," *New York Times*, October 24, 1956, 56.

32. Ginsburg, "The Birth," 9. See also Tony Verna, *Instant Replay: The Day That Changed Sports Forever* (Beverly Hills: Creative Book Publishers International, 2008), 2–3.

33. Val Adams, "C.B.S. Shows Off Tape-Recorded TV," *New York Times*, December 21, 1956, 43.

34. Ginsburg, "The Birth," 9.

35. "N.B.C. Schedules Hour-Long Films," *New York Times*, April 2, 1957, 52.

36. Quoted in Martin, "The Dawn," 55.

37. *Ibid.*, 57.

38. *Ibid.*, 56.

39. Val Adams, "News of TV and Radio," *New York Times*, August 19, 1951, 97.

40. *Ibid.*

41. Powers, *Supertube*, 114.

42. Arledge, *Memoir*, 17–18.

43. Raymond Boyle and Richard Haynes, *Power Play: Sport, Media and Popular Culture* (Harlow: Pearson Education, 2000), 42.

44. *Ibid.*

45. Bert Randolph Sugar, "The Thrill of Victory": *The Inside Story of ABC Sports* (New York: Hawthorn Books, 1978), 99.

46. *Ibid.*, 109.

47. *Ibid.*, 129.

48. Jack Gould, "Telstar Success Spurs U.S. Study," *New York Times*, July 12, 1962, 1.

49. *Ibid.*

50. *Ibid.*

51. "Telstar Gives Japan Hope for TV of 1964 Olympics," *New York Times*, July 12, 1962, 13.

52. "Telstar May Transmit '64 Olympics to U.S.," *New York Times*, August 28, 1962, 47.

53. Richard Witkin, "Live TV of Tokyo Olympics Being Explored," *New York Times*, January 26, 1964, S3.

54. *Ibid.*

55. *Ibid.*

56. Richard Witkin, "Satellite Tested for Olympics TV," *New York Times*, April 24, 1964, 67.

57. *Ibid.*

58. Jack Gould, "Delay in Televising Olympics on Coast Irritates Japanese," *New York Times*, October 11, 1964, 1.

59. *Ibid.*

60. Jack Gould, "When TV Lost the Olympics," *New York Times*, October 18, 1964, X10.

61. *Ibid.*

62. *Ibid.*

63. *Ibid.*

64. *Ibid.*

65. "Biographies," Canadian Communications Foundation. Retrieved from http://www.broadcasting-history.ca/personalities/personalities.php?id=289.

66. Val Adams, "Tape Recorders for TV a Big Hit," *New York Times*, April 20, 1956, 51.

67. Arledge, *Memoir*, 38.

68. *Ibid.*, 39.

69. Powers, *Supertube*, 127.

70. Verna, *Instant Replay*, 14.

71. Margaret Morse, "Sport on Television: Replay and Display," in *Regarding Television* ed. E. Ann Kaplan (Frederick, MD: University Publications of America, 1983), 48.

72. *Ibid.*

73. Geneviève Rail, "Seismography of the Postmodern Condition: Three Theses on the Implosion of Sport," in *Sport and Postmodern Times*, ed. G. Rail (Albany: State University of New York Press, 1998), 154.

74. Morse, "Sport," 51–54.

75. Fielding, Newsreel, 92. Writing for the New Yorker on September 22, 1934, Morris Mackey contributed a feature on newsreels that presented two examples of the use of slow motion cameras revealing errors by officials. The first involved a Chicago baseball game in the early 1930s in which Jimmy Dykes was called out while sliding into third base, "thereby changing the whole complexion of the game." The second example involved a 1932 soccer game between Newcastle United and Arsenal, played at Wembley Stadium. United's winning goal was scored after its kicker was shown to have been standing outside the lines. In both cases, the public furor over the missed calls was enough to force owners and league officials to bar slow motion cameras from ballparks." Slow motion pictures of the Zev–In Memoriam match race at Churchill Downs in Louisville, Kentucky, on November 17, 1923, show that In Memoriam nosed out Zev, that year's winner of the Kentucky Derby and the International Race against Papyrus, in what the New York Times called "the most thrilling match race ever witnessed in this country."

76. "Kennedy Will Appear on TV at Football Award Fete Dec. 5," *New York Times*, November 23, 1961, 71. The pertinent piece is subtitled "Disputed Play on WPIX."

77. Stuart Hall, "The Treatment of 'Football Hooliganism' in the Press," in *Football Hooliganism in the Wider Context*, ed. R. Ingham (London: Inter-Action Imprint, 1978), 17.

78. Boyle, *Journalism*, 67.

79. Schultz, *Broadcasting*, 232.

80. Powers, *Supertube*, 147.

81. MacCambridge, *America's Game*, 279.

82. *Ibid.*

83. Klatell and Marcus, *Sports*, 226.

84. *Ibid.*, 229.

85. Neal-Lunsford, "In the Land," 72.

86. McCarthy, "The Front Row," 32.

87. *Ibid.*, 37.

88. *Ibid.*, 43.

89. Garry Whannel, *Fields in Vision: Television Sport and Cultural Transformation* (New York: Routledge, 1992), 23.

90. Robert Hughes and Jay Coakley, "Mass Society and the Commercialization of Sport," *Sociology of Sport Journal* 1.1 (March 1984): 58.

91. *Ibid.*, 59.

92. *Ibid.*

Chapter 6

1. Rasmussen, *Junkies*, 23.

2. "Satellite & Cable Television." Retrieved from http://history.sandiego.edu/gen/recording/television3.html.

3. Rasmussen, *Junkies*, 46.

4. Michael Goodwin, "TV Sports Money Machine Falters," *New York Times*, January 26, 1986, SM26.

5. Neil Amdur, "The Television Dollars Foster New Perceptions," *New York Times*, October 30, 1982, 9.

6. Frank Litsky, "Review Is Refused of Cable TV Ruling," *New York Times*, January 12, 1982, B11.

7. Henry Geller, "Fairness, Common Sense and the Superstation Issue," *New York Times*, December 16, 1984, S2.

8. Amdur, "Television Dollars," 9.

9. *Ibid.*

10. Frank J. Prial, "Sports Channel Adds Business News," *New York Times*, February 5, 1983, 47.

11. Neil Amdur, "NBC Bids to Revive Appeal of Tennis," *New York Times*, June 7, 1983, B13.

12. Peter Alfano, "CBS Concentrates on Playoffs," *New York Times*, May 17, 1983, B11.

13. Sally Bedell Smith, "'Monday Night Football' Rating Slips," *New York Times*, December 31, 1983, 43.

14. Michael Goodwin, "Highlights Aren't Enough," *New York Times*, November 26, 1985, A25.

15. Michael Goodwin, "The Perils of Slapdash Journalism," *New York Times*, December 16, 1986, D35.

16. Richard Sandomir, "At ESPN After 25 Years, Happy Birthday to Us," *New York Times*, September 7, 2004, D1.

17. *Ibid.*

18. Reginald Stuart, "Age of Domestic Phone Satellites Dawns," *New York Times*, September 22, 1975, 53.

19. *Ibid.*

20. *Ibid.*

21. *Ibid.*

22. Dave Kindred, *Sound and Fury: Two Powerful Lives, One Fateful Friendship* (New York: Free Press, 2006), 90.

23. ESPN SportsCentury, http://espn.go.com/sportscentury/features/00134700.html.

24. Rasmussen, *Junkies*, 70–74.

25. John Noble Wilford, "The Day Satcom 2 Wobbled in Orbit," *New York Times*, November 20, 1979, C1.

26. Michael Freeman, *ESPN: The Uncensored History* (Dallas: Taylor Publishing, 2000), 70.

27. *Ibid.*, 74.

28. Quoted in Freeman, *ESPN*, 68.

29. *Ibid.*

30. Philip H. Dougherty, "New Sports Network's Clients," *New York Times*, September 25, 1979, D18.

31. "Display Ad 319—No Title," *New York Times*, November 13, 1980, D17.

32. Freeman, *ESPN*, 82.

33. Dougherty, "Clients," D18.

34. Parton Keese, "Bristol Hits the Big League in Sports TV," *New York Times*, December 9, 1979, CN1.

35. Quoted in Rasmussen, *Junkies*, 15.

36. Red Smith, "Cable TV for Sports Junkies," *New York Times*, December 3, 1979, C3.

37. *Ibid.*

38. Keese, "Bristol," CN1.

39. Les Brown, "From the Air: Programs by Satellite and Cable," *New York Times*, February 17, 1980, F1.

40. *Ibid.*

41. "Television: The Big Daddy of Nearly All Sports," *New York Times*, December 30, 1979, S7.

42. Freeman, *ESPN*, 104.

43. Gerald Eskenazi, "All-Sports TV Adds Canadian Football," *New York Times*, June 10, 1980, B18.

44. "World Cup on Home TV," *New York Times*, June 6, 1982, S3.

45. Freeman, *ESPN*, 103–106.

46. *Ibid.*, 103.

47. "Display Ad 90—No Title," *New York Times*, April 29, 1980, B23.

48. Peter Alfano, "A Faulty Tack on Covering the Races," *New York Times*, September 27, 1983, B12.

49. *Ibid.*

50. *Ibid.*

51. Tony Schwartz, "Cable TV Programmers Find Problems Amid Fast Growth," *New York Times*, September 28, 1982, A1.

52. Justice Stevens, "'From the Opinion,' Excerpts from Supreme Court Opinions in NCAA Case," *New York Times*, June 28, 1984, B8.

53. *Ibid.*

54. *Ibid.*

55. *Ibid.*

56. *Ibid.*

57. *Ibid.*

58. *Ibid.*

59. *Ibid.*

60. Gordon S. White, Jr., "Ruling Adds Options for Colleges and Television," *New York Times*, June 28, 1984, B7.

61. Gordon S. White, Jr., "Football Playoffs Rejected," *New York Times*, June 30, 1984, 31.

62. Peter W. Kaplan, "Rush Likely to Sign Up More Games," *New York Times*, June 28, 1984, B7.

63. Gordon S. White, Jr., "Colleges May Find TV's Gold Egg Is Tarnished," *New York Times*, August 26, 1984, S9.

64. Lawrie Mifflin, "TV Season Is One of Discontent," *New York Times*, October 15, 1984, C11.

65. *Ibid.* PBS had agreed to televise nine Ivy League games to the Northeast in a deal that would net the eight schools more than $1 million.

66. Amdur, "Television Dollars," 9.

67. *Ibid.*

68. *Ibid.*

69. Joseph Durso, "Get Ready for Those Anthology Shows," *New York Times*, January 31, 1984, B12.

70. William N. Wallace, "Instant Replay Likely in USFL," *New York Times*, February 11, 1985, C8.

71. Amdur, "Television Dollars," 9.

72. *Ibid.*

73. *Ibid.*

74. Michael Katz, "Boxing Novelty: Computerizing Punches," *New York Times*, February 12, 1985, B15.

75. *Ibid.*

76. *Ibid.*

77. *Ibid.*

78. *Ibid.*

79. Michael Katz, "Below-the-Belt Blows Aimed at Boxing," *New York Times*, July 23, 1985, A25.

80. *Ibid.*

81. *Ibid.*

82. *Ibid.*

83. *Ibid.*

84. Goodwin, "Highlights," A25.

85. *Ibid.*

86. *Ibid.*

87. Goodwin, "The Perils," D35.

88. *Ibid.*

89. Gerald Eskenazi, "NBC Plans to Take Tougher Approach," *New York Times*, March 9, 1988, D28.

90. *Ibid.*

91. *Ibid.*

92. Peter Alfano, "Battling Athletes Hurt Sports' Image," *New York Times*, February 8, 1988, C1.

93. *Ibid.*

94. Amdur, "Revive Appeal," B13.

95. Deirdre Carmody, "Female Reporter Sues Over Locker-Room Ban," *New York Times*, December 30, 1977, A17.

96. *Ibid.*

97. "Kuhn Reacts to Suit of Female Writer," *New York Times*, December 31, 1977, 24.

98. Roger Kahn, "Some Modest Proposals," *New York Times*, February 13, 1978, C8.

99. Melissa Ludtke Lincoln, "Locker Rooms: Equality with Integrity," *New York Times*, April 15, 1979, S2.

100. Kahn, "Modest Proposals," C8.

101. Red Smith, "Another View on Equality," *New York Times*, January 9, 1978, C4.

102. Lincoln, "Locker Rooms," S2.

103. *Ibid.*

104. "The Right Place for Women," *New York Times*, October 4, 1990, A28.

105. Thomas Rogers, "Kiam Apologizes After Joking About the Olson Incident," *New York Times*, February 7, 1991, B17.

106. Timothy W. Smith, "Tagliabue Waffles on Lisa Olson File," *New York Times*, May 31, 1992, S7.

107. For a complete discussion on the politics inherent in the Lisa Olson case, see Lisa Disch and Mary Jo Kane, "When a Looker Is Really a Bitch: Lisa Olson, Sport, and the Heterosexual Matrix,"

Signs: Journal of Women in Culture and Society 21.21 (Winter 1996), 278–308.

108. Michael Janofsky, "NFL Faces a New Economy," *New York Times*, March 17, 1987, D30.

109. Bedell Smith, "Rating Slips."

110. *Ibid.*

111. *Ibid.*

112. Goodwin, "Money Machine," SM26.

113. Richard W. Stevenson, "Rates Flat for Sports Programs," *New York Times*, September 2, 1986, D11.

114. Peter Kerr, "Madison Ave.'s Football Woe," *New York Times*, September 22, 1984, 39.

115. John Amis, Trevor Slack, and Tim Berrett, "Sport Sponsorship as Distinctive Competence," *European Journal of Marketing* 33.3/4 (1999), 250–272.

116. David L. Andrews, "Introduction," in *Sport, Culture and Advertising: Identities, Commodities and the Politics of Representation*, ed. D.L. Andrews and S.J. Jackson (New York: Routledge, 2005), 13.

117. Goodwin, "Money Machine," SM26.

118. *Ibid.*

119. Freeman, *ESPN*, 117.

120. Michael Goodwin, "NFL Becomes a Telethon," *New York Times*, November 10, 1987, D32.

121. Geraldine Fabrikant, "It's First and Goal for ESPN," *New York Times*, June 9, 1987, D1.

122. Freeman, *ESPN*, 139.

123. *Ibid.*, 232.

124. Klatell and Marcus, *Sports*, 215.

125. Disch and Kane, "Looker," 282.

126. Susan Tyler Eastman and Andrew C. Billings, "Sportscasting and Sports Reporting: The Power of Gender Bias," *Journal of Sport & Social Issues* 24.2 (May 2000), 192–213.

127. Freeman, *ESPN*, 115.

128. Sandomir, "Happy Birthday," D1.

Chapter 7

1. Martzke and Cherner, "Channeling."

2. Freeman, ESPN, 93. ESPN's first SportsCenter program did not use a single highlight clip. Highlights were shown at 11:30 p.m. on a show called Sports Recap. One of the problems ESPN faced was securing highlights from the networks. NBC and ABC readily agreed to open their video archives because they did not view ESPN as competition. When CBS refused, ESPN began taking them without permission until the older network relented (105–106).

3. Martzke and Cherner, "Channeling." That figure goes beyond watching sportscasts, however; it includes all ESPN programming on its numerous television channels—ESPN, ESPN2, ESPNU, ESPN Classic, ESPNEWS, ESPN Radio, ESPN.com and ESPN Deportes.

4. Richard Sandomir, "At ESPN, the Revolution Was Televised," *New York Times*, September 7, 1999, D1.

5. "Annie Roboff Web Site Interview." http://www.geocities.com/aroboff/interview2.html.

6. Pat Eaton-Robb, "ESPN's Sports-Center Goes on Walkabout." http://www.boston.com/sports/other_sports/articles/2007/01/ 15/espns_sportscenter_goes_on_walkabout.html.

7. *Ibid.*

8. For a complete analysis of anchors' catchphrases, see Grant Farred, "'Cool as the Other Side of the Pillow': How ESPN's SportsCenter Has Changed Television Sports Talk," *Journal of Sport & Social Issues* 24.2 (May 2000).

9. Chris Harris, "Welcome to the SportsCenter Altar." http://www.sportscenteraltar.com.

10. Chris Berman, "A ... Picture ... Is ... Worth ... A ... Thousand ... Words." In *ESPN Ultimate Highlight Reel: The 365 Wildest, Weirdest, Most Unforgettable SportsCenter Moments of All Time* (New York: ESPN Books, 2006), i.

11. Hirshberg, *ESPN 25*, 12.

12. Berman, "Picture," *Ultimate Highlight Reel*, ii.

13. Hirshberg, *ESPN 25*, 12.

14. David L. Andrews, "Excavating Michael Jordan: Notes on a Critical Pedagogy of Sporting Representation," in *Sport and Postmodern Times*, ed. G. Rail (Albany: State University of New York Press, 1998), 195.

15. Sandomir, "Happy Birthday," D1.

16. Prial, "Sports Channel."

17. *Ibid.*

18. *Ibid.*

19. Peter Alfano, "ESPN Struggling, but Making an Impact," *New York Times*, May 24, 1983, B12.

20. Steve Knoll, "More Coverage for Olympics Fans," *New York Times*, July 22, 1984, H22.

21. Michael Katz, "ESPN's Public Service at Cooperstown," *New York Times*, July 30, 1985, B6.

22. *Ibid.*

23. Steve Schneider, "Everything about the Game—Except the Game," *New York Times*, January 26, 1986, H32.

24. *Ibid.*

25. Freeman, *ESPN*, 133–148.

26. Hirshberg, *ESPN 25*, 89.

27. *Ibid.*, 90.

28. Guy Debord, *Society of the Spectacle* (Detroit: Black and Red, 1966), 1.

29. Quoted in Farred, "Other Side of the Pillow," 100. See also Rail, "Postmodern," and Timothy W. Luke, *Screens of Power: Ideology, Domination, and Resistance in Information Society* (Urbana: University of Illinois Press, 1989).

30. Steven Barnett, *Games and Sets: The Changing Face of Sport on Television* (London: British Film Institute, 1990), 8.

31. For a complete discussion of the music video form, see E. Ann Kaplan, *Rocking Around the Clock: Music Television, Postmodernism & Consumer Culture* (New York: Methuen, 1987).

32. *Ibid.*, 50.

33. Rail, "Postmodern," 151.

34. Berman, "Introduction," *Ultimate Highlight Reel*, ii.

35. John Bloom, "No Fall from Grace: Grace Thorpe's 'Athlete of the Century' Campaign for Her Father," in *Native Athletes in Sport & Society: A Reader*, ed. C.R. King (Lincoln: University of Nebraska Press, 2005), 234.

36. Quoted in Freeman, ESPN, 2.

37. *Ibid.*

38. Jim Shea, "The King: How ESPN Changes Everything," *Columbia Journalism Review*, January/February 2000.

39. Klatell and Marcus, *Sports*, 219. See also Boyle, Journalism.

40. "ESPN Sports Attitude Mixing Dedication and Irreverence," *Advertising Age*, October 23, 1995, 3.

41. *Ibid.*

42. Anthony Vagnoni, "Jock Yocks: A New Promo Campaign for ESPN Gives Fun-Loving Sports Stars a 'Spinal Tap,'" *Advertising Age's Creativity*, November 1, 1995, 15.

43. ESPN 25 DVD that accompanied the book by Hirshberg, ESPN 25.

44. Bob Garfield, "The Best Awards; ESPN Scores Best in Show," *Advertising Age*, May 27, 1996, S1.

45. Jon Rappoport, "The Marketing 100; ESPN Judy Fearing," *Advertising Age*, June 24, 1996, S3.

46. Quoted in Shea, "The King," 3.

47. *Ibid.*

48. "Vote: which commercial is your favorite?" http://proxy.espn.go.com/chat/sportsnation/polling?event_id=3266.

49. Wayne Friedman, "Young Stars Give Fresh Spin to ESPN Classic Programs: Ads Feature Contemporary Celebs Touting Heroes of Past," *Advertising Age*, May 31, 1999, 75.

50. David Goetzl, "ESPN Ad Effort Hails a Cab; Adapt Media's Pilot Program Driving in NYC," *Advertising Age*, May 28, 2001, 8.

51. Warren Berger, "Equal Sequels," *Creativity*, May 1, 1999, 30.

52. *Ibid.*

53. Melanie Shortman, "ESPN: Know Thyself (and Thine Audience)," *Creativity*, October 1, 2005, 57.

54. Sandomir, "Revolution," D1.

55. Richard Linnett, "The Buzz; What We're Talking About," *Advertising Age*, January 19, 2004, 33.

56. Wade Paulsen, "Mike Hall Wins ESPN's 'Dream Job.'" http://www.realitytvworld.com/news/mike-hall-wins-espn-dream-job-2421.php.

57. Richard Sandomir, "'Dream Job' the Nightmare, Showing Now on ESPN," *New York Times*, March 6, 2004, D4.

58. Ted McCartan, "ESPN 'Dream Job' Contestants Remain Only Amateurs," *The Daily Iowan*, March 30, 2004, 4. "Punt, Pass & Kick" (PPK) is a competition sponsored by the NFL and Pepsi for youngsters aged 8–15.

59. Sandomir, "Dream Job," D4.

60. *Ibid.*

61. Alexander Marciniak, "'Dream Job' Winner Gets Prime Spot with New ESPNU." http://media.www.theeastcarolinian.com/media/storage/paper915/news/2005/02/01/UndefinedSection/dream.Job.Winner.Gets.Prime.Spot.With.New.Espnu-2209902.shtml.

62. Andrew Wernick, Promotional Culture: Advertising, Ideology and Symbolic Expression (London: Sage, 1991).

63. Geneviève Rail, "Introduction," in *Sport and Postmodern Times*, ed. G. Rail (Albany: State University of New York Press, 1998).

Chapter 8

1. Jenkins, *Convergence*, 13.

2. Seth Schiesel, "Cable TV Lacks Competition, FCC Notes," *New York Times*, January 14, 1998, D6.

3. Linda Saslow, "New Channels and New Costs for Cable TV," *New York Times*, April 6, 1997, L11.

4. Eric A. Taub, "The Big Picture on Digital TV: It's Still Fuzzy," *New York Times*, September 12, 2002, G1.

5. "Live from France on World Wide Web," *New York Times*, June 9, 1998, C4.

6. Jenkins, *Convergence*, 61–62.

7. "CBS to Acquire 22% of Sportsline USA," *New York Times*, March 6, 1997, D10.

8. Steve Lohr, "Joining the New Media: ABC News Begins and On-Line Service," *New York Times*, May 12, 1997, D9.

9. Richard Sandomir, "NFL's Internet Deal Will Be Largest Ever," *New York Times*, July 11, 2001, D2.

10. Bob Tedeschi, "NFL's Site Gets Hits, as Well as Blocks and Tackles," *New York Times*, December 13, 2000, H12.

11. Matt Richtel, "For Fanatics, Sports Webcasts," *New York Times*, March 19, 1998, G9.

12. Amy Harmon, "On the Office PC, Bosses Opt for All Work, and No Play," *New York Times*, September 22, 1997, A1.

13. John D. Solomon, "The Sports Market Is Looking Soggy," *New York Times*, April 21, 2002, B1.

14. Jere Longman, "Pro Leagues' Ratings Drop; Nobody Is Quite Sure Why," *New York Times*, July 29, 2001, SP1.

15. Richard Sandomir, "The Decline and Fall of Sports Ratings," *New York Times*, September 10, 2003, D1.

16. "Customer Snapshot: Media, Entertainment & Internet Services." Retrieved from http://www.sun.com/customers/service/mlbam.xml.

17. *Ibid.*

18. Felicity Barringer, "Baseball Is Trying to Limit How New Coverage Is Used," *New York Times*, March 31, 2001, D6.

19. Jerry Schwartz, "Olympics Stung by Technology's False Starts," *New York Times*, July 22, 1996, D1.

20. *Ibid.*

21. *Ibid.*

22. Ken Brown, "Catching the Atlanta Games on Line," *New York Times*, July 8, 1996, D4.

23. *Ibid.*

24. *Ibid.*

25. *Ibid.*

26. "Live from France on World Wide Web," *New York Times*, June 9, 1998, C4.

27. Bill Carter with Richard Sandomir, "NBC's Ratings for Olympics Are Worst Ever," *New York Times*, September 20, 2000, A1.

28. *Ibid.*

29. Bill Carter, "Chief Lauds NBC Olympic Performance," *New York Times*, September 28, 2000, S2.

30. Bonnie Rothman Morris, "Making Room Online for Young Olympic Fans," *New York Times*, September 21, 2000, G6.

31. Carter and Sandomir, "Ratings," A1.

32. Saul Hansell, "The Medium Gets the Message," *New York Times*, August 14, 2000, C1.

33. *Ibid.*

34. *Ibid.*

35. Lohr, "Joining," D9.

36. *Ibid.*

37. "Disney Names Head of Internet Group," *New York Times*, September 9, 1999, C6.

38. Tedeschi, "NFL's Site," H12.

39. "NFL Says Fans Like Internet Site," *New York Times*, November 12, 1998, G3.

40. *Ibid.*

41. Tedeschi, "NFL's Site," H12.

42. *Ibid.*

43. Sandomir, "NFL's Internet Deal," D2.

44. *Ibid.*

45. Harmon, "Exploration of World Wide Web Tilts from Eclectic to Mudane," *New York Times*, August 28, 2001, 11.

46. *Ibid.*

47. Jeff Jensen, "Steve Kalin: ESPN Internet Ventures," *Advertising Age*, June 1, 1998, S22.

48. *Ibid.*

49. *Ibid.*

50. Harmon, "On the Office PC," A1.

51. Richtel, "For Fanatics," G9.

52. *Ibid.*

53. *Ibid.*

54. *Ibid.*

55. Lawrie Mifflin, "Watch the Tube or Watch the Computer?" *New York Times*, February 1, 1999, C8.

56. *Ibid.*

57. *Ibid.*

58. Judith Zimmer, "Exercise Meets Entertainment on a Virtual-Reality Bike," *New York Times*, August 21, 1996, C3.

59. Verne G. Kopytoff, "Hitting the Virtual Slopes All Year Round," *New York Times*, November 26, 1998, G10.

60. Sreenath Sreenivasan, "From Masters to Duffers, There's Golf on the Web," *New York Times*, April 7, 1997, D8.

61. Barbara Lloyd, "Putting the America's Cup at One's Fingertips," *New York Times*, August 8, 1999, SP12.

62. J.C. Herz, "It's a Video Game, It's TV, and You're the Star," *New York Times*, July 2, 1998, G4.

63. *Ibid.*

64. Saul Hansell, "ESPN Brings Video Clips to High-Speed Net Users," *New York Times*, October 14, 2002, C2.

65. *Ibid.*

66. Nat Ives, "At ESPN.com, New Technology Comes with Commercials," *New York Times*, February 21, 2003, C5.

67. Jenkins, *Convergence*, 63.

68. John Schwartz, "Leisure Pursuits of Today's Young Men," *New York Times*, March 29, 2004, C1.

69. *Ibid.*

70. Saul Hansell, "Baseball Test May Soon Show If Time Is Right for Web Video," *New York Times*, January 27, 2003, C1.

71. *Ibid.*

72. *Ibid.*

73. "EarthLink Bundles Subscription-Only Sports Features from Popular Web Sites," *New York Times*, April 12, 2004, C6.

74. "Earthlink Partners with Synacor to Launch Earthlink Premium Sports." Retrieved from http://www.synacor.com/entries/view/earthlink_partners_with_synacor_to_launch_earthlink_premium_sports.

75. *Ibid.* The term is the same used by Sports Center for its music video segment, as well as the title of a book published by ESPN Books in 2006.

76. "Customer Snapshot: Media, Entertainment & Internet Services." Retrieved from http://www.sun.com/customers/service/mlbam.xml.

77. *Ibid.*

78. Hiawatha Bray, "ESPN Selling Premium Content to Net Providers," *The Boston Globe*, June 15, 2006, D1.

79. *Ibid.*

80. Matt Stump, "ESPN Broadband Goes 360." Retrieved from http://www.multichannel.com/article/CA513756.html?display=Supplement#ESPN%20Broadband%20Goes%20360.

81. *Ibid.*

82. Barry Jackson, "ESPN Gives Heat-Bulls Opener 'Full Circle' Coverage." Retrieved from http://www.miami.com/mld/miamiherald/sports/14392805.htm.

83. Mike Shields and Anthony Crupi, "ESPN Unveils Multiplatform MNF Plans, Bronx Series," MediaWeek.com. Retrieved from http://www.mediaweek.com/mw/news/spotlight/article_display_spot2.jsp?vnu_content_id=1002313144.

84. Marc Weingarten, "A Live Ballgame Unfolds on a Cellphone Screen," *New York Times*, October 24, 2002, G3.

85. *Ibid.*

86. *Ibid.*

87. Seth Schiebel, "For Wireless, the Beginnings of a Breakout," *New York Times*, January 13, 2005, G1.

88. *Ibid.*

89. "VCAST V Pak—Free Offer." http://products.vzw.com/index.aspx?id=fnd_toolsApps_vpak.

90. "Setanta Sports North America Offers Rugby World Cup 2007 on V CAST Video from Verizon Wireless." Retrieved from http://news.vzw.com/news/2007/09/pr2007-09-06f.html.

91. "Verizon Wireless Customers Can Score Big with NHL Mobile Video Alerts." Retrieved from http://news.vzw.com/news/2007/11/pr2007-11-26.html.

92. *Ibid.*

93. Richard Sandomir, "NCAA Is Pursuing an Increase in Billions," *New York Times*, September 10, 1999, D4.

94. Schultz, *Broadcasting*, 231.

95. "The HD Experience." Retrieved from http://hd.espn.com/hd/pdfs/playbook.pdf.

96. *Ibid.*

97. *Ibid.*

98. Rudy Martzke, "Instant Replay Gets 'Matrix'-Like View of Key Plays," *USA Today*, January 23, 2001, D2.

99. *Ibid.*

100. Richard Sandomir, "By the Numbers, the College Bowl Games Have Less Action," *New York Times*, January 7, 2004, D2.

101. *Ibid.*

102. Barringer, "Baseball," D6.

103. *Ibid.*

104. *Ibid.*

105. Mike Reiss, "Local Stations Shut Out by NFL," *The Boston Globe*, April 14, 2006, D1.

106. *Ibid.*

107. *Ibid.*

108. Michael McCarthy, "NFL Taking Bold Steps to Control What Fans See," *USA Today*, September 7–9, 2007, A2.

109. *Ibid.*

110. *Ibid.*

111. "ESPN Looks to Score iTunes Deal." Retrieved from http://news.zdnet.com2102-1035_22-5982937.html.

112. Alice Z. Cuneo, "More Football Fans Hit ESPN's Mobile Site Than Its PC Pages," *Advertising Age*, January 7, 2008, 17.

113. *Ibid.*

114. Kenneth J. Gergen, *The Saturated Self: Dilemmas of Identity in Contemporary Life* (New York: Basic Books, 1991), 73–74.

115. *Ibid.*

116. Marc Gunther, "ESPN's Playbook," *Fortune*. Retrieved from http://money.cnn.com/2005/12/06/news/fortune500/espn_fortune.

117. *Ibid.*

118. Manuel Castells, *The Rise of the Network Society* (Malden, MA: Blackwell, 1996), 373.

119. *Ibid.*

Chapter 9

1. International Football Association Board, "Laws of the Game," 2018/2019: 102. Retrieved from https://www.theifab.com/laws/latest/video-assistant-referee-var-protocol/.

2. *Ibid.*

3. Louis Doré, "Was Referee Right to Give France Penalty for Perisic Handball? VAR Controversy Hits World Cup Final," *iNews*, The Essential Daily Briefing, July 15, 2018. Retrieved from https://inews.co.uk/sport/football/world-cup/france-penalty-wolrd-cup-final-croatia-referee-var-handball-perisic-griezmann-176828.

4. International Football Association Board, "133rd Annual General Meeting," 2019. Retrieved from https://nebotpaez-abogados.com/en/the-international-football-association-board-aprueba-las-nuevas-reglas-del-futbol-2032019/.

5. See David L. Altheide, "Media Logic, Social Control, and Fear," Communication Theory 23 (2013): 230; Michael Bérubé, "Afterword: High-definition Sports Capitalism," in *Marxism, Cultural Studies, and Sport*, ed. B. Carrington and I. McDonald (London: Routledge, 2008), 232–241; Michael Messner, *Taking the Field: Women, Men and Sports* (Minneapolis: University of Minnesota Press, 2002).

6. See FIFA Uncovered, directed by Daniel Gordon, 2022, Netflix Series.

7. Jonathan Finn, "Timing and Imaging Evidence in Sport: Objectivity, Intervention and the Limits of Technology," *Journal of Sport and Social Issues* 40.6 (2016): 459–476.

8. Harry Collins, "The Philosophy of Umpiring and the Introduction of Decision-Aid Technology," *Journal of the Philosophy of Sport* 37 (2010): 138.

9. Raymond Boyle and Richard Haynes, *Power Play: Sport, the Media & Popular Culture* (Harlow: Pearson Education, 2000); John Hoberman, Mortal Engines: The Science of Performance and the Dehumanization of Sport (Caldwell, NJ: Blackburn Press, 1992).

10. Collins, "Philosophy."

11. *Ibid.*, 144.

12. "Nine FIFA Officials and Five Corporate Executives Indicted for Racketeering Conspiracy and Corruption," Department of Justice Office of Public Affairs, May 27, 2015. Retrieved from https://www.justice.gov/opa/pr/nine-fifa-officials-and-five-corporate-executives-indicted-racketeering-conspiracy-and.

13. Jay David Bolter and Richard Grusin, *Remediation: Understanding New Media* (Cambridge: MIT Press, 1999).

14. See Christopher Hanson, "The Instant Replay Time and Time Again," *Spectator* 28.2 (2008): 51–60.

15. Charles Hirshberg, *ESPN 25: 25 Mind-Bending, Eye-Popping, Culture-Morphing Years of Highlights* (New York: Hyperion Books, 2004).

16. Alan Clarke and John Clarke, "Highlights and Action Replays—Ideology, Sport and the Media," in *Sport, Culture and Ideology*, ed. Jennifer Hargreaves (London: Routledge and Kegan Paul, 1982), 62–87.

17. Tony Verna, *Instant Replay: The Day That*

Changed Sports Forever (Minneapolis: Creative Book Publishers International, 2008).

18. Michael J. Medhurst, "Propaganda Techniques in Documentary Film and Television: AIM vs. PBS," in *Television Studies: Textual Analysis*, ed. G. Burns and R.J. Thompson (New York: Praeger, 1989), 183–204.

19. Preben Raunsbjerg and Henrik Sand, "TV Sport and Rhetoric," *Nordicom Review* 19.1 (1998): 160.

20. Henry Jenkins, *Convergence Culture: Where Old and New Media Collide* (New York: New York University Press, 2006).

21. Guy Debord, *Society of the Spectacle* (Detroit: Black and Red, 1967); Douglas Kellner, *Media Spectacle* (London: Routledge, 2003).

22. Bolter and Grusin, *Remediation*, 68.

23. *Ibid.*

24. "Laws of the Game," 2018/2019, 138.

25. Mitchell N. Berman, "Replay," California Law Review 99.6 (2011): 1683–1744.

26. Collins, "Philosophy," 137.

27. Bolter and Grusin, *Remediation*, 188.

28. Dave Anderson, "Replay Instant Replay," *New York Times*, March 10, 1997, B11.

29. Bolter and Grusin, *Remediation*, 71.

30. Mark Andrejevic, *Infoglut: How Too Much Information Is Changing the Way We Think and Know* (New York: Routledge, 2013), 139.

31. Benoit B. Mandelbrot, *The Fractal Geometry of Nature* (New York: W.H. Freeman and Company, 1977); Michael Schwarz and Bill Jersey, "Hunting the Hidden Dimension," PBS's *Nova*, WGBH, Boston, Massachusetts, 2008. Retrieved from http://www.pbs.org/wgbh/nova/transcripts/3514_fractals.html.

32. Raymond Fielding, *The American Newsreel: A Complete History, 1911–1967* (Jefferson, NC: McFarland, 2006).

33. Stuart Wolpin, "Tape Recording Was Introduced 70 Years Ago Today," Recode (May 16, 2016). Retrieved from https://www.recode.net/2016/5/16/11672678/tape-recording-70th-anniversary-jack-mullin.

34. Erik Barnouw, *The Golden Web: A History of Broadcasting in the United States, Vol. II 1933–1953* (Oxford: Oxford University Press, 1968).

35. Hanson, "Instant Replay," 53.

36. Margaret Morse, "Sport on Television: Replay and Display," in *Regarding Television*, ed. E. Ann Kaplan (Frederick, MD: University Publications of America, 1983), 44–66.

37. David Rowe, *Sport, Culture and the Media: The Unruly Trinity* (Buckingham: Open University Press, 1999), 71.

38. Sarah Ahmed, "Affective Economies," *Social Text* 7922.2 (2004): 119.

39. See Hoberman, *Mortal Engines*.

40. *Ibid.*, 82.

41. Timothy Luke, *Screens of Power: Ideology, Domination and Resistance in Informational Society* (Urbana: University of Illinois Press, 1989), 34.

42. Pierre Bourdieu, *On Television*, trans. P.P. Ferguson (New York: The New Press, 1998).

43. Benjamin G. Rader, *In Its Own Image: How Television Has Transformed Sports* (New York: Free Press, 1984), 5.

44. Luke, Screens of Power.

45. Ahmed, "Affective Economies," 120.

46. Andrejevic, Infoglut.

47. Peter Denyer-Simmons, "Tackling Abuse of Officials: Attitudes and Communication Skills of Experienced Football Referees." Conference Paper, Empowerment, Creativity and Innovation—Challenging Media and Communication in the 21st Century (ANZCA), Adelaide, New Zealand, https://researchoutput.csu.edu.au/en/publications/tackling-abuse-of-officials-attitudes-and-communication-skills-of. See also Peter Denyer-Simmons and Ian Cunningham, "Communication and Sport Officials," in *Handbook of Sport Communication*, ed. P.M. Pedersen (New York: Routledge, 2012), 461–470.

48. See Werner Helsen and Jean-Baptiste Bultynck, "Physical and Perceptual-Cognitive Demands of Top-Class Refereeing in Association Football," *Journal of Sports Sciences* 22 (2004): 179–189. Duncan Mascarenhas, Dave Collins, and Patrick Mortimer, "The Art of Reason Versus the Exactness of Science in Elite Refereeing: Comments on Plessner and Betsch" (2001), *Journal of Sport Exercise Psychology* 24 (2005): 328–333. A.M. Nevill, N.J. Balmer, and A.M. Williams, "The Influence of Crowd Noise and Experience upon Refereeing Decisions in Football," *Psychology of Sport and Exercise* 3.4 (2002): 261–272. Jochim Spitz, Koen Put, Johan Wagemans, A. Mark Williams, and Werner Helsen, "Does Slow Motion Impact on the Perception of Foul Play in Football?" *European Journal of Sport Science* 17.6 (2017): 748–756.

49. Mohammed N. Nazaradin, Mohd R. Abdullah, and M.S.O. Fauzee, "Developing a Decision-Making Test for the Rugby Referees," *Malaysian Journal of Sports, Recreation and Education* 2.1 (2015): 77–85.

50. Berman, "Replay."

51. Jack de Menezes, "World Cup 2018 Final Referee: Nestor Pitana in VAR Controversy as Penal Decision Headlines France vs. Croation," *Independent*, July 16, 2018. Retrieved from https://www.independent.co.uk/sport/football/world-cup/world-cup-final-referee-nestor-pitana-var-penalty-decision-video-watch-antoine-griezmann-ivan-a8448431.html.

52. "Laws of the Game," 2018/2019, 140.

53. Collins, "Philosophy."

54. Harry Collins and Robert Evans, "You Cannot Be Serious! Public Understanding of Technology with Special Reference to 'Hawk-Eye,'" *Public Understanding of Science* 17.3 (2008).

55. Collins, "Philosophy," 142.

56. Berman, "Replay."

57. Spitz et al., "Does Slow Motion Impact on the Perception of Foul Play in Football?"

58. Helsen and Bultynck, "Physical and Perceptual-Cognitive Demands."

59. Nazaradin, Abdullah, and Fauzee, "Developing."

60. *Ibid.*, 83.

61. Denyer-Simmons, "Tackling Abuse of Officials."

62. *Ibid.*

63. Denyer-Simmons and Cunningham, "Communication and Sport Officials," 468.

64. *Ibid.*

65. Spitz et al., "Does Slow Motion Impact on the Perception of Foul Play in Football?"

66. Berman, "Replay," 1715.

67. Eugene M. Caruso, Zachary C. Burns, and Benjamin A. Converse, "Slow Motion Increases Perceived Intent," *Proceedings of the National Academy of Sciences of the United States of America* 113.33 (2016): 9250–9255. Retrieved from https://doi.org/10.1073/pnas.1603865113.

68. ESPN FC, "Ivan Perisic Penalty Decision: Did Referee Get World Cup Final Call 'Shockingly' Wrong?" July 15, 2018. Retrieved from https://www.youtube.com/watch?v=sRdDIrRcwio.

69. Berman, "Replay," 1699.

70. *Ibid.*

71. R. Askins, "Common Myths about Officiating," *Referee* 26.10 (2001): 44–47. Jeremy Grunska, "Yeah, You're Good … But You Can Be Better," *Referee* 26.6 (2001): 51–60.

72. Collins, "Philosophy."

73. Andrew Das, "How France Won Its Second World Cup Title," *New York Times*, July 16, 2018, D4.

74. Ian Crouch, "Baseball Replay Works—And It's Terrible," *New Yorker*. Retrieved from https://www.newyorker.com/news/sporting-scene/baseball-replay-worksand-its-terrible.

75. J. Surujlal and D.B. Jordaan, "Goal Line Technology in Soccer: Are Referees Ready for Technology in Decision Making?" *African Journal for Physical, Health Education, Recreation and Dance* 19.2 (2013): 245–257.

76. Collins, "Philosophy," 138.

77. Berman, "Replay," 1755.

78. Hoberman, *Mortal Engines.*

79. David B. Sullivan, "Broadcast Television and the Game of Packaging Sports," in *Handbook of Sports and Media*, ed. A.A. Raney and J. Bryant (Mahwah, NJ: Lawrence Erlbaum, 2006), 131–145.

80. Garry Whannel, *Fields of Vision: Television Sport and Cultural Transformation* (London: Routledge, 1992), 93.

81. Peter Shawn Taylor, "Video Replay Is Ruining Professional Sports," *Maclean's*, May 7, 2017. Retrieved from https://www.macleans.ca/sports/video-replay-is-ruining-professional-sports/.

82. See Eric Laurier and Stuart Reeves, "The Revelations of the Action-Replay: Video and the Optical Unconscious," Working Paper, 2011. Retrieved from https://ericlaurier.co.uk/resources/Writings/Action-replay.pdf. See also Malcolm Turvey, *Doubting Vision: Film and the Revisionist Tradition* (Oxford: Oxford University Press, 2008).

83. Hanson, "Instant Replay," 58.

84. Collins, "Philosophy," 137.

85. Timothy Revell, "A[rtificial] I[ntelligence] Can Doctor Videos to Put Words in the Mouths of Speakers," *New Scientist*, May 19, 2017. Retrieved from https://www.newscientist.com/article/2131716-ai-can-doctor-videos-to-put-words-in-the-mouths-of-speakers/.

86. Collins, "Philosophy," 142.

87. Andrejevic, *Infoglut*, 3.

88. David L. Andrews and Mike L. Silk, "Sport and Neoliberalism: An Affective-Ideological Articulation," *Journal of Popular Culture* 51.2 (2018): 513.

89. Collins, "Philosophy," 138.

90. See Frederic Jameson, *Postmodernism: Or the Cultural Logic of Late Capitalism* (Durham: Duke University Press, 1991).

Chapter 10

1. Ian McDonald, "Situating the Sport Documentary," *Journal of Sport & Social Issues* 31.3 (2007): 208–225.

2. Samantha Sheppard and Travis Vogan, "Introduction," in *Sporting Realities: Critical Readings of the Sports Documentary*, ed. S. Sheppard and T. Vogan (Lincoln: University of Nebraska Press, 2020), 5.

3. For a definition of the economy of death, see Jay W. Baird, *To Die for Germany: Heroes in the Nazi Pantheon* (Bloomington: Indiana University Press, 1990). See also Harald Höbusch, "Rescuing German Alpine Tradition: Nanga Parbat and Its Visual Afterlife," *Journal of Sport History* 29. 1 (Spring 2002): 49–76.

4. National Geographic Channel. Quoted in Hugh Barnard, "Mountain Film: An Analysis of the History and Characteristics of a Documentary Genre" (master's thesis, University of Otago, Dunedin, New Zealand, 2011), 43.

5. Susan Birrell, "Approaching Mt. Everest: On Intertextuality and the Past as Narrative," *Journal of Sport History* 34.1 (2007): 17.

6. Tracy Edwards, email to the author, December 16, 2022.

7. Steve Neal, "Questions of Genre," *Screen* 31.1 (1990): 46.

8. See Jay David Bolter and Richard Grusin, *Remediation: Understanding New Media* (Cambridge: MIT Press, 2000).

9. *Ibid.*, 68.

10. *210 Days: Around the World with Jessica Watson*, produced by A. Fraser (2010, Sony Music Entertainment Australia), DVD.

11. *Maidentrip*, directed by Jillian Schlesinger (2013, New York: Wild Shot Films Productions), DVD.

12. Sarah Crawley, "Gender, Class and the Construction of Masculinity in Professional Sailing,"

Review for the Sociology of Sport 33.1 (1998): 33–42.

13. See Lee McGinnis, Julia McQuillan, and Constance L. Chapple, "I Just Want to Play: Women, Sexism, and Persistence in Golf," *Journal of Sport & Social Issues* 29.3 (August 2005): 313–337.

14. Louise Bricknell, "The Trouble with Feelings: Gender, Sexualities, and Power in a Gender Regime of Competitive Sailing," *Journal of Sport & Social Issues* 23 (1999): 421–438.

15. Gayle Jennings, "Caught in the Irons: One of the Live Experiences of Long-Term Ocean Cruising Women," *Tourism Review International* 9 (2005): 177–193. See also Marilyn Porter, "The Mermaids Are Out There, So Why Aren't We? Women and Sailing," *Canadian Women's Studies* 15.4 (1995): 102–105.

16. Helene de Burgh-Woodman and Janice Brace-Govan, "Marketing and the Other: A Study of Women in the Sailing Marketplace and Its Implications for Marketing Discourse," *European Advances in Consumer Research* 8 (2007): 189–195.

17. Barbara Cox and Shona Thompson, "Multiple Bodies: Sportswomen, Soccer, and Sexuality," *International Review for the Sociology of Sport* 35.1 (2000): 18.

18. George Rosenwald and Richard Ochberg, "Introduction: Life Stories, Cultural Politics, and Self-Understanding," in *Storied Lives: The Cultural Politics of Self-Understanding*, ed. G. Rosenwald and R. Ochberg (New Haven: Yale University Press, 1992), 1–18.

19. Bill Nichols, *Representing Reality: Issues and Concepts in Documentary* (Bloomington: Indiana University Press, 1991).

20. Peter Varley, "Confecting Adventure and Playing with Meaning: The Adventure Commodification Continuum," *Journal of Sport & Tourism* 11.2 (2006): 182–83; 188–91. See also Jean Baudrillard, *The Ecstasy of Communication*, trans. Bernard Schutze and Caroline Schutze (New York: Columbia University Press, 1988).

21. Bill Nichols, *Introduction to Documentary* (Bloomington: Indiana University Press, 2001).

22. Tracy Edwards and Tim Madge, *Maiden* (London: Simon & Schuster, 1990), 162.

23. *Ibid.*, 216.

24. Deborah Battaglia, "On Practical Nostalgia: Self-Prospecting Among Urban Trobrianders," in *Rhetorics of Self-Making*, ed. D. Battaglia, 77–96 (Berkley: University of California Press, 1995), 1.

25. Ann Davison, *Last Voyage* (London: Grafton Books, 1951), ii.

26. Davison, 235.

27. Edwards & Madge, *Maiden*, 13.

28. Naomi James, *At One with the Sea* (London: Hutchinson, 1979), 73.

29. Peter Berger, *The Sacred Canopy* (New York: Anchor Books, 1967), 43.

30. *Ibid.*, 44.

31. Jessica Watson, *True Spirit* (New York: Atria, 2010), 278.

32. Barnard, "Mountain Film," 2, 6.

33. *Ibid.*, 42.

34. James, *At One with the Sea*, 39.

35. Watson, *True Spirit*, 68–69.

36. Barnard, "Mountain Film," 32–41.

37. Ellen MacArthur, *Taking on the World: The Official Story*, directed by R. Simmons (2001, APP Broadcast). Retrieved from https://www.youtube.com/watch?v=0bxt-FzEsnA.

38. Kay Cottee: *First Lady*, directed by Peter Sutton (1989, Showboat Productions).

39. Barnard, "Mountain Film," 34.

40. Laura Dekker, *One Girl, One Dream* (Sydney: HarperCollins, 2014), 189.

41. Edwards, *Maiden*, 127.

42. Andre Bazin, *What Is Cinema?* Trans. Hugh Gray. Berkeley: University of California Press, 1971. See also Barnard, 25–32.

43. Bazin, 162.

44. Ellen MacArthur, *Full Circle: My Life and Journey* (London: Penguin, 2010), 211.

45. Edwards, *Maiden*, 72.

46. *First Lady*, directed by P. Sutton.

47. Watson, *True Spirit*, 159–60.

48. MacArthur, *Full Circle*, 175, 177.

49. Cottee, *First Lady*, 50.

50. Lisa Clayton, *At the Mercy of the Sea* (London: Orion, 1996), 63.

51. Dekker, *One Girl, One Dream*, 98–99.

52. James, *At One with the Sea*, 12.

53. See Robert B. Neveldine, *Bodies at Risk: Unsafe Limits in Romanticism and Postmodernism* (Albany: University of New York Press, 1998); Regina Hewitt, *The Possibilities of Society: Wordsworth, Coleridge, and the Sociological Viewpoint of English Romanticism* (Albany: State University of New York Press, 1997); and Jeffrey C. Robinson, *The Walk: Notes on a Romantic Image* (Norman: University of Oklahoma Press, 1989).

54. Neil Lewis, "The Climbing Body, Nature, and the Experience of Modernity," *Body & Society* 6.3–4 (2000): 65.

55. Davison, *Last Voyage*, 123–24.

56. James, *At One with the Sea*, 72.

57. Cottee, *First Lady*, 199.

58. *First Lady*, directed by P. Sutton.

59. Edwards, *Maiden*, 186.

60. Dean K. Simonton, *Greatness: Who Makes History and Why* (New York: Guilford Press, 1984), 6.

61. Dekker, 315.

62. MacArthur, 327.

63. Lori Holyfield, "Manufacturing Adventure: The Buying and Selling of Emotions," *Journal of Contemporary Ethnography* 28.3 (1999): 3–32.

64. Madge, *Maiden*, 132.

65. Edwards, email to the author.

66. Rosenwald and Ochberg, "Introduction: Life Stories, Cultural Politics, and Self-Understanding," 1.

67. Birrell, "Approaching Mt. Everest," 12–13.

68. Watson, True Spirit, 332.

69. Lewis, "The Climbing Body," 63.

70. Tracy Edwards, online interview. Retrieved from Video | Moments (themaidenfactor.org).

Chapter 11

1. Amelia H. Arsenault, "The Datafication of Media: Big Data and the Media Industries," *International Journal of Media & Cultural Politics* 13.1–2 (March 2017): 7–24.

2. *Ibid.*, 20.

3. Hibai Lopez-Gonzalez and Mark D. Griffiths, "Understanding the Convergence of Online Sports Betting Markets," *International Review for the Sociology of Sport* (2017): 11.

4. Baker Hostetler, "The Future of Legal Sports Gambling: What Everyone Needs to Know About Murphy v. NCAA," *Holt Hackney Sports Litigation Alert*, 2 August 2018, 1.

5. Lopez-Gonzalez and Griffiths, 7–8.

6. Retrieved from Fantasy sports market size U.S. 2021 | Statista.

7. Richard G. Lomax, "Fantasy Sports: History, Game Types, and Research," in *Handbook of Sports and Media*, ed. A.A. Raney and J. Bryant (Florence, KY: Lawrence Erlbaum Associates, 2006), 383.

8. Retrieved from Industry Demographics—Fantasy Sports & Gaming Association (thefsga.org).

9. Bill Ain, "We Had No Idea," *ESPN The Magazine*, February 23, 2010. Retrieved from ESPN The Magazine—Morty Ain—An oral history of Rotisserie Baseball.

10. Lomax, "Fantasy Sports," 383–392.

11. *Ibid.*, 386–87.

12. Nickolas W. Davis and Margaret Carlisle Duncan, "Sports Knowledge Is Power: Reinforcing Masculine Privilege Through Fantasy Sport League Participation," *Journal of Sport and Social Issues* 30 (2006): 247.

13. *Ibid.*, 252.

14. Donald P. Roy and Benjamin D. Goss, "A Conceptual Framework of Influences on Fantasy Sports Consumption," *Marketing Management Journal* 15.2 (2007): 106.

15. Davis and Duncan, 254.

16. Andrew Billings, Brody James Ruihley, and Yiyi Yang, "Fantasy Gaming on Steroids? Contrasting Fantasy Sport Participation by Daily Fantasy Sport Participation," *Communication & Sport* 5.6 (2017): 735.

17. *Ibid.*, 746.

18. Joey Gawrysiak, Brendan Dwyer, Brendan, and Rick Burton, "Understanding Baseball Consumption Via In-Home Gaming," *Journal of Applied Sport Management* 6.3 (Fall 2014): 83.

19. Michael Trippiedi, "Daily Fantasy Sports Leagues: Do You Have the Skill to Win at These Games of Chance?" *UNLV Gaming Law Journal* 5.20 (2015): 220.

20. *Ibid.*

21. *Ibid.*, 221.

22. Brian Hourigan, "The 'Math' Behind Going Pro in DFS." Retrieved from The "Math" Behind Going Pro in DFS (rotogrinders.com).

23. Lia Nower, Dylan Adam Pickering, Kyle Caler, Alex Blaszczynski, "Daily Fantasy Sports Players: Gambling, Addiction, and Mental Health Problems," *Journal of Gambling Studies* 34.3 (2018): 727–737.

24. *Ibid.*

25. Joseph M. Kelly, "Living in a Fantasy," *Gaming Law Review* 12.4 (2008): 315.

26. Nerilee Hing, Alex Myles Thomas Russell, Matthew Lamont, and Peter Vitartas, "Bet Anywhere, Anytime: An Analysis of Internet Sports Bettors' Responses to Gambling Promotions during Sports Broadcasts by Problem Gambling Severity," *Journal of Gambling Studies* 33.4 (2017): 1051–1065.

27. Quoted in Hibai Lopez-Gonzalez, Mark O. Griffiths, and Susana Jimenez-Murcia, "The Symbolic Construction of Sports Betting Products," *International Gambling Studies* (May 2021): 506.

28. Hing, Griffiths, and Jimenez-Murcia, 513.

29. *Ibid.*, 515.

30. *Ibid.*

31. "FOX MLB Analyst David 'Big Papi' Ortiz Steps to the Plate for FOX Bet Super 6," PRNewswire, June 14, 2021. Accessed from https://www.prnewswire.com/news-releases/fox-mlb-analyst-david-big-papi-ortiz-steps-to-the-plate-for-fox-bet-super-6-301311474.html.

32. Hibai Lopez-Gonzalez and Mark D. Griffiths, "Understanding the Convergence of Online Sports Betting Markets," *International Review for the Sociology of Sport* 53.7 (2018): 819.

33. *Ibid.*, 818.

34. Hing, et. al., "Bet Anywhere," 3.

35. *Ibid.*, 9.

36. Nerilee Hing, Matthew Lamont, Peter Vitartas, and Elian Fink, "Sports-Embedded Gambling Promotions: A Study of Exposure, Sports Betting Intention and Problem Gambling Amongst Adults," *International Journal of Mental Health and Addiction* 13 (2015): 130.

37. *Ibid.*, 131.

38. Richard Woolley, "Mapping Internet Gambling: Emerging Modes of Online Participation in Wagering and Sports Betting," *International Journal of Gambling* 3.1 (January 2003): 18.

39. Quoted in Sarah Wolter, "Conceptual Framework for Sports Media in the 21st Century: Content, Platform, Media System, and Political System," *Journal of Sports Media* 15.2 (Fall 2020): 97.

40. *Ibid.*, 98.

41. Lopez-Gonzalez and Griffiths, 14–15.

42. *Ibid.*, 8–9.

43. *Ibid.*, 6.

44. Lance Pugmire, "Step Inside the Future of Betting in U.S. Sports Venues," *USA Today Sports+*, March 7, 2022. Retrieved from Inside Phoenix Suns' Footprint Center and the future of sports betting (usatoday.com).

45. Thomas P. Oates, "Race, Economics, and the

Shifting Politics of Sport Media," *Radical History Review* 125 (May 2016): 162–165.

46. *Ibid.*, 161.
47. Quoted in Oates, 163.
48. *Ibid.*, 165.
49. Arsenault, "The Datafication of Media," 8.
50. *Ibid.*
51. *Ibid.* 9.
52. Andrejevic, Infoglut, 58.
53. Hing, et al., "Bet Anywhere," 13.

54. Retrieved from FOX MLB Analyst David "Big Papi" Ortiz Steps to the Plate for FOX Bet Super 6 (prnewswire.com).
55. Gaming America, "Tennessee Reports $405m in Monthly Sports Wagers for October," Sports Betting Online, November 11, 2022. Retrieved from Tennessee reports $405m in monthly sports wagers for October (gamingamerica.com).

Bibliography

Primary Sources

Films

"Columbia" Winning the Cup. October 24, 1899, Thomas A. Edison, Inc.; producer J. Stuart Blackton, Albert E. Smith.

Corbett and Courtney Before the Kinetograph. November 17, 1894 (filmed September 7), Wm. K.L. Dickson/Edison, Kinetoscope Exhibition Company.

Corbett-Fitzsimmons Fight. March 17, 1897, Veriscope Company.

Ellen MacArthur, Taking on the World: The Official Story. APP Broadcast, director R. Simmons (2001). Retrieved from https://www.youtube.com/watch?v=0bxt-FzEsnA.

Jeffries-Johnson World's Championship Boxing Contest, Held at Reno, Nevada, July 4, 1910. December 7, 1910, J. & J. Co., Photographed by Vitagraph, supervised by J. Stuart Blackton.

Jeffries-Sharkey Contest. November 4, 1899, American Mutoscope & Biograph.

Kay Cottee: First Lady. 1989, Showboat Productions, director Peter Sutton.

Leonard-Cushing Fight. June 14, 1894, Edison/the Kinetoscope Exhibition Company.

Lisa Clayton: Alone Around the World. August 22, 1995; Television Documentary Programme, London: BBC, producer E. Keil.

Maiden. 2019, Sony Pictures Classic, director Alex Holmes.

Maidentrip. 2013, Wild Shot Films Production, director Jillian Schlesinger.

Racing at Sheepshead Bay. July 31, 1897, Thomas A. Edison, Inc.; producer, James White.

This Is Your life—Lisa Clayton. September 13, 1995, BBC, Television Programme, S36, E2, M. Aspel (Host).

210 Days: Around the World with Jessica Watson. 2010, Sony Music Entertainment Australia, producer A. Fraser.

Willard-Johnson Boxing Match. May 4, 1915 (April 5 date of fight), Pantomimic Corp. Fred Mace/L. Lawrence Weber.

World Championship, Jack Johnson vs. Stanley Ketchell [sic]. October 24, 1909, J.W. Coffroth/Kalem, Kleine Optical Company/MPPC and Gaumont, U.K.

Books and Periodicals

"About Carlisle Athletics." *Carlisle Arrow,* September 8, 1908.

Abramson, J.P. "U.S. Athletes Fail 4 Times at Olympics." *New York Herald Tribune,* August 3, 1928, 1.

Adams, Val. "C.B.S. Shows Off Tape-Recorded TV." *New York Times,* December 21, 1956, 43.

_____. "News of TV and Radio." *New York Times,* August 19, 1951.

_____. "Tape Recorders for TV a Big Hit." *New York Times,* April 20, 1956.

_____. "Television Film Men Question Scope of New Tape Recorder." *New York Times,* April 16, 1956.

_____. "TV Football Pact Voided by Court." *New York Times,* July 21, 1961.

_____. "TV Is Put on Tape by New Recorder." *New York Times,* April 15, 1956.

Alfano, Peter. "Battling Athletes Hurt Sports' Image." *New York Times,* February 8, 1988.

_____. "CBS Concentrates on Playoffs." *New York Times,* May 17, 1983.

_____. "ESPN Struggling, but Making an Impact." *New York Times,* May 24, 1983.

_____. "A Faulty Tack on Covering the Races." *New York Times,* September 27, 1983.

"Almost a Lynching Over Gans's Victory." *New York Times,* September 5, 1906.

Amdur, Neil. "History Gives Hope in USFL Venture." *New York Times,* July 20, 1982.

_____. "NBC Bids to Revive Appeal of Tennis." *New York Times,* June 7, 1983.

_____. "The Television Dollars Foster New Perceptions." *New York Times,* October 30, 1982.

"American Athletes Win." *New York Times,* July 15, 1900.

"'American Forum' to Debate What's Wrong with College Football, on Oct. 7." NBC News, October 2, 1951.

"The Americans Ahead." *New York Times,* April 8, 1896.

Anderson, Dave. "Replay Instant Replay." *New York Times,* March 10, 1997, B11.

"Around the Bulletin Boards." *New York Times,* October 21, 1899.

Article 1, No Title. *New York Times,* July 6, 1910.

"At Stag Houses Only." *New York Tribune,* July 11, 1910.

Austin, Sam C. "Lively Bidding for the Jeffries-Sharkey Fight." *Police Gazette,* July 29, 1899.

"Bar Fight Pictures to Avoid Race Riots." *New York Times,* July 6, 1910.

"Barred in San Francisco." *New York Times,* July 7, 1910.

Barringer, Felicity. "Baseball and Editors' Group Compromise to End Dispute." *New York Times,* April 14, 2001.

_____. "Baseball Is Trying to Limit How New Coverage Is Used." *New York Times,* March 31, 2001.

_____. "Internet News Fanatics Prefer Television Sites." *New York Times,* November 30, 1998.

"Baseball Telecast." *Broadcasting,* September 1, 1939.

Bray, Hiawatha. "ESPN Selling Premium Content to Net Providers." *The Boston Globe,* June 15, 2006.

Brown, Ken. "Catching the Atlanta Games on Line." *New York Times,* July 8, 1996.

Brown, Les. "From the Air: Programs by Satellite and Cable." *New York Times,* February 17, 1980.

Carmody, Deidre. "Female Reporter Sues Over Locker-Room Ban." *New York Times,* December 30, 1977.

Carter, Bill. "Chief Lauds NBC Olympic Performance." *New York Times,* September 28, 2000.

_____. "Where the Boys Are." *New York Times,* January 31, 1999.

_____, with Richard Sandomir. "NBC's Ratings for Olympics Are Worst Ever." *New York Times,* September 20, 2000.

"CBS to Acquire 22% of Sportsline USA." *New York Times,* March 6, 1997.

"Charged the Grand Jury. Judge Depue Wants the Corbett Fight Investigated." *Newark Daily Advertiser,* September 11, 1894.

Clayton, Lisa. *At the Mercy of the Sea.* London: Orion, 1996.

"Colorful Early-Day Sportscaster, Bill Munday, Will Recall Famous Wrong-Way Rose Bowl Touchdown on 'Silver Jubilee.'" NBC–New York, News Release, August 8, 1951.

Congressional Record. July 19, 1912, 9305.

Cottee, Kay. *First Lady: A History-Making Solo Voyage Around the World.* South Melbourne, Australia: Macmillan, 1989.

"Court Limits Pro Football's Control of Television to the Area of Home Games." *New York Times,* November 13, 1953.

Daley, Arthur. "Sports of the *Times.*" *New York Times,* November 13, 1953.

_____. "When the Ringside Becomes the Fireside." *New York Times,* March 27, 1949.

Das, Andrew. "How France Won Its Second World Cup Title." *New York Times,* July 16, 2018, D4.

Davison, Ann. *Last Voyage.* London: Grafton Books, 1951.

_____. *My Ship Is So Small.* London: Peter Davies, 1956.

Dekker, Laura. *One Girl One Dream.* Sydney: HarperCollins, 2013.

De Menezes, Jack. "World Cup 2018 Final Referee: Nestor Pitana in VAR Controversy as Penal Decision Headlines France vs. Croatia." *Independent,* July 16, 2018. https://www.independent.co.uk/sport/football/world-cup/world-cup-final-referee-nestor-pitana-var-penalty-decision-video-watch-antoine-griezmann-ivan-a8448431.html.

"Detectives to Aid Olympic Photo Ban." *New York Times,* May 27, 1928.

"Disney Names Head of Internet Group." *New York Times,* September 9, 1999.

"Display Ad 19." *New York Times,* October 19, 1923.

"Display Ad 90, No Title." *New York Times,* April 29, 1980.

"Display Ad 17." *New York Times,* October 18, 1923.

"Display Ad 319, No Title." *New York Times,* November 13, 1980.

Doré, Louis. "Was Referee Right to Give France Penalty for Perisic Handball? VAR Controversy Hits World Cup Final." *iNews, The Essential Daily Briefing,* July 15, 2018.

Dougherty, Philip H. "New Sports Network's Clients." *New York Times,* September 25, 1979.

Dunlap, Orrin E., Jr. "Watching a Battle." *New York Times,* June 4, 1939.

Durso, Joseph. "Get Ready for Those Anthology Shows." *New York Times,* January 31, 1984.

"EarthLink Bundles Subscription-Only Sports Features from Popular Web Sites." *New York Times,* April 12, 2004.

Edwards, Tracy. Email to the author, 2022.

_____, and Tim Madge. *Maiden.* London: Simon & Schuster, 1990.

Eskenazi, Gerald. "All-Sports TV Adds Canadian Football." *New York Times,* June 10, 1980.

_____. "NBC Plans to Take Tougher Approach." *New York Times,* March 9, 1988.

ESPN FC. "Ivan Perisic Penalty Decision: Did Referee Get World Cup Final Call 'Shockingly' Wrong?" July 15, 2018. https://www.youtube.com/watch?v=sRdDIrRcwio.

Fabrikant, Geraldine. "It's First and Goal for ESPN." *New York Times,* June 9, 1987.

"Fights Race Film with Smoke and Sun." *New York Times,* October 21, 1923.

"The Films That Failed." *The Phonoscope,* May 1899.

"First Television of Baseball Seen." *New York Times,* May 18, 1939.

"'Football Kickoff, 1951': Lou Little, Charles Caldwell, Jack Lavelle and Others to Preview Season on Special NBC-TV Program." NBC Television, WNBT New York, News Release, September 11, 1951.

"FOX MLB Analyst David 'Big Papi' Ortiz Steps to the Plate for FOX Bet Super 6." *PRNewswire,* June 14, 2021. https://www.prnewswire.com/news-releases/fox-mlb-analyst-david-big-papi-ortiz-steps-to-the-plate-for-fox-bet-super-6-301311474.html.

"French to Admit U.S. Camera Men." *New York Times,* May 10, 1924.

Geller, Henry. "Fairness, Common Sense and the

Superstation Issue." *New York Times,* December 16, 1984.

"General Motors to Sponsor Coast-to-Coast Telecasts of College Football Games on NBC." NBC-TV News, August 25, 1952.

Goodwin, Michael. "ESPN Ends Season in Middle of Pack." *New York Times,* December 29, 1987.

_____. "Highlights Aren't Enough." *New York Times,* November 26, 1985.

_____. "NFL Becomes a Telethon." *New York Times,* November 10, 1987.

_____. "The Perils of Slapdash Journalism." *New York Times,* December 16, 1986.

_____. "TV Sports Money Machine Falters." *New York Times,* January 26, 1986.

Gould, Jack. "Delay in Televising Olympics on Coast Irritates Japanese," *New York Times,* October 11, 1964.

_____. "Football on Video." *New York Times,* November 15, 1953.

_____. "The News of Radio." *New York Times,* August 25, 1947.

_____. "Radio News." *New York Times,* March 11, 1948.

_____. "The Roller Derby: Is It Television, Sport or Narcotic?" *New York Times,* June 5, 1949.

_____. "Television, in Big Strides, Advances Across the Nation." *New York Times,* April 24, 1949.

_____. "Telstar Success Spurs U.S. Study." *New York Times,* July 12, 1962.

_____. "TV: Color Film on Tape." *New York Times,* October 24, 1956.

_____. "When TV Lost the Olympics." *New York Times,* October 18, 1964.

"Graziano Slugfest on WJZ Tonight." Display Ad 100, *New York Times,* January 18, 1946.

Hansell, Saul. "ESPN Brings Video Clips to High-Speed Net Users." *New York Times,* October 14, 2002.

Harmon, Amy. "Exploration of World Wide Web Tilts from Eclectic to Mundane." *New York Times,* August 26, 2001.

_____. "On the Office PC, Bosses Opt for All Work, and No Play." *New York Times,* September 22, 1997.

Herz, J.C. "It's a Video Game, It's TV, and You're the Star." *New York Times,* July 2, 1998.

"The International Race." *New York Times,* October 19, 1923.

Ives, Nat. "At ESPN.com, New Technology Comes with Commercials." *New York Times,* February 21, 2003.

James, Naomi. *At One with the Sea.* London: Hutchinson, 1979.

Janofsky, Michael. "NFL Faces a New Economy." *New York Times,* March 17, 1987.

"Jeffries Cries 'Foul.'" *New York Herald,* November 4, 1899.

"Johnson-vs.-Ketchell Bout of 1909 to Be Telecast." NBC–New York, Press Release, August 10, 1951.

"Jones Wins U.S. Open for the Fourth Time as 10,000 Look On." *New York Times,* July 13, 1930.

Kahn, Roger. "Some Modest Proposals." *New York Times,* February 13, 1978.

Kaplan, Peter W. "Rush Likely to Sign Up More Games." *New York Times,* June 28, 1984.

Katz, Michael. "Below-the-Belt Blows Aimed at Boxing." *New York Times,* July 23, 1985.

_____. "Boxing Novelty: Computerizing Punches." *New York Times,* February 12, 1985.

_____. "ESPN's Public Service at Cooperstown." *New York Times,* July 30, 1985.

Keese, Parton. "Bristol Hits the Big League in Sports TV." *New York Times,* December 9, 1979.

"Keith's New Theatre." *Boston Herald,* September 22, 1896.

"Kennedy Will Appear on TV at Football Award Fete Dec. 5." *New York Times,* November 23, 1961.

Kerr, Peter. "Madison Ave.'s Football Woe." *New York Times,* September 22, 1984.

"The Kinetograph." *New York Sun,* May 28, 1891.

"The Kinetograph—A New Industry Heralded." *The Phonogram* (October 1892): 217–218.

"Knocked Out by Corbett." *New York Sun,* September 8, 1894.

Knoll, Steve. "More Coverage for Olympics Fans." *New York Times,* July 22, 1984.

Knox-Johnston, Robin. *A World of My Own.* London: Norton, 1969/2013.

Kopytoff, Verne G. "Hitting the Virtual Slopes All Year Round." *New York Times,* November 26, 1998.

"Kuhn Reacts to Suit of Female Writer." *New York Times,* December 31, 1977.

Lasch, Christopher. "The Corruption of Sports." *New York Review of Books* 24.7: 24–30.

"Lindsey Nelson Appointed Assistant Sports Director for NBC." *Trade News,* July 23, 1952.

Litsky, Frank. "Review Is Refused of Cable TV Ruling." *New York Times,* January 12, 1982.

"Live from France on World Wide Web." *New York Times,* June 9, 1998.

Lloyd, Barbara. "Putting the America's Cup at One's Fingertips." *New York Times,* August 8, 1999.

Lohman, Sidney. "Coverage of Sports." *New York Times,* April 24, 1949.

_____. "News of TV and Radio." *New York Times,* September 17, 1950.

Lohr, Steve. "Joining the New Media: ABC News Begins and On-Line Service." *New York Times,* May 12, 1997.

"London Is Shocked by Decisive Defeat." *New York Times,* October 21, 1923.

Longman, Jere. "Pro Leagues' Ratings Drop; Nobody Is Quite Sure Why." *New York Times,* July 29, 2001.

"Louis vs. Walcott." Display Ad 39, *New York Times,* June 23, 1948.

Ludtke Lincoln, Melissa. "Locker Rooms: Equality with Integrity." *New York Times,* April 15, 1979.

MacArthur, Ellen. *Full Circle: My Life and Journey.* London: Penguin, 2010.

"Magic Lantern Kinetoscope." *New York Sun,* April 21, 1895.

Martzke, Rudy. "Instant Replay Gets 'Matrix'-Like View of Key Plays." *USA Today,* January 23, 2001.

_____, and Reid Cherner. "Channeling How to View Sports." *USA TODAY,* August 17, 2004.

"May the Better Horse Win." *New York Times,* October 20, 1923.

McCarthy, Michael. "NFL Taking Bold Steps to Control What Fans See." *USA TODAY,* September 7–9, 2007.

Mifflin, Lawrie. "TV Season Is One of Discontent." *New York Times,* October 15, 1984.

_____. "Watch the Tube or Watch the Computer?" *New York Times,* February 1, 1999.

"Mitchell Demands Zev Race My Own." *New York Times,* October 1, 1923.

"My Own Is Coming by Special Train." *New York Times,* October 19, 1923.

"National Football League Denied Plea to Delay Voiding TV Pact." *New York Times,* July 29, 1961.

"N.B.C. Schedules Hour-Long Films." *New York Times,* April 2, 1957.

"NBC-TV Provides Weekly Sports Reel for Stations." NBC–New York, Press Release, September 25, 1951.

"NBC's Football Staff Plans for Complete Schedule of College Games to Be Televised by Network." NBC-TV News, July 29, 1952.

"News of Radio." *New York Times,* June 23, 1948.

"N.F.L. Gains Right to Pool TV Pacts." *New York Times,* October 1, 1961.

"NFL Says Fans Like Internet Site." *New York Times,* November 12, 1998.

"No Moaning for Loser." *New York Times,* June 26, 1948.

"No Women Olympians for American Team." *New York Times,* March 31, 1914.

"Notables Will See Match Race Today." *New York Times,* October 20, 1923.

"Olympic Body Will Supply Photographs of the Games." *New York Times,* January 10, 1924.

"Olympic Prizes Lost; Thorpe No Amateur." *New York Times,* January 28, 1913.

"Our Athletes in Paris." *New York Times,* July 12, 1900.

"Picture Men to Fight." *New York Times,* July 7, 1910.

"Picture Rights Let for Olympic Games." *New York Times,* November 28, 1923.

"Pictures and Pugilism." *Motion Picture World,* December 18, 1909.

"Plan to Charge $60,000 for Olympic Rights Draws U.S. Protest and May Bar Films Here." *New York Times,* May 16, 1928.

Prial, Frank J. "Sports Channel Adds Business News." *New York Times,* February 5, 1983.

"Pro Charge Annoys U.S. Rugby Players." *New York Times,* May 8, 1924.

"Pro Football Seeks Dismissal of TV Suit." *New York Times,* October 30, 1951.

"Protest UFA Monopoly." *New York Times,* January 24, 1928.

"Race No Fair Test, Say London Critics." *New York Times,* October 22, 1923.

"Radio and Television." *New York Times,* May 31, 1949.

Reiss, Mike. "Local Stations Shut Out by NFL." *The Boston Globe,* April 14, 2006.

Richtel, Matt. "For Fanatics, Sports Webcasts." *New York Times,* March 19, 1998.

"Rickard Explains 'Secret' Session." *New York Times,* December 5, 1909.

"The Right Place for Women." *New York Times,* October 4, 1990.

Rogers, Thomas. "Kiam Apologizes After Joking About the Olson Incident." *New York Times,* February 7, 1991.

"Roller Derby: An Industry Made by Television." *Business Week,* June 4, 1949.

Rothman Morris, Bonnie. "Making Room Online for Young Olympic Fans." *New York Times,* September 21, 2000.

"Ruling on TV Rights Favors 2 Pac-10 Teams." *New York Times,* September 11, 1984.

Sandomir, Richard. "At ESPN After 25 Years, Happy Birthday to Us." *New York Times,* September 7, 2004.

_____. "At ESPN, the Revolution Was Televised." *New York Times,* September 7, 1999.

_____. "By the Numbers, the College Bowl Games Have Less Action." *New York Times,* January 7, 2004.

_____. "The Decline and Fall of Sports Ratings." *New York Times,* September 10, 2003.

_____. "'Dream Job,' the Nightmare, Showing Now on ESPN." *New York Times,* March 6, 2004.

_____. "NCAA Is Pursuing an Increase in Billions." *New York Times,* September 10, 1999.

_____. "NFL's Internet Deal Will Be Largest Ever." *New York Times,* July 11, 2001.

_____. "Pepsi Gets $50 Million Deal for Major League Baseball." *New York Times,* March 20, 1997.

Saslow, Linda. "New Channels and New Costs for Cable TV." *New York Times,* April 6, 1997.

"Satellite & Cable Television." http://history.sandiego.edu/gen/recording/television3.html.

Schiebel, Seth. "Cable TV Lacks Competition, FCC Notes." *New York Times,* January 14, 1998.

_____. "For Wireless, The Beginnings of a Breakout." *New York Times,* January 13, 2005.

Schneider, Steve. "Everything About the Game— Except the Game." *New York Times,* January 26, 1986.

Schwartz, John. "Leisure Pursuits of Today's Young Men." *New York Times,* March 29, 2004.

_____. "Olympics Stung by Technology's False Starts." *New York Times,* July 22, 1996.

Schwartz, Tony. "Cable TV Programmers Find Problems Amid Fast Growth." *New York Times,* September 28, 1982.

"The Screen." *New York Times,* October 22, 1923.

Shepard, Richard F. "U.S. Will Study Sports TV Pacts." *New York Times,* July 26, 1961.

Smith, Red. "Another View on Equality." *New York Times,* January 9, 1978.

_____. "Cable TV for Sports Junkies." *New York Times,* December 3, 1979.

Smith, Sally Bedell. "'Monday Night Football' Rating Slips." *New York Times,* December 31, 1983.

Smith, Timothy W. "Tagliabue Waffles on Lisa Olson File." *New York Times,* May 31, 1992.

Solomon, John D. "The Sports Market Is Looking Soggy." *New York Times,* April 21, 2002.

"Special Pre-Game and Post-Game Football Programs to Complement NBC-TV's Gridiron Coverage." NBC–New York, NBC-TV News Release, September 10, 1951.

Sreenivasan, Sreenath. "From Masters to Duffers, There's Golf on the Web." *New York Times,* April 7, 1997.

Stevens, John Paul. "'From the Opinion,' Excerpts from Supreme Court Opinions in NCAA Case." *New York Times,* June 28, 1984.

Stevenson, Richard W. "Rates Flat for Sports Programs." *New York Times,* September 2, 1986.

Stuart, Reginald. "Age of Domestic Phone Satellites Dawns." *New York Times,* September 22, 1975.

"The Suburban." *New York Herald,* June 24, 1896.

Taub, Eric A. "The Big Picture on Digital TV: It's Still Fuzzy." *New York Times,* September 12, 2002.

"Ted Husing to Give Pre-Game Warmup of College Football Telecasts on Saturdays." NBC-New York, NBC-TV News Release, September 27, 1951.

Tedeschi, Bob. "NFL's Site Gets Hits, as Well as Blocks and Tackles." *New York Times,* December 13, 2000.

"Television: The Big Daddy of Nearly All Sports." *New York Times,* December 30, 1979.

"Telstar May Transmit '64 Olympics to U. S." *New York Times,* August 28, 1962.

"Top Football Games Will Be Telecast by NBC in Fall; More Than 50 Stations to Carry NCAA Events." NBC Television News, August 10, 1951.

Turnock, Rob. "The Arrival of Videotape." http://www.birth-of-tv.org/birth/assetView.do?asset=123173128_1117789877.

"TV Names Gobel Best Newcomer." *New York Times,* March 8, 1955.

"U.S. Doubts Legality of TV Sports Pacts." *New York Times,* July 28, 1961.

United States of America, Plaintiff v. National Football League et al., Defendants, 196 F. Supp.445; 1961 U.S. Dist. Lexis 5184; 1961 Trade Cas. (CCH) P70,082, July 20, 1961.

"U.S. Rugby Players Threaten to Quit." *New York Times,* May 9, 1924.

United States v. National Football League et al. 116 F. Supp. 319; 1953 U.S. Dist. Lexis 2218.

Vecsey, George. "All Leagues Look Alike." *New York Times,* January 5, 1983.

"Video Status Confused, Agency Finds." *Broadcasting,* August 12, 1946.

Wallace, William N. "Instant Replay Likely in USFL." *New York Times,* February 11, 1985.

"Watching a Televised Baseball Game." *New York Times,* September 3, 1939, X10.

Watson, Jessica. *True Spirit.* Sydney: Simon & Schuster, 2010.

Weingarten, Marc. "A Live Ballgame Unfolds on a Cellphone Screen." *New York Times,* October 24, 2002.

White, Gordon S., Jr. "Colleges May Find TV's Gold Egg Is Tarnished." *New York Times,* August 26, 1984.

_____. "Football Playoffs Rejected." *New York Times,* June 30, 1984.

_____. "Ruling Adds Options for Colleges and Television," *New York Times,* June 28, 1984.

Wilford, John Noble. "The Day Satcom 2 Wobbled in Orbit." *New York Times,* November 20, 1979.

Witkin, Richard. "Live TV of Tokyo Olympics Being Explored." *New York Times,* January 26, 1964.

_____. "Satellite Tested for Olympics TV." *New York Times,* April 24, 1964.

"World Cup on Home TV." *New York Times,* June 6, 1982.

"Zev, Champion Colt, Injures His Hoof." *New York Times,* September 11, 1923, 11, 23.

"Zev Is Selected to Meet Papyrus in Match Race." *New York Times,* October 6, 1923.

Zimmer, Judith. "Exercise Meets Entertainment on a Virtual-Reality Bike." *New York Times,* August 21, 1996.

Newsreels (chronological)

"Highlights in the World of Sports for 1929." *Universal Newsreels,* January 1, 1930.

"'Babe' Gets a New Bat as He and 'Missus' Invade Southern Links." *Universal Newsreels,* January 18, 1930.

"US Team First in International Bob-Sled Race." *Universal Newsreels,* February 12, 1930.

"Girl Mat Gladiator Wins Smashing Bout with Man Rival." *Universal Newsreels,* February 26, 1930.

"Sharkey Knocks Out Phil Scott in Three Rounds." *Universal Newsreels,* March 1, 1930.

"Seattle Girl Sets Three World Marks for Swim Crown." *Universal Newsreels,* March 19, 1930.

"Welsh Rugby Team Beats France 11–0, as Crush Imperils Fans." *Universal Newsreels,* May 3, 1930.

"Sharkey-Schmeling Preview." *Universal Newsreels,* May 14, 1930.

"Predict Child Golf Wonder, 3, Will Be Second Bobby Jones." *Universal Newsreels,* June 8, 1930.

"Bobby Jones Victor in British Amateur After Close Finish." *Universal Newsreels,* June 14, 1930.

"Schmeling Wins on Foul by Sharkey in World Title Bout." *Universal Newsreels,* June 14, 1930.

"Jones Wins U.S. Open After Sensational Holing of 40-Foot Putt." *Universal Newsreels,* July 14, 1930.

"Women's Tennis Title Won for Fourth Year by Helen Wills Moody." *Universal Newsreels,* July 14, 1930.

"Tilden Wins Singles Against Borotha But U.S. Loses Davis Cup." *Universal Newsreels,* August 4, 1930.

"Dot Dickinson Wins 2-Mile Swim in New Time, 55' 16½"." *Universal Newsreels*, August 18, 1930.

"Betty Nuthall Wins U.S. Tennis Crown in One-Sided Match." *Universal Newsreels*, August 25, 1930.

"Lipton's Hopes Wane as 'Enterprise' Again Humbles 'Shamrock.'" *Universal Newsreels*, September 15, 1930.

"'Shamrock' Fails in Last Gallant Try for America's Cup." *Universal Newsreels*, September 18, 1930.

"Jones Wins Amateur; Holds All British and U.S. Golf Titles." *Universal Newsreels*, September 29, 1930.

"Record Crowds See Cards and Mackmen Battle for Title." *Universal Newsreels*, October 6, 1930.

"Notre Dame Sinks Penn 60–20 in Pigskin Rout." *Universal Newsreels*, November 10, 1930.

"Hockey Ushered in with American Win Over Montreal." *Universal Newsreels*, November 17, 1930.

"Trojans Lose to Notre Dame Fighting Irish, 27–0, in Gridiron Upset." *Universal Newsreels*, December 8, 1930.

"Disputes Mark Olympics." *Universal Newsreels*, February 2, 1948.

"U.S. Third in Olympics." *Universal Newsreels*, February 9, 1948.

"Olympics Round-Up." *Universal Newsreels*, February 16, 1948.

"Yanks Gain in Track and Swimming." *Universal Newsreels*, August 5, 1948.

"Highlights of the Olympics: Yanks Forge Ahead Crushing Opposition." *Universal Newsreels*, August 9, 1948.

"Thrills from the Olympics; Dispute Mars Relay." *Universal Newsreels*, August 12, 1948.

"Olympic Heroes Come Home." *Universal Newsreels*, August 16, 1948.

"Winter Olympics at Oslo—U.S. Team Off to Good Start." *Universal Newsreels*, February 18, 1952.

"U.S. Sweeps 500-Meter Race." *Universal Newsreels*, February 21, 1952.

"Norway Wins Winter Olympics." *Universal Newsreels*, February 25, 1952.

"Olympics Open—Russia Competing for First Time in Soviet Era." *Universal Newsreels*, July 21, 1952.

"Helsinki Olympics—Zatopek Wins Rare Double." *Universal Newsreels*, July 24, 1952.

"U.S. Dominates Track and Field Events." *Universal Newsreels*, July 28, 1952.

"Records Fall as Games Near End." *Universal Newsreels*, July 31, 1952.

"U.S. Wins Over Reds in Unofficial Point Scoring." *Universal Newsreels*, August 4, 1952.

Secondary Sources

Ahmed, Sarah. "Affective Economies." *Social Text* 7922.2 (2004): 79–117.

Ain, Bill. "We Had No Idea." *ESPN The Magazine*, February 23, 2010.

Allen, Frederick Lewis. *Only Yesterday: An Informal History of the Nineteen-Twenties*. New York: Blue Ribbon Books, 1931.

Allen, Robert C., and Douglas Gomery. *Film History: Theory and Practice*. New York: Knopf, 1985.

Altheide, David L. "Media Logic, Social Control, and Fear." *Communication Theory* 23, 223–238.

Amis, John, Trevor Slack, and Tim Berrett. "Sport Sponsorship as Distinctive Competence." *European Journal of Marketing* 33.3–4 (1999): 250–272.

Andrejevic, Mark. *Infoglut: How Too Much Information Is Changing the Way We Think and Know*. New York: Routledge, 2013.

Andrews, David L. "Excavating Michael Jordan: Notes on a Critical Pedagogy of Sporting Representation." In *Sport and Postmodern Times*, edited by Geneviève Rail, 185–220. Albany: State University of New York Press, 1998.

_____, and Steven J. Jackson. "Introduction: Sport Celebrities, Public Culture and Private Experience." In *Sport Stars*, edited by David L. Andrews and Steven J. Jackson, 1–19. London: Routledge, 2001.

_____, and Mike L. Silk. "Sport and Neoliberalism: An Affective-Ideological Articulation." *Journal of Popular Culture* 51.2 (2018): 511–533.

Arledge, Roone. *Roone: A Memoir*. New York: HarperCollins, 2003.

Arsenault, Amelia H. "The Datafication of Media: Big Data and the Media Industries." *International Journal of Media & Cultural Politics* 13.1–2 (March 2017): 7–24.

Askins, R. "Common Myths About Officiating." *Referee* 26.10 (2001): 44–47.

Baechlin, Peter, and Maurice Muller-Strauss. *Newsreels Across the World*. Paris: UNESCO, 1952.

Baird, Jay. *To Die for Germany: Heroes in the Nazi Pantheon*. Bloomington: University of Indiana Press, 1990.

Barnard, Hugh. *Mountain Film: An Analysis of the History and Characteristics of a Documentary Genre*. Unpublished dissertation. University of Otago, New Zealand, 2011.

Barnett, Steven. *Games and Sets: The Changing Face of Sport on Television*. London: British Film Institute, 1990.

Barnouw, Eric. *The Golden Web: A History of Broadcasting in the United States*, Vol. II 1933–1953. Oxford: Oxford University Press, 1968.

_____. *A Tower in Babel: A History of Broadcasting in the United States to 1933*. New York: Oxford University Press, 1966.

Barthes, Roland. "From Word to Text." In *Image, Music, Text*, edited Roland Barthes, translated by S. Heath, 155–164. New York: Noonday Press, 1988.

_____. *The Pleasure of the Text*, translated by R. Miller. New York: Hill and Wang, 1975. (Original work published in 1973).

_____. "Theory of the Text." In *Untying the Text:*

A Poststructuralist Reader, edited by Robert Young, 31–47. Boston: Routledge and Kegan Paul, 1981.

Battaglia, Deborah. "On Practical Nostalgia: Self-Prospecting Among Urban Trobrianders." In *Rhetorics of Self-Making,* edited by D. Battaglia, 77–96. Berkley: University of California Press, 1995.

Baudrillard, Jean. *The Ecstasy of Communication,* translated by B. Schutze and C. Schutze. New York: Columbia University Press, 1988.

_____. *Fatal Strategies.* New York: Semiotext(e), 1983.

_____. *Passwords,* trans. Chris Turner. New York: Verso, 2003.

_____. *Revenge of the Crystal.* London: Pluto, 1990.

_____. "The Virtual Illusion." *Theory, Culture & Society* 12: 97–107.

Bazin, Andre. *What Is Cinema?* translated by H. Gray. Berkeley: University of California Press, 1971.

Becker, A. "ESPN's Mobile Trials." *Broadcasting & Cable,* 2006. http://www.broadcastingcable.com/article/CA6327095.html?display=News.

Berger, Peter L. *The Sacred Canopy: Elements of a Sociological Theory of Religion.* New York: Doubleday, 1967.

Berger, Warren. "Equal Sequels." *Creativity,* May 1, 1999.

Berman, Mitchell N. "Replay." *California Law Review* 99.6 (2011): 1683–1744.

Bérubé, Michael. "Afterword: High-definition Sports Capitalism." In *Marxism, Cultural Studies, and Sport,* edited by B. Carrington and I. McDonald, 232–241. London: Routledge, 2008.

Betts, John R. *America's Sporting Heritage: 1850–1950.* Reading, MA: Addison-Wesley, 1974.

Biel, Michael. "Time Shifting by the Networks." http://members.aol.com/jeff560/am2.html.

Billings, Andrew, Brody James Ruihley, and Yiyi Yang. "Fantasy Gaming on Steroids? Contrasting Fantasy Sport Participation by Daily Fantasy Sport Participation." *Communication & Sport* 5.6 (2017): 732–750.

Bird, S. Elizabeth, and Robert W. Dardenne. "Myth, Chronicle, and Story." In *Media, Myths and Narratives: Television and the Press,* edited by James W. Carey, 67–86. Newbury Park, CA: Sage, 1988.

Birrell, Susan. "Approaching Mt. Everest: On Intertextuality and the Past as Narrative." *Journal of Sport History* 34.1 (2008): 1–22.

Bloom, John. "No Fall from Grace: Grace Thorpe's 'Athlete of the Century' Campaign for Her Father." In *Native Athletes in Sport & Society: A Reader,* edited by C. Richard King, 228–244. Lincoln: University of Nebraska Press, 2005.

Bolter, Jay D., and Richard Grusin. *Remediation: Understanding New Media.* Cambridge: MIT Press, 2000.

Bourdieu, Pierre. *On Television,* translated P.P. Ferguson. New York: The New Press, 1998.

Boyle, Raymond, and Richard Haynes. *Power Play: Sport, the Media & Popular Culture.* Essex: Pearson Education Limited, 2000.

_____. *Sports Journalism: Context and Issues.* London: Sage, 2006.

Bricknell, Louise. "The Trouble with Feelings: Gender, Sexualities and Power in a Gender Regime of Competitive Sailing." *Journal of Sport and Social Issues* 23 (1999): 421–438.

Brooks, Tim, and Earle Marsh. *The Complete Directory to Prime Time TV Shows, 1946–Present.* New York: Ballantine, 1981.

Bryant, Jennings, and Andrea M. Holt. "A Historical Overview of Sports and Media in the United States." In *Handbook of Sports and Media,* edited by Arthur A. Raney and Jennings Bryant, 21–44. Mahwah, NJ: Lawrence Erlbaum Associates, 2006.

Buehler, Branden. "The Documentary as 'Quality' Sports Television." *Sporting Realities: Critical Readings of the Sports Documentary,* edited by Samantha N. Sheppard and Travis Vogan, 11–34. Lincoln: University of Nebraska Press, 2020.

Burke, Kenneth. *A Grammar of Motives.* Berkeley: University of California Press, 1966.

_____. *The Philosophy of Literary Form.* Berkeley: University of California Press, 1941.

Byers, Walter. *Unsportsmanlike Conduct: Exploiting College Athletes.* Ann Arbor: University of Michigan Press, 1995.

Caruso, Eugene M., Zachary C. Burns, and Benjamin A. Converse. "Slow Motion Increases Perceived Intent." *Proceedings of the National Academy of Sciences of the United States of America* 113.33 (2016): 9250–9255. https://doi.org/10.1073/pnas.1603865113.

Carvalho, Anabela. "Media(ted) Discourse and Society." *Journalism Studies* 9.2 (2016): 161–177.

Castells, Manuel. *The Rise of the Network Society.* Oxford: Blackwell, 1996.

Clarke, Alan, and John Clarke. "Highlights and Action Replays—Ideology, Sport and the Media." In *Sport, Culture and Ideology,* edited by Jennifer Hargreaves, 62–87. London: Routledge and Kegan Paul, 1982.

Clarke, John. "Football and Working-class Fans: Tradition and Change." In *Football Hooliganism in the Wider Context,* edited by Roger Ingham, 37–60. London: Inter-Action Imprint, 1978.

Cohn, Lawrence. *Movietone Presents the Twentieth Century.* New York: St. Martin's Press, 1976.

Collins, Harry. "The Philosophy of Umpiring and the Introduction of Decision-aid Technology." *Journal of the Philosophy of Sport* 37 (2010): 135–146.

_____, and Robert Evans. "You Cannot Be Serious! Public Understanding of Technology with Special Reference to 'Hawk-Eye.'" *Public Understanding of Science* 17.3 (2008): 283–308.

Cormack, Michael J. *Ideology.* Ann Arbor: University of Michigan Press, 1992.

Cox, Barbara, and Shona Thompson. "Multiple Bodies: Sportswomen, Soccer and Sexuality." *International Review for the Sociology of Sport* 35.1 (2000): 5–20.

Crawley, Sara. "Gender, Class and the Construction of Masculinity in Professional Sailing." *Review for the Sociology of Sport* 33.1 (1998): 33–42.

Cressman, Dale L., and Lisa Swenson. "The Pigskin and the Picture Tube: The National Football League's First Full Season on the CBS Television Network." *Journal of Broadcasting & Electronic Media* 51.3 (Fall 2007): 479–497.

Critcher, Chas. "Football Since the War." In *Working-Class Culture: Studies in History and Theory,* edited by John Clarke, Chas Critcher, and Richard Johnson, 161–184. New York: St. Martin's, 1979.

Crouch, Ian. "Baseball Replay Works—And It's Terrible." *New Yorker.* https://www.newyorker.com/news/sporting-scene/baseball-replay-worksand-its-terrible.

Cuneo, Alice Z. "More Football Fans Hit ESPN's Mobile Site Than Its PC Pages." *Advertising Age,* January 7, 2008.

Daddario, Gina. *Women's Sport and Spectacle: Gendered Television Coverage and the Olympic Games.* Westport, CT: Praeger, 1998.

Davis, Nickolas W., and Margaret Carlisle Duncan. "Sports Knowledge Is Power: Reinforcing Masculine Privilege Through Fantasy Sport League Participation." *Journal of Sport and Social Issues* 30 (2006): 244–264.

Dayan, Daniel, and Elihu Katz. *Media Events: The Live Broadcasting of History.* Cambridge: Harvard University Press, 1992.

Debord, Guy. *Society of the Spectacle.* Detroit: Black and Red, 1967.

De Burgh-Woodman, Helene, and Janice Brace-Govan. "Marketing and the Other: A Study of Women in the Sailing Marketplace and Its Implications for Marketing Discourse." *E—European Advances in Consumer Research* 8 (2007): 189–195.

Denyer-Simmons, Peter. "Tackling Abuse of Officials: Attitudes and Communication Skills of Experienced Football Referees." Conference Paper, Empowerment, Creativity and Innovation—Challenging Media and Communication in the 21st Century, Adelaide, New Zealand.

Denyer-Simmons, Peter, and Ian Cunningham. "Communication and Sport Officials." In *Handbook of Sport Communication,* edited by P.M. Pedersen, 461–470. New York: Routledge, 2021.

Disch, Lisa, and Mary Jo Kane. "When a Looker Is Really a Bitch: Lisa Olson, Sport, and the Heterosexual Matrix." *Signs: Journal of Women in Culture and Society* 21.21 (Winter 1996): 278–308.

Dyreson, Mark. "Aggressive America: Media Nationalism and the 'War' Over Olympic Pictures in Sports 'Golden Age.'" *The International Journal of the History of Sport* 22.6 (November 2005): 974–989.

_____. "American Ideas About Race and Olympic Races from the 1890s to the 1950s: Shattering Myths or Reinforcing Scientific Racism?" *Journal of Sport History* 28.2 (Summer 2001): 173–215.

_____. "The Emergence of Consumer Culture and the Transformation of Physical Culture: American Sport in the 1920s." *Journal of Sport History* 16.3 (Winter 1989): 261–281.

_____. "Icons of Liberty or Objects of Desire? American Women Olympians and the Politics of Consumption." *Journal of Contemporary History* 38.3 (Autumn 2003): 435–460.

_____. "Marketing National Identity: The Olympic Games of 1932 and American Culture." *OLYMPIKA: The International Journal of Olympic Studies* IV (1995): 23–48.

_____. "Melting-Pot Victories: Racial Ideas and the Olympic Games in American Culture During the Progressive Era." *International Journal of the History of Sport* 6.1 (1989): 49–61.

Early, Gerald. *The Culture of Bruising: Essays on Prizefighting, Literature and Modern American Culture.* Hopewell, NJ: Ecco Press, 1994.

Eastman, Susan Tyler, and Andrew C. Billings. "Sportscasting and Sports Reporting: The Power of Gender Bias." *Journal of Sport & Social Issues* 24.2 (May 2000): 192–213.

Eco, Umberto. *The Role of the Reader: Explorations in the Semiotics of Texts.* Bloomington: Indiana University Press, 1979.

"ESPN and SANYO Team for Inaugural Mobile ESPN Handset; Multimedia SANYO MVP Offers Ultimate Wireless Experience for Ultimate Sports Fans." http://www.findarticles.com/p/articles/mi_m0EIN/is_2005_ Sept_27/ai_n15633862.

"ESPN Looks to Score iTunes Deal." http://news.zdnet.com/2100-1035_22-5982937.html.

"ESPN Sports Attitude Mixing Dedication and Irreverence." *Advertising Age,* October 23, 1995.

Farred, Grant. "'Cool as the Other Side of the Pillow': How ESPN's *SportsCenter* Has Changed Television Sports Talk." *Journal of Sport & Social Issues* 24.2 (2000): 96–117.

Fielding, Raymond. *The American Newsreel: A Complete History, 1911–1967.* Jefferson, NC: McFarland, 2006.

_____. *A Technological History of Motion Pictures and Television.* Berkeley: University of California Press, 1967.

Finn, Jonathan. "Timing and Imaging Evidence in Sport: Objectivity, Intervention and the Limits of Technology." *Journal of Sport and Social Issues* 40.6 (2016): 459–476.

Fiske, John. "The Semiotics of Television." *Critical Studies in Mass Communication* (June 1985): 176–183.

Freeman, Michael. *ESPN: The Uncensored History.* Dallas: Taylor Publishing, 2000.

Friedman, Wayne. "Young Stars Give Fresh Spin to ESPN Classic Programs: Ads Feature Contemporary Celebs Touting Heroes of Past." *Advertising Age,* May 31, 1999.

Gallico, Paul. *Farewell to Sport.* 1938. Reprint, Freeport, NY: Books for Libraries Press, 1970.

Garfield, Bob. "The Best Awards; ESPN Scores Best in Show." *Advertising Age,* May 27, 1996.

Gawrysiak, Joey, Brendan Dwyer, and Rick Burton. "Understanding Baseball Consumption Via In-Home Gaming." *Journal of Applied Sport Management* 6.3 (Fall 2014): 76–97.

Gergen, Kenneth J. *The Saturated Self: Dilemmas of Identity in Contemporary Life.* New York: Basic Books, 1991.

Ginsburg, Charles P. "The Birth of Video Recording." Paper first delivered at the 82nd Convention of the Society of Motion Picture and Television Engineers on October 5, 1957. http://www.labguysworld.com/VTR_BirthOf.htm.

Gitelman, Lisa. "Introduction: Media as Historical Subjects." In *Always Already New: Media, History and the Data of Culture* (work in progress). Quoted in Jenkins.

Giulianotti, Richard. "The Fate of Hyperreality: Jean Baudrillard and the Sociology of Sport." In *Sport and Modern Social Theorists,* edited by Richard Giulianotti, 225–239. New York: Palgrave, 2004.

Goetzl, David. "ESPN Ad Effort Hails a Cab; Adapt Media's Pilot Program Driving in NYC." *Advertising Age,* May 28, 2001.

Gorn, Eliott, and Wallace J. Goldstein. *A Brief History of American Sports.* New York: HarperCollins, 1993.

Grierson, John. *Grierson on Documentary,* edited by F. Hardy. New York: Praeger, 1966.

Grieveson, Lee. "Fighting Films: Race, Morality, and the Governing of Cinema, 1912–1915." *Cinema Journal* 38.1 (Fall 1988): 40–72.

Grossberg, Lawrence. *We Gotta Get Out of This Place: Popular Conservatism and Postmodern Culture.* London: Routledge, 1992.

Gruneau, Richard. "Making Spectacle: A Case Study in Television Sports Production." In *Media, Sports, and Society,* edited by Lawrence A. Wenner, 134–154. Newbury Park: Sage, 1989.

Grunska, Jeremy. "Yeah, You're Good … But You Can Be Better." *Referee* 26.6 (2001): 51–60.

Guttmann, Allen. *From Ritual to Record: The Nature of Modern Sports.* New York: Columbia University Press, 1978.

_____. *Sports: The First Five Millennia.* Amherst: University of Massachusetts Press, 2004.

_____. *A Whole New Ball Game: An Interpretation of American Sports.* Chapel Hill: University of North Carolina Press, 1988.

Hall, Stuart. "The Treatment of 'Football Hooliganism' in the Press." In *Football Hooliganism in the Wider Context,* edited by Roger Ingham, 15–36. London: Inter-Action Imprint, 1978.

Handy, Robert J. *A Christian America: Protestant Hopes and Historical Realities.* New York: Oxford University Press, 1971.

Hanson, Christopher. "The Instant Replay Time and Time Again." *Spectator* 28.2 (2008): 51–60.

Hargreaves, Jennifer. "Theorising Sport: An Introduction." In *Sport, Culture and Ideology,* edited by Jennifer Hargreaves, 1–29. London: Routledge and Kegan Paul, 1982.

Harris, Janet C. *Athletes and the American Hero Dilemma.* Champaign, IL: Human Kinetics, 1994.

Hegarty, Paul. *Jean Baudrillard: Live Theory.* London: Continuum, 2004.

Helsen, Werner, and Jean-Baptiste Bultynck. "Physical and Perceptual-Cognitive Demands of Top-Class Refereeing in Association Football." *Journal of Sports Sciences* 22 (2004): 179–189.

Hewitt, Regina. *The Possibilities of Society: Wordsworth, Coleridge, and the Sociological Viewpoint of English Romanticism.* Albany: State University of New York Press, 1997.

Hing, Nerilee, Alex Myles Thomas Russell, Matthew Lamont, and Peter Vitartas. "Bet Anywhere, Anytime: An Analysis of Internet Sports Bettors' Responses to Gambling Promotions during Sports Broadcasts by Problem Gambling Severity." *Journal of Gambling Studies* 33.4 (2017): 1051–1065.

_____, Matthew Lamont, Peter Vitartas, and Elian Fink. "Sports-Embedded Gambling Promotions: A Study of Exposure, Sports Betting Intention and Problem Gambling Amongst Adults." *International Journal of Mental Health and Addiction* 13 (2015): 115–135.

Hirshberg, Charles. *ESPN 25: 25 Mind-Bending, Eye-Popping, Culture-Morphing Years of Highlights.* New York: Hyperion Books, 2004.

Hoberman, John. *Mortal Engines: The Science of Performance and the Dehumanization of Sport.* Caldwell, NJ: The Blackburn Press, 1982.

Höbusch, Harald. "Rescuing German Alpine Tradition: Nanga Parbat and Its Visual Afterlife." *Journal of Sport History* 29.1 (2002): 49–77.

Holyfield, Lori. "Manufacturing Adventure: The Buying and Selling of Emotions. *Journal of Contemporary Ethnography* 28.3 (1999): 3–32.

Horowitz, Ira. "Market Entrenchment and the Sports Broadcast Act." *The American Behavioral Scientist* 21.3 (January/February 1978): 415–430.

Hostetler, Baker. "The Future of Legal Sports Gambling: What Everyone Needs to Know About Murphy v. NCAA." *Holt Hackney Sports Litigation Alert,* 2 August 2018, 1–8.

Hourigan, Brian. "The 'Math' Behind Going Pro in DFS." https://rotogrinders.com/blog-posts/the-math-behind-going-pro-in-dfs-178641.

Huggins, Mike. "'And Now, Something for the Ladies': Representations of Women's Sport in Cinema Newsreels 1918–1939." *Women's Historical Review* 16.5 (November 2007): 681–700.

Hughes, Robert, and Jay Coakley. "Mass Society and the Commercialization of Sport." *Sociology of Sport Journal* 1 (1984): 57–63.

International Football Association Board. "Laws of the Game." 2018/2019. https://www.theifab.com/laws/latest/video-assistant-referee-var-protocol/.

_____. "133rd Annual General Meeting." 2019.

Jackson, Stephen J., and David L. Andrews.

"Introduction: The Contemporary Landscape of Sport Advertising." In *Sport, Culture and Advertising,* edited by Steven J. Jackson and David L. Andrews, 1–23. London: Routledge, 2005.

Jameson, Frederic. *Postmodernism: Or the Cultural Logic of Late Capitalism.* Durham: Duke University Press, 1991.

Jenkins, Henry. *Convergence Culture: Where Old and New Media Collide.* New York: New York University Press, 2006.

Jennings, Gayle. "Caught in the Irons: One of the Lived Experiences of Long-term Ocean Cruising Women." *Tourism Review International* 9 (2005): 177–193.

Jensen, Klaus B. "Contexts, Cultures and Computers." In *A Handbook of Media and Communication Research: Qualitative and Quantitative Methodologies,* edited by Klaus B. Jensen, 171–190. London: Routledge, 2002.

Johnson, Melissa A. "Pre-Television Stereotypes: Mexicans in U.S. Newsreels, 1919, 1932." *Critical Studies in Mass Communication* 16 (1999): 417–435.

Kaplan, E. Ann. *Rocking Round the Clock: Music Television, Postmodernism, and Consumer Culture.* New York: Methuen, 1987.

Kellner, Douglas. *Media Spectacle.* London: Routledge, 2003.

_____. "Sports, Media Culture, and Race—Some Reflections on Michael Jordan." *Sociology of Sport Journal* 13 (1996): 458–467.

Kelly, Joseph M. "Living in a Fantasy." *Gaming Law Review* 12.4 (2008): 310–317.

Kindred, Dave. *Sound and Fury: Two Powerful Lives, One Fateful Friendship.* New York: Free Press, 2006.

Kinkema, Kathleen M., and Janet C. Harris. "MediaSport Studies: Key Research and Emerging Issues." In *MediaSport,* edited by Lawrence A. Wenner, 27–56. London: Routledge, 1998.

Klatell, David A., and Norman Marcus. *Sports for Sale: Television, Money and the Fans.* New York: Oxford University Press, 1988.

Lasch, Christopher. *The Culture of Narcissism: American Life in an Age of Diminishing Expectations.* New York: Norton, 1979.

Laurier, Eric, and Stuart Reeves. "The Revelations of the Action-Replay: Video and the Optical Unconscious." Working Paper, 2011. https://ericlaurier.co.uk/resources/Writings/Action-replay.pdf.

Lewis, Neil. "The Climbing Body, Nature and the Experience of Modernity." *Body & Society* 6.3–4 (2000): 58–80.

Linnett, Richard. "The Buzz; What We're Talking About." *Advertising Age,* January 19, 2004.

Lippman, Walter. *Public Opinion.* New York: Free Press, 1922.

Lomax, Richard G. "Fantasy Sports: History, Game Types, and Research." In *Handbook of Sports and Media,* edited by A.A. Raney & J. Bryant, 383–392. Mahwah, NJ: Lawrence Erlbaum, 2006.

Lopez-Gonzalez, Hibai, and Mark D. Griffiths.

"Understanding the Convergence of Online Sports Betting Markets." *International Review for the Sociology of Sport* 53.7 (2018): 807–823.

Lopez-Gonzalez, Hibai, Mark O. Griffiths, and Susana Jimenez-Murcia. "The Symbolic Construction of Sports Betting Products." *International Gambling Studies* (May 2021): 498–515.

Lowes, Mark D. "Sports Page: A Case Study in the Manufacture of Sports News for the Daily Press." *Sociology of Sport Journal* 14 (1997): 143–59.

Luke, Timothy W. *Screens of Power: Ideology, Domination, and Resistance in Informational Society.* Urbana: University of Illinois Press, 1989.

MacCambridge, Michael. *America's Game: The Epic Story of How Pro Football Captured a Nation.* New York: Random House, 2004.

Mandelbrot, Benoit B. *The Fractal Geometry of Nature.* New York: W.H. Freeman and Company, 1977.

Martin, Jeff. "The Dawn of Tape: Transmission Device as Preservation Medium." *The Moving Image* 5.1 (2005): 45–66.

Mascarenhas, Duncan, Dave Collins, and Patrick Mortimer. "The Art of Reason Versus the Exactness of Science in Elite Refereeing: Comments on Plessner and Betsch (2002)." *Journal of Sport Exercise Psychology* 24 (2005): 328–333.

McCarthy, Anna. "'The Front Row is Reserved for Scotch Drinkers': Early Television's Tavern Audience." *Cinema Journal* 34.4 (Summer 1995): 31–49.

McDonald, Ian. "Situating the Sport Documentary." *Journal of Sport & Social Issues* 31.3 (2007): 208–225.

McGinnis, Lee, Julia McQuillan and Constance L. Chapple. "I Just Want to Play: Women, Sexism, and Persistence in Golf." *Journal of Sport & Social Issues* 29.3 (August 2005): 313–337.

McKernan, Luke. "Witnessing the Past." In *Researcher's Guide to British Newsreels,* Volume III, edited J. Ballentyne. London: BUFVC, 1983.

Medhurst, Michael J. "Propaganda Techniques in Documentary Film and Television: *AIM vs. PBS.*" In *Television Studies: Textual Analysis,* edited by Gary Burns and Richard J. Thompson, 183–204. New York: Praeger, 1989.

Messner, Michael A. *Taking the Field: Women, Men and Sports.* Minneapolis: University of Minnesota, 2002.

Messner, Michael A., Margaret C. Duncan, and Cheryl Cooky. "Silence, Sports Bras and Wrestling Porn: Women in Televised Sports News and Highlight Shows." *Journal of Sport & Social Issues* 27.1 (2003): 38–51.

Messner, Michael A., Margaret C. Duncan, and Karen Jensen. "Separating the Men from the Girls: The Gendered Language of Televised Sports." *Gender & Society* 7.1 (1993): 121–137.

Moen, Margaret. "Broadcast Bomber." *Air & Space.* http://www.airspacemag.com/issues/2007/august/oldies_and_oddities.php.

Morse, Margaret. "Sport on Television: Replay and

Display." In *Regarding Television*, edited by E.A. Kaplan, 44–66. Frederick, MD: University Publications of America, 1983.

Morton, Gerald W., and George M. O'Brien. *Wrestling to Rasslin: Ancient Sport to American Spectacle*. Bowling Green, OH: Bowling Green University Popular Press, 1985.

Musser, Charles. *Edison Motion Pictures, 1890–1900: An Annotated Filmography*. Washington, D.C.: Smithsonian Institution Press, 1997.

_____. *The Emergence of Cinema: The American Screen to 1907*. New York: Scribner's, 1990.

Nazaradim, Mohammed N., Mohd R. Abdullah, and M.S.O. Fauzee. "Developing a Decision-Making Test for the Rugby Referees." *Malaysian Journal of Sports, Recreation and Education* 2.1 (2015): 77–85.

Neal-Lunsford, Jeff. "Sport in the Land of Television: The Use of Sport in Network Prime-Time Schedules 1946–1950." *Journal of Sport History* 19.1 (Spring 1992): 56–76.

Neale, Steve. "Questions of Genre." *Screen* 31.1 (1990): 45–66.

Neveldine, Robert Burns. *Bodies at Risk: Unsafe Limits in Romanticism and Postmodernism*. Albany: State University of New York Press, 1998.

Nevill, A.M., N.J. Balmer, and A.M. Williams. "The Influence of Crowd Noise and Experience upon Refereeing Decisions in Football." *Psychology of Sport and Exercise* 3.4 (2002): 261–272.

Nichols, Bill. *Introduction to Documentary*. Bloomington: Indiana University Press, 2001.

_____. *Representing Reality: Issues and Concepts in Documentary*. Bloomington: Indiana University Press, 1991.

Nower, Lia, Dylan Adam Pickering, Kyle Caler, and Alex Blaszczynski. "Daily Fantasy Sports Players: Gambling, Addiction, and Mental Health Problems." *Journal of Gambling Studies* 34.3 (2018): 727–737.

Oates, Thomas P. "Race, Economics, and the Shifting Politics of Sport Media." *Radical History Review* 125 (May 2016): 159–167.

O'Connor, John E. "Historical Analysis, Stage One: Gathering Information on the Content, Production, and Reception of a Moving Image Document." In *Image as Artifact*, edited by John E. O'Connor, 10–26. Malabar, FL: Robert E. Krieger Publishing Company, 1990.

Oriard, Michael. *King Football*. Chapel Hill: University of North Carolina Press, 2001.

Plymire, Darcy C. "Qualitative Methods in Sport-media Studies." In *Qualitative Methods in Sports Studies*, edited by David L. Andrews, Daniel S. Mason, and Michael L. Silk, 139–164. Oxford: Berg, 2005.

Pope, Steven W. "American Muscles and Minds: Public Discourse and the Shaping of National Identity During Early Olympiads, 1896–1920." *The Journal of American Culture* 15.4 (1992): 105–124.

_____. "Introduction: American Sport History—Toward a New Paradigm." In *The New American Sport History: Recent Approaches and Perspectives*, edited by Steven W. Pope, 1–30. Urbana: University of Illinois Press, 1997.

Porter, Marilyn. "The Mermaids Are Out There, So Why Aren't We? Women and Sailing. *Canadian Women Studies* 15.4 (1995): 102–105.

Powers, Ron. *Supertube: The Rise of Television Sports*. New York: Coward-McCann, 1984.

Pronay, Nicholas. "The Newsreel: The Illusion of Actuality." In *The Historian and Film*, ed. P. Smith, 95–120. Cambridge: Cambridge University Press, 1976.

Pugmire, Lance. "Step Inside the Future of Betting in U.S. Sports Venues." *USA Today Sports+*, March 7, 2022. https://www.usatoday.com/in-depth/sports-betting/2022/03/07/inside-phoenix-suns-footprint-center-and-future-sports-betting/9096465002/.

Rader, Benjamin G. *In Its Own Image: How Television Has Transformed Sports*. New York: Free Press, 1984.

Rail, Geneviève. "Introduction." In *Sport and Postmodern Times*, edited by Geneviève Rail, 3–20. Albany: State University of New York Press, 1998.

_____. "Seismography of the Postmodern Condition: Three Theses on the Implosion of Sport." In *Sport and Postmodern Times*, edited by Genevieve Rail, 143–162. Albany: State University of New York Press, 1998.

Ramsaye, Terry. *A Million and One Nights: A History of the Motion Picture Through 1925*. New York: Touchstone, 1986.

Rappoport, Jon. "The Marketing 100; ESPN Judy Fearing." *Advertising Age*, June 24, 1996.

Rasmussen, Bill. *Sports Junkies Rejoice! The Birth of ESPN*. Hartsdale, NY: QV Publishing, 1983.

Raunsbjerg, Preben, and Henrik Sand. "TV Sport and Rhetoric." *Nordicom Review* 19.1 (1998): 159–174.

Real, Michael R. "MediaSport: Technology and the Commodification of Postmodern Sport." In *MediaSport*, edited by Lawrence A. Wenner, 14–26. London: Routledge, 1998.

Revell, "AI Can Doctor Videos to Put Words in the Mouths of Speakers." *New Scientist*, May 19, 2017. https://www.newscientist.com/article/2131716-ai-can-doctor-videos-to-put-words-in-the-mouths-of-speakers/.

Ricchiardi, Sherry. "Offensive Interference." *American Journalism Review* 26.6 (December 2004/January 2005): 54–59.

Robinson, Jeffrey C. *The Walk: Notes on a Romantic Image*. Norman: University of Oklahoma Press, 1989.

Rosenwald, George, and Richard Ochburg. "Introduction." In *Storied Lives: The Cultural Politics of Self-Understanding*, edited by George Rosenwald and Richard Ochburg, 1–18. New Haven: Yale University Press, 1992.

Rowe, David. *Sport, Culture and the Media: The Unruly Trinity*. Buckingham: Open University Press, 1999.

Roy, Donald P., and Benjamin D. Goss. "A Conceptual Framework of Influences on Fantasy Sports Consumption." *Marketing Management Journal* 15.2 (2007): 96–108.

Sammons, J.T. *Beyond the Ring: The Role of Boxing in American Society.* Chicago: University of Illinois Press, 1988.

Scannell, Paddy. "History, Media and Communication." In *A Handbook of Media and Communication Research: Qualitative and Quantitative Methodologies,* edited by Klaus B. Jensen, 191–205. London: Routledge, 2002.

Schrøder, Kim C. "The Best of Both Worlds? Media Audience Research Between Rival Paradigms." In *Rethinking the Media Audience,* edited by Pertti Alasuutari, 38–68. London: Sage, 1999.

_____. "Discourses of Fact." In *A Handbook of Media and Communication Research: Qualitative and Quantitative Methodologies,* edited by Klaus B. Jensen, 98–116. London: Routledge, 2002.

Schultz, Brad. *Sports Broadcasting.* Boston: Focal Press, 2002.

Schultz, Brad, and Mary Lou Sheffer. "The Changing Role of Local Television Sports." *The Sport Journal* 7.1 (2004): 1–5.

Schwarz, Michael, and Bill Jersey. "Hunting the Hidden Dimension." PBS's *Nova,* WGBH. Boston, Massachusetts, 2008.

Sewell, Philip W. "From Discourse to Discord: Quality and Dramedy at the End of the Classic Network System." *Television & New Media* 11.4 (2012): 235–259.

Shea, Jim. "The King: How ESPN Changes Everything." *Columbia Journalism Review,* January/February 2000.

Sheppard, Samantha N., and Vogan, Travis. "Introduction." In *Sporting Realities: Critical Readings of the Sports Documentary,* edited by S. Sheppard and T. Vogan, 1–10. Lincoln: University of Nebraska Press, 2020.

Shinzawa, Fluto. "Seeing Is Believing with ESPN's Latest Call." *The Boston Globe,* April 21, 2006.

Shortman, Melanie. "ESPN: Know Thyself (And Thine Audience)." *Creativity,* October 1, 2005.

Silk, Michael L., David L. Andrews, and Daniel S. Mason. "Encountering the Field: Sport Studies and Qualitative Research." In *Qualitative Methods in Sports Studies,* edited by David L. Andrews, Daniel S. Mason and Michael L. Silk, 1–20. Oxford: Berg, 2005.

Simonton, Dean Keith. *Greatness: Who Makes History and Why.* New York: Guilford Press, 1994.

Slater, John. "Changing Partners: The Relationship Between the Mass Media and the Olympic Games." *Fourth International Symposium for Olympic Research,* University of Western Ontario, London, Ontario, Canada (October), 49–68, 1998.

Smith, Curt. *Voices of the Game: The First Full-Scale Overview of Baseball Broadcasting, 1921 to the Present.* South Bend, IN: Diamond Communications, 1987.

Spitz, Jochim, Koen Put, Johan Wagemans, A. Mark Williams, and Werner Helsen. "Does Slow Motion Impact on the Perception of Foul Play in Football?" *European Journal of Sport Science* 17.6 (2017): 748–756.

Stam, Robert. "Television News and Its Spectator." In *Regarding Television: Critical Approaches—An Anthology,* edited by E. Ann Kaplan, 23–43. Frederick, MD: University Publications of America, 1983.

Startt, James D., and William David Sloan. *Historical Methods in Mass Communication.* Northport, AL: Vision Press, 2003.

Stone, Philip. "A Dark Tourism Spectrum: Towards a Typology of Death and Macabre Related Touring Sites, Attractions and Exhibitions." *Tourism* 54.2 (2006): 145–160.

Streible, Daniel G. *A History of Prizefight Films.* Ph.D. Dissertation. University of Texas at Austin, 1994.

Stump, M. "ESPN Broadband Goes 360." http://www.multichannel.com/article/CA513756.html?display=Supplement#ESPN%20Broadband%20Goes%20360.

Sugar, Bert Randolph. *"The Thrill of Victory": The Inside Story of ABC Sports.* New York: Hawthorn Books, 1978.

Sullivan, David B. "Broadcast Television and the Game of Packaging Sports." In *Handbook of Sports and Media,* edited by Arthur A. Raney and Jennings Bryant, 131–145. Mahwah, NJ: Lawrence Erlbaum, 2006.

Surujlal, J., and D.B. Jordaan. "Goal Line Technology in Soccer: Are Referees Ready for Technology in Decision Making?" *African Journal for Physical, Health Education, Recreation and Dance* 19.2 (2013): 245–257.

Taylor, Peter Shawn. "Video Replay Is Ruining Professional Sports." *Maclean's,* May 7, 2017. https://www.macleans.ca/sports/video-replay-is-ruining-professional-sports/.

Trippiedi, Michael. "Daily Fantasy Sports Leagues: Do You Have the Skill to Win at These Games of Chance?" *UNLV Gaming Law Journal* 5.20 (2015): 201–223.

Tuggle, C.A. "Differences in Television Sports Reporting of Men's and Women's Athletics: ESPN SportsCenter and CNN Sports Tonight." *Journal of Broadcasting & Electronic Media* 41.1 (1997): 14–25.

Turnock, Rob. "The Arrival of Videotape." http://www.birth-of-tv.org/birth/assetView.do?asset=123173128_111778977.

Turvey, Malcolm. *Doubting Vision: Film and the Revisionist Tradition.* Oxford: Oxford University Press, 2008.

Vagnoni, Anthony. "Jock Yocks: A New Promo Campaign for ESPN Gives Fun-Loving Sports Stars a 'Spinal Tap.'" *Creativity,* November 1, 1995.

Varley, Peter. "Confecting Adventure and Playing with Meaning: The Adventure Commodification Continuum." *Journal of Sport & Tourism* 11.2 (2006): 173–194.

Verna, Tony. *Instant Replay: The Day That Changed Sports Forever.* Beverly Hills: Creative Book Publishers International, 2008.

Von Schilling, James. *The Magic Window: American Television, 1939–1953.* New York: The Haworth Press, 2003.

Walker, James A., and Robert V. Bellamy, "Baseball on Television: The Formative Years 1939–1951." *Nine: A Journal of Baseball and Culture* 11.2 (2002): 1–15.

Walter, J.A. "Death as Recreation: Armchair Mountaineering." *Leisure Studies* 3.1 (1984): 67–76.

Welky, David B. "Viking Girls, Mermaids and Little Brown Men: U.S. Journalism and the 1932 Olympics." *Journal of Sport History* 24.1 (Spring 1997): 24–49.

Wernick, Andrew. *Promotion Culture: Advertising, Ideology and Symbolic Expression.* London: Sage, 1991.

Whannel, Garry. *Fields in Vision: Television Sport and Cultural Transformation.* London: Routledge, 1992.

_____. "Reading the Sports Media Audience." In *MediaSport,* edited by Lawrence A. Wenner, 221–232. London: Routledge, 1998.

Wheeler, Raymond W. *Jim Thorpe: The World's Greatest Athlete.* Norman: University of Oklahoma Press, 1975.

Wiggins, David K., and Daniel S. Mason. "The Socio-Historical Process in Sports Studies." In *Qualitative Methods in Sports Studies,* edited

by David L. Andrews, Daniel S. Mason, and Michael L. Silk, 39–64. Oxford: Berg, 2005.

Williams, Raymond. *Television: Technology and Cultural Form.* New York: Schocken Books, 1975.

Wolpin, Stewart. "The Race to Video." *Invention and Technology* (Fall 1994): 52–72.

_____. "Tape Recording Was Introduced 70 Years Ago Today." *Recode,* May 16, 2016.

Wolter, Sarah. "Conceptual Framework for Sports Media in the 21st Century: Content, Platform, Media System, and Political System." *Journal of Sports Media* 15.2 (Fall 2020): 93–115.

"Women Buy 55% of U.S. Good, Study Indicates." *Advertising Age,* January 26, 1950.

Wood, Chris, and Vince Benigni. "The Coverage of Sports on Cable TV." In *Handbook of Sports and Media,* edited by Arthur A. Raney and Jennings Bryant, 147–169. Mahwah, NJ: Lawrence Erlbaum, 2006.

Woolley, Richard. "Mapping Internet Gambling: Emerging Modes of Online Participation in Wagering and Sports Betting." *International Journal of Gambling* 3.1 (January 2003): 3–21.

Zettl, Herbert. "The Graphication and Personification of Television News." In *Television Studies: Textual Analysis,* edited by Gary Burns and Robert J. Thompson, 121–136. New York: Praeger, 1989.

_____. *Sight Sound Motion: Applied Media Aesthetics.* Belmont, CA: Wadsworth.

Index